ACCOUNTING AND CONTROL FOR SUSTAINABILITY

STUDIES IN MANAGERIAL AND FINANCIAL ACCOUNTING

Series Editor: Marc J. Epstein

Recent Volumes:

Volume 10:	Organizational Change and Development in Management Control Systems: Process Innovation for Internal Auditing and Management Accounting
Volume 11:	US Individual Federal Income Taxation: Historical, Contemporary and Prospective Policy Issues
Volume 12:	Performance Measurement and Management Control: A Compendium of Research
Volume 13:	Information Asymmetry: A Unifying Concept for Financial and Managerial Accounting Theories
Volume 14:	Performance Measurement and Management Control: Superior Organization Performance
Volume 15:	A Comparative Study of Professional Accountants' Judgements
Volume 16:	Performance Measurement and Management Control: Improving Organizations and Society
Volume 17:	Non-Financial Performance Measurement and Management Practices In Manufacturing Firms: A Comparative International Analysis
Volume 18:	Performance Measurement and Management Control: Measuring and Rewarding Performance
Volume 19:	Managerial Attitudes Toward a Stakeholder Prominence within a Southeast Asia Context
Volume 20:	Performance Measurement and Management Control: Innovative Concepts and Practices
Volume 21:	Reputation Building, Website Disclosure and the Case of Intellectual Capital
Volume 22:	Achieving Global Convergence of Financial Reporting Standards: Implications from the South Pacific Region
Volume 23:	Globalization and Contextual Factors in Accounting: The Case of Germany
Volume 24:	An Organizational Learning Approach to Process Innovations: The Extent and Scope of Diffusion and Adoption in Management Accounting Systems
Volume 25:	Performance Measurement and Management Control: Global Issues

STUDIES IN MANAGERIAL AND FINANCIAL ACCOUNTING VOLUME 26

ACCOUNTING AND CONTROL FOR SUSTAINABILITY

EDITED BY

LUCREZIA SONGINI
Department of Economics and Business, Eastern Piedmont University, Italy

ANNA PISTONI
Deparment of Economics, Insubria University, Italy

CHRISTIAN HERZIG
Nottingham Business School, Nottingham Trent University, UK

United Kingdom – North America – Japan
India – Malaysia – China

Emerald Group Publishing Limited
Howard House, Wagon Lane, Bingley BD16 1WA, UK

First edition 2013

British Library Cataloguing in Publication Data
A catalogue record for this book is available from the British Library

ISBN: 978-1-78052-766-6
ISSN: 1479-3512 (Series)

CONTENTS

PART II: INTEGRATING SUSTAINABILITY INTO BUSINESS PRACTICE: WHAT IS THE ROLE OF MANAGERIAL CONTROL SYSTEMS AND ACCOUNTANTS?

LIST OF CONTRIBUTORS

Gerald Avondo Bodino	SCAME Parre SpA, Italy
Michael Burkert	Faculty of Economics and Social Sciences, University of Fribourg, Fribourg, Switzerland
Maurizio Cisi	Department of Management, University of Torino, Torino, Italy
Laura Corazza	Department of Management, University of Torino, Torino, Italy
Nathalie Crutzen	HEC Management School – University of Liege, Liege, Belgium
Giovanni Battista Derchi	Department of Accounting and Control, HEC Lausanne, Faculty of Business and Economics, University of Lausanne, Lausanne, Switzerland
Francesco Gangi	Department of Economics, Seconda Università di Napoli, Naples, Italy
Christian Herzig	Nottingham Business School, Nottingham Trent University, Nottingham, UK
Daniel Oyon	Department of Accounting and Control, HEC Lausanne, Faculty of Business and Economics, University of Lausanne, Lausanne, Switzerland
Cristiana Parisi	Copenhagen Business School, Frederiksberg, Denmark
Anna Pistoni	Deparment of Economics, University of Insubria, Varese, Italy
Simone Domenico Scagnelli	Department of Management, University of Torino, Torino, Italy

Stefan Schaltegger	Centre for Sustainability Management (CSM), Leuphana University Lüneburg, Lüneburg, Germany
Silvana Signori	Department of Management, Economics and Quantitative Methods, University of Bergamo, Bergamo, Italy
Lucrezia Songini	Department of Economics and Business, Eastern Piedmont University, Novara, Italy
Carmen Trotta	Department of Economics, Seconda Università di Napoli, Naples, Italy
Dimitar Zvezdov	Centre for Sustainability Management (CSM), Leuphana University Lüneburg, Lüneburg, Germany

INTRODUCTION

Sustainability and corporate social responsibility (CSR) refer to a company's activities which include social and environmental concerns in business operations and various forms of interaction with its stakeholders. Transparency, public disclosure, stakeholder engagement and management, business model, information management, and so on should all be tailored to be in line with the context and specific objectives of sustainability and CSR pursued by a company.

In this context, sustainability accounting is seen to play a central role as it can support the implementation of the sustainability strategy, embedding sustainability into day-to-day operations and decision making, and developing relationships with stakeholders based on trust and legitimacy. It comprises, in fact, internal and external accounting practices and mechanisms devoted to measure, represent and communicate the company's performance, and embraces environmental, social, and economic aspects of the business life and their relationships. Among these mechanisms, sustainability/CSR disclosure has become a prominent phenomenon, consistently with the legitimacy theory and the stakeholder theory. Such theories consider the company as part of an open system where different subjects interact with each other. This system-oriented understanding of the company highlights the role of information and disclosure in the relations among organizations, institutions, individuals, and groups. In particular, legitimacy theory postulates that a company aims to measure and communicate its performance consistently with the expectations of different societal groups in order to (re)gain or maintain its social acceptance and legitimacy. Stakeholder theory provides another useful frame for understanding the existence, role, and nature of CSR disclosure. In fact, information and communication represent some of the most important ways through which the company engages with different stakeholder groups in order to obtain their support and approval, or, vice versa, to try to remove their opposition and disapproval.

The debate on the drivers of sustainability/CSR disclosure is quite heated in managerial literature. Some authors, for example, highlighted the diffusion and features of various practices and determinants of disclosure. Numerous studies suggest that firms provide more informative disclosure, in addition to a sense of responsibility toward their stakeholders, to overcome adverse selection, or moreover, as in the case of companies with above average performance, to favorably distinguish themselves from other firms, thereby increasing demand for their securities and decreasing their cost of capital.

The need to pay attention to performance measurement and communication is also found in the concept of accountability. It has been widely used in management and business studies mainly as the basis for explaining and justifying the role and nature of the practices of social (and environmental) reporting. Social accounting and its techniques, furthermore, are the means by which it is possible to increase the democracy of society and contribute to the idealization and implementation of economic and social systems based more on the principles of sustainable development.

CSR/sustainability disclosure mainly falls into the voluntary sphere, since specific and comprehensive legislation in this field has not yet widely been spread, with the exception of a few countries such as Denmark, France, South Africa, or Sweden.[1] Consequently, the ways and the forms chosen by firms are, very often, a direct effect of the relevance which management attributes to the principles of CSR and sustainability and to the importance given to the information needs of all stakeholders.

Although sustainability disclosure has been received growing attention from academics and practitioners alike in recent years, relatively few organizations seem to have implemented comprehensive systems up to date. In the last few years, such issue has been in part filled up by initiatives of different organizations and institutions, both national and international, which have proposed various schemes for measuring and reporting CSR/sustainability performance, such as the framework developed by the Global Reporting Initiative (GRI)[2] or guidance documents published by the accountancy bodies.

The GRI Sustainability Reporting Guidelines are periodically reviewed to provide the best and most up-to-date guidance for effective sustainability reporting. Recently G4, the fourth such update, was developed, to be universally applicable to all organizations, large and small, across the world. The G4 guidelines aim "to help reporters prepare sustainability reports that matter, contain valuable information about the organization's most critical sustainability-related issues, and make such sustainability reporting standard practice. Together with the aim of being more user-friendly than previous versions of the Guidelines, G4 was developed to increase emphasis on the need for organizations to focus the reporting process and final report on those topics that are material to their business and their key stakeholders. This 'materiality' focus will make reports more relevant, more credible and more user-friendly. This will, in turn, enable organizations to better inform markets and society on sustainability matters."[3]

Also the European Union promotes a European framework for CSR performance measurement and indicates the so-called "triple bottom line" reporting as good practice, that is the idea that the overall performance of a company should be represented according to three perspectives: financial, social, and environmental.

The most recent initiative in this field is represented by the movement toward the so called "One report." It suggests that companies integrate both compulsory financial disclosure and voluntary social and environmental information (Eccles & Krzus, 2010). In this context, the International Integrated Reporting Council (IIRC) has launched in 2010 a project aimed to develop a global standard of disclosure which combines actual compulsory and voluntary disclosure guidelines and proposals into a single Integrated Reporting (IR) framework. IIRC's mission is to "create the globally accepted International [IR] Framework that elicits from organizations material information about their strategy, governance, performance and prospects in a clear, concise and comparable format. The Framework will underpin and accelerate the evolution of corporate reporting, reflecting developments in financial, governance, management commentary and sustainability reporting. The IIRC will seek to secure the adoption of [IR] by report preparers and gain the recognition of standard setters and investors."[4]

Notwithstanding the various initiatives promoting sustainability disclosure, relevant issues have not been yet enough considered by research, and practitioners, such as the effectiveness and quality of sustainability disclosure, its impacts on internal processes, managerial practices and mechanisms, the effects on organizational responsibilities, and, above all, the relationship between CSR/sustainability disclosure and managerial control systems.

In fact, while research has generated a sizeable body of insights into sustainability reporting and disclosure practices, quite a little is known about the relationship between external sustainability reporting and internal managerial accounting and reporting. Even less is known about the integration of sustainability into management control and its uses for strategic management, although there is a wide recognition that sustainability managerial accounting can play a central role in supporting the implementation of the sustainability strategy, embedding sustainability into day-to-day operations and decision making, and developing relationships with internal stakeholders based on trust and legitimacy. Paying more attention to this field appears to be even more sensible in today's environment where the linkage between business strategy and sustainable strategy has become more relevant as a consequence of the actual financial and economic crisis, which asks strongly for a new strategic paradigm, more focused on the ethical conduct of the firm, the social and environmental impact of its activities, and its duties and responsibilities toward all stakeholders. Moreover, previous research has shown that sustainability, effectively embedded, measured and communicated, has a positive correlation with higher profitability, lower risk, and better returns on the capital market.

A company that intends to integrate the sustainable principles into practice needs to use internal systems to influence people's behaviour and to align individual objectives with the company's goals and strategies. Management control systems (MCSs) and performance measurement systems (PMSs) can play a fundamental role to pursue those objectives which managers are responsible for and upon which they are evaluated and rewarded. PMSs, in particular, deal with the identification of the drivers of past and future performance and the related indicators, favouring the alignment between business strategy and sustainable strategy.

Clearly, redefining the actual role of MCSs as well designing, implementing and using MCSs focused on sustainability asks a company a big effort. The involvement of Accounting, Finance, and Control (AFC) department, and, within this the role of the controller in sustainability disclosure, performance measurement, and managerial control represent a relatively neglected topic in the research on accounting and control for sustainability. It also seems that practice has devoted little attention on questions of how to embed sustainability and CSR in MCSs and PMSs in order to align business strategy and sustainable strategy, as well the role of AFC department(s) and its relationship with the CSR/sustainability unit is very often an open issue. In fact, the empirical research shows that only a few companies have adopted MCSs and PMSs oriented to CSR and sustainability (such as the sustainability balanced scorecard) and have involved the AFC department and the controller in the sustainability issues.[5]

Starting from these premises, the aim of this book is to explore new challenges and new prospects in studies on accounting for sustainability, and discuss future directions of research.

In particular, this book aims to critically review and advance theorizations and methodological applications in the study of accounting and control for sustainability, highlighting the relevance of different theories and research approaches, issues which have not yet been analyzed jointly before, highlighting the potential richness of this stream of research for both sustainability and accounting studies. A large spectrum of theoretical lenses, such as legitimacy theory, stakeholder theory, resource-based view (RBV) theory, institutional theory, positive accounting theory, proprietary cost theory, agency theory, and theory of asymmetric information as well different research methods, have been brought together, and various types of organizational settings and practices in different countries have been explored. The book features both conceptual and empirical articles using various methodologies, such as univariate analysis, multivariate analysis, but also case study analysis. The empirical articles draw on different samples and contexts, consisting mainly of European companies, such as large enterprises and SMEs in Italy, large enterprises in the United Kingdom and Germany, and a large Danish company.

The book is divided in two parts, which respectively deal with the two main issues related to CSR/sustainability accounting and performance measurement: the mechanisms devoted to the external communication, and internal managerial accounting and control.

The first part of this volume is entitled "Sustainability Disclosure: Determinants and Practices." It aims to increase our understanding of sustainability's role for and impact on voluntary disclosure and corporate reporting. It presents the more diffused practices of sustainability reporting adopted by companies, and the main determinants of sustainability and CSR disclosure. It highlights both the similarities and differences among different industries, countries, and types of enterprises. In particular, it copes with the lack of knowledge in the field of sustainability disclosure in small and medium sized enterprises (SMEs). A more specific and emerging form of accountability, water-related accounting and accountability, is also discussed.

Chapters in the first part of this volume cover the following topics: corporate social responsibility determinants and the relation with CSR disclosure (Pistoni and Songini); the determinants of corporate social disclosure through a multiperspective approach, focusing on evidences from the target companies of socially responsible funds (Gangi and Trotta); the sustainability disclosure in SMEs (Scagnelli, Corazza, and Cisi); and water management and accounting (Signori and Avondo Bodino).

This volume also intends to contribute to the debate on the relationship between sustainability and management accounting, focusing on MCSs and PMSs. Managerial accounting, in fact, represents a field in accounting for sustainability that requires greater attention from both accounting and sustainability scholars, primarily due to the limited number of contributions in this area and the benefits that embedding sustainability in MCSs and PMSs can offer to companies. Concerning the relations between sustainability and MCSs and PMSs, the second part of this volume, entitled "Integrating Sustainability into Business Practice: The Role of Managerial Control Systems and Accountants," deals with the following topics: a review of the empirical research in management control, strategy and sustainability (Crutzen and Herzig); a review of the evidence and claims for future research on eco-control mechanisms (Derchi, Burkert, and Oyon); the use of causal mapping in the design of sustainability PMSs, based on the evidence from Novo Nordisk (Parisi); the role of accountants in controlling sustainability information (Schaltegger and Zvezdov).

A summary of the main contents of the different chapters is provided in the following.

Pistoni and Songini contribute to the debate on determinants of CSR and their impact on performance measurement and communication systems. They analyze the relationship between the reasons why firms adopt CSR and the importance given to voluntary CSR disclosure. Referring to the frameworks proposed by the body of theories, which deal with CSR issues, such as legitimacy theory, stakeholder theory, and institutional theory, two main categories of CSR determinants have been identified: the external ones, coming from the environment outside the firm, and the internal determinants, which are linked to some specific characteristics of the enterprise and to the objectives it pursues. The CSR drivers have been used to explain the reasons why firms decide to report and communicate their CSR and sustainability performance. The analyzed sample consists of 120 large Italian manufacturing and nonmanufacturing enterprises. Main results point out that in companies giving importance to CSR disclosure, the internal drivers are more relevant than the external ones in determining the attitude toward CSR. Among the internal determinants, drivers related to company and management values and ethics, are seen to be relevant.

Starting from the main theoretical frameworks on corporate social disclosure (CSD), such as the legitimacy theory, the stakeholder-based approach, the agency theory, the theory of asymmetric information and the institutional perspective, Gangi and Trotta empirically investigate the determinants of CSD. The study is based on the analysis of the sustainability reports of 80 companies participated by the European socially responsible funds (SRFs) listed on the Morningstar platform during 2008–2009. Research findings show that the breadth of disclosure is associated with multiple factors both external and internal to the firm, such as country of origin, industry reputation, firm size, frequency of the SRFs participation, and corporate social performance. For a comprehensive understanding of the deeper causes of the variations in CSD, the outcome of the survey supports an interpretative approach that enables to look at the CSD through different perspectives.

Scagnelli, Corazza, and Cisi provide insights on SMEs' involvement in sustainability reporting and the variables influencing the choice of reporting guidelines. On the basis of a survey carried out among all Italian companies which were certified in 2011, as having adopted both environmental and social management systems, their research demonstrates that, in most cases, SMEs prefer to use simple guidelines which are mandatory under management systems certification. Some exceptions are represented by SMEs within a group of companies or when a significant amount of time has passed since the certification date. Such findings drive the authors to develop an interpretative framework of the firms' behavioral drivers according to legitimacy theory.

The paper written by Signori and Avondo Bodino introduces and discusses a specific form of accountability, recognizing a right to water-related information. After a presentation of the risks and responsibilities connected with water issues, mainly from a business point of view, the chapter focuses on water management and accounting. In particular, the need for shared forms of water accountability is highlighted. Moreover, an analysis of the potentials offered by the developments of the Australian General Purpose Water Accounting (GPWA) standard setting, as a form of global and multi-stakeholder accountability, is presented. The results of Signori and Avondo Bodino's research demonstrate that significant progress is still to be made on disclosing water-related data in a more uniform and comparable manner, even though promising developments are emerging, such as GPWA.

The role of management control for supporting strategies orientated toward sustainability has increasingly been discussed in the literature. In their literature review paper, Crutzen and Herzig explore the theoretical frameworks and models used in 27 empirical papers as well as the research questions and methods applied to empirically explore this emerging research area. The review shows that, even if a growing body of empirical research has emerged over the last decade, our current knowledge about how companies design or use management control to support environmental or sustainability strategy appears to be limited in several ways, providing scope for further research. For example, using the framework developed by Tucker et al. (2009), Crutzen and Herzig show that a disproportionate part of the empirical studies investigate how management control design supports sustainability strategy implementation and that other "relationships" (such as management control use and strategy content) have been less frequently examined. Overall, this first attempt to structure this emerging body of empirical literature provides guidance in structuring the state of our knowledge in this area and in guiding future research efforts.

Derchi, Burkert, and Oyon state that organizations' increasing concern for environmental results requires appropriate accounting mechanisms that take into account relevant flows of environment-related information. Today, both managers and researchers are promoting environmental management accounting (EMA) mechanisms as a means to incorporate the full spectrum of environment-related data into day-to-day business decisions and foster green management execution. However implementation remains a challenge and many of the difficulties are associated with conceptual and practical problems in integrating "green" information and providing guidance on how to effectively execute green management. In this context academics have room to provide further explanations on how to achieve excellence in both environmental and financial performance, and contribute to management accounting research. The authors reviewed the growing body of research on EMA mechanisms in order to give insights on what has been studied to date. They indicate the necessity for further theoretical and empirical work. In addition, they make suggestions of areas for future investigation. In particular researchers might explore the concept of environmental performance and the application of different forms of green management control within organizations. Moreover accounting scholars have the opportunity to further examine the role of EMA mechanisms in companies that do not seem to pursue environmental results for specific economic benefits.

Parisi's study advances the understanding of the relationship between sustainability and financial results in three ways: theoretically, methodologically, and empirically. On the theoretical side, it aims at opening the black box of the RBV to extend the literature on the operationalization of sustainability. More specifically, a model is presented in which ethical and sustainable practices are analyzed as mediating factors in the relationship between sustainability and financial returns. To support the definition of the empirical model, the study draws upon the recent formulation of the RBV framework linking social and environmental challenges to organizational resources, that is, the so-called "natural RBV." Methodologically, Parisi's study aims at overcoming the lack of consensus on the relationship between sustainability and financial results, which also relates to measurement issues, the omission of variables, and a lack of clear direction of causality between social and financial performance by using a multi-method approach, the causal map. The study uses two methods to build causal maps, that is, aggregate and congregate mapping, in order to capture managerial cognition. The resulting causal map is a prerequisite and serves as a building block for the design of the organization's Strategic Performance Measurement Systems (SPMS) for sustainability. Finally, Parisi's study shows that the use of the ad hoc methodology of causal mapping can support the process of quantifying the financial returns related to CSR. Empirically, the research relies on qualitative, deductive research that was undertaken at a leading international pharmaceutical company, Novo Nordisk, in order to provide more robust findings than those provided by previous studies. This setting is particularly relevant for the risk related to the management of sustainability in the pharmaceutical industry and the related problems of designing an effective SPMS. In addition, Novo Nordisk's unique ownership structure, which is controlled by the Novo Nordisk Foundation that has a purely humanitarian mission, allows the company to focus on sustainability beyond the boundaries of a traditional normative approach, making it a relevant case for the present research.

The paper written by Schaltegger and Zvezdov, finally, analyze the accountants' involvement in environmental and sustainability management. Starting from the evidence of the continuous take-up of sustainability issues by companies and with the growing experience companies gain in dealing with this topic, the chapter raises the question whether accountants are involved in a way different than previously reported and if yes, what their role is in social accounting practice. The authors empirically investigate and discuss the accountant's contribution to sustainability information management, which can help overcome organizational challenges impeding companies to successfully implement sustainability measures. Based on 58 interviews with corporate practitioners, the chapter first explores the roles in the social accounting practice in companies which are considered to be leading in sustainability reporting in the United Kingdom and Germany. Second, the role of professional accountants is analyzed from a power theory perspective. Main findings suggest that professional accountants are partially involved in social accounting practice but mainly exert a gate keeping role between sustainability managers and higher management. Practical implications of the research show that accountants have no other option but to act like gatekeepers; accounting education will play a major role in overcoming this deficiency in the pursuit of improved sustainability knowledge and performance. If, on the other hand, it is the defensive stance of accounting professionals and the fear of losing power in corporate structures which motivates them to act as gatekeepers, mechanisms to motivate them to cooperate should be researched.

To conclude, the points of strength of this volume concern the variety of topics, contexts, and research methodologies covered, which confirms the increasing interest of scholars in issues of accounting and control for sustainability, as well as the potential of this stream of research to inform both accounting and sustainability studies. Sustainability disclosure and corporate reporting as well as relevant aspects in managerial accounting are addressed, the latter of which have been rather underdeveloped in previous studies. We believe that MCSs and PMSs for sustainability, in particular, represent a research field that could attract greater interest in the future. Consequently, we also consider that the impact embedding sustainability within MCSs and PMSs can have on the accounting profession, and especially on the role of controller, remains an open question that future research should explore in greater depth.

Lucrezia Songini
Anna Pistoni
Christian Herzig
Volume Editors

NOTES

1. On March 1, 2010 the Johannesburg Stock Exchange (JSE) adopted the King III principles as part of its listing requirements. Listed companies in South Africa have to apply King III principles, which recommend Integrated Reporting (IR) and hence the requirements for listed companies to issue integrated reports. South Africa is leading the way internationally with regard to IR, being the first country in the world to take on integrated reporting on scale.
2. See www.globalreporting.org.
3. See https://www.globalreporting.org/reporting/g4/g4-developments/Pages/default.aspx.
4. See http://www.ifrs.org/Use-around-the-world/Pages/Use-around-the-world.aspx.
5. Case studies of enterprises which have embedded sustainability among strategic planning and MCSs, and have involved the AFC department in sustainability issues are presented in the book: "Mainstreaming Corporate Responsibility: Cases and Text for Integrating Corporate Responsibility across the Business School Curriculum," edited by N. C. Smith and G. Lenssen, Wiley, 2009. In particular, see the chapters "Enel: CSR and performance measurement," by A. Pistoni and L. Songini.

REFERENCES

Eccles, R. G., & Krzus, M. (2010). *One report: Integrated reporting for a sustainable strategy*. New York, NY: Wiley.

Tucker, B., Thorne, H., & Gurd, B. (2009). Management control systems and strategy: What's been happening? *Journal of Accounting Literature*, *28*, 123–133.

PART I
SUSTAINABILITY DISCLOSURE: DETERMINANTS AND PRACTICES

CORPORATE SOCIAL RESPONSIBILITY DETERMINANTS: THE RELATION WITH CSR DISCLOSURE

Anna Pistoni and Lucrezia Songini

ABSTRACT

Purpose – *This chapter intends to contribute to the debate on the determinants of corporate social responsibility (CSR) and their impact on performance measurement and communication systems. It aims at analyzing the relationship between the reasons why firms adopt CSR and the importance given to voluntary CSR disclosure.*

Methodology – *Two main categories of CSR determinants have been identified: the external ones, coming from the environment outside the firm, and the internal determinants, which are linked to some specific characteristics of the enterprise and to the objectives it pursues.*

The analyzed sample consists of 120 large Italian manufacturing and nonmanufacturing enterprises. The research hypotheses concerning the relationship between external and internal determinants of CSR and

Accounting and Control for Sustainability
Studies in Managerial and Financial Accounting, Volume 26, 3–32

ISSN: 1479-3512/doi:10.1108/S1479-3512(2013)0000026001

CSR disclosure were verified using an independent sample t-*test, evaluating the equal variances of clusters using the Levene's test.*

Findings – *Main results point out that in companies giving importance to CSR disclosure, the internal drivers are more relevant than the external ones in determining the attitude toward CSR. Among the internal determinants, drivers related to company and management values and ethics are quite relevant.*

Research limitations – *This study is subject to the limitations that generally apply to cross-sectional survey-based research.*

Originality/Value of chapter – *Our research findings show that legitimacy theory represents the most relevant theory in explaining CSR disclosure practices of Italian large firms, as well as the operational implementation of stakeholder theory, such as stakeholder management. On the contrary, institutional theory only partially explains CSR disclosure, with respect to the pressures coming from financial markets.*

Keywords: CSR determinants; CSR disclosure; CSR performance measurement and communication; CSR internal drivers; CSR external drivers; large Italian companies

INTRODUCTION

Over the last few decades a growing awareness of the role of firms in society has emerged. The concern is justified. One the one hand, a number of firms have caused negative impacts on society and the environment, even though they have contributed to economic and technological progress. On the other hand, issues such as pollution, waste, resource depletion, product quality and safety, labor conditions, human rights, and status of workers have gained growing attention and concern.

In this context, companies have been increasingly urged to become accountable to the complex of stakeholders. Besides, public awareness in environmental and social issues and increased attention in mass media have resulted in more social disclosures from corporations.

Corporate social responsibility (CSR) refers to a company's activities – voluntary by definition – demonstrating the inclusion of social and environmental concerns in business operations and in interaction with its stakeholders (CEC, 2001). Within this general concept, there are many definitions of CSR provided by literature (Bowen, 1953; Carroll, 1991; Carroll & Shabana, 2010; Frederick, 1960; Renneboog, Ter Horst, & Zhang, 2008). However, in more than four decades of research and practice on CSR, a single and agreed definition of the term CSR has not yet been developed by researchers and the business community (Hayes & Walker, 2005; Thomas & Nowak, 2006). In fact, the concepts of CSR, sustainability, corporate citizenship, and business ethics are often used as synonyms (Maon, Lindgreen, & Swaen, 2010; Mercer Investment Consulting, 2007); all of them highlight the relevance of different issues, such as transparency, public disclosure, stakeholder engagement, societal approach to business, human capital, and so on (Lenssen, Perrini, Tencati, & Lacy, 2007).

Different theories have coped with CSR related issues, which have been classified by Garriga and Melé (2004) into four main groups:

- Instrumental theories, which assume that the only firm's social responsibility is wealth creation. Consequently, CSR is considered as a mere means to the end of profits.
- Political theories, which emphasize the firm's social power and its responsibility in the political environment associated with this power. CSR is the mean which the corporation accepts its social duties and rights or participate in social cooperation.
- Integrative theories, which consider that enterprises have to integrate social demands, through CSR, because they depend on society for their continuity and growth as well as for the existence of the business itself.
- Ethical theories, which consider the relationship between business and society embedded with ethical values. CSR assumes an ethical perspective and, as a consequence, firms have to accept social responsibilities as an ethical obligation.

All these theories highlight different reasons why firms engage in CSR initiatives. According to Wood (1991, p. 709), enterprises apply the principles of CSR for three main reasons: "(a) *institutional* – to uphold the legitimacy of business in society, (b) *organizational* – to improve the firm's adaptability and fit with its environment, and (c) *moral/ethical*, to create a culture of ethical choice."

In the last few years, motivation for companies to implement CSR initiatives has become a popular area of research, which has highlighted multiple and different drivers of CSR (Buehler & Shetty, 1974), such as: firm's proximity to the social issue in question (Pedersen & Neergaard, 2008), company's economic and organizational resources and skills, competitive environment and competitors' strategy (Wokutch & Shepard, 1999), national cultural values (Matten & Moon, 2008), self-enlightened motivation of management and owners, legal compliance (Moon, 2004), image creation, and improvement of future profits and goodwill (McWillam & Siegel, 2002).

The central idea of CSR is that business and society are not distinct entities: society has expectations about firms' behavior and their social impact and, to be defined socially sound, firms have to take into consideration and give an adequate response to the various social issues (Davis, 1973). Consequently, there is a considerable and diverse body of literature – and a less extensive but clearly identifiable set of practices – which rests on a broader conception of the accountability appropriate to economic agents and entities.

Included in this extensive category is literature addressing the development and implementation of social and environmental accounting, sustainability reporting, and auditing practices. In various ways, this literature assigns economic entities with an extra-contractual obligation, and hence it takes a broad view of the extent of accountability, which is appropriate for economic entities (Shearer, 2002). A number of studies have dealt with CSR performance measurement and communication, emphasizing different aspects of such issue (Cormier, Gordon, & Magnan, 2004; Deegan, 2002; Eccles & Krzus, 2010; Hinna, 2002; Lehman, 1995, 1999; Roberts, 1992; Rusconi, 1988; Ullman, 1985; Unerman, Bebbington, & O'Dwyer, 2007; Wood, 2010). Among these studies, a significant body of literature has focused on CSR disclosure (Deegan, 2006; Hackston & Milne, 1996; Gray, Owen, & Adams, 1996; Larrinaga-Gonzales, 2007). According to Reverte (2009) three types of studies have been produced among the empirical research on CSR disclosure. The first one relates to "descriptive studies," which analyze the nature and extent of CSR disclosure and make comparison among different countries and time periods; the second type is based on "explicative studies," which pay attention to the determinants of social and environmental disclosure; finally, the third one focuses on the "impact of social and environmentnal information" on various users, mainly on market reaction.

Our study falls within the second group, as it aims at analyzing whether the reasons why a firm engages in CSR affect the CSR disclosure practices of firms.

As stated by Van Staden and Hooks (2007), much has been written about what motivates organizations to disclose information about their interactions with the environment (Deegan, 2002; Mathews, 2003). Adams (2002) highlighted that previous literature on the factors that influence disclosure focused on three main aspects: corporate characteristics (including size, industry, financial/economic performance, share trading volume, price and risk), general contextual factors (such as country of origin, time, specific events, media pressures, stakeholders, and finally social, political, cultural, and economic contexts), and the internal context (including the identity of company chair and the existence of a social reporting committee).

Beyond the descriptive analysis, studies have begun to extend the empirical CSR disclosure (CSD) literature by focusing on a number of corporate characteristics, which are potential determinants of CSR disclosure practices. In reviewing these studies, Gray, Kouhy, and Lavers (1995) noted that a number of empirical studies have shown strong associations between disclosure and firm size, and between disclosure and type of industry. Such studies concluded that CSD is not related to profitability in the same period, but it may be related to lagged profits. CSD does appear to be related to company size, while industry appears to affect CSD, even though studies are not clear or consistent enough to determine such effects precisely. In addition, the country, in which the company reports or where the firm's ownership is established, appears to be related to CSD. Finally, capital intensity, age, senior executive attitudes, and social responsibility committees may be related to CSD.

Moving on from such preliminary remarks, this chapter intends to contribute to the debate on the impact of CSR on performance measurement and communication systems. It focuses on CSR disclosure, aiming at analyzing the relationship between the reasons why firms adopt CSR and the importance given to voluntary CSR disclosure. Based on the framework proposed by different theories, two main categories of CSR determinants have been identified: the external ones, coming from the environment outside the company, and the internal determinants, which are linked to some specific characteristics of the enterprise and to the objectives it pursues.

The analyzed sample consisted of 120 large Italian manufacturing and nonmanufacturing enterprises. The research hypotheses concerning the relationship between CSR disclosure and external and internal determinants of CSR were verified using an independent sample *t*-test, evaluating the equal variances of clusters using the Levene's test. Findings show that in companies giving importance to CSR disclosure, the internal drivers are more relevant than the external ones in determining the firm's attitude toward CSR. Among the internal determinants, both drivers related to company and management values and ethics, as well as the improvement of the company image are relevant.

The chapter proceeds in five sections. Firstly, the theoretical mainstreams on the determinants of CSR and CSR disclosure are outlined. Secondly, the research propositions and hypotheses are highlighted. Thirdly, the research design and methods are described. In the fourth section, findings are presented. Finally, implications and limitations of the study are discussed.

THEORETICAL BACKGROUND

Even though a great number of studies have dealt with the issue of what are the determinants of both CSR and CSR disclosure, a common and recognized theoretical framework has not yet been developed. Previous literature shows an overlap among theories and studies, which focused on both CSR determinants and the drivers of CSR disclosures.

Gray et al. (1995) argued that corporate social and environmental reporting determinants may be explained through three main broad groups of theories, focused on organization-society information flows: (1) decision – usefulness studies, (2) economic theory studies, and (3) social and political theory studies.

Holder-Webb,Cohen, Nath, and Wood (2009) suggested four main theoretical streams, as main reference frameworks to understand the why of CSR activity and CSR disclosures, such as: neo-classical economics, studies on marketing strategy, political economy, and institutional theory. They stated that: "the choice of broad theoretical framework depends on whether the researcher approaches the question of CSR from an economic or an ethical standpoint" (Holder-Webb et al., 2009, p. 499). Ethical theories affirm that CSR activities and disclosures "should be promoted because they are the right thing to do" (Holder-Webb et al., 2009, p. 499). On the contrary, these authors suggest that economic theories highlight the role of CSR and disclosure in creating shareholder wealth. However, both theoretical approaches suggest that "it is not enough to partake of a CSR action, it is necessary then to disseminate information about the action that has been taken" (Holder-Webb et al., 2009, p. 499), pointing out a strong relationship between CSR and related disclosure. However, "it is difficult, from an academic and theoretical perspective, to disentangle the differences between a firm's decision to engage in CSR activities and the decision on why, how and when to report on those activities to stakeholders" (Holder-Webb et al., 2009, p. 499).

Different disciplinary and theoretical streams have been proposed, concerning the determinants of CSR and CSR disclosure. CSR drivers have been studied in the context of political economy theory, stakeholder theory, legitimacy theory, economic theory, and institutional theory, while other theories have coped more specifically with the determinants of disclosure (both accounting and CSR one), such as positive accounting theory, proprietary cost theory, and decision-usefulness studies.

In particular, political economy and economic theory can be considered as more general frameworks, while stakeholder theory, legitimacy theory, and positive accounting theory can be classified as second-level theories.

In this study, to cope with the analysis of the determinants of both CSR and disclosure, we have adopted mainly the framework of legitimacy theory, stakeholder theory, positive accounting theory, and institutional theory, even though the theoretical approaches of proprietary cost theory and decision-usefulness studies have been also considered.

Legitimacy theory highlights the existence of different contracts between the company and the society (Dowling & Pfeffer; 1975; Luthans, 1985; Mathews, 1997). According to such theory, to achieve legitimacy an organization should operate within the norms and expectations of the society within which it acts. When the company's objectives are aligned with those of society, the social contract is effectively pursued and the enterprise obtains legitimacy. Conversely, the existence of the company is threatened if society feels that it did not respect the social contract, operating in an unacceptable and illegitimate way. In such case, the society could revoke the contract, preventing the company from continuing its activity, causing, as a consequence, customer losses, reduction in product demand, interruption of labor and capital supplies, and pressure on governmental bodies to pass measures that punish actions not aligned with the community's expectations.

Legitimacy is defined as a condition or status that exists when the value system of an entity is consistent with the wider value system of the society to which it belongs (Lindblom, 1994). Legitimacy is also an essential resource for an organization's survival, even though the organization itself can influence and manipulate it. Consistently with the resource dependence theory (Pfeffer & Salancik, 1978), legitimacy theory suggests that when managers realize that the availability of a particular resource is vital for the company's survival, they have to undertake actions and measures aimed at guaranteeing its availability. Particularly, the ways a company can obtain trust in its activities, in the case of threats to legitimacy, are numerous. The enterprise can adapt its output, objectives, and management methods to conform to the prevalent definition of legitimacy. Through communication, a firm can try to be identified with strongly legitimated symbols, values, or institutions. Therefore, to gain and maintain legitimacy in the eye's of society, communication plays a relevant role (Lindblom, 1994). Thus, legitimacy theory has been used as an underlying theory also in environmental and social disclosure research. According to Suchman (1995), strategic organizational legitimacy views legitimacy as a resource that management can use by manipulating and deploying evocative symbols to obtain societal support. As a result, legitimacy management is heavily dependent on communication between the organization and its various audiences. Disclosure is necessary to demonstrate legitimacy, on the one hand, but, on the other hand, organizations may face a legitimacy threat if society is not aware that they are operating within its norms and expectations.

Considering an olistic vision of the company, legitimacy theory highlights the role of information and disclosure in the relations among organizations, institutions, individuals, and groups (Dowling & Pfeffer, 1975; Jones, 1999; Luthans, 1985; Mathews, 1997). Likewise, Patten (1991) argues that social disclosure represents one of the methods that firms can use to influence the public policy process. The desired effect is to reduce the exposure of the company to the social and political environment.

Legitimacy theory states that companies can follow a proactive or reactive approach toward achieving legitimacy. Many studies have found evidence of the reactive approach, meaning that companies publish environmental and social information in reaction to some event or crisis facing either the company or the industry. Verrecchia (1983) and Dye (1986) argued that firms use accounting disclosure to overcome adverse selection. According to Deegan (2002) the need to counter threats to an organization's legitimacy is a strong driver of CSR disclosure. In fact, the publication of the environmental and social report could represent an answer to the negative propaganda of media, as a consequence of environmental or social incidents, or to a negative evaluation of rating agencies. On the contrary, the proactive approach, which considers disclosure designed to prevent legitimacy concerns from arising, has been neglected in the literature, even though economic rationality could force companies to adopt CSR disclosure to impact positively on business activities, improving the company's image (Deegan, 2002). "The benefit from an enhanced reputation that we are thinking of is not that it reduces the perceived riskiness of the future cash flows, nor that it induces investors to expect higher cash flows because they are less skeptical, nor that the company will have a more accurate market value. The benefit is improved competitive advantage and ease of doing business" (Armitage & Marston, 2008). Firms with above-average performance use disclosure to favorably distinguish themselves from other firms, thereby increasing demand for their securities and decrease their cost of capital. The research of Herremans, Parporn, and McInnes (1993) showed that CSR, effectively measured and communicated, has a positive correlation with higher profitability, lower risk, and better returns on the capital market.

According to stakeholder theory, among a number of reasons suggested by literature to explain why companies would disclose voluntary environmental and social information, the desire to be legitimated with powerful stakeholders is pointed out. This implies that organizations make voluntary disclosure in order to gain legitimacy from or maintain legitimacy with relevant stakeholders or public. Gelb and Strawser (2001) pointed out that firms may provide more informative disclosure as a consequence of a sense of responsibility to their stakeholders. Particularly, they found that companies engaged in CSR activities adopt more informative and extensive disclosure than do enterprises less focused on CSR. As a consequence, disclosure is a form of socially responsible behavior. Accordingly, stakeholder theory (Donaldson & Preston, 1995; Freeman, 1984; Freeman & Reed, 1983) gives a useful mainframe in understanding the role of CSR disclosure. As the firm acts within a complex and dynamic network of people and groups, its survival depends on its ability to create value through the satisfaction of the stakeholders' interests. Individuals and groups are in fact willing to give the firm the resources it needs only if the relationship with the firm is perceived as fair and convenient. The immediate consequence is the need for the firm to balance the different interests of the various groups of stakeholders. Indeed, the financial perspective alone is not able to guarantee firm's decisions, actions, and behaviors aligned with stakeholder satisfaction. Therefore, information represents one of the most important ways for the enterprise to deal with different stakeholder groups, in order to obtain their support and approval, or, vice versa, to remove their opposition and disapproval (Deegan, Rankin, & Voght, 2000). In other words, information is shared for strategic reasons, rather than for recognized responsibility. The stakeholders' approach is consistent with the drive toward accountability, which requires that individuals take responsibility for their actions: "the giving and demanding of reasons for conduct" (Roberts & Scapens, 1985). Indeed, accountability requires enterprises to account for the outcomes of decisions and actions in a transparent and objective way. On the one hand, accountability benefits from the relationship with objective and scientific characteristics of accounting methods (Gambling, 1977;

Hopwood, 1984); on the other hand, it requires an agreement about what is good conduct and acceptable performance. It states that a firm has to register all the business operations that can influence the risk position of third parties, whose interests converge in the firm, but who do not directly participate in the operations mentioned.

Discussing the reduced importance given by companies to accountability and transparency, when compared to management advantage, some authors have proposed the concept of "managerial capture" (Bebbington, 1997; Owen, Gray, & Bebbington, 1997; Owen, Swift, Humphrey, & Bowerman, 2000; Power, 1991). It refers to "the concept that sees management take control of the whole process (including the degree of stakeholder inclusion) by strategically collecting and disseminating only the information it deems appropriate to advance the corporate image, rather than being truly transparent and accountable to the society it serves. This is not to say that managerial capture results only in a myopic and limited number of stakeholders being included. On the contrary, managerial capture may also result in over-inflated promises of accountability to an all-encompassing and essentially meaningless set of 'stakeholders'" (Owen et al., 2000, p. 85).

Theoretical arguments developed by both legitimacy theory and stakeholder theory aimed at explaining CSR activities and disclosure, under the more general framework and lens of the political economy (Campbell, 2003; Deegan & Gordon, 1996; Guthrie & Parker, 1990; Maignan & Ralston, 2002). "However, in the area of CSR it is difficult to distinguish between the drivers and the implications of legitimacy theory versus stakeholder theory, as the target population according to both theories will be the community of individuals providing access to resources, or those in a position to enhance or diminish the firm's ability to access resources" (Holder-Webb et al., 2009, pp. 500–501).

CSR disclosure may be not only the outcome of a decision-making rational process by organizations acting independently, rather it could become institutionalized, determining to some extent the choice of organizations (Larrinaga-Gonzales, 2007). In fact, institutional theory suggests that organizations will adapt their structures and operations to conform with external expectations about what is acceptable. This process is referred to as "isomorphism" and causes institutions to become increasingly similar (DiMaggio & Powell, 1983, 1991). Isomorphism may have implications for both CSR activities and disclosure. "To the extent that managers… have been inculcated with the belief that CSR activity is necessary… it is possible that the surge in this type of activity – and related disclosure – represents a form of normative isomorphism. To the extent that the upsurge in such activity is perceived by managers to be a competitive requirement irrespective of the need to deploy ethical principles or to derive gains from specific resources it may be mimetic" (Holder-Webb et al., 2009, p. 499).

According to Larrinaga-Gonzales (2007), there is an overlap between institutional theory and legitimacy theory, that allow to say that the former is richer than the latter. Deegan (2006, p. 305) states that institutional theory provides a complementary perspective, to both stakeholder theory and legitimacy theory, to investigate voluntary corporate reporting practices, and to understand how organizations comprehend and respond to changing social and institutional pressures and expectations. It could be argued that while legitimacy theory is more useful for determining in the short term why a given organization is making particular CSR disclosure, institutional theory is more helpful in the explanation of why given CSR disclosure practices become common in a particular context.

Legitimacy theory, with respect to the proactive approach, and stakeholders theory highlight mainly the internal determinants of CSR disclosure, which are related to company's values, objectives, and strategies; the relevance given to different groups of stakeholders; and issue related to economic rationality, such as company image and risk aversion. However, if a reactive approach is followed, legitimacy theory focuses on external determinants of CSR.

Instead, institutional theory focuses mainly on external factors that can encourage enterprises to enrich their performance measurement systems with CSR elements. It highlights that among factors determining CSR initiatives there are practices followed by competitors or enterprises in the same industry (Harrison & Freeman, 1999). Moreover, in a number of companies programs aimed at reinforcing the relationship with institutional investors have outlined the need to pursue a strategy based on disclosure. Sparkes and Cowton (2004) have highlighted that socially responsible investing (SRI) could play a crucial role in obliging and influencing quoted companies to address social issues. Again, the information requests coming from the financial markets that are becoming more and more sensitive to the social and environmental conduct of the listed firms move firms to disclose CSR information. Disclosure for the financial markets significantly considers all aspects of company performance, increasing the number and kind of information communicated by enterprises, from the financial indicators to the environmental and social ones (Di Piazza & Eccles, 2002; Eccles & Krzus, 2010).

As CSR disclosure requires, on the one hand, to integrate and communicate financial and nonfinancial information, on the other hand to collect, process, elaborate, and communicate a great mass of data and information, which represent typical responsibilities and competences of the accounting profession, it can be useful to consider also accounting theory when studying the determinants of CSR disclosure. In particular, in order to understand why and how managers and companies implement CSR measurement and communications practices, three main theoretical streams can be proposed: decision-usefulness studies, positive accounting theory, and proprietary cost theory.

The studies developed according to the decision-usefulness framework relate to the usefulness of accounting information, and can be grouped into two categories. The first group has argued that CSR has gained perceived importance among the information set considered by the financial community in order to support the investment decision processes (Belkaoui, 1984; Benjamin & Stanga, 1977; Chenall & Juchau, 1977; Firth, 1984). The second group of studies has attempted to investigate whether CSR disclosure is treated as information by stock market participants (Aupperle, 1984; Belkaoui, 1980; Bowman, 1973; Shane & Spicer, 1983; Spicer, 1978) and has proposed some investigations of information effects on share prices. However, the decision-usefulness approach has been considered largely unsatisfactory to investigate CSR disclosure (Gray et al., 1995) for two main reasons. On the one side, the criticism is a consequence of the theoretical problems with decision usefulness itself, because it lacks a theoretical backing; on the other side, it depends on the fact that the involvement in CSR disclosure could not be motivated mainly by the needs of the financial participants but from other nonfinancial motives of the corporations. In fact, apart from the pressures coming from the financial markets, and the willingness to be aligned with the requests of its own industry or with particular codes of conduct, other external drivers can impact on CSR disclosure. Deegan (2002) has pointed out that the need to be aligned with the body of legislation can be considered an external driver which forces enterprises to disclose CSR. Even though legislative recommendations often cannot put strong pressure on enterprises, due to the absence of a specific body of legislation on social and environmental disclosure and related control systems in most countries, Holland and Foo (2003) highlighted that elements of the legal and regulatory framework of each country impact on environmental and social disclosures. Also national business systems, which are characterized by specific and different political, financial, education, labor, and cultural systems, may explain differences among CSR definitions, initiatives, and practices adopted by companies of different countries (Matten & Moon, 2008).

Moreover, positive accounting theory, in particular the political cost hypothesis, can be suggested to explain why firms make voluntary social disclosures. Based on the original work of Watts and Zimmerman (1978, 1986), several empirical studies (e.g., Belkaoui & Karpik, 1989; Ness & Mirza, 1991) have directly sought to establish evidence for the political cost hypothesis as an explanation for firms' social disclosure. The objective of positive accounting theory is to describe, explain, and predict accounting practice of managers. This theory is an expression of neo-classical economic theory, being based on the belief in human rationale choice and the opportunistic behavior as the basis for all economic activities. According to positive accounting theory, self-interest is considered the main reason for the choice of accounting methods and techniques as well as policy decisions. Such theory considers the firm as a nexus of contracts that are necessary in order to motivate the individuals (managers, lenders of capital, and employees) to cooperate and to act to maximize the shareholders value. However, as there are contracting costs associated with the contracts (e.g., cost of negotiation and of involved parties' performance monitoring), positive accounting theory holds that firms will seek to minimize these costs. This will affect the policies adopted, including the accounting policies. In order to minimize the contracting costs, firms will be driven to publish certain information like corporate social disclosure.

In the context of research on social and environmental disclosure, Gray et al. (1995) dismissed the positive accounting arguments and literature on the grounds of the underlying assumptions of this theoretical framework. As they suggested, positive theories are not about what social reporting should be but rather about what it is. As a basis for change and improvement, positive theories are seen to offer little or no development of corporate social reporting.

Finally, proprietary cost theory states that enterprises limit voluntary disclosure due to the existence of some disclosure costs (Darrough & Stoughton, 1990; Dye, 1986; Verrecchia, 1983, 1990; Wagenhofer, 1990). Such theory states that the probability of a company communicating information is negatively correlated with the costs of disclosure, and positively correlated with its benefits. The costs of disclosure are related to data and information measurement, elaboration and communication, and the diffusion of strategic information, which can give competitors an advantage or can be used against the company's interests. Armitage and Marston (2008) highlighted that the bulk of costs of disclosure is staff time and management time, as well as incremental creation and provision of information. Holland (2006) lists the perceived costs of communication in the United Kingdom as

Table 1. Different Theories' Focus.

<table>
<tr><th>Focus/Theory</th><th>CSR Determinants</th><th>Disclosure Determinants</th><th>Internal Determinants</th><th>External Determinants</th></tr>
<tr><td>Legitimacy Theory</td><td style="background:gray"></td><td style="background:gray"></td><td style="background:gray">Proactive approach</td><td style="background:gray">Reactive approach</td></tr>
<tr><td>Stakeholder Theory</td><td style="background:gray"></td><td style="background:gray"></td><td style="background:gray"></td><td></td></tr>
<tr><td>Institutional Theory</td><td style="background:gray"></td><td style="background:gray"></td><td></td><td style="background:gray"></td></tr>
<tr><td>Decision-usefulness studies</td><td></td><td style="background:gray"></td><td></td><td style="background:gray"></td></tr>
<tr><td>Positive Accounting Theory</td><td></td><td style="background:gray"></td><td></td><td style="background:gray"></td></tr>
<tr><td>Proprietary Cost Theory</td><td></td><td style="background:gray"></td><td style="background:gray"></td><td></td></tr>
</table>

proprietary costs, including possible competitive disadvantage and information-production costs. According to Armitage and Marston (2008) the main cost of disclosure is seen as the cost of creating the information.

To summarize, we propose that different theories have highlighted different determinants of CSR and CSR disclosure. Legitimacy theory, stakeholder theory, and institutional theory, have dealt with both determinants of CSR and disclosure, while positive accounting theory, decision usefulness studies and proprietary cost theory focused mainly on disclosure and its drivers (Table 1). Moreover, stakeholder theory has highlighted mainly the internal drivers of CSR and its disclosure, as well as proprietary cost theory, while institutional theory, positive accounting theory, and decision usefulness studies can be considered mainly focused on external drivers. Legitimacy theory has showed both external determinants of CSR, when a reactive approach is carried out, and the internal ones, when a proactive approach is pursued. According to all such theories, it can be argued that internal determinants of CSR and CSR disclosure are linked to specific firms' characteristics, such as company values, objectives, and strategies; the relevance given to various stakeholders; top management values and commitment; and kind of ownership. Instead, external drivers come from the environment outside the firm and comprise practices followed by competitors in the same industry, particular code of conducts of the related industry, legislative recommendations, legal and regulatory framework of the country, national business system, pressures coming from financial markets, SRI, opinions groups, and media.

Following main analyzed theories, in this study we adopt a multitheoretical framework in order to explain the drivers of companies' CSR and disclosure practices (Cormier, Michel, & Van Velthoven, 2005).

RESEARCH HYPOTHESES

Starting from the reasons why firms adopt a CSR approach, this chapter aims to explore firms' attitude toward the CSR disclosure, which causes the enterprises to measure and communicate CSR performance notwithstanding legal obligations (Verrecchia, 1983; Wagenhofer, 1990). In this study, determinants of CSR disclosure have been derived indirectly, by using the drivers of CSR, consistently with Holder-Webb et al. (2009), who stated the difficulty to disentangle the determinants of CSR and the decision on CSR disclosure. Moving on from the evidence of previous literature which considers CSR disclosure a relevant aspect of the firm's CSR strategy and initiatives, this chapter aims at analyzing the relationship between the drivers of the firms' attitude toward CSR and CSR disclosure practices. Based on the different theories discussed in the previous paragraph, two main categories of CSR determinants have been identified: the external drivers and the internal ones.

According to stakeholder theory and the proactive approach suggested by legitimacy theory, internal drivers of CSR have been identified referring to firms' specific characteristics, such as company values, objectives, and strategies; the relevance given to various stakeholders; top management values and commitment; and kind of ownership. Consistently, we would propose the following hypothesis:

H1. Firms that adopt CSR as a consequence of the internal determinants give importance to CSR disclosure.

Referring to institutional theory and the reactive approach of legitimacy theory, external CSR determinants have been identified as variables that come mainly from the environment and consist of various pressures which a company has to face, such as public and private regulations, public incentives, the presence of nongovernmental and other independent organizations, the evolution of financial markets, especially SRI, among the others (Sparkes & Cowton, 2004).

In particular, considering the suggestion of both decision-usefulness studies and positive accounting theory, we have focused especially on the role of the financial community/markets in influencing CSR disclosure. Moreover, according to Deegan (2002), and considering that CSR disclosure is a voluntary activity, we exploit also the role of body of legislation as a driver of CSR disclosure. Hence, we propose the following hypotheses:

H2. Firms that adopt CSR as a consequence of the influence of financial markets give importance to CSR disclosure.

H3. Legislative recommendations concerning CSR issues do not have any impact on the importance given to CSR disclosure by companies.

Finally, consistently with stakeholder theory and the proactive approach supported by legitimacy theory, we propose the last hypothesis:

H4. Internal determinants of CSR have a greater impact on CSR disclosure than external ones.

RESEARCH DESIGN

Sample

It has been argued that large companies are more involved in CSR than SMEs (Branco & Rodrigues, 2008; Gray & Bebbington, 2000). Moreover, Watts and Zimmerman (1986) argued that large companies are more visible to the public, have more market power, and are more newsworthy. Large corporations do have a bigger impact on the community, and therefore have a bigger exposure toward the stakeholders' influence. From an empirical perspective various studies have found a positive relationship between CSR disclosure and firm size.

Consistently with this evidence, the initial sample of the research consisted of 4,222 large Italian manufacturing and nonmanufacturing enterprises drawn from the AIDA database (by Bureau Van Dijk Electronic Publishing), defined at the four-digit level of the ATECO91 Classification System. Large enterprises here are defined as firms that have either more than 250 employees, or an annual turnover exceeding 40 million Euros. These criteria are consistent with those identified by the EU to define company size (employees and turnover), up to 2005, and to discriminate between SMEs and large enterprises. The initial sample consisted of 2,749 service enterprises (65% of total sample) and 1,473 manufacturing firms (35% of total sample). Among manufacturing industries, we distinguished the following sectors: food, textiles, raw material transformation, chemical, mechanical, and electronics. As far as nonmanufacturing industries are concerned, they were classified into: public utilities, building, trade, tourism, transportation, telecommunications, and knowledge-intensive firms.

Procedure

Data collection proceeded in three phases. Firstly, measurement scales were developed by reviewing relevant literature and by completing some on-site interviews with CFOs from large firms. Next, the preliminary version of the questionnaire was pretested with a few CFOs. These pretests led to the revision of several items to improve their clarity as well as to the addition of some new items identified during the interviews, resulting in the final version of the questionnaire. In the final stage, the questionnaire was mailed to the companies included in the sampling frame described further. We addressed the surveys to the firm's CFO and the cover letter requested explicitly that it had to be completed by the CFO. As the focus of our research was on CSR disclosure, and thus on the use of mechanisms, such as environmental, social, and/or sustainability report/balance sheets, we involved the CFO, being she/he the manager specifically in charge of performance measurement and communication activities and mechanisms. We have assumed that the CFO is involved not only in financial compulsory disclosure, but also in nonfinancial one, playing a relevant role in CSR disclosure process, as pointed out by recent surveys (Ernst & Young, 2012; KPMG, 2012).

Finally, the importance of the most significant aspects, related to CSR and CSR disclosure, was measured on a five-point scale, with 5 being the most important.

Achieved Sample

Stratified phase sampling was carried out in order to ensure an error of 3.5% and design a sample that was representative of the reference population, according to the redemption rate typical of these kinds of surveys. From the initial sample, 800 companies were identified, to whom the questionnaire was sent; the companies were selected through random extraction and were representative of the reference population in terms of turnover, employees, industries, and geographical areas and for whom addresses were obtained.

A total of 120 completed questionnaires were returned, representing a response rate of about 15%. This response rate is comparable with those found in large-scale surveys involving executives (Powell & Dent-Micallef, 1997; Robertson, Rymon, & Eliashberg, 1995). It is reasonable given the setting of the survey (large firms), firm diversity, the positions of the respondents, and the sensitivity of the information.

Referring to the revenues, 45% of the sample companies have a turnover of up to 100 million Euros, 18% from 101 to 250, and 37% over 250 million Euros. With regard to the number of employees, 9% of enterprises have up to 100 employees, 23% from 101 to 250, 34% from 251 to 500, and 34% over 500. Of the sample companies, 76% belong to a group, with an Italian holding for two thirds of the sample companies and with a foreign one for the other third. With regard to ownership, most firms are family-owned businesses or entrepreneurial ones (about 51%), 28% of the enterprises are private with shareholders that are not an entrepreneur or a family (such as: other companies, financial institutions, and pension funds), 8% are cooperative enterprises, 7% public companies, and about 7% state-owned enterprises. Of the companies, 33% are quoted on the stock exchange. The sample of 120 enterprises is almost representative of large Italian enterprises according to the categories mentioned earlier (industry, turnover, employees, and geographical areas). The public utilities, food industries, and textile industries are somewhat overrepresented, while knowledge-intensive firms, chemical companies, and mechanical companies are a bit underrepresented.

Measures

In order to test the research hypotheses, we defined the following constructs, using some descriptive variables: CSR disclosure, internal determinants of CSR, and external determinants of CSR.

CSR Disclosure

This construct was defined using five variables: the annual report integrated by CSR and sustainability information, the environmental report, the environmental balance sheet, the social balance sheet, and the sustainability report (Cronbach's $\alpha = 0.8646$). Companies were asked about the importance given to these performance measurement and communication mechanisms oriented to CSR, measured on a five-point scale.

Internal Determinants of CSR

According to the proactive approach proposed by legitimacy theory, as well as stakeholder theory, to study the internal determinants of CSR, we used two constructs (corporate objectives and width of stakeholders' definition) and a descriptive variable (company and management's values).

The construct "corporate objectives" was measured using five variables, related to the following reasons why the company adopts CSR: "CSR is a must for the firm's future development"; "CSR is a must for the firm's sustainable development"; "CSR allows new competitive and business opportunities to be created"; "CSR is important for the company's reputation"; and "CSR is required by the parent company/holding company" (Cronbach's $\alpha = 0.7785$). Respondents were asked to rate the importance of each given reason, measured on a five-point scale.

The construct "width of stakeholders' definition" was measured using variables, concerning the importance given to different stakeholder categories by the company, measured on a five-point scale (Cronbach's $\alpha = 0.7110$).

For the descriptive variable "company and management's values" respondents were asked about the importance given to the following reason for adopting CSR: "CSR is consistent with the company and management's value system." This variable was measured on a five-point scale.

External Determinants of CSR

Consistently with literature and especially institutional theory, and the reactive approach suggested by legitimacy theory, external determinants of CSR were defined with regard to the "legislative recommendations" and the "influence of financial markets." In particular, the construct "legislative recommendations" was measured using two variables, related to the following reasons why the company adopts CSR: "CSR is an answer to external rules and instructions" and "CSR allows the company to benefit from public and fiscal incentives" (Cronbach's $\alpha = 0.6808$). The respondents were asked about the importance given to each reason, measured on a five-point scale. Lastly, the "influence of financial markets" was identified and respondents were asked to rate the importance given to the variable "CSR allows to get financial resources," measured on a five-point scale.

Control Variables

Due to the fact that previous literature highlighted the influence of company size (Branco & Rodrigues, 2008), industry (Gray et al., 1995), and ownership structure (i.e., family versus non family firms, listed companies, etc.) (Chau & Gray, 2002) on the decision of a company to engage in CSR and also in CSR disclosure, we considered the following control variables: size of the company, industry, and kind of ownership. In fact, as highlighted before, the analyzed sample comprises large companies, which can be classified into different categories with regard to revenues and number of employees, who operate in different industries, and are characterized by different kind of ownership.

To test the research hypotheses, we considered that about 70 firms out of 120 either gave an importance score of 1 to the construct "CSR disclosure" (which presents a mean of 1.68 and a median of 1) or did not reply to all or some of the questions related to this construct. Thus, we considered only the replies of one or more than one and did not consider any missing values. We divided the sample into two groups: the group of companies that did not give importance to CSR disclosure (important score of 1) and the group of enterprises that gave some importance to it (importance score of more than 1, i.e., significant, high, and very high). The research hypotheses about the relation between CSR disclosure and external and internal determinants of CSR were verified using an independent sample *t*-test, evaluating the equal variances of the two groups using the Levene's test.

RESULTS

In this section, we report and comment on the results regarding the relationships between CSR determinants and CSR disclosure. Data analysis shows that H1–3 are verified (Table 2).

Table 2. The relation between Internal and External Determinants of CSR and CSR Disclosure.

CSR Determinants	Importance of CSR Disclosure	No.	Mean	Std. Deviation	*t*	sig.
Corporate objectives	>1.00	47	3.8851	0.5560	2.0335	0. 0456
	≤1.00	42	3.5933	0.7674		
Width of stakeholder's definition	>1.00	46	3.9312	0.5218	2.5510	0.0131
	≤1.00	40	3.5583	0.7859		
Legislative recommendations	>1.00	45	3.4000	0.7657	0.3785	0.7061
	≤1.00	39	3.3333	0.8377		
Influence of financial markets	>1.00	45	3.4889	0.7575	2.5494	0.0130
	≤1.00	37	3.0000	0.9428		
Company and management's values	>1.00	46	4.3261	0.7009	2.1438	0.0353
	≤1.00	38	3.9737	0.7880		

Enterprises that give importance to CSR disclosure also give more importance to all the CSR determinants, differently from companies not interested in CSR disclosure. In particular, the differences in mean values are significant (sigma lower than 0.05) with regard to the following variables and constructs: "corporate objectives," "width of stakeholders' definition," "influence of financial markets" and "company and management's values." By contrast, they are not significant with regard to "legislative recommendations."

Therefore, H1 (Firms that adopt CSR as a consequence of the internal determinants give importance to CSR disclosure), H2 (Firms that adopt CSR as a consequence of the influence of financial markets give importance to CSR disclosure), and H3 (Legislative recommendations concerning CSR issues do not have any impact on the importance given to CSR disclosure by companies) are verified.

To test H4 (Internal determinants of CSR have a greater impact on CSR disclosure than external ones), we analyzed the differences in mean values related to the importance given to the CSR determinants, considered two by two, considering only companies that gave importance to CSR disclosure (Table 3).

In Table 3, significant differences in means (sig.<0.05) are represented by a colored cell, which identifies a situation where one of the two determinants of CSR disclosure considered has a mean significantly higher than the other one. In particular, the cell is colored in dark gray when the difference in mean values is significant and the mean by column is higher than

Table 3. Analysis of Differences in Mean Values of CSR Determinants.

	Corporate Objectives	Width of Stakeholder's Definition	Legislative Recommendations	Influence of Financial Markets	Company and Management's Values
Corporate Objectives					
Width of Stakeholder's Definition	−0.03				
Legislative Recommendations	0.48	0.51			
Influence of Financial Markets	0.39	0.42	−0.09		
Company and Management's Values	−0.42	−0.39	−0.91	−0.82	

the mean by row; vice versa, it is light gray when the difference in mean values is significant and the mean by row is higher than the mean by column. Differences in mean values that are not significant are shown in white cells.

The following results are shown:

- the determinant "company and management's value (E)" highlights significant differences, as for the means, in respect to the other CSR determinants: "corporate objectives (A)," "width of stakeholder's definition (B)," "legislative recommendations (C)," and "influence of financial markets (D)";
- the determinants "corporate objectives (A)" and "width of stakeholder's definition (B)" do not show significant differences between their means, but there are significant differences in terms of the means of the determinants "legislative recommendations (C)" and "influence of financial markets (D)";
- the drivers "legislative recommendations (C)" and "influence of financial markets (D)" do not show any significant differences between their means.

Based on the above results, we can define a relationship between the CSR determinants with regard to their impact on CSR disclosure:

$$E > A/B > C/D$$

Findings show that in companies giving importance to CSR disclosure, the internal determinants of CSR have a greater importance than external ones. Among the internal determinants both drivers related to company and management values and ethics are quite relevant.

All research findings remain stable after controlling for size, industry, and ownership.

DISCUSSION AND CONCLUSIONS

This study intended to contribute to the debate on the impact of CSR on performance measurement and communication systems. It focused on the determinants of CSR and the relation with CSR disclosure, aiming at analyzing the reasons why CSR is adopted by enterprises and its relationship with external reporting toward the stakeholders. Main findings pointed out that in companies giving importance to CSR disclosure, the internal determinants of CSR have a greater importance than external drivers. Among the latter, the impact of legislative recommendations is not relevant, while the financial markets exert a great pressure. Among the internal determinants drivers related to company and management values and ethics are relevant. It can be said that notwithstanding numerous recommendations by international, European, and Italian institutional bodies regarding CSR disclosure, internal determinants are the most important drivers of CSR disclosure, especially those related to company's values and the width of the stakeholders' definition. Moreover, large Italian firms report on CSR activities mainly in order to build or sustain corporate legitimacy.

Our research findings show that legitimacy theory represents the most relevant theory in explaining CSR disclosure practices of Italian large firms, as well as the operational implementation of stakeholder theory, such as stakeholder management (Roberts, 1992). On the contrary, institutional theory only partially explains CSR disclosure, with respect to the pressures coming from financial markets. Our research findings suggest that factors influencing CSR practices of large Italian firms are not significantly different from those that influence CSR disclosure in other countries. In fact, similar evidence has been highlighted by Reverte (2009), with reference to a sample of Spanish listed companies.

However, our findings refer to about half of the sample companies, which are more involved in CSR. By contrast, the other half of the sample enterprises stated that they were not quite interested in CSR disclosure. This very limited CSR orientation of external reporting systems may be the consequence of both the fact that disclosure on CSR is voluntary and the values and orientation of Italian top management, often involved in family-owned businesses, which are less willing to reveal information about company performance. Besides this, under-performing companies in particular are unlikely to disclose information unless it is made compulsory, which is consistent with proprietary costs theory (Darrough & Stoughton, 1990; Dye, 1986; Verrecchia, 1983, 1990; Wagenhofer, 1990). In addition to the voluntary characteristics of disclosure and the orientation and values of Italian top management, other reasons why large Italian enterprises seem to be unlikely to disclose voluntary information may be as follows:

- the cognitive orientation and limited involvement in CSR of the Financial department and the CFO. We asked the CFO to compile the questionnaire, accepting the point of view and perspective of this specific professional manager (Petrick & Scherer, 1993), being he/she the manager in charge of performance measurement and communication issues. Maybe, the involvement of other top management's representatives should have caused different findings;

- the phase in the life cycle of CSR diffusion among Italian companies, at the time when our research was carried out, which was at a very early stage, especially with regard to CSR performance measurement and communication;
- the relative immaturity of the Italian financial market: in other contexts, such as the Anglo-Saxon one, financial markets and their control bodies are increasing their requests with regard to compulsory disclosure, which include CSR disclosure, forcing companies to conform;
- data gathering and processing costs and technical issues (e.g., IT investments) regarding the information to be provided.

As CSR disclosure is a firms' voluntary initiative, its wider diffusion needs to be supported by an effective incentive system. Now only listed companies, through their appreciation on the stock exchange, can achieve real benefits from disclosure. Failing incentives, CSR disclosure will continue to depend on the top management's values and decisions and on the firm's culture. Furthermore, an important role could be played by universities, schools of management, industrial associations, training institutions, institutional bodies, etc., which can work toward spreading CSR culture and promote a greater level of accountability of the firms. This is an important step toward achieving the satisfaction of all stakeholder groups.

Although we have presented evidence from a large number of firms in a varied set of industries, this study is subject to the limitations that generally apply to cross-sectional survey-based research. The first one is the redemption rate, which appears to be quite low when compared with North American and other countries' surveys. However, it is in line with rates that are normally obtained in Italy and other European countries. A second limitation concerns the fact that the research was conducted on large Italian enterprises; studies in other countries might show different results due to the influence of national culture (Hofstede & Bollinger, 1987). Thirdly, the under-representation of services could have partially impacted the research findings. Finally, several issues concerning the relationship between CSR determinants and disclosure need to be investigated in greater depth. On the one hand, determinants of CSR disclosure have been derived indirectly, by using the drivers of CSR, in accordance with legitimacy theory, which considers disclosure one of the consequences of honoring the social contract between the enterprise and its stakeholders. It could be of interest to investigate directly the determinants of CSR disclosure. On the other hand, the involvement of the CFO, as respondent, could have influenced the results by her/his professional perspective. It could be of interest to involve other top management roles, in order to find out their point of view. Moreover, among the internal determinants, company and management values were jointly considered, assuming the convergence of their value systems. This is in contrast with the evidence that management's decisions are driven by personal values and interests, besides the company's objectives and values (Hemingway & Maclagan, 2004). In fact, with particular regard to CSR, it was stated that it can be adopted as a consequence of the behavior of some managers, influenced by their personal values and beliefs (Wood, 1991). For instance, Harris and Crane (2002) showed the importance of managers' personal beliefs in the adoption of a green culture, which can be different from the company's objectives.

As a direct extension of this research, several issues could be further investigated. Empirical studies have shown that CSR disclosure varies across companies, industries, and time (Gray, Javad, Power, & Sinclair, 2001; Gray et al., 1995; Hackston & Milne, 1996). They have also shown that it is determined by a variety of firm and industry characteristics, which influence the relative costs and benefits of disclosing such information (Belkaoui & Karpik, 1989; Cormier and Magnan, 2003; Patten, 2002; Reverte, 2009). The analysis of a wider sample of companies could allow to understand the impact on CSR disclosure of some variables, not considered in this study, such as: company size (SMEs), age, company ownership (i.e., family-owned businesses), company strategy, and so on. Secondly, although heterogeneity in a sample is a condition for empirical generalization, it would be useful for country-level studies to validate these results. Finally, further investigation could elaborate on the relationships between CSR disclosure and social, environmental, and financial performance of the company (Balabanis, Phillips, & Lyall, 1998; Waddoch & Graves, 1997).

REFERENCES

Adams, C. A. (2002). Internal organisational factors influencing corporate social and ethical reporting. Beyond current theorizing. *Accounting, Auditing and Accountability Journal*, *15*(2), 223–250.

Armitage, S., & Marston, C. (2008). Corporate disclosure, cost of capital and reputation: Evidence from finance directors. *The British Accounting Review*, *40*, 314–336.

Aupperle, K. E. (1984). An empirical measure of corporate social orientation. *Research in Corporate Social Performance and Policy*, *6*, 27–54.

Balabanis, G., Phillips, H. C., & Lyall, J. (1998). Corporate social responsibility and economic performance in the top British companies: Are they linked? *European Business Review, 98*(1), 25–44.

Bebbington, J. (1997). Engagement, education and sustainability: A review essay on environmental accounting. *Accounting Auditing and Accountability Journal, 10*(3), 365–381.

Belkaoui, A. (1980). The impact of socio-economic accounting statements on the investment decision: An empirical study. *Accounting Organizations and Society, 5*(3), 263–83.

Belkaoui, A. (1984). *Socio-economic accounting*. Connecticut: Quorum Books, Westport.

Belkaoui, A., & Karpik, R. G. (1989). Determinants of the corporate decision to disclose social information. *Accounting, Auditing & Accountability Journal, 2*(1), 36–51.

Benjamin, J. J., & Stanga, K. G. (1977). Difference in disclosure needs of major users of financial statements. *Accounting and Business Research, Summer*, 187–92.

Bowen, H. (1953). *Social responsibilities of the businessman*. New York, NY: Harper.

Bowman, E. H. (1973). Corporate social responsibility and the investor. *Journal of Contemporary Business, Winter*, 21–43.

Branco, M. C., & Rodrigues, L. L. (2008). Social responsibility disclosure: A study of proxies for the public visibility of Portuguese banks. *The British Accounting Review, 40*, 161–181.

Buehler, V. M., & Shetty, Y. K. (1974). Motivations for corporate social actions. *Academy of Management Journal, 17*(4), 767–771.

Campbell, D. (2003). Intra- and intersectoral effects in environmental disclosures: Evidence for legitimacy theory. *Business Strategy and the Environment, 12*(6), 357–371.

Carroll, A. B. (1991). The pyramid of the corporate social responsibility. *Business Horizons, 34* (June–August), 39–48.

Carroll, A. B., & Shabana, K. M. (2010). The business case for corporate social responsibility: A review of concepts, research and practice. *International Journal of Management Reviews, 12*(1), 85–105.

Chau, G. K., & Gray, S. J. (2002). Ownership structure and corporate voluntary disclosure in Hong Kong and Singapore. *The International Journal of Accounting, 37*, 247–265.

Chenall, R. H., & Juchau, R. (1977). Investor information needs: An Australian study. *Accounting and Business Research, 26*(Spring), 111–119.

Commission of the European Communities (CEC). (2001). *Promoting a European framework for corporate social responsibilities*. Green Paper. Brussels, COM (2001), 366 final.

Cormier, D., Gordon, I. M., & Magnan, M. (2004). Corporate environmental disclosure: Contrasting management's perceptions with reality. *Journal of Business Ethics, 49*(2), 143–165.

Cormier, D., & Magnan, M. (2003). Environmental reporting management: A continental European perspective. *Journal of Accounting and Public Policy, 22*(1), 43–62.

Cormier, D., Michel, M., & Van Velthoven, B. (2005). Environmental disclosure quality in large German companies: Economic incentives, public pressures or institutional conditions? *European Accounting Review, 14*(1), 3–39.

Darrough, M. N., & Stoughton, N. M. (1990). Financial disclosure policy in an entry game. *Journal of Accounting and Economics, 12*, 219–243.

Davis, K. (1973). The case for and against business assumption of social responsibilities. *Academy of Management Journal, 16*, 312–322.

Deegan, C. (2002). Introduction – The legitimising effect of social and environmental disclosures – A theoretical foundation. *Accounting, Auditing & Accountability Journal, 15*(3), 282–311.

Deegan, C. (2006). *Financial accounting theory*. North Ryde: McGraw-Hill.

Deegan, C., & Gordon, B. (1996). A study of the environmental disclosure practices of Australian corporations. *Accounting and Business Research*, *26*, 187–199.

Deegan, C., Rankin, M., & Voght, P. (2000). Firms' disclosure reactions to major social incidents: Australian evidence. *Accounting Forum*, *24*(1), 101–130.

DiMaggio, P. J., & Powell, W. W. (1983). The iron cage revisited: Institutional isomorphism and collective rationality in organizational fields. *American Sociological Review*, *48*(2), 147–160.

DiMaggio, P. J., & Powell, W. W. (1991). Institutional isomorphism and collective rationality. In W. W. Powell & P. J. DiMaggio (Eds.), *The new institutionalism in organizational analysis* (pp. 147–160). London: University of Chicago Press.

Di Piazza, S. A., & Eccles, R. G. (2002). Building public trust. *The future of corporate reporting*. New York, NY: Wiley.

Donaldson, T., & Preston, L. E. (1995). The stakeholder theory of the corporation: Concepts, evidence and implications. *Academy of Management Review*, *20*(1), 65–92.

Dowling, J., & Pfeffer, J. (1975). Organizational legitimacy: Social values and organisational behavior. *Pacific Sociological Review*, *January*, 122–136.

Dye, R. A. (1986). Proprietary and non-proprietary disclosures. *Journal of Business*, *59*(2), 331–366.

Eccles, R. G., & Krzus, M. P. (2010). *One report. Integrated reporting for a sustainable strategy*. Hoboken, NJ: Wiley.

Ernst & Young. (2012). *Ernst & Young's excellence in integrated reporting awards 2012*. Retrieved from http://www.ey.com/Publication/vwLUAssets/Excellence_in_Integrated_Reporting_Awards_2012/$FILE/120830%20Excellence.indd.pdf

Firth, M. (1984). The extent of voluntary disclosure in corporate annual reports and its association with security risk measures. *Applied Economics*, *16*, 269–77.

Frederick, W. (1960). The growing concern over business responsibility. *California Management Review*, *60*, 54–61.

Freeman, R. E. (1984). *Strategic management: A stakeholder approach*. Boston, MA: Pitman Publishing Inc.

Freeman, R. E., & Reed, D. (1983). Stockholders and stakeholders: A new perspective on corporate governance. *Californian Management Review*, *25*(2), 88–106.

Gambling, T. (1977). Magic, accounting and morale. *Accounting, Organizations and Society*, *2*(2), 141–151.

Garriga, E., & Melé, D. (2004). Corporate social responsibilities theories: Mapping the territory. *Journal of Business Ethics*, *53*, 51–71.

Gelb, D. S., & Strawser, J. A. (2001). Corporate social responsibility and financial disclosure: An alternative explanation for increased disclosure. *Journal of Business Ethics*, *33*(1), 1–13.

Gray, R., Javad, M., Power, D. M., & Sinclair, C. D. (2001). Social and environmental disclosure and corporate characteristics: A research note and extension. *Journal of Business Finance and Accounting*, *2*(3/4), 327–356.

Gray, R. H., & Bebbington, J. (2000). Environmental accounting, managerialism and sustainability: Is the planet safe in the hands of business and accounting? *Advances in Environmental Accounting and Management*, *1*(1), 1–44.

Gray, R. H., Kouhy, R., & Lavers, S. (1995). Corporate social and environmental reporting: A review of the literature and a longitudinal study of UK disclosure. *Accounting, Auditing & Accountability Journal*, *8*(2), 47–77.

Gray, R. H., Owen, D., & Adams, C. (1996). *Accounting and accountability: Changes and challenges in corporate social and environmental reporting*. Englewood Cliffs, NJ: Prentice Hall.

Guthrie, J., & Parker, L. D. (1990). Corporate social disclosure practice: A comparative international analysis. *Advances in Public Interest Accounting*, *3*, 159–75.

Hackston, D., & Milne, M. J. (1996). Some determinants of social and environmental disclosures in New Zealand companies. *Accounting, Auditing and Accountability Journal*, *9*(1), 77–108.

Harris, L. C., & Crane, A. (2002). The greening of organizational culture: Management views on the depth, degree and diffusion of change. *Journal of Organizational Change Management*, *15*(3), 214–234.

Harrison, J. S., & Freeman, R. E. (1999). Stakeholders, social responsibility, and performance: Empirical evidence and theoretical perspectives. *Academy of Management Journal*, *42*(5), 479–485.

Hayes, B., & Walker, B. (2005). Corporate responsibility or core competence? *Development in Practice*, *15*(3/4), 405–412.

Hemingway, C. A., & Maclagan, P. W. (2004). Managers' personal values as drivers of corporate social responsibility. *Journal of Business Ethics*, *50*(1), 33–44.

Herremans, I. M., Parporn, A., & McInnes, H. (1993). An investigation of corporate social responsibility reputation and economic performance. *Accounting, Organization and Society*, *18*(7/8), 587–604.

Hinna, L. (Ed.). (2002). *Il bilancio sociale*. Milano: Il Sole 24 Ore.

Hofstede, G., & Bollinger, D. (1987). *Les différences culturelles dans le management*. Paris: Les Editions d'Organisation.

Holder-Webb, L., Cohen, J., Nath, L., & Wood, D. (2009). The supply of corporate social responsibility disclosures among U.S. firms. *Journal of Business Ethics*, *84*(4), 497–527.

Holland, J. (2006). *A model of corporate financial communications*. Edinburgh: The Institute of Chartered Accountants of Scotland.

Holland, L., & Foo, J. B. (2003). Differences in environmental reporting practices in the UK and the US: The legal and regulatory context. *The British Accounting Review*, *35*, 1–18.

Hopwood, A. (1984). Accounting and the pursuit of efficiency. In A. Hopwood & C. Tomkins (Eds.), *Issues in public sector accounting* (pp. 167–186). Oxford: Philip Allan Publishers Limited.

Jones, M. T. (1999). The institutional determinants of social responsibility. *Journal of Business Ethics*, *20*, 163–179.

KPMG. (2012). *Turning global risk into opportunity: Key priorities for consumer company CFOs*. Retrieved from http://www.kpmg.com/Global/en/IssuesAndInsights/Articles Publications/Documents/consumer-company-cfo-priorities.pdf

Larrinaga-Gonzales, C. (2007). Sustainability reporting: Insights from neoinstitutional theory. In J. Unerman, J. Bebbington, & B. O'Dwyer (Eds.), *Sustainability accounting and accountability* (pp. 150–167). London: Routledge.

Lehman, G. (1995). A Legitimate concern for environmental accounting. *Critical Perspectives on Accounting*, *6*(5), 393–413.

Lehman, G. (1999). Disclosing new worlds: A role for social and environmental accounting and auditing. *Accounting, Organizations and Society*, *24*(3), 217–242.

Lenssen G., Perrini, F., Tencati, A., & Lacy, P. (Eds.). (2007). Corporate responsibility and strategic management. Guest editorial. *Corporate Governance: The International Journal of Business in Society*, 7(4), 344–354.

Lindblom, C. K. (1994). The implications of organizational legitimacy for corporate social performance and disclosure. Paper presented at the Critical Perspectives on Accounting Conference, New York, NY.

Luthans, F. (1985). *Organizational behaviour*. New York, NY: Mc Graw-Hil.

Maignan, I., & Ralston, D. A. (2002). Corporate social responsibility in Europe and the U.S.: Insights from businesses' self-presentations. *Journal of International Business Studies, 33*, 497–515.

Maon, F., Lindgreen, A., & Swaen, V. (2010). Organizational stages and cultural phases: A critical review and a consolidative model of corporate social responsibility development. *International Journal of Management Reviews, 12*(1), 20–38.

Mathews, M. R. (1997). Towards a mega-theory of accounting. *Asia-Pacific Journal of Accounting, 4*(2), 273–289.

Mathews, M. R. (2003). A history of social and environmental accounting through the research literature. *AFAANZ conference*, Brisbane.

Matten, D., & Moon, J. (2008). "Implicit" and "Explicit" CSR: A conceptual framework for a comparative understanding of corporate social responsibility. *Academy of Management Review, 33*(2), 404–424.

McWillam, A., & Siegel, D. (2002). Additional reflections on the strategic implications of corporate social responsibility. *The Academy of Management Review, 27*(1), 15–16.

Mercer Investment Consulting. (2007). *The language of responsible investment – An industry guide to key terms and organisations*. London: Mercer Investment Consulting.

Moon, J. (2004). *Government as a driver of corporate social responsibility – The UK in comparative perspectives*. ICCSR Research Paper Series No. 20. University of Nottingham, Nottingham; Watts and Zimmerman: Englewood Cliffs, N.J.

Ness, K. E., & Mirza, A. M. (1991). Corporate social disclosure: A note on a test of agency theory. *British Accounting Review, 23*(3), 211–18.

Owen, D. L., Gray, R. H., & Bebbington, J. (1997). Green accounting: Cosmetic irrelevance or radical agenda for change? *Asia Pacific Journal of Accounting, 4*(2), 175–198.

Owen, D. L., Swift, T. A., Humphrey, C., & Bowerman, M. (2000). The new social audits: Accountability, managerial capture or the agenda of social champions? *European Accounting Review, 9*(1), 81–98.

Patten, D. M. (1991). Exposure, legitimacy and social disclosure. *Journal of Accounting and Public Policy, 10*(4), 297–308.

Patten, D. M. (2002). Give or take on the internet: An examination of the disclosure practices of insurance firm web innovators. *Journal of Business Ethics, 36*(3), 247–259.

Pedersen, E. R., & Neergaard, P. (2008). From periphery to center: How CSR is integrated in mainstream performance management frameworks. *Measuring Business Excellence, 12*(2), 4–12.

Petrick, J., & Scherer, R. (1993). Competing social responsibility values and the functional roles of managers. *Journal of Managerial Psychology, 8*(3), 14–21.

Pfeffer, J., & Salancik, G. R. (1978). *The external control of organizations: A resource dependence perspective*. New York, NY: Harper and Row.

Powell, T. C., & Dent-Micallef, A. (1997). Information technology as competitive advantage: The role of human, business, and technology resources. *Strategic Management Journal, 18*, 375–405.

Power, M. (1991). Auditing and environmental expertise: Between protest and professionalisation. *Accounting, Auditing and Accountability Journal, 4*(3), 30–42.

Renneboog, L., Ter Horst, J., & Zhang, C. (2008). Socially responsible investments: Institutional aspects, performance, and investor behavior. *Journal of Banking and Finance, 32*, 1723–1742.

Reverte, C. (2009). Determinants of corporate social responsibility disclosure ratings by spanish listed firms. *Journal of Business Ethics, 1988*(2), 351–366.

Roberts, J., & Scapens, R. (1985). Accounting systems and systems of accountability. Understanding accounting practices in their organizational context. *Accounting, Organizations and Society*, *10*(4), 443–456.

Roberts, R. W. (1992). Determinants of corporate social responsibility disclosure: An application of stakeholder theory. *Accounting, Organizations and Society*, *17*(6), 595–612.

Robertson, T. S., Rymon, T., & Eliashberg, J. (1995). New product announcement signals and incumbent reactions. *Journal of Marketing*, *59*, 1–15.

Rusconi, G. (1988). *Il bilancio sociale d'impresa*. Milano: Giuffrè.

Shane, P., & Spicer, B. (1983). Market response to environmental information produced outside the firm. *The Accounting Review*, *July*, 521–538.

Shearer, T. (2002). Ethics and accountability: From the for-itself to the for-the-other. *Accounting, Organizations and Society*, *27*(6), 541–573.

Sparkes, R., & Cowton, C. J. (2004). The maturing of socially responsible investment: A review of the developing link with corporate social responsibility. *Journal of Business Ethics*, *52*(1), 45–57.

Spicer, B. H. (1978). Accounting for corporate social performance: Some problems and issues. *Journal of Contemporary Business*, *Winter*, 151–67.

Suchman, M. C. (1995). Managing legitimacy: Strategic and institutional approaches. *Academy of Management Review*, *20*(3), 571–610.

Thomas, G., & Nowak, M. (2006). *Corporate social responsibility: A definition*. Working Paper No. 62, Graduate School of Business, Curtin University of Technology, Australia.

Ullman, A. H. (1985). Date in search of a theory: A critical examination of the relationships among social performance, social disclosure and economic performance of U.S. firms. *Academy of Management Review*, *10*(3), 540–557.

Unerman, J., Bebbington, J., & O'Dwyer B. (Eds.). (2007). *Sustainability accounting and accountability*. London: Routledge.

Van Staden, C. J., & Hooks, J. (2007). A comprehensive comparison of corporate environmental reporting and responsiveness. *The British Accounting Review*, *39*, 197–210.

Verrecchia, R. (1983). Discretionary disclosure. *Journal of Accounting and Economics*, *5*(3), 179–194.

Verrecchia, R. (1990). Information quality and discretionary disclosure. *Journal of Accounting and Economics*, *12*(4), 365–380.

Waddoch, S. A., & Graves, S. B. (1997). The corporate social performance – Financial performance link. *Strategic Management Journal*, *18*(4), 303–319.

Wagenhofer, A. (1990). Voluntary disclosure with a strategic opponent. *Journal of Accounting and Economics*, *12*(4), 341–363.

Watts, R. L., & Zimmerman, J. L. (1978). Toward a positive theory of determination of accounting standards. *The Accounting Review*, *LIII*(1), 112–134.

Watts, R. L., & Zimmerman, J. L. (1986). *Positive accounting theory*. Prentice-Hall.

Wokutch, R. E., & Shepard, J. M. (1999). The maturing of the Japanese economy: Corporate social responsibility implications. *Business Ethics Quarterly*, *9*(3), 527–540.

Wood, D. J. (1991). Corporate social performance revisited. *Academy of Management Review*, *16*(4), 691–718.

Wood, D. J. (2010). Measuring corporate social performance: A review. *International Journal of Management Reviews*, *12*(1), 50–84.

DETERMINANTS OF CORPORATE SOCIAL DISCLOSURE THROUGH A MULTI-PERSPECTIVE APPROACH: EVIDENCES FROM THE TARGET COMPANIES OF SOCIALLY RESPONSIBLE FUNDS☆

Francesco Gangi and Carmen Trotta

ABSTRACT

Purpose – *The research aims to empirically investigate the determinants of the breadth of the corporate social disclosure (CSD).*

Design/methodology/approach – *The study adopts a multi-perspective approach, referring to different theoretical frameworks on CSD, such as the legitimacy theory, the stakeholder theory, the agency model, the asymmetric information theory, and the institutional perspective.*

☆Although the study is the result of a joint effort, Carmen Trotta treated the section on univariate analysis, while Francesco Gangi oversaw all the other sections.

Accounting and Control for Sustainability
Studies in Managerial and Financial Accounting, Volume 26, 33–75

ISSN: 1479-3512/doi:10.1108/S1479-3512(2013)0000026002

The empirical research is based on the sustainability reports of 80 companies in which investments were made by European socially responsible funds (SRFs) listed on the Morningstar platform during the years 2009–2008.

The theoretical hypotheses are tested by a univariate and multivariate analysis.

Findings – *The breadth of the CSD depends on multiple factors, both external and internal, such as the country of origin, the industry reputation, the firm size, the frequency of the SRFs participation, the corporate social performance.*

Research limitations/implications – *Limits inherent in this type of research are the comparability of the CSR reports and the systematization of the categories of content to be analyzed.*

Practical implications – *The chapter identifies several factors that lead to a greater completeness of the CSD, exploiting the capacity of the social reporting to trigger benefits for the firms such as a stronger social legitimacy and the reduction of asymmetric information.*

Social implications – *The research supports the investigation of the levers of CSD to meet the demand for a broader accountability.*

Originality/value – *The reference to firms in which SRFs participated allows to focus on companies ascertained as socially responsible in accordance with a "certification function" of these funds. Findings support an approach which is not one-sided, thus enabling to look at the determinants of the CSD through different theoretical perspectives.*

Keywords: Corporate Social Responsibility; corporate social disclosure; sustainability reports; determinants of CSD; CSD variations

INTRODUCTION

In recent years, companies have started paying more attention toward corporate social responsibility disclosure (CSD) as a further opportunity to interact with their internal and external environment. This trend has occurred with the development of the theme of corporate social responsibility (Jones, 1980; McGuire, 1963; McWilliams & Siegel, 2001; Windsor, 2006) that over time has been enriched with new practical and theoretical matters (Jamali, Safieddine, & Rabbath, 2008; Sweeney & Coughlan, 2008). Moreover, the recognition of a specific identity and usefulness of CSR reporting has gradually increased along with the higher demand for sustainability of corporate decisions. In this sense, an important role can be attributed to the voluntary social disclosure in acquisition of new intangible resources, such as trust and good reputation (Brammer & Pavellin, 2007).

Furthermore, the several corporate scandals and the deep financial crises of the past decade, which produced effects over the boundaries of the capital markets, have contributed to renewing the search for the equilibrium between ethics, social responsibility, and economic affairs (Argandona, 2011). Therefore, this equilibrium requires companies to strengthen the communication of their commitment toward a wider social task (van der Laan Smith, Adhikari, & Rasoul, 2005).

Finally, the development of socially responsible investors is another important factor that increases the interest toward CSR disclosure (Gangi & Trotta, 2011; Jamali et al., 2008; MacMillan, Money, Downing, & Hillenbrand, 2004; Rhodes, 2010). In fact, by applying selection policies that combine financial evaluation with ethical and social demands, these specialized investors further increase the range of those who are interested in the quality of voluntary disclosure adopted by companies.

Several reasons justify the interest in the management of information within social reporting, in particular because of the existence of different factors that affect CSD. This issue has practical and scientific implications. With respect to the first aspect, it's useful to know which drivers can interfere with the management of CSD. For example, it is useful to (a) know whether the context is more or less sensitive to CSR initiatives, (b) understand whether CSD can be a tool for the exchange of information and the sharing of values in larger companies, (c) assess the effect of disclosure on the information asymmetries, and (d) verify the relationship between social performances and the CSR reporting. All these factors can lead to a greater awareness and completeness of the topics discussed. This aspect plays an important role in exploiting the potential capability of social reporting in triggering economic benefits such as the gain of a stronger social legitimacy; the support of key stakeholders; the strengthening of the organizational identity; the reduction in the adverse selection; the improvement in company reputation. After all, the interest in the most appropriate levers of social communication to meet the growing demand for a broader accountability is confirmed by the same companies that have responded providing a continuous production of data (Perrini, 2005), exploiting the greater variety of media that are available thanks to the innovation of information and communication technologies (Cormier, Ledoux, & Magnan, 2009; Sweeney & Coughlan, 2008; Trabelsi, Labelle, & Dumontier, 2008).

Consequently, the growth of demand and supply of information has provided new incentives to the academic studies about the CSD, which explore the theoretical frameworks that fit with the interpretation of the variety of the CSD between the firms. In this regard, the study of the determinants of CSD may fall within a broader debate on the convergence or divergence of corporate responsibility (CR) (Chapple & Moon, 2005; Chen & Bouvain, 2008; Stohl, 2001). Indeed, while some companies demonstrate a long tradition in reporting nonfinancial information, others provide only a limited disclosure or, in some cases, no information. As noticed by previous studies, the CSR reports differ based on the country and the type of industry (Kolk, 2005; Kolk, Walhain, & Van de Wateringen, 2001; Sweeney & Coughlan, 2008), but findings are not totally conclusive or it is difficult to compare these surveys owing to the methodological differences (Graafland, Eiffinger, & Smid, 2004).

From our research on existing literature emerge, among others, two main lines of study. The first concerns the use of multiple theoretical perspectives for interpreting the CSD, such as the social legitimacy theory (Archel, Husillos, Larrinaga, & Spence, 2009; Guthrie & Parker, 1989; Lindblom, 1984, 1993; Owen, 2008; Patten, 1992), the stakeholder theory (Gray, Kouhy, & Lavers, 1995a, 1995b; Perrini, 2005; Roberts, 1992; Sweeney & Coughlan, 2008; Ullmann, 1985; van der Laan Smith et al., 2005), the agency theory (Naser & Al-Khatib, 2000; Naser, Al-Husaini, Al-Kwari, & Nuseibeh, 2006; Wallace, Naser, & Mora, 1994), the information asymmetries theory (Di Giulio, Migliavacca, & Tencati, 2011; Dye, 1985; Verrecchia, 1999) and the institutional perspective (Aguilera & Cuervo-Cazurra, 2004; Aguilera, Williams, Conley, & Rupp, 2006; Chen & Bouvain, 2008; van der Laan Smith et al., 2005). Notwithstanding the specific assumptions, these general theories allow to look at the CSD from multiple points of view. It is an incontrovertible observation that comes from the excursus of previous contributions. In this regard, it's not disputed that the different analytical lenses retain their identity.

Having clarified that point, the second line of academic research concerns the empirical analysis of the determinants of the CSD. In particular, based on the above-mentioned general theories, these studies have focused on the context (Chen & Bouvain, 2008; Roberts, 1992; van der Laan Smith et al., 2005), the industry (Gao, Heravi, & Xiao, 2005; Sweeney & Coughlan, 2008; Waddock & Graves, 1997) and some firm-specific characteristics as the corporate size (Belkaoui & Karpik, 1989; Gray, Javad,

Power, & Sinclair, 2001; Naser et al., 2006), the participation of institutional investors to the ownership structure (Chen & Bouvain, 2008; Naser et al., 2006), the membership to institutional initiatives that stimulate socially sustainable policies (Cetindamar & Husoy, 2007; Chen & Bouvain, 2008), the level of the social responsibility of the firm (Roberts, 1992; Ullmann, 1985). So, from time to time these works refer to the general theories mentioned earlier in order to explain the existing differences in CSD. However, these analyses are not conclusive and are often based on the annual reports produced by companies in single countries, with a predominant focus on the US context.

Our study, which belongs to the second line of research, tries to provide a further contribution through an empirical investigation of the determinants that may affect the breadth and the concentration of the CSD, with reference to the social reporting of companies across different industries and countries. In particular, with the term "breadth" we intend to refer to the capacity of the corporate social reporting to cover a broad range of themes. So, the greater the number of themes addressed within the reporting, the greater the breadth of the CSD. On the contrary, with the term "concentration" we intend to focus on certain areas and topics of disclosure with respect to other ones. So, the lesser the homogeneity of distribution of themes treated within the reporting, the higher the concentration of the CSD.[1]

Therefore, through a univariate and multivariate analysis, our survey includes the study of the effects of both macro- and firm-specific determinants of CSD, such as the economic model of the country of origin; the reputation of the industry; the size of the company; the participation of institutional investors; the membership to institutional initiatives that stimulate socially sustainable policies; the level of social responsibility of firms expressed in terms of social performance. More in particular, our investigation concerns the study of the CSR reports produced by 80 companies between 2008 and 2009. Assuming a "certification and monitoring" function of the socially responsible investment funds, the sample is composed by firms participated by European socially responsible funds (SRFs) reported on the Morningstar Direct platform. This means that the empirical analysis is based on firms ascertained as socially responsible.

So, the work is composed of six parts: the first is a brief overview of the main theoretical backgrounds that it's possible to find in previous investigations; the second is dedicated to the development of the hypotheses for our empirical analysis; the third concerns the explanation of the methodology; the fourth and the fifth describe and discuss the results of the analysis; finally, the last part contains the general conclusions of the study.

THEORETICAL BACKGROUNDS ON DETERMINANTS OF CSD

At a theoretical level, CSD includes a wide range of diverse information concerning the activities and the public image of the company with respect to the environment, the community, the employees, the customers, the product safety (Gray et al., 1995a), and it also includes information on corporate governance[2] and investor relations (Perrini, 2005; Perrini, Russo, Tencati, & Vurro, 2011) in accordance with CR continuum (Bhimani & Soonawalla, 2005; Jamali et al., 2008). These aspects show that voluntary disclosure can be considered as an important meeting point between the demand for a greater sensitivity toward the context and the need for a greater awareness (Vurro & Perrini, 2010). However, the variety of information and the diversity of those potentially interested in the CSD represent two motivations of the various efforts to apply and to systematize different general theories provided by the literature over the years with the aim of defining logical categories widely accepted and comparable[3] (see Table 1).

Starting from the vision of the company as a socioeconomic system (Carroll, 1994), the social legitimacy theory is one of the fundamental references in the literature to interpret the function and the variants of the CSD (Guthrie & Parker, 1989; Owen, 2008; Patten, 1992). Following this approach, the CSD becomes a media that companies can use to increase the "fitting" with their environment (Hannan & Freeman, 1989), legitimizing the existence in the long term, thanks to the demonstration that their own values are congruent with the value system of the larger social context of which they are a part (Lindblom, 1984, 1993). In this way an enterprise acquires and defends its *right of citizenship*, a concept that can be traced back to the contribution of McGuire (1963), for which the company must look after the welfare of the community by acting as a true "citizen." Some years later Carroll (1998) spoke about the multiple faces of the corporate citizenship (economic, legal, ethical, philanthropic), putting this concept in relation with a multilevel model of social responsibility (Carroll, 1991). In this perspective, the CSD should contribute to the legitimacy of the firm,

Table 1. Behind the CSD: Theoretical Frameworks and Determinants.

Theoretical Framework	CSD Scope	CSD Determinants	Authors
Legitimacy theory (Carroll, 1994; Hannan & Freeman, 1977, 1989)	Legitimacy of the company existence to society	External institutional influence; values/habitus of the society	Archel et al. (2009), Frost and Seamer (2002), Guthrie and Parker (1989), Lindblom (1984, 1993), Owen (2008), Patten (1992, 2002)
Stakeholder theory (Donaldson, 1992; Freeman, 1984; Preston, Donaldson, & Broks, 1999)	Gain the support of the social groups that can influence the company success	Countries values; claims of social groups; interests of internal/ external stakeholders; industry reputation; managerial approach	Gray et al. (1995a; 1995b), Perrini (2005), Roberts (1992), Sweeney and Coughlan (2008), Ullmann (1985), van der Laan Smith et al. (2005)
Agency theory (Jensen & Meckling, 1976)	Reduction of agency costs	Ownership structure; size; governance models	Naser (1998), Naser and Al-Khatib (2000), Naser et al. (2006), Wallace et al. (1994)
Information asymmetry theory (Akerlof, 1970; Spence, 1973)	Reduction of information asymmetry; avoidance of adverse selection; perception of company as less risky	Market capital relationships; institutional investors participation; SRFs investments	Di Giulio et al. (2011), Dye (1985), Naser et al. (2006), Perrini (2005), Verrecchia (1983, 1999)
Institutional perspective (DiMaggio & Powell, 1983; Hall & Soskice, 2001; Scott, 2001; Selznick, 1948)	Convergence of external influences and organizational arrangements (isomorphism)	Country; capitalistic model; cultural context; membership to institutional initiatives on CSR	Aguilera and Cuervo-Cazurra (2004), Aguilera et al. (2006), Cetindamar and Husoy (2007), Chen and Bouvain (2008), Cooper and Sherer (1984), Kolk et al. (2001), Meek et al. (1995), Roberts (1992), van der Laan Smith et al. (2005)

by giving more information along those different dimensions of the corporate citizenship. Therefore, companies could be encouraged to implement a voluntary social disclosure in order to provide a constructive response to the pressures coming from the society,[4] "pacifying" the questions about their business, and gaining the support of the social reference groups (Archel et al., 2009; Guthrie & Parker, 1989; Patten, 1992).

Next to the mentioned vision of the CSD, the other important analytical perspective widely adopted to interpret the social disclosure is represented by the stakeholder theory (Donaldson, 1992; Donaldson & Dunfee, 1994; Donaldson & Preston, 1995; Freeman, 1984; Preston et al., 1999). Knowing that there isn't a single definition of stakeholders (Mitchell, Agle, & Wood, 1997), we refer to any social group or individual who can affect, or is affected by the achievement of corporation's purpose (Freeman, 1984). From this derives the vision of the company as a nexus of relationships with a wide range of stakeholders. Therefore, the set of objectives that the firm has to face is expanded in parallel with the evolution from a narrow view (including those who have a direct interest in the life of the firm) to a broader view of the stakeholders (including those who influence business decisions or are influenced by them, while not participating directly in the firm activities). In this perspective, the capacity to respond positively to pressures coming from different kinds of stakeholders, on the base of the power, the actuality, and the legitimation of their interests, becomes important (Clarkson, 1995; Mitchell et al., 1997). As a consequence we arrive at a dynamic vision of the stakeholders because their role and their impact can change over time with the occurrence of certain events (think of the environmental disasters) or in function of the activity, the size, the ownership, and the origin of the firm. Therefore, the social disclosure can be interpreted as a tool to gain the support of the stakeholders involved in a process of an enlarged value creation (Roberts, 1992; Sweeney & Coughlan, 2008; Ullmann, 1985; van der Laan Smith et al., 2005). Moreover, this theoretical framework is useful to categorize the main themes of a voluntary disclosure (Gray et al., 1995a; Perrini, 2005; van der Laan Smith et al., 2005), contributing to understand the variations existing in the CSD in function of the dynamic nature of the relationship with the stakeholders and due to the differences in managerial sensitivity with respect to the interests of the different social groups. From this last perspective several studies (Cowen, Ferreri, & Parker, 1987; Roberts, 1992; Ullmann, 1985) hypothesize that there exists a positive relationship between the quality/quantity of social disclosure and the capacity of the firm to reach a higher social performance that is assumed as the extent to which an organization is able to meet needs and demands of different stakeholders. In this way, the firms that obtain better results from their CSR activities are expected to have an incentive to disclose their commitment toward the instances of various stakeholders.[5]

Through a broader view, the stockholders represent a social group with specific interests. However, unlike the other primary stakeholders, their remuneration is not fixed by a formal contract. This characteristic makes them residual claimants and this is a problematic point of the stakeholder theory (Jensen, 2002). Having said this, emphasizing the role of the ownership structure and the size of the organization, some studies (Naser & Al-Khatib, 2000; Naser et al., 2006; Wallace et al., 1994) interpret the function of the CSD by using the agency theory (Fama, 1980; Fama & Jensen, 1983; Jensen & Meckling, 1976). As known, this theoretical model is potentially applied to every kind of social interaction between actors involved in a cooperative effort.[6] In our case the agency model is concerned with the governance and the size of the firm. In particular, when the shareholders are more fragmented (e.g., the public companies) and the complexity of the business increases with the size growth, the firm needs to acquire more managerial competences based on contracts inherently incomplete (Grossman & Hart, 1982). The underlying risk is represented by the potential conflict of interest that arises whenever managers (agent) behave in an opportunistic and self-serving manner with respect to the objectives of the owners (principal). In this case the incomplete nature of the contracts feeds the cost of control (agency costs) of actors potentially at odds (Benn & Bolton, 2011). Moreover, the agency costs increase as firm size increases (Jensen & Meckling, 1976). In fact, if the residual claimants coincide with the holders of the decision-making power, it's possible to avoid the cost associated with the monitoring of decisions, but, when there isn't this perfect coincidence and the size of the firm grows, it's necessary to separate the decision-making across multiple level of hierarchy where each agent is required to check the decision taken at a lower level. That being said, previous studies (Naser & Al-Khatib, 2000; Naser et al., 2006) noticed how, with regard to larger companies, the managers have an incentive to implement more extensive and detailed voluntary disclosure in order to reduce the agency costs. This may happen in order to facilitate the monitoring in progress, demonstrating the performances achieved through the decision-making delegation and improving in this way the relationship with shareholders and investors in general.

With reference to the latter issue, the voluntary disclosure can be read as an attempt to reduce the wider problem of asymmetric information

(Akerlof, 1970) that interferes with the access to capital markets (Di Giulio et al., 2011; Dye, 1985; Verrecchia, 1999, 2001). As known, a market is efficient when all the relevant and ascertainable information are widely and cheaply available to all the actors. Therefore, far from a perfect competition we face an information asymmetry situation that causes adverse selection problems, with an increase in the transaction costs among operators differently informed. The consequence is a potential exclusion or undervaluation of the better initiatives from the financial facilities, with a growth of the burdensome of the investments (e.g., including CSR initiatives) due to the increase in the cost of funding. So, referring to Verrecchia (2001), the information asymmetry can be seen as an additional component to the cost of capital that the firm should have interest in reducing through disclosure solutions.[7] This aspect becomes even more important when the firms aim to compete to attract new investors in a scenario of capital rationing. Indeed, in a market characterized by the asymmetric information, the firm risks to pay a "premium" to become more attractive toward the investors, sustaining an additional cost. So, the ability of the management to transfer the right signals to the markets becomes even more relevant. Namely, in our case, the integration of CSD practices in a wider public disclosure system can represent an additional signal coming from the company in order to demonstrate its ability to meet the expectations of a broader set of stakeholders, presenting itself as potentially less risky and less exposed to future social costs (Perrini et al., 2011; Vurro & Perrini, 2011). In this way the companies can become more attractive toward the investors in general and toward the SRFs specifically. A proxy of this positive response can be the presence of such institutional investors into the equity of companies recognized as socially responsible, which means an additional incentive to the CSD.

Finally, including the investors among the various categories of stakeholders, in accordance with the fact that the social groups may have different degrees of salience (Dunfee, 2008; Mitchell et al., 1997), several studies consider that the pressure coming from the stakeholders on the CSD may also vary in relation to the cultural and economic context in which the company operates (Aguilera & Cuervo-Cazurra, 2004; Aguilera et al., 2006; Chen & Bouvain, 2008; van der Laan Smith et al., 2005). In this sense, the differences in the CSD between firms may depend on the diversity existing between the countries in terms of emphasis on the social issues, distinguishing the contexts with a higher "stakeholder orientation" from the ones with a marked preference for a "shareholder orientation" (van der Laan Smith et al., 2005). The comparison is connected with an institutional approach that recognizes the variety of the capitalistic models (Albert, 1990; Hall & Soskice, 2001). In particular, this perspective distinguishes between the Anglo-Saxon systems, where the role of the financial markets is prominent, and the German model (also called Rhine model), where the interlacing between banks, corporations, unions, managers, and workers tends to feed a potentially wider stakeholder orientation. On this line, Hall and Soskice (2001) separate the liberal market economies (LMEs), which are overlapped with the Anglo-Saxon systems, from the coordinated market economies (CMEs).[8] So, recognizing that the coordination between the firm and its stakeholders can be problematic because of the agent/principal relationship, Hall and Soskice define the economies of liberal markets as the systems where firms coordinate their activities primarily via competitive market arrangements (the United Kingdom, Ireland, Canada, Australia, New Zealand), while in the CMEs (Germany, Austria, Belgium, Netherlands, Scandinavian countries, Japan) the firms depend more on nonmarket relationships to coordinate their endeavors with other actors (Hall & Soskice, 2001).[9] Summarizing, the differences emerging between these capitalistic models concern several social and economic spheres that can explain the variety of the CSD among firms across countries (Aguilera et al., 2006; van der Laan Smith et al., 2005). However, as shown in previous studies (Chen & Bouvain, 2008), the relation between the institutional perspective and the CSD needs to take into account global initiatives and standards for nonfinancial reporting that represent another face of the institutionalist perspective. Indeed, their diffusion is an indicator of the "institutionalization" of social reporting (Rossi, 2010). Moreover, the involvement of National or sovra-National institutions enrich the panel of proactive actors in the definition of reporting guidelines and in the promotion of sustainability practices. So, the membership to these institutional initiatives, where the most famous is the United Nations Global Compact (UNGC), can represent an additional incentive that companies may receive to improve the completeness of the contents of the CSD. In this case the assumption is that behind the reporting standards there exists a set of values and principles that can be applied to any business anywhere in the world (Chen & Bouvain, 2008).

In conclusion, the *excursus* of previous literature outlines a broad picture of theories to explain the determinants of the CSD. Therefore, these frameworks are useful to define our next hypotheses on the breadth and on the concentration of the sustainability reports, looking at this issue from different perspectives.

RESEARCH HYPOTHESES

Our hypotheses are grouped in three areas, such as the *country*, the *industry*, and the *firm-specific characteristics*.

Following an approach that goes from the general to the particular, the first area of investigation concerns the country. In particular, referring to an institutionalist perspective, as mentioned, the country where the company has been founded and developed, or where is its headquarter, may be a factor that can influence the CSD (Chen & Bouvain, 2008; Roberts, 1992; van der Laan Smith et al., 2005). There are several reasons and interrelated factors that together contribute to bring out a country effect, such as the cultural values, the financial systems, and the governance models. In the first place, the sociocultural values may interfere with the management values. So, the countries where there is a strong concern for community issues can provide more incentives toward the commitment for social disclosure.[10] In the second place, there are better conditions for favoring a greater quality of CSD in countries more oriented toward all the social groups (van der Laan Smith et al., 2005), for example, without a marked preference for the financial ones with respect to the other stakeholders. This distinction can be associated with the variety of the capitalistic models seeking to explore the differences of CSR practices across countries (Chen & Bouvain, 2008; Matten & Moon, 2004). In particular, the Anglo-Saxon financial systems are historically characterized for a stronger orientation toward the shareholder value and the financial reporting (Aguilera & Cuervo-Cazurra, 2004; Aguilera et al., 2006; van der Laan Smith et al., 2005). A similar argument can be made for the governance systems, distinguishing between models that are based on a "contractarian" view and those who are inspired by a "communitarian" approach.[11] In fact, the first one characterizes primarily the so-called "liberal" market economies, typical of the Anglo-Saxon countries (Hall & Soskice, 2001), where the orientation toward the stockholders expectations is prevalent (van der Laan Smith et al., 2005). Instead, the communitarian perspective characterizes the "coordinated" market economies (Hall & Soskice, 2001), where the company is seen not only as a *nexus* of contracts between managers and shareholders, but rather as an organization that struggles constantly to balance social and economic interests, aiming at the creation and diffusion of an enlarged value that embraces the entire network of stakeholders. As a result, in this case the managers should be encouraged to respect a broad social responsibility that is reflected in the breadth of

CSR reports. Therefore, distinguishing between the "liberal" market economies and the "coordinated" market economies (Hall & Soskice, 2001), the hypothesis is as follows:

> **H1.** The context affects the voluntary disclosure. In particular, firms in countries with a coordinated market economy confer a greater breadth and a lower concentration at the social disclosure than firms in countries with a liberal market economy.

The second aspect of our empirical analysis is represented by the industry. The premise is that different industries have different characteristics regarding the effects that they can generate toward society (Gao et al., 2005). In theory, the companies belonging to a given industry can demonstrate a different sensitivity with respect to their own social responsibility simply for the nature of the activities characterizing that industry (Boutin-Dufresne & Savaria, 2004). Several empirical studies have examined this issue, with interpretations and results not always convergent. In fact, some studies do not confirm that the disclosure changes significantly in relation to the industry (Cowen et al., 1987), while other works seem to prove the existence of an industry effect on the CSD (Gao et al., 2005; Sweeney & Coughlan, 2008; Waddock & Graves, 1997). In the first place, the industries are characterized by different risks in terms of environmental impact. So, the most sensitive industries with respect to this factor may provide more incentives in terms of social disclosure (Deegan & Gordon, 1996). In the second place, following a stakeholder-based perspective, some studies show that companies belonging to different industries can focus their operational and communication activities toward different groups of interest, distinguishing between primary and secondary stakeholders to which they can direct their attention (Sweeney & Coughlan, 2008). Finally, retrieving to the wider concept that connects CSD with the public image of the firm (Gray et al., 2001), authors notice that the practices of CSR are particularly important for industries with a bad reputation (Yoon, Gürhan-Canli, & Schwarz, 2006). Therefore, companies belonging to these industries should show a greater interest toward CSD in order to improve their image and to affirm their citizenship right (Carroll, 1998; Matten & Crane, 2005; McGuire, 1963). Traditionally, this last motivation has been linked to sectors like the energy and oil industries (Arnold, 2001; Sweeney & Coughlan, 2008), especially for the risks and the environmental disasters that frequently involved these kinds of firms.[12] Furthermore, due to the recent financial scandals and the serious social consequences, another industry that has drastically worsened its reputation is the banking and financial one. So, also in this case, the companies should be encouraged to demonstrate a stronger sensitivity toward social responsibility. In this regard, previous studies (Hamid, 2004; Sweeney & Coughlan, 2008) reveal that these companies focus their disclosure in particular on customers and employees as primary stakeholders. However, the issue of the reputation effect remains controversial. In fact, other research show that companies which belong to an industry that can have a negative impact on a specific area tend not to give much space to the communication on this area, paying more attention to other issues where they have a positive impact, such as charitable contributions (Mitnick, 2000). If verified, this approach could also lead to the production of more concentrated reports by companies that, on the contrary, should theoretically provide a broader disclosure because of the industry reputation. Therefore, given the controversial effect related to the industry, it is possible to propose two antagonistic hypotheses as follows:

H2. The industry affects the voluntary disclosure. In particular (a) firms in industries with a bad reputation confer a greater breadth and a lower concentration at the social disclosure than firms in industries with a good reputation; on the contrary (b), firms in industries with a bad reputation confer a lower breadth and a greater concentration at the social disclosure than firms in industries with a good reputation.

The third and last direction of our empirical analysis focuses on the effect of several firm-specific characteristics. In particular, we intend to refer to the size of the companies, the participation of institutional investors, the membership to institutional initiatives like the UNGC, the level of the commitment toward the CSR expressed in terms of social performance.

In the past, the size effect has already been associated with the voluntary social disclosure (Belkaoui & Karpik, 1989; Cowen et al., 1987). More recently, some works confirm that larger firms with a higher profile make a wider disclosure than smaller ones (Gray et al., 2001). At the same way, other authors emphasize the existence of a CSR gap between bigger and smaller companies (Perrini & Minoja, 2008). So, considering the social vision of the firm, the thesis is that larger companies can theoretically be more sensitive to the CSR and its disclosure. This is based on the belief that these organizations have a greater social impact because they employ more people, produce more goods, and consume more resources (Carlisle & Faulkner, 2004). Then, such companies usually have a greater publicity that further stimulates the interest of the community toward their social behavior (Graafland et al., 2004). Furthermore, larger firms mean more transactions and relations in general with the internal and the external stakeholders. Consequently this means more opportunities but also more risks and costs. So, larger firms should be more willing to engage CSR practices, including voluntary social disclosure, to cover these increased risks and costs than smaller firms. Finally, assuming that larger companies also tend to achieve more complex ownership structures, as shown in the previous section, another theoretical justification of the increasing attention of these firms toward the CSD is represented by the agency model (Fama, 1980; Fama & Jensen, 1983; Jensen & Meckling, 1976). In fact, due to the increase in the expenses for monitoring, which depends on the firm size (Jensen & Meckling, 1976), the disclosure can become a tool to contain the agency costs (Naser et al., 2006), in the sense that it facilitates the reduction of the information gap between "insiders" and "outsiders" in the management of the company.

For all the reasons outlined, we expect that larger companies produce a broader and more detailed disclosure than smaller sized companies. Therefore, the hypothesis is:

> **H3.** The size of the firm affects the voluntary disclosure. In particular, larger firms confer a greater breadth and a lower concentration at the social disclosure than smaller firms.

Remaining anchored to the agency theory, it is possible to recognize that institutional investors play an important role in monitoring of management behavior (Chen & Bouvain, 2008), whereby their presence can be interpreted as an incentive to disclose more information (Naser et al., 2006). In a similar way, an inducement can derive from the aim to reduce the cost of capital through the containment of the information asymmetries (Verrecchia, 2001). Moreover, this pressure can become even stronger and more targeted if the investors are SRFs. In fact, the latter are characterized by a shareholder activism with respect to ethical and social issues,[13] in addition to the strictly financial aims (Cowton, 1999). Therefore, the disclosure, insofar as it reduces information asymmetries, can contribute to a perception of the company as less risky.[14] On one hand, this can make easier and cheaper the access to the capital market (Di Giulio et al., 2011; Perrini et al., 2011), on the other hand, it may also facilitate the attraction of the socially responsible investors (Bauer et al., 2005; Gangi & Trotta, 2010; Renneboog, Ter Horst, & Zhang, 2008). So, on the basis of these premises, the hypothesis is as follows:

> **H4.** The participation of socially responsible investors affects the voluntary disclosure. In particular, the firms participated by a higher number

of SRFs confer a greater breadth and a lower concentration at the social disclosure than firms participated by a lower number of SRFs.

The other firm-specific characteristic that we intend to investigate is the adhesion to institutional initiatives that aim to stimulate socially sustainable policies and reporting standards. Recent years have witnessed a growing diffusion of corporate social reporting, with an increase in the variety in terms of volume and type of disclosure.[15] These trends have in turn reinforced the need for institutional initiatives to introduce a "CSR language" (Donaldson, 1992), most common and standardized, so as to reduce a gap of comparability (Perrini, 2005) between the social reporting. The confirmation of this need stems from the development of initiatives that on one hand are addressed to stimulate the CSR, and on the other hand are directed to provide guidelines for a common "grammar" of social reporting (Painter-Morland, 2006; Rossi, 2010). Although these are nonbinding proposals, the diffusion of such initiatives should contribute to the creation of a framework and a shared language that allows firms to adopt and compare the best practices for the collection and the communication of their social performance (DiMaggio & Powell, 1983). Therefore, the application of institutional reporting practices (Brammer & Pavellin, 2007) can be considered as an additional source to recognize and to legitimize the corporate socially responsible behavior (Suchman, 1995). Moreover, going beyond the reporting standards, one of the well-known institutional initiatives to promote the compliance with the social responsibility is the UN Global Compact,[16] which dates back to 1999. As supposed in previous studies (Chen & Bouvain, 2008), the adhesion to this initiative can represent an additional incentive for monitoring the social performances. In particular, the Global Compact is a program that supports the member companies for the implementation and disclosure of environmental, social, and governance policies. To confirm this, in October 2006 the UNGC and the Global Reporting Initiative (GRI) have developed a strategic alliance known as the "UNGC-GRI Value Platform" on the basis of the complementary aspects of the two initiatives.[17] So the fifth hypothesis is as follows:

H5. The membership to institutional initiatives that stimulate socially sustainable policies affects the voluntary disclosure. In particular, firms adhering to UNGC confer a greater breadth and a lower concentration at the social disclosure than firms that don't adhere to UNGC.

The last but not less important firm-specific characteristic that we intend to analyze is the impact on the CSD generated by the level of the commitment and awareness toward the CSR. As known it's not easy to assess the quality of the CSR within the management approaches. In particular, we refer to the interaction among the principles of social responsibility and the policies developed by firms to address the social issues (Wortick & Cochran, 1985)). The outcome of this interaction is the so-called "Corporate Social Performance" (CSP) that can be assimilated to the results reached by putting in practice the compliance toward the corporate social responsibility (Maron, 2006). So, the CSP belongs to the operational dimension of the CSR. In fact, the latter pertains to the principles applicable to practices socially sustainable, while the former embraces the policies and the activities within this domain (De Bakker, Groenewegen, & Den Hond, 2005). In this sense, the CSP represents a media that assesses the CSR practices with respect to a wide range of concerns that are relevant to the social field (van Beurden & Gossling, 2008). Hence, on the basis of these characteristics, CSR and CSP seem to be "faces of the same coin," and the two terms are frequently considered as interchangeable (Barnett, 2007). Similarly, the CSP is difficult to measure, due to the necessity of a multidimensional assessment of the organizational behavior that involves the natural environment, workers, customers, human rights, and the community in general. In this regard, as mentioned, Ullmann (1985) states that social performances refer to the extent to which an organization is able to meet the expectations of certain external constituencies beyond those linked to the company's products/markets. In this respect, there can be a correlation between the level of social disclosure and the socially responsible behavior. In particular, considering the CSD as another component of the operational dimension of the CSR, hence a "proxy" of such behaviors, the assumption is a positive relationship between the quantity and the quality of a firm's social disclosure and its social performance (Cowen et al., 1987; Roberts, 1992; Ullmann, 1985). In particular, this approach considers that a higher quality of CSD ought to reflect a higher level of CSR, where the latter is expressed in terms of better social performance. So the sixth hypothesis is the following:

> **H6.** The CSR affects the voluntary disclosure. In particular, firms with a higher level of CSR confer a greater breadth and a lower concentration at the social disclosure than firms with a lower level of CSR.

METHODOLOGY

In this chapter, we identify the CSD through the CSR reports, also intended as sustainability reports (Chen & Bouvain, 2008; Hou & Reber, 2011; Vurro & Perrini, 2010).[18] In particular, the study is based on nonfinancial reporting of 80 companies in the period 2009–2008. The typology of the sample is an aspect that characterizes this study. In fact, recognizing a function of "certification and monitoring" of CSR to the socially responsible investment funds, the sample has been composed of 80 companies drawn from the portfolios of 78 SRFs listed on European markets, which are reported on Morningstar platform over the considered period (2009–2008). This database provides information about companies that compose the portfolio of investment funds, indicating the industry and the percentage of shares held by the investors. Therefore, based on the information available in the Morningstar database, we have built a cumulative portfolio consisting of the firms in which SRFs have invested. This step has returned a first set of 346 companies stratified by industry.[19] In addition, since a same company can be owned by more than one fund, for each industry we have organized the companies in decreasing order, according to the number of SRFs participating in a single firm. Finally, based on the number of companies, we have calculated the weight that each industry has inside the cumulative panel.

So, the sample of 80 companies replicates the stratification and the weight of the industries that compose the cumulative portfolio (see Table 2).

In particular, for the purpose of companies extraction, the criterion of the "frequency of the SRFs presence" has been adopted. This criterion is defined as the number of different funds that participated in the same company in the years 2008 and 2009. Therefore, for each industry, companies have been extracted proceeding by a decreasing order in accordance with the number of SRFs present in the risk capital and cutting off the extraction when the industry has reached the percentage weight retained within the cumulative portfolio.

Table 2. Composition of the Sample by Industry.

Industries	Companies (No.)	%
Consumer goods	12	15
Industrial goods	19	24
Hardware	3	4
Software	3	4
Health	7	9
Consumer and industrial services	6	8
Tlc and media	6	8
Oil and energy	12	15
Finance	12	15
Total	80	100

In summary, the construction of the sample is carried out through the following steps: step 1 = identification of SRFs listed on the European markets and identified by Morningstar platform in the period 2008–2009; step 2 = construction of a cumulative portfolio of all SRFs, stratified by industry; step 3 = for each industry, organization of firms in decreasing order according to the number of SRFs participating in the capital; step 4 = extraction of the 80 companies that composed the sample stratified by industry.

Consistently with other previous work (Gray et al., 1995b; Naser et al., 2006; Perrini, 2005; van der Laan Smith et al., 2005), the analysis of the CSD has been based on the following six key areas of disclosure[20]: (i) environment; (ii) human resources; (iii) community; (iv) customers; (v) suppliers; (vi) corporate governance.[21]

For each theme of the six identified areas, through the study of CSR reports, it has been noted whether the company has made (yes = 1) or not (no = 0) the disclosure during the period 2009–2008. So, for each area of the disclosure we have measured an *incidence rate* (Perrini, 2005) that is a *ratio* between the number of the themes reported and the total themes referring to a given area (Vurro & Perrini, 2010). Next, similarly to previous studies (Naser et al., 2006) to measure the amplitude of the CSD, for each firm a global index called CSD breadth is constructed. In particular, as shown in recent works (Vurro & Perrini, 2010), since the number of themes for single area can be considered arbitrary, the CSD index has been determined as the sum of the six *ratios* referring to the six areas. In particular, these *ratios* are obtained dividing the number of themes reported by the firm for a given area and the total number of the issues assigned to that area.[22] In addition, for a further verification of the variety of disclosure between the firms, in order to measure the distribution of themes reported (CSD concentration), for each company the Gini coefficient with respect to the six ratios is calculated.[23]

The test of the hypotheses has been performed by a univariate (Mann–Whitney test) and a multivariate analysis (OLS model). With regard to the first, in order to verify the statistical significance of the differences in terms of breadth and concentration of the CSD, we have classified the firms in two subgroups on the basis of five criteria (see Table 3). In particular, the sampled companies have been classified from time to time in accordance with the following principles:

- [Test 1] Country = belonging to a "liberal" market economy (Anglo-Saxon countries) or to a "coordinated" market economy (other European countries and Japan);

Table 3. Classification of the Sample Firms.

	Subgroups	Companies (No.)	%
Macro factors	*Country*		
	Coordinated market economies	40	50
	Liberal market economies	40	50
	Total	80	100
	Industry		
	Bad reputation	24	30
	Good reputation	56	70
	Total	80	100
Firm-specific characteristics	*Size*		
	Large/Medium	52	65
	Small	28	35
	Total	80	100
	SRFs participation		
	High/Medium	40	50
	Low	40	50
	Total	80	100
	UN-Global Compact membership		
	Yes	47	59
	No	33	41
	Total	80	100
	Level of CSR		
	Higher level	38	48
	Lower level	42	52
	Total	80	100

- [Test 2] Industry = belonging to an industry characterized by "bad reputation" (oil, energy, finance) or to other industries;
- [Test 3] Size = medium and large size or small size;
- [Test 4] SRFs participation = medium and high frequency of participation or low frequency of participation;
- [Test 5] UNGC = membership or not to the institutional initiative UNGC;
- [Test 6] CSR = higher and lower level of CSR.

Therefore, as in previous studies (Chen & Bouvain, 2008; van der Laan Smith et al., 2005), to measure the country-effect, we have distinguished the firms in relation to the socioeconomic model which draws the country of origin (see Table 4). In particular, following the classification of Hall and Soskice (2001), we have distinguished between a "liberal" market model, which is considered as more shareholder oriented and characterizing the

Table 4. Classification of the Sample by Countries.

Countries	Companies (No.)	Capitalistic Model
US	21	"Liberal" market economy
UK	18	
Australia	1	
Total	40	
Scandinavian countries	12	"Coordinated" market economy
Holland	1	
Germany	4	
Austria	1	
Switzerland	4	
France	10	
Spain	2	
Italy	1	
Japan	5	
Total	40	

Anglo-Saxon countries, and a "coordinated" market model, which is assumed as more stakeholder oriented.

For the industry-effect, the reference is to the bad reputation of the oil and energy industries (Sweeney, 2009; Yoon et al., 2006), to which we have added the financial industry because of the scandals that have recently marked the international crises.

For the size-effect, as in previous studies (Naser et al., 2006), we have adopted the average of total assets during the years 2009–2008. In particular, consistent with other surveys (van der Laan Smith et al., 2005), for each industry the companies of the sample are classified as "medium or large," if the total asset is included respectively between the 26th and 75th percentile and the 76th and 100th percentile, while the sampled companies are classified as "small" ones if the total asset is included between the 1st and the 25th percentile reported always at single industry.[24] Similarly, based on the frequency of participation of SRFs measured by the number of funds present in the capital, for each industry the companies have been classified as firms with a "medium or high" frequency of participation, if the number of funds is included between the 26th and 75th percentile and between the 76th and 100th percentile, and as companies with a "low" frequency of participation, if the number of funds that set in the capital is included between the 1st and 25th percentile.[25] Moreover, to evaluate the effect generated by the membership to institutional initiatives that stimulate socially sustainable policies, as in previous studies (Chen & Bouvain, 2008), the firms in the sample have been classified between those who adhere formally to UNGC and those who do not. Finally, with the reference to the time horizon 2009–2008, for each company we have extracted from the dataset ASSET4-ESG a global indicator of the social performance obtained as a sum of the single scores attributed during the period 2009–2008 to the following categories[26]: environment, human rights, corporate governance, customers, and employment. In particular, given that all the sampled firms are acknowledged as socially responsible according to the participation of SRFs, the companies have been classified as firms with a "higher level of CSR," if the total score is higher than the median of the panel, and as companies with a "lower level of CSR," if the total score is lower than or equal to the median of the panel. Subsequently, for a deeper study of the determinants, we have performed a multivariate analysis with dependent variables – the CSD breadth and the Gini coefficient (CSD concentration).

So, the models are formalized as follows:

Mod. 1: CSD (breadth) $= \beta_1$Country $+ \beta_2$Industry $+ \beta_3$Size $+ \beta_4$SRFsParticipation $+ \beta_5$UNGCmembership $+ \beta_6$CSR

Mod. 2: CSD (concentration) $= \beta_1$Country $+ \beta_2$Industry $+ \beta_3$Size $+ \beta_4$SRFsParticipation $+ \beta_5$UNGCmembership $+ \beta_6$CSR

The explanatory variables are the same for both the regression models. In particular, *Country* is a dummy that takes value 1 if the country to which companies belong refers to a coordinated market economy, and 0 in the case of Anglo-Saxon countries ("liberal" market economy). *Industry* is a dummy that measures the reputation. It takes value 1 in the case of companies belonging to industries with a bad reputation (oil, energy, and finance) and 0 otherwise. *Size* is a dummy that measures the size-effect and takes value 1 in the case of "medium and large" companies and the value 0 for the sampled firms classified as "small" ones. *SRFs participation* is a variable corresponding to the number of different funds participating in the same company. It measures the influence of institutional investors on the CSD. *UNGC membership* is a dummy that takes the value 1 in case of the membership to the UN Global Compact, and 0 in the other cases. Finally, *CSR* is a dummy that measures the effect of the level of the CSR (through the proxy represented by a global social performance indicator) on the CSD. This dummy takes value 1 in the case of companies with a "higher level of Social Responsibility" and the value 0 for the sampled firms classified for a "lower level of Social Responsibility." The indicator of the global CSP, as a proxy of the level of CSR, is obtained from the data-base ASSET4-ESG already adopted for the univariate analysis. Therefore, on the basis of the research hypothesis, in the first model we expect a positive relationship between the explanatory variables and the CSD breadth index. As countercheck, in the second model we expect an inverse relationship between the same variables and the Gini concentration coefficient (CSD concentration).

UNIVARIATE ANALYSIS

Through the Mann–Whitney test (see Table 5), in this section we verify if there are statistically significant differences in terms of amplitude and concentration of the CSD in relation to the socioeconomic context (*country*), the industry reputation (*industry*), the *size*, the *SRFs participation*, the *UNGC membership*, the level of *CSR*.

Starting from the analysis of the socioeconomic and institutional context, the results highlight significant differences in the breadth of CSD between CMEs and LMEs. In fact, companies that have their headquarters in countries with a CME show a wider amplitude of information about CSR practices in their sustainability reports than firms that refer to LME (in the first case the median of the CSD breadth is equal to 3.389 while in the second case it is equal to 3.223). So, this finding seems to confirm that in countries less polarized toward a shareholder orientation, managers tend to implement a higher disclosure within the social report, offering more information on the different areas of the CSD. At the same time, companies belonging to LME are more inclined toward a greater concentration on certain areas within the report (the median of the concentration coefficient is equal to 0.230 compared to 0.179 related to CMEs). It means a less homogeneous distribution of information between the different themes and areas of CSD. Therefore, the results of the test are consistent with the first research hypothesis.

Passing to the study of the industry-effect, relatively to the reputation, we find a significant difference in terms of the breadth of disclosure between the firms belonging to sectors with a "bad reputation" and those with a "good reputation." In particular, in this last case firms show a greater breadth of the CSD (median equal to 3.654) than firms of the other group (median 3.010). In addition, as countercheck, companies that operate in industries with a bad reputation tend to concentrate information only on some areas of CSR, presenting a concentration coefficient of the disclosure that is higher than companies belonging to industries with a good reputation. In fact, in the first case the median is equal to 0.29

Table 5. Mann–Whitney Test on CSD Breadth and CSD Concentration.

	CSD Breadth		CSD Concentration	
	Coordinated market economies (CMEs)	Liberal market economies (LMEs)	Coordinated market economies (CMEs)	Liberal market economies (LMEs)
Country				
Median	3.589	3.223	0.179	0.230
Mann–Whitney test H0: Me (CME)=Me(LME)	−2.098**		−2.011**	
Industry	Bad reputation (BR)	Good reputation (GR)	Bad reputation (BR)	Good reputation (GR)
Median	3.010	3.654	0.291	0.193
Mann–Whitney test H0: Me (BR)=Me(GR)	−2.194**		−1.669*	
Size	Large/Medium (L/M)	Small (S)	Large/Medium (L/M)	Small (S)
Median	3.664	3.292	0.199	0.208
Mann–Whitney test H0: Me (L/M)=Me(S)	−2.128**		−1.674*	
SRFs participation	High/Medium (H/M)	Low (L)	High/Medium (H/M)	Low (L)
Median	3.768	3.401	0.173	0.229
Mann–Whitney test H0: Me (H/M)=Me(L)	−2.358**		−2.425**	
UN Global Compact membership	Yes (Y)	No (N)	Yes (Y)	No (N)
Median	3.601	3.349	0.204	0.207
Mann–Whitney Test H0: Me (Y)=Me(N)	−1.735*		−1.334	
Level of CSR	Higher (H)	Lower (L)	Higher (H)	Lower (L)
Median	3.667	3.280	0.185	0.231
Mann–Whitney test H0: Me (H)=Me(L)	−2.312**		−2.794***	

Significant level: ***1%; **5%; *10%.

while in the second case it is equal to 0.193. Therefore, the results seem to support the thesis (Mitnick, 2000) for which companies belonging to the industries that have or may have a negative impact on a specific area of CSR (e.g., the environment for companies in the oil industry) tend to avoid providing information on this item, in order to focus their disclosure in the areas where they are able to demonstrate a favorable impact in terms of social performance (e.g., the charitable contributions). Moreover, this approach can contribute to determine a higher concentration of the CSD. So, in relation to the significance of the industry effect, the findings are consistent with the second (H2b) of the two antagonistic hypotheses.

Then, through the analysis of firm-specific characteristics, starting from the size of the company, we highlight statistically significant differences between companies with a "large or medium" size and the "small" sized ones. In fact, looking at the amplitude of the CSD, it is clear that firms with a larger size provide more information in different areas of the CSD (the median is equal to 3.664, against the median of the CSD index of the smaller firms which is equal to 3.292). This finding is consistent with the thesis for which larger firms generally have a higher social impact and at the same time they are designed to reduce the higher agency costs that accompany their growth. Consequently, looking at the concentration of the CSD, it is possible to note that smaller firms provide more focused information, clearly restricting the disclosure only to certain areas of CSR (the median of the CSD concentration of smaller sized firms is equal to 0.208 against a median of larger firms that is equal to 0.199). In this sense, smaller firms in contrast to larger companies confirm a gap in terms of CSR disclosure. Probably they solve the costs and benefits trade-off of the disclosure on social performance, concentrating the information on more restricted areas that attract the attention of their stakeholders. Therefore, the results of the test are consistent with the third hypothesis.

Subsequently, the analysis of the participation of SRFs highlights statistically significant differences in the amplitude of CSD comparing the high or medium participation of these investors with the low frequency of participation. In fact, where there is a higher presence of SRFs, it is possible to detect even a greater breadth of information in different areas of the CSR (the median is equal to 3.768 compared to a median equal to 3.401 for the companies with a lower participation). This is consistent with the argument that the SRFs encourage companies to adopt a wider disclosure characterized by a lower level of concentration (the median of the Gini coefficient is equal to 0.173 for companies with a higher presence of SRFs, against a median equal to 0.229 for companies less participated by socially responsible investors). Therefore, confirming that the increased presence of SRFs corresponds to a significantly broader and homogeneous disclosure, the results are consistent with the fourth research hypotheses.

Moreover, the analysis of the membership to institutional initiatives, such as the UN-Global Compact, shows a statistically significant difference only in terms of the breadth of the CSD between members and nonmembers of this initiative, even if with a lower degree of significance. In particular, the median of the CSD breadth for companies that adhere to UN-Global Compact is higher (equal to 3.601) than the median relative to nonmembers (equal to 3.349). This seems to confirm that the adhesion to UN-Global Compact encourages better monitoring and reporting activities, resulting in a larger collection of data and information concerning the social performance. Therefore, with regard to the breadth, the test is consistent with the fifth research hypothesis.

Finally, as expected, the level of CSR makes the difference in terms of breadth and concentration of the social reporting. In fact, in the first case the median of the CSD breadth for companies with a higher level of CSR is significantly higher (equal to 3.667) than the median relative to firms with a lower level of CSR (equal to 3.280). At the same time, the median of the CSD concentration is significantly lower for companies with a higher level of CSR (0.185) with respect to the firms characterized for a lower level of CSR (0.231). So, in both cases we find a very significant statistical difference that supports the sixth and last hypothesis.

In summary, the overall results confirm the hypotheses and strengthen the thesis about the usefulness of an interpretative approach that considers different perspectives to explain the causes of the disclosure variation between firms. Therefore, we further deepen this topic in the next section specifically dedicated to a multivariate analysis of the determinants of CSD.

MULTIVARIATE ANALYSIS

The results of the multivariate analysis (see Table 6) are consistent with the previous statistical tests, confirming the existence of several factors, macro and firm-specific, that can significantly affect the variety of the CSD between different companies.

In the first place, we find that the country has an important influence on social disclosure, confirming that between the firm and its context there is

Table 6. The Determinants of CSD Breadth and CSD Concentration.

Explanatory Variables	Model 1		Model 2	
	Dependent variable: CSD breadth		Dependent variable: CSD concentration	
	Standardized coefficient	*t*-statistic	Standardized coefficient	*t*-statistic
Country				
[Coord. economies (1); lib. economies (0)]	0.285***	2.854	−0.241**	−2.397
Industry				
[Bad reputation (1); good reputation (0)]	−0.261***	−2.682	0.212**	2.162
Size				
[Large/medium (1); small (0)]	0.197**	1.975	−0.184*	−1.829
SRFs participation				
(No. of funds)	0.188*	1.946	−0.198**	−2.035
UN Global Compact membership				
[Yes (1); No (0)]	0.134	2.565	−0.118	−1.133
Level of CSR				
[Higher (1); Lower (0)]	0.258***	1.302	−0.320***	−3.149
No. of observations	480		480	
	R^2	Adjusted R^2	R^2	Adjusted R^2
	0.330	0.275	0.320	0.264
ANOVA test	*F* 5.994***		*F* 4.355***	

Significant level: ***1%; **5%; *10%.

an exchange of values that can influence the priorities underlying the aims and the policies of communication among the various social groups. In fact, in line with an institutionalist perspective (Albert, 1990; Hall & Soskice, 2001; Soskice, 1989), consistent with other empirical research (Chen & Bouvain, 2008; van der Laan Smith et al., 2005), results show that the belonging of the firm to a country based on a coordinated market model, less shareholder-oriented and with governance systems more consistent with a communitarian vision (Lashgari, 2004), determines a positive influence on the amplitude of the disclosure and the homogeneity of the themes distribution. Moreover, in terms of comparison with other positive predictors, we find that the country is the most statistically significant determinant of the CSD breadth. Therefore, the first hypothesis is confirmed.

Second, referring to its reputation, the industry also influences the disclosure. However, unlike the theoretical perspective that assigns a counterbalance function of the bad reputation to the practices of CSR and voluntary disclosure (Yoon et al., 2006), this last characteristic seems to affect negatively the breadth of the CSD and, in turn, has a positive effect on the concentration of the themes represented in the reporting systems. Thus, the second interpretive perspective that discriminates the industries on the basis of their reputation seems to prevail. In particular, companies that have weakness in some areas of disclosure (e.g., the environment) tend to reduce the information and the space dedicated to these issues (Mitnick, 2000), determining a lower breadth of the CSD as a whole. Therefore, the second and antagonistic hypothesis is confirmed.

Third, measured by the total asset, the size is the other factor that with a significant weight is able to positively influence the breadth of the disclosure. In fact, consistent with other research (Gao et al., 2005; Gray et al., 1995b; Hou & Reber, 2011; Naser et al., 2006; Sweeney, 2009), the larger the size the higher the CSD breadth index and the lower the concentration coefficient of CSR reports. This confirms that with the increase in dimension, firms tend to discover a wider range of themes and information. So, in a theoretical perspective, the existence of a CSR gap for smaller companies (Perrini & Minoja, 2008), the need to contain the higher agency costs that accompany the size growth (Jensen & Meckling, 1976), and finally the aim to meet the expectations of a wider range of interest groups (Carroll, 1994; Freeman, 1984; Preston et al., 1999) may all represent the reasons that contribute to justify the positive relationship between the breadth of the CSD and the size of the company. Accordingly, the third hypothesis is confirmed.

Fourth, the greater or lesser presence of institutional investors is an additional explanatory factor for the variety of disclosure between different companies. In fact, given that all firms in the sample are participated by SRFs, when the number of SRFs that invest in the same company increases, the breadth of the CSD increases and the degree of concentration of the themes discussed is reduced. More specifically, with regard to the latter, it should be noted that the participation of SRFs is a negative predictor of the disclosure concentration. Thus, the empirical evidence shows that the function of certification and monitoring of CSR undertaken by SRFs represents an incentive for the breadth of social disclosure. Moreover, CSD, contributing to reduce information asymmetries on the risk exposure of the company to future social costs (Di Giulio et al., 2011; Perrini et al., 2011), legitimates the presence of investors theoretically interested to a better equilibrium between ethics and business as well as to financial performance and CSP. Therefore, the fourth hypothesis is confirmed.

In the fifth place, as shown in other studies (Chen & Bouvain, 2008), to be a member of an institutional initiatives like the UNGC has positive influence on CSD; however, in our model this effect is not statistically significant. The same result, but with an opposite sign, we can find for the impact on the CSD concentration. Therefore, the fifth hypothesis is not confirmed.[27]

Finally, the level of CSR makes a significant difference among the social reports. In fact, the higher is the level of social performance, higher is the breadth of the CSD and, at the same time, lower is the degree of concentration. So, consistent with the literature that assumes a positive relationship between the social performance and the quality of the disclosure (Cowen et al., 1987; Roberts, 1992; Ullmann, 1985), our findings fully support the sixth and last hypothesis.

In summary, the multivariate study substantially confirms the previous general conclusion coming from the univariate analysis. Namely, there are empirical evidences that a wide range of variables can act as determinants of the CSD. Moreover, the different nature of these factors strengthens an approach that looks at this phenomenon through different analytical lenses.

CONCLUSIONS

This study aimed to verify empirically which factors can act as determinants of the breadth and of the concentration of the CSD. According to this objective, the analysis identifies several factors, both external and internal, that are able to explain the existing variety in the CSD between different companies. For an exhaustive interpretation, our empirical survey looks at this phenomenon from different perspectives, consistently with the existing literature that draws diverse general theories. As mentioned, the main references found are the legitimacy theory, the stakeholder theory, the agency model, the theory of the information asymmetries, and the institutionalist perspective. It being understood the specific identity of these theoretical frameworks, from our excursus derives a vision of the CSD as tool to reach different economic objectives. For example, it's possible to make reference to: the reinforcing of the social legitimacy of the firm; the support of key stakeholders; the reduction of the agency costs and the adverse selection problems. So, in this process it's important to verify the predictors of the CSD that can make the difference between the firms.

In our case we have been focusing simultaneously on macro- and firm-specific factors, such as: the country and the industry to which the enterprise belongs; the size of the company; the frequency of participation of the SRFs; the membership to the UNGC; and the level of CSR.

With regard to the methodology, the empirical study is based on a stratified sample composed by 80 firms in which European SRFs have invested in during the period 2008–2009. This is a characteristic that distinguishes the research with respect to previous contributions. In fact, the SRFs participation, as basic criterion for the sample composition, allows to focus on firms ascertained as socially responsible, in accordance with a certification and monitoring function of these nonconventional funds.

Moreover, for a measure of the variations of the voluntary disclosure, the survey adopted two indicators defined as CSD-breadth and CSD-concentration. Regard to these two parameters, the findings are consistent with the hypotheses defined.

In the first place, proceeding from the general to the particular, it is confirmed that the country of origin is a very important predictor of the quality of voluntary disclosure measured in terms of themes represented in the CSR reports. In this regard, assuming that the social values of the context interact with the aim of legitimacy of the firm, the belonging to a market economy less polarized on the shareholders groups determines a greater breadth of disclosure. This may have important implications not only for the companies that operate locally in order to be accredited as socially responsible, but also for larger companies with a global business that are called to a greater effort to understand the expectations of the different social contexts in which they operate.

In the second place, our findings provide insights into the controversial theses on the industry effect. In fact, the public reputation of the industry helps to differentiate the breadth of the CSD. More particularly, the assumption for which the worst reputation can be offset by a greater propensity to disclosure is not confirmed. Rather, the antagonistic hypothesis seems to prevail for which firms that are known to be weak in one or more areas tend to reduce information about these themes in order to focus on other areas, such as donations or other initiatives of public interest. In this regard, a special attention can be paid to the degree of consistency between the information on socially responsible activities that the company decides to communicate and its core business.

In the third place, among the factors that we have defined as firm specific, firm size is confirmed as one of the major determinants of the amplitude of the disclosure. In fact, the results of the tests show that larger firms are more likely to produce wider CSD, having probably to deal with both a stronger political and social pressure, due to a higher visibility and a higher need for reduction of agency costs connected to their greater dimension. At the same time, the survey shows that the activism of socially responsible investors is a predictor of CSD. In fact, due to a mix of financial, ethical, and social evaluation during the allocation process, when the number of SRFs that participate to the ownership structure of the target company increases, the breadth of voluntary social disclosure also increases. Therefore, this indirectly confirms the activism that can be assigned to the SRFs. In particular, the presence of the latter is a reputational signal and a spur for the CSD that may contribute to the reduction of information asymmetries and adverse selection risks, facilitating the relationship between socially responsible companies and the capital market.

In the fourth place, the findings on the membership to the UNGC are not conclusive. In fact the results demonstrate a positive relationship with the breadth of the CSD, but this effect is significant only in the univariate analysis. So the potential incentive deriving from the adhesion to an institutional initiative like the UNGC assume a lower weight if compared with other determinants.

Finally, the companies that with their measurable performance demonstrate to be more sensitive toward the best practices of CSR are also able to translate this attitude in their CSR reports. In other words, the firms with a greater commitment to sustainable policies repaid by higher social results are encouraged to report their CSR performance. This means a positive relationship with the quality of the social disclosure in terms of higher breadth and lower concentration.

Before concluding, it should be noted that the study presents some limitations that are inherent in this type of research. First, there is a shortage of comparability between the CSR reports that can influence the interpretation and the calculation of a synthetic measure as the CSD indexes (breadth and concentration). Second, the reports analyzed are all in English, that, however, doesn't represent the native language for all the sampled companies. Third, even if the six content categories are well accepted in literature and although we have made reference to the GRI for identifying the themes by areas, the number of items for each area of disclosure may be eventually considered arbitrary. Fourth, the study doesn't analyze the volume of the disclosure in terms of pages, even if this method is criticizable due to the intrinsic difficulty of measurement. Finally, the analysis doesn't deepen the relationships between the determinants and the single content categories highlighted.

However, notwithstanding these limitations, the results of our analysis are well supported by different theoretical viewpoints that literature offers for explaining the deeper origins of the differences in disclosure activities. About it, the variety of significant determinants of CSD seems to support the consideration that for an exhaustive discussion it is not suitable a one-sided stance. Rather, we are faced with a management issue that lends itself to be analyzed from different perspectives, while respecting the identity of each specific analytical lens.

NOTES

1. For further details about the concepts and the measurement of the breadth and of the concentration of the CSD, see also the section "Methodology."

2. From a narrow view, the corporate governance (CG) represents a set of mechanisms to solve the potential conflicts of interests between owners and managers, or between the different classes of shareholders (Jensen & Meckling, 1976). From a broader perspective, the CG represents a system to manage corporate interests for the wider good society, the firm organization, and the environmental practices, in accordance with a model that addresses companies' accountability toward a range of stakeholders that includes and goes beyond the stockholders (Benn & Bolton, 2011).

3. Several years ago, Verrecchia stated that there is no comprehensive or unifying theory of disclosure, no central paradigm, and no well-integrated theory (2001). This assertion is probably valid also with reference to the specific field of the CSD.

4. Under this perspective, the company defends its survival by disclosing a wider information in order to prove that it is a good "citizen" (Guthrie & Parker, 1989), demonstrating to honor in this way its social contract (Donaldson & Dunfee, 1994, 1999). In fact, if an organization fails to fulfill the terms of the social synallagma, as a reaction the consumers can reduce or eliminate at all the demand for these products, the suppliers can stop the deliveries, the government can increase taxes or laws for discouraging those productions (Deegan, 2002).

5. Other studies (Vurro & Perrini, 2010, 2011) consider the CSR reporting as a tool to improve the corporate social performance, because it is a means to attract supportive stakeholders and because it allows the control of the social impact of corporate activities. In this sense "the CSR disclosure is expected to predict CSP, in that the former mirrors the latter" (Vurro & Perrini, 2010, p. 7).

6. Due to its cross-cutting nature, the agency model can be applied to different hierarchical relationships where there is a principal and an agent. In this regard Mitnick identifies at least three main areas of study where the agency model can be applied: the theory of the firm, the corporate finance, and the organizational theory (Mitnick, 1992).

7. Following Verrecchia (2001), in theory the best practice should be a "corner solution," which means a full disclosure in order to eliminate any potential component of the cost related to the asymmetric information. However this doesn't

happen. In first place, the markets' agents are different, so it is difficult or impossible for the disclosure to "yield a positive benefit for everyone." In second place, managers define the perimeter of disclosure they have to face with "countervailing economic forces," such as, risk sharing, agency costs, or proprietary costs in general (see, e.g., the diffusion of sensitive information to competitors).

8. In truth, as observed in other studies, this framework can show some shortcomings, such as (Kang, 2006) an overemphasis on the firms with respect to other actors, an excessive determinism, and a strong rational-choice view of institutions.

9. Even some European countries have developed capacities for nonmarket coordination (Italy, France, Spain, Portugal, Greece), the specificity of these arrangements generates an ambiguous economic model sometimes defined as "Mediterranean" (Hall & Soskice, 2001). Nevertheless, apart from this specification, the Mediterranean countries are closer to the coordinated economies than the liberal ones.

10. It is known, for example, that some countries in Northern Europe have focused on the environment for a long time (Halm & Huse, 1997), and in these contexts the attention toward the quality of life, labor policies, and involvement of the community where the company operates prevails (van der Laan Smith et al., 2005).

11. The *contractarian* vision subtends an endorsement of the shareholder sovereignty because their assets (financial capital) are more easily expropriated. This motivates a governance model that stresses the need to primarily protect the shareholders (Cobbaut & Lenoble, 2003). Instead, the *communitarian* model provides for a stakeholder-based approach to governance that may include lenders, suppliers, customers, employees, and the community (Epstein, 2012). The governance structures in countries like Germany, Belgium, Scandinavia, or Japan are quite communitarian, while nations like the United States and other Anglo-Saxon countries show a structure more tipically contractarian (Bradley, Schipani, Sundaram, & Walsh, 1999, Epstein, 2012). This distinction supports the assumption for which the communitarian models can be associated to a "coordinated" market economy, while a contractarian structure belong especially to the "liberal" market economies.

12. The British Petroleum disaster in the Mexican Gulf can be considered as an example of the social risks and costs to which the oil companies can be exposed. In fact, the BP has recently agreed to pay damages and compensations for $4.5 billion and plead guilty to 14 offenses, including manslaughter in 2010 for the explosion of the Deepwater Horizon platform. This disaster cost the lives of 11 workers and caused environmental devastation. Moreover, the last compensation is in addition to 23 billion already paid by BP for damages to the environment and families.

13. The general criteria of ethical and social investors are classified into three categories: (1) "in" or "out" screening; (2) the engagement; (3) the community investing. In particular, since the engagement intends to stimulate or modify specific behaviors of the company in terms of social responsibility, the shareholder activism can be placed in this category.

14. Several studies show that, by reducing information asymmetries, socially responsible funds can offset the theoretical "ethical sacrifice" represented by the restrictions on diversification strategies. This contributes to the attainment of performance even superior to those of conventional funds, especially during the last financial crisis (Bauer, Koedijk, & Otten, 2005; Galema, Plantinga, & Scholtens, 2008; Gangi & Trotta, 2010, 2013).

15. In previous studies it has been highlighted that, although nonfinancial reporting increasingly relies on institutional standards (e.g., GRI), neither a unique format nor a universal language exists for clearer and more comparable reports (Perrini, 2005; Vurro & Perrini, 2010).

16. With over 10,000 corporate participants over 130 countries, the UNGC is recognized as the largest voluntary corporate responsibility initiative in the world. The participation to the UNGC asks companies to embrace values in the areas of *human rights*, *labor standards*, *environment*, and *anti-corruption*. With respect to these domains, the UNGC states 10 principles that constitute the architecture of core values for a sustainable business model. For more details, see www.unglobalcompact.org.

17. Having said the synergies, the UNGC gave a set of principles of organizational behavior, while the GRI provides a framework for translating into information the results of the application of those behavioral principles. Moreover, some empirical evidences show that the membership to these initiatives facilitates the improvement of the corporate image, expanding and strengthening the relationships with stakeholders (Cetindamar & Husoy, 2007).

18. Many works on social voluntary disclosure are based on annual reports as the main communication media between the firm and the society (Gao et al., 2005; Gray et al., 1995a, 1995b; Naser et al., 2006; van der Laan Smith et al., 2005).

19. The organization of the sample by industry reflects the classification provided by the Morningstar platform.

20. The identification of the themes for each area of disclosure is based on the cited literature and on the guidelines issued by the GRI. As known, this last represents the most common standard between the firms. For a detailed description of the themes we refer to the appendix.

21. The reference to the disclosure on corporate governance, which includes the theme of shareholders' rights, is consistent with the model of Corporate Responsibility Continuum proposed by Jamali and Mirshak (2006).

22. For example, if a company shows 5 of the 11 themes referred to the Environment (I ratio = 5/11), 3 of the 9 themes related to the Human Resources (II ratio = 3/9), 5 of the 10 themes reported for the Community (III ratio = 5/10), 7 of the 9 themes related to the area of Customers (IV ratio = 7/9), 2 of the 4 themes related to Suppliers (V ratio = 2/4), and 8 of the 18 themes referred to Corporate Governance (VI ratio = 8/18), then the CSD index is equal to (5/11 + 3/9 + 5/10 + 7/9 + 2/4 + 8/18)=3.01.

23. As it is known, the Gini coefficient varies between 0 and 1, which indicates a maximum equity or a maximum concentration of distribution. Therefore, given that the concentration measurement can be taken as countercheck of the breadth measurement of the disclosure, in the case of a concentration index closest to zero, it means that the themes and the areas of the disclosure are homogeneously treated. Conversely, for a concentration index closest to the unity, it means that the disclosure focuses more on certain topics and less on others. So, this measure can be intended as a proxy of the broader or narrower vision of the CSD.

24. For example, with regard to the industry of consumer goods, we find the following classification (€/million): [0–25 perc.]=8.1–21.5 = Small (S); [26–75 perc.] =21.51–51.5 = Medium (M); [76–100 perc.]=51.51–121 = Large (L). Therefore, we

have obtained the following distribution by the number of firms and classes: 2 (S), 9 (M/L).

25. For example, in the case of the industry of consumer goods, we consider the following classification based on the number of participating funds (no. of SRFs): [0–25 perc.]=1–3 = Low (L); [26–75 perc.]=4–6 = Medium (M); [76–100 perc.] =7–11 = High (H). Therefore, we obtained the following distribution for the number of firms and classes: 4 (L), 8 (M/L).

26. ASSET4-ESG is a database processed by Thomson Reuters that provides objective and systematic information based on 280 key performance indicators (KPIs). The score gives an overall measure of the quality of the practices socially responsible and it represents a useful tool for defining and comparing socially responsible investment strategies. In this sense, it is an indicator very consistent with the nature of our sample. For more details, see www.thomsonreuters.com.

27. Given the synergies, we also tested for the adhesion to GRI (a dummy = 1, if Yes; or = 0, if Not) in substitution of the dummy INGC, but the model returns the same results (outcomes not-reported).

REFERENCES

Aguilera, R. V., & Cuervo-Cazurra, A. (2004). Codes of good governance worldwide: What is the trigger? *Organization Studies*, *25*(3), 415–443.

Aguilera, R. V., Williams, C., Conley, J., & Rupp, D. (2006). Corporate governance and social responsibility: A comparative analysis of the UK and the US. *Corporate Governance: An International Review*, *14*(1), 147–158.

Akerlof, G. A. (1970). The market for 'Lemons': Quality uncertainty and the market mechanism. *Quarterly Journal of Economics*, *84*(3), 488–500.

Albert, M. (1990). *Capitalisme contre capitalisme*. Paris: Seuil.

Archel, P., Husillos, J., Larrinaga, C., & Spence, C. (2009). Social disclosure, legitimacy theory and the role of the state. *Accounting, Auditing and Accountability Journal*, *22*(8), 1284–1307.

Argandona, A. (2011). Three ethical dimensions of the financial crisis. 1st Workshop on Business Ethics. Eiasm conference, Brussels, Belgium, November.

Arnold, M. (2001). Walking the ethical tightrope. *Marketing*, *1*, 17.

Barnett, M. L. (2007). Stakeholder influence capacity and the variability of financial returns to corporate social responsibility. *Academy of Management Review*, *32*(3), 794–816.

Bauer, R., Koedijk, K., & Otten, R. (2005). International evidence on ethical mutual fund performance and investment style. *Journal of Banking and Finance*, *29*, 1751–1767.

Belkaoui, A., & Karpik, P. G. (1989). Determinants of the corporate decision to disclose social information. *Accounting, Auditing and Accountability*, *2*, 36–51.

Benn, S., & Bolton, D. (2011). *Key concepts in corporate social responsibility*. London: Sage.

Bhimani, A., & Soonawalla, K. (2005). From conformance to performance: The corporate responsibilities continuum. *Journal of Accounting and Public Policy*, *24*, 165–174.

Boutin-Dufresne, F., & Savaria, P. (2004). Corporate social responsibility and financial risk. *The Journal of Investing*, *13*, 57–66.

Bradley, M., Schipani, C. A., Sundaram, A. K., & Walsh, J. P. (1999). The purposes and accountability of the corporation in contemporary society: Corporate governance at a crossroads. *Law and Contemporary Problems*, *62*(3), 9–86.

Brammer, S., & Pavellin, S. (2007). Voluntary social disclosures by large UK companies. *Business Ethics: A European Review*, *13*(2), 86–99.

Carlisle, Y., & Faulkner, D. (2004). Corporate social responsibility: A stages framework. *European Business Journal*, *16*(4), 143–152.

Carroll, A. (1991). The pyramid of corporate social responsibility: Toward the moral management of organizational stakeholders. *Business Horizons*, *34*(4), 39–48.

Carroll, A. (1994). Social issues in management research: Experts views, analysis and commentary. *Business and Society Review*, *33*(1), 5–29.

Carroll, A. (1998). The four faces of corporate citizenship. *Business and Society Review*, *100*(1), 1–7.

Cetindamar, D., & Husoy, K. (2007). Corporate social responsibility practices and environmentally responsible behaviour: The case of the United Nations global compact. *Journal of Business Ethics*, *76*(2), 163–176.

Chapple, W., & Moon, J. (2005). Corporate social responsibility (CSR) in Asia: A seven-country study of CSR web site reporting. *Business and Society*, *44*(4), 415–441.

Chen, S., & Bouvain, P. (2008). Is corporate responsibility converging? A comparison of corporate responsibility reporting in the USA, UK, Australia, and Germany. *Journal of Business Ethics*, *87*, 299–317.

Clarkson, M. B. E. (1995). A stakeholder framework for analysing and evaluating corporate social performance. *Academy of Management Review*, *20*(1), 92–117.

Cobbaut, R., & Lenoble, J. (2003). *Corporate governance: An institutionalist approach.* New York, NY: Kluwer.

Cooper, D. J., & Sherer, M. J. (1984). The value of corporate accounting reports: Arguments for a political economy of accounting. *Organizations and Society*, *9*(3), 207–232.

Cormier, D., Ledoux, M. J., & Magnan, M. (2009). The use of Web sites as a disclosure platform for corporate performance. *International Journal of Accounting Information Systems*, *10*(1), 1–24.

Cowen, S. S., Ferreri, L. B., & Parker, L. D. (1987). The impact of corporate characteristics on social responsibility disclosure: A typology and frequency based analysis. *Accounting, Organisation and Society*, *12*(2), 111–122.

Cowton, C. (1999). Accounting and financial ethics: From margin to mainstream? *Business Ethics: A European Review*, *8*(2), 99–107.

De Bakker, F. G. A., Groenewegen, P., & Den Hond, F. (2005). A bibliometric analysis of 30 years of research and theory on corporate social responsibility and corporate social performance. *Business and Society*, *44*(3), 238–317.

Deegan, C. (2002). Introduction: The legitimising effect of social and environmental disclosure – A theoretical foundation. *Accounting, Auditing and Accountability Journal*, *15*(3), 282–311.

Deegan, C., & Gordon, B. (1996). A study of the environmental disclosure practices of Australian corporations. *Accounting and Business Research*, *26*(3), 187–199.

Di Giulio, A., Migliavacca, P., & Tencati, A. (2011). Corporate social performance and cost of capital: A meaningful relationship? In A. Tencati & F. Perrini (Eds.), *Business ethics and corporate sustainability* (pp. 132–146). Cheltenham, UK: Edward Elgar Publishing.

DiMaggio, P. J., & Powell, W. W. (1983). The iron cage revisited: Institutional isomorphism and collective rationality in organizational fields. *American Sociological Review*, *48*(1), 147–160.

Donaldson, T. (1992). The language of international corporate ethics. *Business Ethics Quarterly*, *2*(3), 271–281.

Donaldson, T., & Dunfee, T. W. (1994). Toward a unified conception of business ethics: Integrative social contracts theory. *The Academy of Management Review*, *19*(2), 252–284.

Donaldson, T., & Dunfee, T. W. (1999). *Ties that bind: A social contracts approach to business ethics*. Boston, MA: Harvard Business School Press.

Donaldson, T., & Preston, L. E. (1995). The stakeholder theory of the corporation: Concepts, evidence and implications. *Academy of Management Review*, *20*(1), 65–91.

Dunfee, T. W. (2008). Stakeholder theory: Managing corporate social responsibility in a multiple actor context. In A. Crane, A. McWilliams, D. Matte, J. Moon, & D. Siegel (Eds.), *Corporate Social Responsibility*. Oxford: Oxford University Press.

Dye, R. A. (1985). Disclosure of nonproprietary information. *Journal of Accounting Research*, *23*(1), 123–145.

Epstein, M. J. (2012). Challenges of governing globally. *Strategic Governance*, *1*(July), 27–34.

Fama, E. F. (1980). Agency problems and the theory of the firm. *Journal of Political Economy*, *88*(2), 288–307.

Fama, E. F., & Jensen, M. C. (1983). Separation of ownership and control. *Journal of Law and Economics*, *26*(2), 301–325.

Freeman, R. E. (1984). *Strategic management: A stakeholder approach*. Boston, MA: Pitman.

Frost, G. R., & Seamer, M. (2002). Adoption of environmental reporting and management practices: An analysis of New South Wales public sector entities. *Financial Accountability and Management*, *18*(2), 103–127.

Galema, R., Plantinga, A., & Scholtens, B. (2008). The stocks at stake: Return and risk in socially responsible investment. *Journal of Banking and Finance*, *32*(12), 2646–2654.

Gangi, F., & Trotta, C. (2010). CSR and ethical investments performances. *Euram conference*, Tor Vergata, Rome, May.

Gangi, F., & Trotta, C. (2011). Corporate governance disclosure in a CSR perspective: Empirical evidence from SRFs selection. EIASM (The European Institute for Advanced Studies in Management), Brussels, Belgium, November.

Gangi, F., & Trotta, C. (2013). The ethical finance as a response to the financial crises: An empirical survey of European SRFs performance. *Journal of Management and Governance*, doi:10.1007/s10997013-9264-7.

Gao, S. S., Heravi, S., & Xiao, J. Z. (2005). Determinants of corporate social and environmental reporting in Hong Kong: A research note. *Accounting Forum*, *29*, 233–242.

Graafland, J. J., Eiffinger, S. C. W., & Smid, H. (2004). Benchmarking of corporate social responsibility: Methodological problems and robustness. *Journal of Business Ethics*, *53*, 137–152.

Gray, R., Javad, M., Power, D. M., & Sinclair, C. D. (2001). Social and environmental disclosure and corporate characteristics: A research note and extension. *Journal of Business Finance and Accounting*, *28*(3), 327–356.

Gray, R., Kouhy, R., & Lavers, S. (1995a). Corporate social and environmental reporting: A review of the literature and longitudinal study of UK disclosure. *Accounting, Auditing and Accountability Journal*, *8*(2), 47–77.

Gray, R., Kouhy, R., & Lavers, S. (1995b). Methodological themes: Construction research database of social and environmental reporting by UK companies. *Accounting, Auditing and Accountability Journal*, *8*(2), 78–101.

Grossman, S., & Hart, O. (1982). Corporate financial structure and managerial incentives. In J. J. McCall (Ed.), *The economics of information and uncertainty*. Chicago, IL: University of Chicago Press.

Guthrie, J., & Parker, L. D. (1989). Corporate social practice: A comparative international analysis. *Advances in Public Interest Accounting*, *3*, 159–176.

Hall, P., & Soskice, D. (2001). An introduction to varieties of capitalism. In P. Hall & D. Soskice (Eds.), *Varieties of capitalism: The institutional foundations of comparative advantage* (pp. 1–68). Oxford: Oxford University Press.

Halme, M., & Huse, M. (1997). The influence of corporate governance, industry and country factors on environmental reporting. *Sacndinavian Journal of Management*, *13*(2), 137–157.

Hamid, F. (2004). Corporate social disclosure by banks and finance companies: Malaysian evidence. *Corporate Ownership & Control*, *1*(4), 118–30.

Hannan, M. T., & Freeman, J. (1977). The population ecology of organizations. *American Journal of Sociology*, *82*(5), 929–964.

Hannan, M. T., & Freeman, J. (1989). *Organizational ecology*. Cambridge: Harvard University Press.

Hou, J., & Reber, B. H. (2011). Dimensions of disclosures: Corporate social responsibility (CSR) reporting by media companies. *Public Relations Review*, *37*(2), 166–168.

Jamali, D., & Mirshak, R. (2006). Corporate social responsibility (CSR): Theory and practice in a developing country context. *Journal of Business Ethics*, *72*, 243–262.

Jamali, D., Safieddine, A. M., & Rabbath, M. (2008). Corporate governance and corporate social responsibility synergies and interrelationships. *Corporate Governance: An International Review*, *16*(5), 443–459.

Jensen, M. C. (2002). Value maximization, stakeholder theory and the corporate objective function. *Business Ethics Quarterly*, *12*(2), 235–256.

Jensen, M. C., & Meckling, W. H. (1976). Theory of the firm: Managerial behaviour, agency costs and ownership structure. *Journal of Financial Economics*, *4*(3), 305–360.

Jones, T. M. (1980). Corporate social responsibility revisited, redefined. *California Management Review*, 22(3), 59–67.

Kang, N. (2006). A critique of the "varieties of capitalism" approach. *ICCSR Research Paper Series*, 45.

Kolk, A. (2005). Environmental reporting by multinationals from the triad: Convergence or divergence? *Management International Review*, *45*, 145–166.

Kolk, A., Walhain, S., & Van de Wateringen (2001). Environmental reporting by the Fortune Global 250: Exploring the influence of nationality and sector. *Business Strategy and the Environment*, *10*, 15–28.

Lashgari, M. (2004, September). Corporate governance: Theory and practice. *The Journal of American Academy of Business*, *5*(1), 46–51.

Lindblom, C. E. (1984). The accountability of private enterprise: Private – No. Enterprise – Yes. In A. M. Tinker (Ed.), *Social accounting for corporations*. New York, NY: Marcus Weiner.

Lindblom, C. E. (1993). The implications of organizational legitimacy for corporate social performance and disclosure. *Critical perspectives on accounting conference*, New York, NY.

MacMillan, K., Money, K., Downing, S., & Hillenbrand, C. (2004). Giving your organization spirit: An overview and call to action for directors on issues of corporate governance, corporate reputation and corporate responsibility. *Journal of General Management*, *30*(2), 15–42.

Maron, I. Y. (2006). Toward a unified theory of the CSP-CFP Link. *Journal of Business Ethics*, *67*(2), 191–200.

Matten, D., & Crane, A. (2005). Corporate citizenship: Toward an extended theoretical conceptualization. *The Academy of Management Review*, *30*(1), 166–179.

Matten, D., & Moon, J. (2004). "Implicit" and "Explicit" CSR: A conceptual framework for understanding CSR in Europe. *ICCSR Working Papers* No. 29. ICCSR-International Centre for Corporate Social Responsibility, Nottingham University Business School, Nottingham.

McGuire, J. W. (1963). *Business and society*. New York, NY: McGraw-Hill.

McWilliams, A., & Siegel, D. S. (2001). Corporate social responsibility: A theory of the firm perspective. *Academy of Management Review*, *26*(1), 117–127.

Meek, G. K., Roberts, C. B., & Gray, S. J. (1995). Factors influencing voluntary annual report disclosure by U.S., U.K. and Continental European multinational corporations. *Journal of International Business Studies*, *26*(3), 555–572.

Mitchell, R. K., Agle, B. R., & Wood, D. j. (1997). Toward a theory of a stakeholder identification and salience: Defining the principle of who and what really counts. *Academy of Management Review*, *22*(4), 853–886.

Mitnick, B. M. (1992). The theory of agency and organizational analysis. In N. E. Bowie & R. E. Freeman (Eds.), *Ethics and agency theory*. New York, NY: Oxford University Press.

Mitnick, B. M. (2000). Commitment, revelation and the testaments of belief. The metrics of measurement of corporate social performance. *Business and Society*, *39*(4), 419–456.

Naser, K. (1998). Comprehensiveness of disclosure of non-financial companies listed on the American financial market. *International Journal of Commerce and Management*, *2*(8), 88–119.

Naser, K., & Al-Khatib, K. (2000). Determinants of the depth of voluntary disclosure in the board of directors' statement in a sample of Jordanian listed companies. *Advances in International Accounting*, *13*, 99–118.

Naser, K., Al-Husaini, A., Al-Kwari, D., & Nuseibeh, R. (2006). Determinants of corporate social disclosure in developing countries: The case of Qatar. *Advances in International Accounting*, *19*(1), 1–23.

Owen, D. (2008). Chronicles of wasted time? A personal reflection on the current state of, and future prospects for social and environmental accounting research. *Accounting, Auditing and Accountability Journal*, *21*(2), 240–267.

Painter-Morland, M. (2006). Triple bottom-line reporting as social grammar: Integrating corporate social responsibility and corporate codes of conduct. *Business Ethics: A European Review*, *15*(4), 352–364.

Patten, D. M. (1992). Intra-industry environmental disclosures in response to the Alaskan oil spill: A note on legitimacy theory. *Accounting, Organisation and Society*, *17*, 471–475.

Patten, D. M. (2002). The relation between environmental performance and environmental disclosure: A research note. *Accounting, Organizations and Society*, *27*(8), 763–773.

Perrini, F. (2005). Building a European portrait of corporate social responsibility reporting. *European Management Journal*, *23*(6), 611–627.

Perrini, F., & Minoja, M. (2008). Strategizing corporate social responsibility: Evidence from an Italian medium-sized, family-owned company. *Business Ethics: A European Review*, *17*(1), 47–63.

Perrini, F., Russo, A., Tencati, A., & Vurro, C. (2011). Deconstructing the relationship between corporate social and financial performance. *Journal of Business Ethics*, *102*, 59–76.

Preston, L. E., Donaldson, T., & Broks, L. J. (1999). *Principles of stakeholder management*. Toronto, Canada: The Clarkson Centre for Business Ethics.

Renneboog, L., Ter Horst, J., & Zhang, C. (2008). Socially responsible investments: Institutional aspects, performance, and investor behavior. *Journal of Banking and Finance*, *32*(9), 1723–1742.

Rhodes, M. J. (2010). Information asymmetry and socially responsible investment. *Journal of Business Ethics*, *95*(1), 145–150.

Roberts, R. W. (1992). Determinants of corporate social responsibility disclosure: An application of stakeholder theory. *Accounting, Organization and Society*, *17*, 595–612.

Rossi, P. (2010). Convergence or idiosyncrasy? An analysis of Italian (and Italianized) social reporting guidelines. *Euram conference*, Tor Vergata, Rome, May.

Scott, W. R. (2001). *Institutions and organizations*. Thousand Oaks, CA: Sage.

Selznick, P. (1948). Foundations of the theory of organization. *American Sociological Review*, *13*(1), 25–35.

Stohl, C. (2001). Globalizing organizational communication. In F. M. Jablin & L. Putnam (Eds.), *The new handbook of organizational communication: Advances in theory, research and methods*. Thousand Oaks, CA: Sage.

Soskice, D. (1989). Reinterpreting corporatism and explaining unemployment: Coordinated and non-coordinated market economies. In R. Brunetta & C. Dell'Aringa (Eds.), *Markets, institutions and corporations: Labour relations and economic performance*. London: MacMillan.

Spence, M. (1973). Job market signalling. *The Quarterly Journal of Economics*, *87*(3), 355–374.

Suchman, M. C. (1995). Managing legitimacy: Strategic and institutional approaches. *Academy of Management Review*, *20*, 571–610.

Sweeney, L. (2009). *A study of current practice of corporate social responsibility (CSR) and an examination of the relationship between CSR and financial performance using structural equation modeling (SEM)*. Doctoral thesis, Dublin Institute of Technology, Dublin.

Sweeney, L., & Coughlan, J. (2008). Do different industries report corporate social responsibility differently? An investigation through the lens of stakeholder theory. *Journal of Marketing Communications*, *14*(2), 113–124.

Trabelsi, S., Labelle, R., & Dumontier, P. (2008). Incremental voluntary disclosure on corporate websites, determinants and consequences. *Journal of Contemporary Accounting and Economics*, *4*(2), 120–155.

Ullmann, A. E. (1985). Data in search of a theory: A critical examination of the relationship's among social performance, social disclosure and economic performance of US firms. *Academy of Management Review*, *10*(3), 540–557.

van der Laan Smith, J., Adhikari, A., & Rasoul, H. T. (2005). Exploring differences in social disclosures internationally: A stakeholder perspective. *Journal of Accounting and Public Policy*, *24*, 123–151.

Van Beurden, P., & Gossling, T. (2008). The worth of values – A literature review on the relation between corporate social and financial performance. *Journal of Business Ethics*, *13*(4), 407–424.

Verrecchia, R. E. (1983). Discretionary disclosure. *Journal of Accounting and Economics*, *5*(1), 179–194.

Verrecchia, R. E. (1999). Disclosure and the cost of capital: A discussion. *Journal of Accounting and Economics*, *26*, 271–283.

Verrecchia, R. E. (2001). Essays on disclosure. *Journal of Accounting and Economics*, *32*, 97–180.

Vurro, C., & Perrini, F. (2010). Making the most of corporate social responsibility reporting: Disclosure structure and its impact on performance. *Euram conference*, Tor Vergata, Rome, May.

Vurro, C., & Perrini, F. (2011). Making the most of corporate social responsibility reporting: Disclosure structure and its impact on performance. *Corporate Governance: The International Journal of Business in Society*, *11*(4), 459–474.

Waddock, S. A., & Graves, S. B. (1997). The corporate social performance–financial performance link. *Strategic Management Journal*, *18*(4), 303–319.

Wallace, R. S. O., Naser, K., & Mora, A. (1994). The relationship between the comprehensiveness of annual corporate reports and firm characteristics in Spain. *Accounting and Business Research*, *25*, 41–53.

Windsor, D. (2006). Corporate social responsibility: Three key approaches. *Journal of Management Studies*, *43*(1), 93–114.

Wortick, S. L., & Cochran, P. L. (1985). The evolution of the corporate social performance model. *Academy of Management Review*, *10*(4), 758–769.

Yoon, Y., Gürhan-Canli, Z., & Schwarz, N. (2006). The effect of corporate social responsibility (CSR). Activities on companies with bad reputations. *Journal of Consumer Psychology*, *16*(4), 377–390.

APPENDIX

Areas and Themes of Disclosure		
Environment	*Human Resources*	*Community*
Materials	Total workforce by contracts	Agreements including human rights causes
Energy consumption	Rate of employee turnover	Measures taken to contribute to eliminate child labor
Withdrawal of water	Labor/Management relations	Measures taken to contribute to eliminate forced labor
Emissions	Rates of injury, diseases, and absenteeism	Programs to assess and manage impacts on communities
Waste and spills	Training and education	Actions taken in response to or to prevent corruption
Packaging materials reclaimed	Diversity and equal opportunity	Participation in public policy development
Energy saving	Benefits provided to employees	Employee training on policies concerning human rights
Initiatives for renewable energy	Safety committees	Indigenous rights
Water recycled and reused	Health and safety programs	Contributions to institutions by country
Initiatives to reduce greenhouse gas emissions	Career development review	Charitables giving
Environmental protection expenditures		
Corporate Governance	*Suppliers*	*Customers*
Committees under board of directors for economic tasks	Suppliers under screening on human rights	Safety and health impact on product improvement
Independent and/or nonexecutive committees members	Suppliers management policy	Product information and labelling
Chairman with executive role	Key-suppliers with an Environmental Management System	Marketing communication and promotion
Independent and/or nonexecutive board members	Key-suppliers with an H&S Management System	R&D/Product innovation and quality
Number of board meetings		Voluntary codes concerning H&S

Appendix. (*Continued*)

Areas and Themes of Disclosure	
Mechanisms for shareholders to provide recommendations to the board	Voluntary codes concerning product information
Mechanisms for preserving minority shareholders rights	Practices related to customer satisfaction and loyalty
Capital stock composition	Claims
Top-management compensation linkage with financial and economic performance	Customer privacy
Processes in place to avoid board conflict of interest	
Codes of conduct	
Governance bodies composition according to gender and minority	
Committees under board of directors for environmental and social tasks	
Mechanisms to involve employees into the corporate governance	
Relationship with work councils	
Employees representation in the highest governance body	
Top-management compensation linkage with environmental and social performance	
Procedures through which governance body assess sustainability performance	

HOW SMEs DISCLOSE THEIR SUSTAINABILITY PERFORMANCE. WHICH VARIABLES INFLUENCE THE CHOICE OF REPORTING GUIDELINES?

Simone Domenico Scagnelli, Laura Corazza and Maurizio Cisi

ABSTRACT

Purpose – *Nowadays, social and environmental reporting is approached in different ways, paths and fields by either large-, small-, or medium-sized enterprises (SMEs). However, as demonstrated by previous scholars, SMEs have been critically discussed because they provide lack of proper sustainability disclosure. The fact that the predominant approach of SMEs toward social responsibility is often "sunken" and not "explicit" can drive the lack of disclosure. Furthermore, unstructured communication practices create difficulties in measuring and reporting the sustainability reporting phenomenon in SMEs. The aim of our study is to shed light on the activity of SMEs' sustainability reporting and*

Accounting and Control for Sustainability
Studies in Managerial and Financial Accounting, Volume 26, 77–114

ISSN: 1479-3512/doi:10.1108/S1479-3512(2013)0000026003

disclosure, specifically, by addressing the variables that influence the choice of the guidelines used to prepare sustainability reports.

Design/methodology/approach – *The research has been carried out by using qualitative and quantitative methodologies. The empirical evidence is based on all the Italian companies, mostly SMEs, that were certified in 2011 as having adopted both environmental (i.e., ISO14001 or EMAS) and social (i.e., SA8000) management systems. A multivariate linear regression model has been developed to address the influence of several variables (i.e., financial performance, size, time after achievement of the certifications, group/conglomerate control, etc.) on the guidelines' choice for preparing sustainability reports.*

Findings – *Our findings demonstrate that SMEs prefer to use simple guidelines such as those guidelines that are mandatory under management system certifications. However, the sustainability disclosure driven by the adoption of international guidelines may be more complex if the SME is controlled within a group of companies or if a significant amount of time has passed since the certification date. As such, we developed a taxonomy of their different behavioral drivers according to a legitimacy theory approach.*

Research limitations – *At this stage, our study didn't focus on the contents' quality of the disclosure and reporting practices adopted by SMEs, which is obviously a worthwhile and important area for further research. Furthermore, the analysis took into account the impact of a number of easily accessible variables; therefore, it can be extended to investigate the effect on disclosure of other relevant variables (i.e., nature of the board of directors, age, and industrial sector in which the company operates) as well as contexts prevailing in other countries.*

Practical implications – *The study represents an important contribution for understanding how and why managers might use externally focused disclosure on social and environmental issues to benefit the company's legitimacy.*

Social implications – *Our study provides interesting insights for policy makers who require social or environmental certification when calling for tenders or specific EU contracts, in order to put aside the "brand" or "symbol" and really focus on the disclosed practices.*

Originality/value – *Previous studies have provided only a few evidence about reporting practices and related influencing features of SMEs' sustainability actions. As such, the study wishes to make a significant contribution to the existing literature on Corporate Social Responsibility (CSR) by providing relevant insights about the factors which influence the guidelines used by SMEs in preparing their sustainability reports.*

Keywords: Sustainability; reporting; SMEs; ISO 14001; EMAS; SA8000

INTRODUCTION

There are 23 million small and medium-sized enterprises (SMEs) in the European Union, representing 99% of all businesses and providing around 90 million jobs in the single market. SMEs are the backbone of the European economy and their contribution is essential for pursuing the goals of "Europe 2020," the EU's strategy for smart, sustainable and inclusive growth (Eurobarometer survey, 2012).

At the same time SMEs are responsible for roughly 64% of the industrial pollution in Europe and they find it more difficult to comply with environmental legislation than large companies (Eurobarometer survey, 2012). Nevertheless, according to a recent study carried out by European Commission, up to 33% of SMEs are making efforts to improve resource efficiency because it is one of their top priorities and 25% of SMEs are using an environmental management system to facilitate active engagement in the reduction of their environmental impact (mainly by reducing their energy consumption). Lack of expertise, lengthy approval procedures for new products, and lack of consumer demand are the main obstacles that prevent SMEs from entering green markets. In addition, over half (51%) of SMEs in the EU name financial incentives as the most effective policy measure to promote energy efficiency. However, financial incentives are often linked to an assessment of the investment and performance must be accounted for. Moreover, for SMEs that want to participate in a public tender, it is common practice today that companies be compelled to adhere to environmental requirements. For that reason 34% of SMEs analyzed have created so-called "green jobs," in which the primary responsibility is dealing with information, technology, or materials that preserve or restore environmental quality. This requires specialized skills, knowledge, training, or experience.

In order to be accountable for their sustainability performances, SMEs, exactly as large firms, should integrate this information into their accounts.

The adoption of sustainability practices leads managers to view economic, social, and environmental performance as a balance between three strictly interconnected dimensions (Adams, 1999; Gray, Kouhy, & Lavers, 1995; Gray, Owen, & Adams, 1996; Guthrie & Parker, 1989).

We have decided to carry out an analysis of the variables that affect SMEs in the choice of guidelines for preparing their reports. This choice stems from the fact that in our opinion there is a growing need for financial institutions and regulators to figure out which of the CSR actions are the most attractive for an SME. We also argue that the sustainability report is one of the most common tools for communicating sustainability performances to stakeholders in order to obtain the "license to operate."

The fact that the predominant approach of SMEs toward social responsibility is often "sunken" and not "explicit" generates a generalized lack of disclosure (Del Baldo, 2012; Fuller & Tian, 2006; Matten & Moon, 2008). This lack of communication creates difficulties in measuring and reporting the phenomenon inSMEs. The goal of our analysis is to shed light on the activity of reporting and disclosure on the part of SMEs and in particular on those variables that influence the choice of the guidelines used to prepare the reports. As a matter of fact, having analyzed the existing literature, we have found a lack of information in the studies related to SME sustainability reporting due mainly to a lack of SME reports (Fisher et al., 2009; Fitjar, 2011; Hillary, 2000; Lawrence, Collins, Pavlovich, & Arunachalam, 2006; Lepoutre & Heene, 2006; Nielsen & Thomsen, 2009; Parsa & Kouhy, 2008). With this study we wish to make a contribution to the existing literature on CSR in SMEs, through an analysis of the sustainability reports and disclosure of Italian SMEs.

The results derived from our analysis can be useful for accountants, public regulators, and those involved in implementing sustainability strategies within SMEs. The interest-oriented approach to CSR by SMEs is strongly supported by European policies, so we believe that an analysis of the report can be particularly useful especially in the near future.

In order to better understand what variables influence the choice of the guidelines and, above all, the rationale behind those choices, it was decided to use the legitimacy theory approach.

The remainder of this chapter is organized as follows. The second section presents a summary of the state of the art of the CSR in SMEs and an overview of the accountability behavior of SMEs, analyzing the typical features of SME's CSR-awareness. Third section presents the theoretical background and a reminder of the legitimacy theory. Fourth section presents the research methodology. Fifth section presents the analysis and the discussion of the results and sixth section concludes the study by suggesting a classification of what variables influence the choice of the guidelines for sustainability reporting using the legitimacy theory model. The empirical evidence is based on all the Italian companies certified in 2011 as having adopted both environmental (i.e., ISO14001 or EMAS) and social (SA8000) management systems with related certifications. The reason behind the choice of this sample is that these ethically approved firms have demonstrated an interest in sustainability issues by becoming certified. It is obvious that our sample is quite positively influenced.

LITERATURE REVIEW

Nowadays, the EU Commission's definition of CSR has been extended and broadened as "the responsibility of enterprises for their impacts on society" (Eu Commission, 2011). However, in the European context, SMEs represent the 99% of all European businesses acting as the real engine of the modern economy. The attention of public regulators is also more focused on the SME sector.

A lot is being written on the adoption and interpretation of CSR practices into the SME framework (Fuller & Tian, 2006; Jenkins, 2006; Murillo & Lozano, 2006; Spence, 1999; Spence, Schmidpeter, & Habisch, 2003). On the contrary, there is a lack of literature on the disclosure of these CSR actions through the publication by SMEs of social and environmental reports. We want to clarify this distinction between CSR performance (management) and CSR disclosure. In the following sections, we will present an in-depth review of the existing literature on CSR in SMEs and also of the literature on SME sustainability disclosure and reporting which is in its infancy.

The Specificity of SMEs

Small businesses, although not a homogeneous group, have significantly different behavioral characteristics compared to larger firms in respect of social and environmental management (Brammer, Hoejmose, & Marchant, 2012). In general, SMEs have relatively informal organizational structures, are often managed by owners, and as a result personal choices and attitudes can greatly affect socially responsible behavior among them (Moore, Slack, & Gibbon, 2009; Sarbutts, 2003; Vives, 2006).

SMEs are typically described as independent, cash-limited, immediately exposed to the potential economic loss that may occur from business failure, multitasking, reliant on personal relationships, rich, and communal (Castka et al., 2004; Del Baldo, 2012; Russo & Perrini, 2010; Russo & Tencati, 2009; Spence, 1999; Spence et al., 2003; Vyakarnam, Bailey, Myers, & Burnett, 1997).

"Independence" is understood as a close correlation between the head of the company, who is often the owner (or the head of a family if the company is also a family business), and the role played by his/her personal attitudes and values (Jamali, Safieddine, & Rabbath, 2008; Lange & Fenwick, 2008; Longenecker, Moore, Petty, Palich, & McKinney, 2006; Longo, Mura, & Bonoli, 2005; Nielsen & Thomsen, 2009; Petts, Herd, Gerrad, & Horne, 1999; Redmond, Walker, & Wang, 2008; Schlierer et al., 2012; Worthington, Ram, & Jones, 2006). Personal relations between the owner-manager and employees are often fluid and this enables controlling activities to be performed more informally (Cambra-Fierro, Hart, & Polo-Redondo, 2008; Cassells & Lewis, 2011; Fassin, Rossem, & Buelens, 2010; Fenwick, 2010; Hammann et al., 2009; Rivera-Lirio & Muñoz-Torres, 2010; Russo & Perrini, 2010; Russo & Tencati, 2009).

SMEs face competitive pressure and limited cash flow and so may not be motivated to invest time and resources on ethics. They perceive it "as a business cost with no benefit" (Chiappetta Jabbour & Puppim-de-Oliveira, 2012; Spence & Rutherfoord, 2001, 2003). This implies short- or medium-term strategic planning and a myopic view of the future (Lepoutre & Heene, 2006).

Multitasking pertains to the flexibility of managers who can perform many different daily tasks. In small firms the entrepreneur often participates intensively because he or she suffers from a lack of specialized knowledge (Davies & Crane, 2010; Nooteboom, 2004).

These relationships, built out of trust, reputation and legitimacy with identified stakeholders, represent the lifeblood of an SME only if properly managed. Otherwise they may become a constraint (Courrent & Gundolf, 2009; Graafland, Van de Ven, & Stoffele, 2003; Revell, Stokes, & Chen, 2010; Spence, 1999; Spence et al., 2003). It is without doubt that many small companies are naturally attuned to the values of their founder or owner as well as to a variety of "intangible" components such as the needs of their local communities (Del Baldo, 2012; Fassin et al., 2011; Fuller & Tian, 2006; Perrini, 2006; Russo & Perrini, 2010). Among these intangibles are the company's strategic profile (in terms of initiatives integrated with the overall business strategy), the culture of the enterprise, the processes of accountability (improving systems of collecting and sharing information), and systems of corporate governance (systems of decision-making processes and internal control) (Del Baldo, 2012).

SMEs are especially integrated into the local communities where they operate and there is a sort of "closeness" between the firm and the environment (Del Baldo, 2006, 2012; Fisher, Geenen, Jurcevic, McClintock, & Davis, 2009; Lawrence et al., 2006; Longo et al., 2005; Muller & Kolk, 2009; Niehm, Swinney, & Miller, 2008; Perrini, 2006; Russo & Perrini, 2010; Russo & Tencati, 2009). Scholars define this "closeness" as a core feature of SMEs because their founders and managers are embedded in the organization and involved in community affairs (Perrini, 2006; Williamson, Lynch-Wood, & Ramsay, 2006).

SMEs and CSR Behavior

By definition, SMEs have a smaller scale of operation, and in absolute terms, comparatively modest individual social and environmental impacts. This is reflected in the perceptions of owners and managers in SMEs, who believe that they have little impact on the environment (Gadenne, Kennedy, & McKeiver, 2009). On the contrary, Morsing and Perrini (2009) note "that the 'smallness' of the individual SME is not proportional to the collective 'grandness' of SMEs," because SMEs are the largest contributors to most European economies in terms of employment.

Small businesses exhibit relatively reactive approaches and ethical practices performing CSR actions (Ahmad & Seet, 2009; Lepoutre & Heene, 2006; Udayasankar, 2008; Uhlaner, van Goor-Balk, & Masurel, 2004). Epstein (2007) represents the CSR approach as a continuum starting from compliance behavior (reactivism) to ethical and moral commitment that leads to voluntary actions (proactivism), trying to achieve financial results minimizing negative spillovers and maximizing positive externalities to the environment and society. Firstly, SMEs lack the necessary resources and skills to implement social and environmental practices (Avram & Kühne, 2008; Chiappetta Jabbour & Puppim-de-Oliveira, 2012; Roberts, Lawson, & Nicholls, 2006); secondly, managers-owners find it hard to justify investment into social and environmental management from an economic and competitive viewpoint, as most customers are not willing to pay for environmental-friendly products and processes and find it difficult to publish their efforts (Brammer et al., 2012; Déniz & Suárez, 2005; Torugsa, O'Donohue, & Hecker, 2012; Williamson et al., 2006).

SMEs often misunderstand the meaning of ethical terms such as CSR, sustainability reporting, code of conduct, and ethical codes, and they perceive them as distant, possibly inoperative, or counter-productive (Baden & Harwood, 2013; Fassin, 2008; Grayson, 2004; Murillo & Lozano, 2006; Rivera-Lirio & Muñoz-Torres, 2010). The predominant approach of SMEs toward social responsibility is often "sunken" and "internal" because socially responsible actions will not be formalized by the company or they will not be a part of a strategic process; on the other hand, the same approach could be defined as "proactive" because it stems from voluntary involvement, even if it is not "explicit," given the generalized lack of disclosure (Del Baldo, 2012; Fuller & Tian, 2006; Jenkins, 2004, 2006, 2009; Lynch-Wood, Williamson, & Jenkins, 2009; Matten & Moon, 2008).

Scholars demonstrated a different range of small business behavior. An interesting study by Unioncamere (2003), the union of Italian Chambers of Commerce, identifies five types of Italian CSR-aware companies' behavior: cohesive, multi-certificate, aware, skeptical, and movable. *Cohesive* companies are sensitive to stakeholder expectations, both internally and externally, and their approaches are very focused toward them. *Multi-certificate* companies are entities who decide to invest in both environmental (i.e., ISO14001 and EMAS) and social (i.e., SA8000) management systems. *Aware* companies are certified companies that adopt an opportunistic approach or use an "ethics of self-interest," focusing their efforts on projecting an adequate image rather than fundamentally behaving in social or environmental ways (Cambra-Fierro et al., 2008; Cisi & Scagnelli, 2009). *Skeptical* companies follow a suspicious approach without focusing on activities that promote a socially responsible culture. Finally, *movable* companies are totally passive to CSR topics and tools but can be engaged if they identify some opportunistic interest therein.

A new body of literature is growing on the issue of CSR within the supply chain, especially in relation to SME behavior (Baden & Harwood, 2013; Baden et al., 2009; Gadenne et al., 2009; Jorgensen & Knudsen, 2006; Perrini et al., 2007). Moreover, scholars are beginning to study the phenomenon of business networks as a driver for the diffusion of CSR within SMEs (Battaglia, Bianchi, Frey, & Iraldo, 2010; Fenwick, 2010; von Weltzien Høivik & Shankar, 2011; Jämsä et al., 2011; Moore & Manring, 2009; Spence et al., 2003).

Scholars analyzing worldwide CSR in SMEs found several different behaviors, as reported in Table 1.

Table 1. CSR in SMEs, Recent Literature.

Reference	Key Observations and Findings (*a*) Overall Study (*b*)	Notes on Observations
Ahmad and Seet (2009)	*a*	CSR is perceived as: the need to demonstrate ethical practice in business dealings; honesty and integrity; willingness to admit mistakes and to tell the truth; a commitment to social obligation and social welfare; willingness to give extra service to people; to take responsibility and accountability for one's own action.
Avram and Kühne (2008)	*a*	SMEs will usually experience more difficulties than their larger counterparts when detecting and engaging in business actions, especially regarding issues involving external stakeholders or the natural environment because of a lack of discretionary slack or even financial and personnel resources. Governments and industrial organizations, therefore, play a very important role.
Baden and Harwood (2013)	*a*	Provide a discussion on the ambiguity of the term CSR especially in the view of an SME. They stress a need for a better choice of words and suggestions including a focus on the totality of responsible business practice; use of action verbs that reflect the nature of the engagement with the community; and environment.
Baden et al. (2009)	*b*	Analyze the effect of the supply chain to demonstrate CSR practices.
Baden and Harwood (2013)	*b*	Analyze policies on "downstream" corporate social responsibility activity into the views and actions of SME owner-managers.
Battaglia et al. (2010)	*b*	Suggest a networked approach to foster CSR in SMEs trough industrial clustering.
Cambra-Fierro et al. (2008)	*a*	Behavior of SMEs involved in environmental CSR: complying with the reference legislation, adapting the management to the owner's and/or managers' value system, and trying to make a profit with the effort.

Table 1. (*Continued*)

Reference	Key Observations and Findings (*a*) Overall Study (*b*)	Notes on Observations
Cassells and Lewis (2011)	*a*	Adoption of waste management practices is the most prevalent CSR action. The majority of owner-managers were generally aware of the risk their business activities posed to the environment.
Castka et al. (2004)	*a*	Certifications are a vehicle for the implementation of CSR in SMEs.
Chiappetta Jabbour and Puppim-de-Oliveira (2012)	*a*	Barriers to CSR in SMEs: lack of information and the decline of traditional and environmental-friendly knowledge.
Courrent and Gundolf (2009)	*a*	Ethics has been seen as a management tool for managing corporate reputation and image.
Davies and Crane (2010)	*b*	Descriptive theory of how SMEs implement CSR in their business using human resources management practices.
Del Baldo (2012)	*b*	Identify relationship between social engagement, social statements, and governance.
Del Baldo (2006)	*a*	CSR as actions contributing to sustainability of specific territories.
Déniz and Suárez (2005)	*a*	CSR is seen as a philanthropic activity.
Fassin (2008)	*a*	Informal CSR and lack of awareness of the real meaning of the term CSR. The motivation is intended as doing the right things.
Fassin et al. (2011)	*b*	Owner-manager perception of business ethics.
Fenwick (2010)	*a*	Owners learned CSR by working through three main areas of challenge within everyday practices: positioning SR commitments and affiliations; balancing diverse stakeholders with SR ideals and costs; and negotiating value conflicts within SR practice, as part of "becoming" a particular enterprise of SR engagement. Importance of a networked approach.
Fisher (2009)	*a*	Less documentation of CSR in SMEs. Importance of the community.

Table 1. (*Continued*)

Reference	Key Observations and Findings (*a*) Overall Study (*b*)	Notes on Observations
Fitjar (2011)	*a*	External pressure to improve SMEs' social responsibility. Such pressure stems partly from news reports on their activities and partly from increasing competition.
Fuller and Tian (2006)	*b*	Social and symbolic capital as strategic orientation.
Gadenne et al. (2009)	*a*	Real willingness to voluntarily contribute to environmental organizations. Influenced by suppliers but do not use Environmental Management System.
Graafland et al. (2003)	*a*	CSR is perceived as a dialogue strategy with stakeholders. A lot of attention is paid on expectations and responsiveness.
Grayson (2004)	*a*	The language, codes, and processes of SMEs differ markedly from those of larger organizations and are more heavily driven by the beliefs and values of the people running them, causing a different form of engagement.
Hammann et al. (2009)	*a*	Socially responsible management practices toward employees, customers, and to a lesser extent society have a positive impact on the firm and its performance. Personal values create (economic) value.
von Weltzien Høivik and Shankar (2011)	*a*	Network model (cluster approach) to CSR will motivate the uptake of CSR among SMEs when the network (cluster) is characterized by close geographical proximity and operates in the same sector.
Jamali et al. (2008)	*b*	CSR practices based on ethical/religious motivation.
Jämsä et al. (2011)	*a*	SMEs utilize their networks as a source of opportunities and resources and their networks can serve as an avenue for change toward sustainability. Moreover, learning in the network was identified as a key process through which the enterprises and the network evolve.

Table 1. *(Continued)*

Reference	Key Observations and Findings (*a*) Overall Study (*b*)	Notes on Observations
Jenkins (2006)	*b*	Moral and ethical arguments justify a CSR approach. Internal motivation is more important than external pressures.
Jenkins (2009)	*b*	Moral and ethical arguments to justify a CSR approach. Internal approach.
Jenkins (2004)	*b*	CSR sunken communication.
Jorgensen and Knudsen (2006)	*a*	SMEs face CSR requirements from their buyers much more frequently than they apply such requirements to their own suppliers.
Lange and Fenwick (2008)	*b*	CSR is perceived as the right thing to do.
Lawrence et al. (2006)	*a*	Reporting of practices is virtually nonexistent, but firms tend to be close to their communities and actively engaged in employee and community support.
Lepoutre and Heene (2006)	*b*	CSR focus on the impact of firm size.
Llach et al. (2013)	*a*	Quality management practices have a significant direct impact on market success factors but not on companies' profit and loss statements. There is a significant relationship between Environment Management Practices and financial performance.
Longenecker et al. (2006)	*a*	Ethical values of small firms are not totally different from those of large firms.
Longo et al. (2005)	*b*	Moral and ethical reasons for doing CSR, but also CSR contributes to the growth of the company's value.
Lynch-Wood et al. (2009)	*b*	Externally driven business case (EDBC) for voluntary CSR practices is likely to remain a weak form of pressure for many small firms.
Matten and Moon (2008)	*a*	CSR as implicit vs explicit communication (large firms).
Moore and Manring (2009)	*a*	Networks of SMEs will become essential for addressing the systemic problems that underline industrial ecology, enterprise resilience, and global supply chain sustainability.

Table 1. *(Continued)*

Reference	Key Observations and Findings (*a*) Overall Study (*b*)	Notes on Observations
Muller and Kolk (2009)	*a*	CSR is linked to external factor as the integration of sustainability practices in the global supply chain. CSR depends on the institutional framework in which the firm operates.
Niehm et al. (2008)	*a*	The most important dimension of CSR is the community involvement and commitment.
Nielsen and Thomsen (2009)	*a*	CSR in SMEs is a practice not a strategy. The choice is based on personal values of the SME manager/entrepreneur. Tends to not communicate externally about CSR.
Parsa and Kouhy (2007)	*a*	SMEs report only if they have to enhance reputation. They tend to not report their actions toward stakeholders.
Perrini et al. (2007)	*a*	Importance of the supply chain. Less likely to address environment, employment, and local community involvement.
Perrini (2006)	*b*	CSR as a silent approach.
Petts et al. (1999)		Environment is important to individuals and that environmental compliance is regarded as "the right thing to do."
Redmond et al. (2008)	*a*	Whereas owner-managers of small enterprises express concern regarding the environment, this does not then translate into better waste management practices.
Revell et al. (2010)	*a*	CSR action: recycling, energy efficiency, responsible buying and selling, and efforts to reduce their carbon emissions. Motivation: helps solve environmental problems, the "push" of legislation and the "pull" of potential cost savings, new customers, higher staff retention, and good publicity for their firms.
Rivera-Lirio and Muñoz-Torres (2010)	*b*	Importance of the CSR implementation in government to foster the initiatives in SMEs.
Roberts et al. (2006)	*a*	Barriers of CSR: lack of resources, time, and knowledge. Be excluded from supply chain is the main risk related to CSR.

Table 1. *(Continued)*

Reference	Key Observations and Findings (*a*) Overall Study (*b*)	Notes on Observations
Russo and Perrini (2010)	*b*	CSR–SME relationships accompanied by stakeholder view and stakeholder theory.
Russo and Tencati (2009)	*a*	CSR as formal vs informal communication. CSR is related to the "license to operate" given by the community where the entity operates.
Schlierer et al. (2012)	*a*	SME owner-managers, thus, seem to have a clearer pragmatic picture of the value creation process for all stakeholders. Differences in the perceptions of owner-managers in the countries are analyzed. These differences can be often explained by differences in the countries' national business environments, that is, the institutional structure of the national economy and also wider cultural norms and habits regarding economic activity.
Spence and Rutherfoord (2001)	*a*	Profit is not seen a key motivator, but the involvement in CSR actions is based on social priority and long-term survival.
Spence et al. (2003)	*a*/*b*	CSR and intangible assets: increasing social capital. It is important the action of "wanting to give back" to community also through access to networks.
Spence and Schmidpeter (2003)	*a*/*b*	Importance of a networked approach toward CSR in SMEs. Profit is not seen as a key factor in order to be involved in CSR actions.
Spence et al. (2003)		CSR and intangible assets: increasing social capital.
Spence (1999)	*b*	CSR and intangible assets: reputation and informal relation.
Sarbutts (2003)	*a*	SMEs are better placed than major companies to take advantage of the fact that society and the media revere qualities such as honesty, integrity, and the ability to say sorry.
Torugsa et al. (2012)	*a*	SMEs being able to maximize financial returns while proactively making progress toward CSR.

Table 1. *(Continued)*

Reference	Key Observations and Findings (*a*) Overall Study (*b*)	Notes on Observations
Uhlaner et al. (2004)	*a*	CSR behaviour relies on small acts toward stakeholders. The commitment toward community is given through the job offer and commercial activity.
Vives (2006)	*a*	CSR practices based on ethical/religious motivation. Other motivations: employees benefit and increase profits.
Williamson et al. (2006)	*a*	Drivers of environmental behavior are business performance and public regulations.
Worthington et al. (2006)	*a*	CSR appears driven by personal attitudes. External influence and institutional pressure are not significant in explaining CSR involvement.

SMEs, Social Accounting, and Disclosure

The SMEs CSR-aware behavior is also reflected in their disclosure practices. Some of the scholars underlined that the lack of communication creates difficulties in measuring and reporting the phenomenon in SMEs and often CSR is perceived as "a business cost with no benefit" (Fisher et al., 2009; Fitjar, 2011; Lawrence et al., 2006; Lepoutre & Heene, 2006; Nielsen & Thomsen, 2009; Parsa & Kouhy, 2007; Spence et al., 2003). Hillary (2000) illustrates that SMEs are less likely to report social information by identifying a number of reasons for SMEs' disengagements from environmental issues, among which there are a lack of technical knowledge, a lack of awareness of benefits, and high cost of implementation. In addition, little external pressure from stakeholders is relevant too. Revell and Rutherfoord (2003) argued that the institutional framework is a key element in fostering environmental proactive behavior among SMEs.

Parsa and Kouhy (2007) investigate the prevalent view that SMEs are unlikely to report social information due to their financial constraints and the perception that they have very little social conduct on which to report. They demonstrated that on the contrary, SMEs report social information regardless of their financial constraints. For small companies a good reputation is crucial in attracting resource holders and fulfilling their expectations (Sabate & Puente, 2003).

Unfortunately, there is a general lack of tools dedicated to SMEs that want to adopt CSR disclosure account (i.e., social, environmental, or sustainability reports) (Castka et al., 2004; Russo & Perrini, 2010). Adopted reporting practices include corporate mission, corporate values, and also corporate business strategy and corporate sustainability strategy. The reports are tools used by managers or entrepreneurs to gain a broader overview of short-term corporate performance and to set/integrate/transform future goals into a long-term strategy in order to become "Good Companies." Epstein (2007) underlines that "better companies, are optimisers that continuously seek to perform the economic functions for which society relies upon them in a manner that optimises the firm's usefulness to the diverse stakeholders affected by their actions and to minimise the deleterious effects of their operations."

Enderle (2004) points out that, overall, CSR reporting standards might be inappropriate for small firms because such standards have been developed mainly with large businesses in mind. Besides, from the SMEs' perspective, the possible ineffectiveness of informal tools such as codes of conduct and social and ethical standards might be explained by the requirement of a greater investment in terms of time, funds, and energy. Furthermore, much more study and work is needed in order to develop appropriate ethical tools capable of connecting new theories to small businesses practice (Tilley, 2000).

Lozano (2012) gives an in-depth analysis of the voluntary initiative contribution toward CSR but often SMEs tend to adapt the tools developed for large enterprise to their own needs, even if "SMEs are not little big firms" (Tilley, 2000). This is particularly evident in the case of reporting (Lawrence et al., 2006; Lepoutre & Heene, 2006; Nielsen & Thomsen, 2009; Parsa & Kouhy, 2007; Spence et al., 2003). Despite the many different types of reporting standards that have been developed, none of them seem to meet the increasing needs of SMEs, including even the Global Reporting Initiative (GRI) guidelines (EU & CREM, 2011). Among these tools are Social and Environmental Management System (SEMS) certifications. SEMS and the related certifications have also been very successful in the SME framework, as demonstrated by Bouma and Kamp-Roelands (2000), Castka et al. (2004), Castka and Balzarova (2008a, 2008b), Jirillo, Rocchi, and Martucci (2003), Llach, Bagur-Femenías, Alonso-Almeida, and Perramon (2012), and Miles and Munilla (2004).

An environmental management system can be described as being a system comprising people, instruments, and activities aimed at collecting and

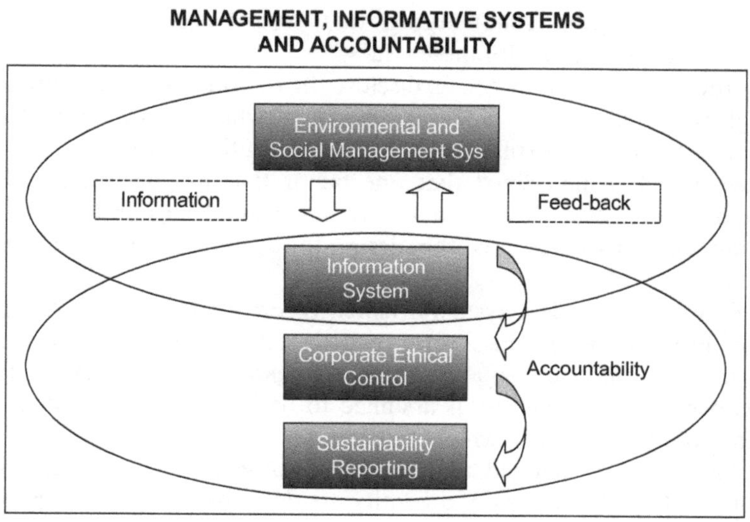

Fig. 1. Social and Environmental Management systems and Accountability.

processing data in order to provide environmental information for decision-making or accountability purposes (see van der Woerd, 1997). These systems identify, analyze, calculate, classify, record, summarize, and report environmental data. We use the term SEMS applying the presented definition also to the social dimension. As seen further on in this chapter (Fig. 1), even though the accountability activity is the last part of a process of SEMS, it is important in order to be accountable to stakeholders and be legitimated (Bouma & Kamp-Roelands, 2000). The adoption of sustainability practices leads managers to observe economic, social, and environmental performance as equilibrium of three tightly connected dimensions (Adams, 1999; Gray et al., 1995, 1996; Guthrie & Parker, 1989).

THEORETICAL BACKGROUND

The Legitimacy Theory Approach

As Gray et al. (1998) argued, the need for new accounting and new accounting methods has been driven by the increasing concern with stakeholders and the growing importance of corporate social responsibilities and ethical values in management practices. Among scholars there is common agreement on the fact that environmental issues cannot be separated from social issues. Deegan (2002) argued that "social accounting, indeed, is designed to deal exactly with these issues."

In order to explain how SMEs disclose their sustainability performances through the publication of a social report and what are the rationales, we would like to make an explicit reference to the legitimacy theory.

Deegan (2002) underlined that one factor that has been embraced in recent times by researchers as a key reason behind corporate social and environmental disclosures is the desire to legitimize an organization's operations.

Legitimacy theory is a system-oriented theory that helps to explain the role of information and disclosure in the relationship between organizations, the state, individuals, and groups (Deegan, 2002; Gray et al., 1996). In this perspective, the entity is assumed to be influenced by, and to have influence on, the society in which it operates.

Suchman (1995) defined legitimacy as "a generalised perception or assumption that the actions of an entity are desirable, proper, or appropriate within some socially constructed system of norms, values, beliefs and definitions."

The legitimation is perceived as the respect of a social contract between the entity and the society (Shocker & Sethi, 1973). Deegan (2002) argued that corporate disclosure practices are considered the most important means by which managers can influence external perceptions of their organizations. If an entity perceives a legitimation gap between the entity itself and society, managers and entrepreneurs can react in order to strategically manage these gaps (Deegan, 2002; O'Dwyer, Owen, & Unerman, 2011; Suchman, 1995). Deegan (2002) goes further, describing how corporate disclosure plays an active role as:

1. The organization can adapt its output, goals, and methods of operation to conform to prevailing definitions of legitimacy;
2. The organization can attempt to alter the definition of social legitimacy so that it conforms to the organization's present practices, outputs, and values; and
3. The organization can attempt to become identified with symbols, values, or institutions, which have a strong base of legitimacy.

Lindblom (1994) suggested that if an organization perceives that there is an issue related to its legitimacy it can also adopt a number of strategies. The organization can:

1. Educate and inform its "relevant public" about changes in organizational performance and activities;

2. Change the perceptions of the "relevant public" but not change its behaviors;
3. Manipulate the perception by deflecting attention from the issue; and
4. Change the external expectations of its performances.

The aim of this chapter is to explain SME sustainability disclosure practices through the analysis of the variables that influence the adoption of the reporting guidelines. We will also try to explain the lack of SME reports (Bebbington, Larrinaga, & Moneva, 2008). Furthermore, we will explain these behaviors in light of the legitimacy theory.

RESEARCH METHODOLOGY

The research has been carried out on 357 Italian companies that at the end of July 2011 had adopted specific environmental (i.e., ISO14001, EMAS[1]) and social (i.e., SA8000[2]) management systems and achieved related certification. This research approach is consistent with the sample selection used in our previous research (Cisi & Scagnelli, 2009) but this time it is more focused on SMEs.

Information about the certified companies was collected by cross-selecting the data available on the SA8000, EMAS, and ISO14001 certifying authorities. CSR-related information and sustainability reports of the selected companies were searched on their own websites while their financial data was collected using financial databases (i.e., Bureau Vand Djik AIDA).

Given the aim of this study, we developed a regression model to analyze which variables may influence the CSR behavior and practices of the multi-certified companies in our sample.

As such, we designed a dependent variable to take into account the quality of sustainability reporting available on the websites of the entities analyzed. The quality is intended as the magnitude of reporting guidelines. The term "magnitude" identifies those guidelines that are mono-stakeholders directed (i.e., SA8000 reports). For example, the GRI guidelines takes into account several different Key Performance Indicators (KPIs) and these have been designed to answer the accounting needs of different stakeholders. It is not the goal of this study to provide an analysis of the efficacy of the application of the guidelines, but only an analysis of those variables that influence the choice of the guidelines.

We found companies for which it was not possible to assess disclosure as they don't have any website, or websites that don't provide any information on their social/environmental strategies or policies; companies with CSR policies available or declared on their websites but not providing reports as well as other companies that provided CSR related reports.

Specifically, we collected and analyzed the following reports:

- Mandatory reports or management system driven reports (i.e., SA8000 reports, EMAS reports, EU Reg. 761/2001);
- Voluntary nonfinancial reports that don't follow a common reporting framework ("self-defined methodology") or nonfinancial reports that follow a national reporting framework (i.e., not-for-profit scheme for social reporting[3], GBS reports[4]); and
- Voluntary sustainability reports that follow an international reporting framework or international guidelines (i.e., Global Reporting Initiative, United Nations Global Reporting principles).

As such, we designed our dependent variable in relation to the level of CSR disclosure (CSR_d) on a rating scale based on the scores provided in Table 2.

Importantly, the resulting average values will be used as cutoffs for addressing the level of SME disclosure (i.e., poor/good) when cross-tabulating with other variables.

Moreover, in order to address the role of the different variables that might influence the level of disclosure of the multi-certified companies, we applied statistical multivariate analysis. Specifically, we tested for the influence of qualitative factors (i.e., age, achieved experience, belonging to a Group/Conglomerate structure and size) and quantitative financial features

Table 2. CSR Disclosure Assigned Rating (Dependent Variable).

CSR Disclosure Rating	Behavior
5	Sustainability reporting based on international standards (i.e., GRI, UN GR).
4	Sustainability reporting based on Italian standards or self-defined methodologies.
3	EMAS or SA8000 reporting scheme.
2	Documents on policies or actions (ref. to SA8000/EMAS/ISO14001/ Integrated Policy).
1	Disclosure of CSR actions without accountability tools.
0	No CSR information, no website.

(i.e., sales, total assets, and financial leverage). Given that we wanted to address such different features within the same population, consistent with previous literature (Aupperle & Van Pham, 1989; Lanis & Richardson, 2012; Raar, 2007; Reddy, Locke, & Fauzi, 2013; Ullmann, 1985), instead of using multiple ANOVA models, we developed one multiple linear regression model that addresses comprehensively the level of the disclosure rating (CSR_d). The use of linear regression is preferable if compared to logit and probit models because the independent variable assumes categorical values from 0 to 5 and it does not measure probability. Furthermore, cubic or quadratic regressions were discarded because of the use of multiple dependent variables whose impact is unpredictable.

Therefore, the linear model can be summarized by the following equation:

$$\begin{aligned}\text{CSR\_d}_i = {} & \beta_0 + \beta_1\text{Age} + \beta_2\text{Exp1} + \beta_3\text{Exp2} + \beta_5\text{Grp} + \beta_6\text{Assets} + \beta_7\text{Lev} \\ & + \beta_8\text{Sales} + \beta_9\text{SME} + \varepsilon_i\end{aligned}$$

where

CSR_d	is the rating score of the CSR disclosure for company *i*;
Age	is the age of the company, in years, at the time of first certification;
Exp1	is the time span in years between the analysis and the time of first certification, acts as marker of the experience achieved in using the environmental/social management system;
Exp2	is the time span in years between the analysis and the time of first certification, acts as marker of the experience achieved in using the broad environmental/social management system;
Grp	is the dummy variable that measures the extent to which the company belongs to a structured group of companies;
Assets	represents the total amount of assets of the company, data available from financial statements at the end of 2010;
Lev	represents the financial leverage of the company, computed as total liabilities divided by total equity, amounts available from financial statements at the end of 2010;
Sales	represents the total amount of sales of the company, data available from financial statements at the end of 2010; and
Size	is the dummy variable, which controls for the size of the company, it is 1 for SMEs and 0 for larger companies.

FINDINGS AND DISCUSSION

At end of July 2011, we found that the number of certifications achieved by Italian companies increased dramatically if compared to the end of 2006. The increase ranges between 20% and 59%, with a major increase for the EMAS certification (+59%). The number of companies that adopted more than one certification and that can be considered "multi-certified" increased from 185 in 2007 to 397 in 2011 (115% increase). This finding is consistent with previous literature, which highlighted relevant increases in the European adoption of these certifications; the main driver being the increase in public institutions and governmental organisations requiring for such standardizations when they advertise tenders or public contracts (Botta, Comoglio, & Petrosillo, 2013; Evangelinos & Skouloudis, 2012).

The complete breakdown of the growing trend of certified and multi-certified companies is provided in Table 3.

Data about 357 companies were available and cross-selected; therefore, our sample comprises 357 such companies. The breakdown by size of the sample is provided in Table 4. As can be seen, more than half of the multi-certified companies can be considered an SME according to the EU definition[5] (65%).

Table 5 provides the distribution of the *disclosure* score. The breakdown is provided according to the size (SME or large) of the multi-certified companies.

If we compare the score's means between SMEs and larger companies we see that large companies provide more disclosure with a mean of 2.74 (std. dev. 1.51) if compared with SMEs (mean 1.74, std dev. 1.34), the

Table 3. Numbers of Italian Companies Adopting Environmental and Social Management Systems.

	2006	2011	⊗	⊗ (%)
SA 8000 Certified entities	701	858	*157*	*22*
ISO 14001 Certified entities	11,730	14,055	*2,325*	*20*
EMAS Certified entities	705	1,118	*413*	*59*
SA8000 + EMAS	5	1	*−4*	*−80*
SA8000 + ISO14001	167	368	*201*	*120*
SA8000 + ISO14001 + EMAS	13	28	*15*	*115*
"Multi-certified companies"	**185**	**397**	***212***	***115***

Table 4. Size of the Multi-Certified Companies in the Sample.

Multi-Certified Companies	2007	2011	%	⊗ (%)
SME	128	231	*65*	*81*
Large	57	126	*35*	*11%*
Total	**185**	**357**	***100***	

Table 5. Distribution of the CSR Disclosure Score According to the Size of the Company.

CSR Disclosure	0 (%)	1 (%)	2 (%)	3 (%)	4 (%)	5 (%)	Total (%)	Mean
SMEs	23	24	20	26	4	3	*100*	*1.74*
Large	6	16	24	24	10	19	*100*	*2.74*

difference between the two groups' means is statistically significant (*t*-value 6.43, $p \leq 0.01$).

This can confirm that SMEs are still providing less sustainability disclosure/reporting compared to larger companies. Various authors have tried to explain this difference by referring to their unstructured practices and therefore sunken CSR approach (Del Baldo, 2012; Fuller & Tian, 2006), their lack of communication and propensity to be misunderstood (Murillo & Lozano, 2006; Rivera-Lirio & Muñoz-Torres, 2010) and more specifically due to the fact that sustainability reporting standards have been developed for larger companies which are consistently different from SMEs (Enderle, 2004; Tilley, 2000).

However, SA 8000 and EMAS require mandatory reports, which are often not provided by SMEs, representing a possible failure in the legitimization of their CSR practices. Therefore, in order to better understand the factors influencing the SMEs' lower disclosure and to address their legitimization approach, we applied the linear regression model discussed in the previous section. The model accounts for variables such as membership of a group/conglomerate, age, the time since certification, and financial data. We checked for possible collinearities in order to exclude some variables but none were found.

Descriptive statistics of the variables accounted for in the model are presented in Table 6, while the model's results are presented in Table 7.

As it can be seen by the R^2 value computed in the model, the overall variance on the CSR disclosure explained by all the accounted variables is 33.4%. This means that other factors for which we did not account and

Table 6. Descriptive Statistics of the Study's Variables.

	N	Min	Max	Mean	Std. Dev.
Rating of CSR disclosure	357	0	5	2.09	1.477
Age at the year of first certification (Age)	357	0	77	19.92	14.975
Years since the 1st certification (Exp1)	357	0	12	4.84	2.630
Years since the 2nd certification (Exp2)	337	0	12	2.99	2.175
Belonging to a group (Grp)	357	0	1	.34	.474
Total 2010's assets (Assets)	357	200,247	13,676,767,000	163,780,339	1,053,118,965
Financial leverage (Lev)	353	.02	570.61	10.98	36.21
Total 2010's Sales (Sales)	357	131,848	5,421,992,000	96,379,575	453,964,486
SME or not (SME)	357	0	1	.65	.478

Table 7. Linear Regression Results (Dependent Variable = Rating of CSR Disclosure).

Variables	Expected Sign	β	Std. Error
Intercept		1.190	0.223
Age	+	0.006	0.004
Exp1	+	-0.447^{*}	0.229
Exp2	+	0.047	0.033
Grp	+	0.860^{**}	0.167
Assets	+	0.000	0.000
Leverage	–	−0.002	0.003
Sales	+	0.000	0.000
SME	–	-0.623^{**}	0.166
R^2	0.334		

$^{*}p \leq 0.05$, $^{**}p \leq 0.01$.

which still need to be investigated have an influence on the level of disclosure/reporting of the multi-certified companies.

The preliminary results confirm our findings, namely that size is an important variable in driving the level of CSR disclosure. As explained by the coefficient of the dummy variable SME, which is significantly negative, if a multi-certified company is an SME it has a high probability to have lower levels of CSR disclosure compared to larger companies. However, the coefficients of the other variables must be taken into account in order to have a clearer picture.

Hence, if we focus on the other coefficients, some variables don't seem to have any significant influence on the level of disclosure while others do. Specifically, financials such as the amount of assets, sales, and leverage ratio (Assets, Lev, Sales) don't have a defined influence on the level of CSR disclosure of the multi-certified companies. Previous studies agree that SMEs adopt CSR despite financial constraints (Parsa & Kouhy, 2008) and there is no direct link between social and environmental activity and economic reward (Choi & Pae, 2011; Longo et al., 2005; Russo & Perrini, 2010).

The age of the company and the time span since it's second certification (Exp2) don't play a significant role in the disclosure level. Previous studies have shown that the age of directors and managers turns out to be an important driver for the voluntary adoption of environmental management systems (McKeiver & Gadenne, 2005). However, manager and director turnover in a company can result in undefined outcomes under the disclosure perspective.

Indeed, the only variables that significantly influence the level of CSR disclosure are Expl and Grp. Importantly, Expl measures the time span since the first certification date, which means that the more certification experience a company has, the greater its level of disclosure is. Experienced companies are able to provide specific documents and sustainability reports according to national and international guidelines. At the beginning, companies decide to legitimize their activity by identifying themselves with some commonly recognized symbols (i.e., the adoption of the first environmental/social management system) (Dowling & Pfeffer, 1975, p. 127), afterward they achieve experience and understand the power and the importance that disclosure can play in changing external perceptions (Cormier & Gordon, 2001) and, therefore, provide more disclosure by preparing specific reports (i.e., social and environmental reports).

Another positive stimulus for CSR disclosure is the fact of belonging to a group or conglomerate. Usually, large conglomerates increase their competitiveness over the supply chain by acquiring control of the suppliers, often SMEs, and this control requires standardization of the processes, sometimes requiring appropriate social/environmental certifications. Institutional pressure encourages organizations to conform and standardize in order to improve the relationship with important stakeholders (i.e., the group or the supply chain) (Gray et al., 1996, p. 45), failure to undertake this isomorphic process may generate significant obstacles to company survival (DiMaggio & Powell, 1983, p. 149). However, when only a minimal threat is perceived no disclosure is deemed necessary (Bebbington et al., 2008; Deegan, 2002). Although group control can be seen as an important driver to disclose and report, a minority of SMEs, maybe because just entered into a group, or companies belonging to specific unregulated industries, still do not achieve good levels of disclosure even if they do belong to a group.

Since we found that the relevant factors affecting social and environmental disclosure and reporting were time span in managing the first certification and membership of a conglomerate/group of companies, Table 8 shows how the SMEs included in our sample behave in such terms.

Building on these results we can outline a classification of SME disclosure and reporting behavior under a legitimacy perspective. Namely, we identified six behaviors as follows:

Table 8. SMEs Disclosure Levels According to Experience and Group Membership.

SMEs	Experience		Total	Members of a Group		Total
	High (≥4 years)	Low (<4 years)		Yes	Not	
Good disclosure (rating values ≥3)	58 (75%)	19 (25%)	**77** (100%)	32 (59%)	22 (41%)	**54** (100%)
Poor disclosure (rating values <3)	56 (36%)	98 (64%)	**154** (100%)	13 (9%)	131 (91%)	**144** (100%)
Total	114 (49%)	117 (51%)	**231** (100%)	45 (23%)	153 (77%)	**198** (100%)

- *Immature*: the environmental and social management systems have just been adopted; however, this results in a lack of experience and, therefore, poor performance in term of related disclosure. These companies are young, are not controlled by groups or conglomerates, cannot leverage the experience developed by other entities, and have to build up their CSR practice on their own. The behavior is driven by the need to comply to some community expectations and to legitimize the organization's operations in line with commonly recognized values (Deegan, 2002); however, it fails in providing sufficient account of social and environmental performance because of this early stage adoption.
- *Pioneer*: even if the environmental and social management systems have just been adopted, the approach is taken seriously and the company is providing disclosure and reporting. Their efforts must be praised as they are not part of large groups and can't leverage the experience developed by others. The underlying legitimization behavior reflects the view that people have a inalienable right to information that should be satisfied regardless of the associated costs (Donaldson & Preston, 1995; Freeman & Reed, 1983; Freeman, 1984).
- *Gattopardian*: environmental and social management systems have been in place for several years; however, such companies don't provide sufficient disclosure and reporting. Because these companies are not part of a group and do not face related competitive issues, they seem disinclined to increase their accountability practices. They behave like the Italian family pictured in the famous book *Il Gattopardo* (*The Leopard*), which is more focused in showing off rather than adopting and developing actual strategies to overcome its financial and cultural crisis. They tried to achieve legitimization by approaching certification in an opportunistic

manner (Jermier & Forbes, 2003; Sarbutts, 2003) hoping to avail of the business advantages in appearing to do the "right thing," building a false reputation, rather than believing in any environmental or social responsibility of the business (Friedman, 1962).

- *Systematic*: the experience gained throughout the adoption of the environmental and social management systems led to the development of good practices in providing relevant disclosure and reporting. These companies requested legitimization throughout their social and environmental certifications long ago. However, legitimacy relies on current and updated external perceptions (Cormier & Gordon, 2001). Information and communication are tools for changing perceptions hence altering the definitions of social legitimacy (Lindblom, 1994). These companies systematically provide updated disclosure and reports because of the importance in maintaining or changing the achieved legitimacy (O'Donovan, 2002).
- *Imitative*: the adoption of environmental and social management systems pursuant to pressure from corporate HQ. This is an isomorphic and passive behavior, which does not provide sufficient disclosure because the threat of not maintaining legitimacy is minimal (O'Donovan, 1999, 2002), for example, the focus of media and community is on the parent company's actions and not on the SME involved. Collaborating with other parties who in themselves are considered to be legitimate might be the only focus of such companies (Fiedler & Deegan, 2002).
- *Copycat*: the adoption of environmental and social management systems is driven by pressure from the group resulting in total implementation of

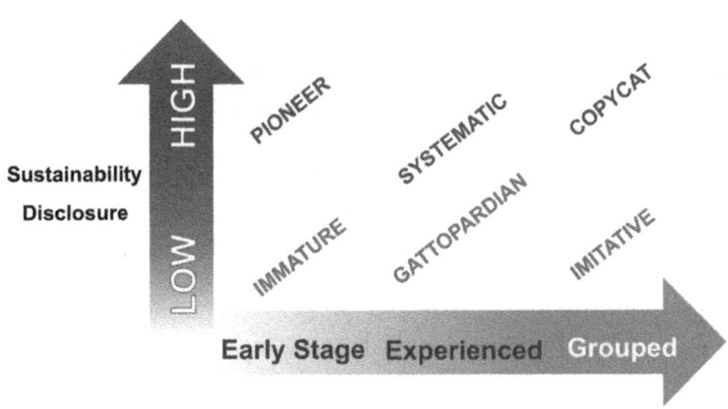

Fig. 2. Classification of Multi-Certified SMEs Disclosure Behaviors.

group-wide quality in terms of disclosure and reporting. Legitimization occurs when an entity's value system is congruent with the value system of the larger social system of which the company is part (Lindblom, 1994). Indeed, the more important the stakeholder is for the company (i.e., the group), the more effort will be applied in targeting the disclosure by agreeing and conforming to its practices (Gray et al., 1996, p. 45).

Features of the classified behaviors are summarized in Fig. 2.

CONCLUSIONS

The aim of this chapter was to address the behavior of SMEs in sustainability disclosure. Specifically, this study focused on the analysis of the factors influencing social and environmental disclosure/reporting of SMEs. The evidence is based on a sample of Italian "multi-certified" companies, in other words small- and medium-sized enterprises that adopted both environmental (i.e., ISO14001 or EMAS) and social (i.e., SA8000) management systems and related certifications. The analysis was carried out by developing a statistical model aimed at measuring the impact on disclosure/reporting, of different factors, such as the age of the company, the time span since certification (experience), membership of a group/conglomerate, and financial data (i.e., total assets, sales, and financial leverage).

Our main findings confirm that SMEs still suffer from of a lack of social and environmental disclosure and reporting if compared to larger companies. However, the use of the multi-certified sample suggests that variables such as the time span since certification and the integration into a group structure are important factors in stimulating disclosure and reporting.

Furthermore, by focusing on such findings we classified their disclosure behaviors from a legitimacy perspective and found six interesting patterns. Because legitimacy is considered to be a strategic resource for survival and building reputation (Dowling & Pfeffer, 1975), it can lead to different outcomes depending on the way it has been supplied and manipulated by managers (Woodward, Edwards, & Birkin, 2001). In the chapter, we are acknowledging CSR practices as tools of legitimization for SMEs, and, therefore, we have provided a classification of their disclosure behavior based on our analysis. However, legitimacy is based on managers' perceptions of social contracts and potential breaches, it cannot predict the outcomes of the legitimization approaches. Indeed, it can provide relevant insights on management decision-making regarding steps taken to build up the company's reputation (Deegan, 2002). Therefore, the study represents an important contribution for understanding how and why managers might use externally focused disclosure on social and environmental issues to benefit the company's legitimacy. Furthermore, the study provides interesting insights for policy makers who require social or environmental certification for national tenders or specific community contracts putting aside the "brand" or "symbol" and really focusing on the disclosed practices.

This study is not free from limitations and may be subject to further improvements. Firstly, we did not focus on the quality of the contents of disclosure and reporting practices adopted by SMEs, which is obviously a worthwhile and important area for further research.

Secondly, the rating used to address the level of disclosure/reporting has been developed by our research team in line with previous literature, which might affect the applicability of the results in other contexts. Thirdly, the study can be extended to investigate the effect on disclosure of other relevant variables (i.e., nature of the board of directors, age and industrial sector in which the company operates) as well as contexts prevailing in other countries.

NOTES

1. In order to be certified under the Eco-Management and Audit Scheme (EMAS) an organization shall: (a) conduct an environmental review of its activities, products, and services and implement an environmental management system; (b) carry out, or cause to be carried out, environmental auditing; (c) prepare an environmental statement. The statement shall pay particular attention to the results achieved by an organization against its environmental objectives and targets and the appropriate requirement of continuing to improve its environmental performance, and shall consider the information needs of relevant interested parties; (d) have the environmental review, if appropriate, management system, audit procedure, and environmental statement examined to verify that they meet the relevant requirements of this regulation and have the environmental statement validated by the environmental verifier; (e) forward the validated environmental statement to the competent body of the member state in which the organization seeking registration is located and, after registration, make it publicly available.

2. Social Accountability 8000 (SA8000) has been developed by Social Accountability International (SAI), a not-for-profit affiliate of the Council on Economic Priorities (CEP). SA8000 is promoted as a voluntary, universal standard for companies interested in auditing and certifying labor practices in their facilities and those of their suppliers and vendors. It is designed for independent third-party certification. SA8000 is based on the principles of international human rights norms

as described in International Labour Organisation conventions, the United Nations Convention on the Rights of the Child and the Universal Declaration of Human Rights. It measures the performance of companies in eight key areas: child labor, forced labor, health and safety, free association and collective bargaining, discrimination, disciplinary practices, working hours and compensation. SA8000 also provides for a social accountability management system to demonstrate ongoing compliance with the standard. Although it is recognized as a social responsibility certification, it is mainly directed at a single stakeholder (human resources).

3. In Italy is provided by Agenzia per le Onlus (updated in 2011).

4. Since 1998, Gruppo di Studio per il Bilancio Sociale (GBS) was formally established as a nonprofit research group with the mission of "developing and promoting scientific research on topics related to social and responsible management of business processes to foster the spread of corporate social responsibility and its application in the national and international context". In 2001, GBS published the first edition of their social reporting guideline namely "Principi di redazione del Bilancio Sociale." Since 2001 it has published separate social reporting standards for not-for-profit associations, public sector, business conglomerations, etc.

5. Recommendation 2003/361/EC. It defines the category of Small and Medium-sized Enterprises according to three criteria: staff headcount, annual amount of sales and assets. Specifically, an SME is an autonomous enterprise which (i) employs fewer than 250 people and (ii) which has annual sales not exceeding 50 million euro, and/or (iii) annual total assets not exceeding 43 million euro. An autonomous enterprise is totally independent (there is no participation in other enterprises and no enterprise has a participation in it) or it holds less than 25% of the capital or voting rights in one or more other enterprises and/or outsiders do not have a stake of 25% or more of the capital or voting rights in the enterprise.

REFERENCES

Adams, C. (1999). *The nature and processes of corporate reporting on ethical issues*. London: CIMA.

Ahmad, N. H., & Seet, P. (2009). Developing competitive advantage through ethical and SR practices: The case of SME in Australia and Malaysia. *International Business Research*, *2*(4), 116–124.

Aupperle, K. E., & Van Pham, D. (1989). An expanded investigation into the relationship of corporate social responsibility and financial performance. *Employee Responsibilities and Rights Journal*, *2*(4), 263–274.

Avram, D. O., & Kühne, S. (2008). Implementing responsible business behavior from a strategic management perspective: Developing a framework for Austrian SMEs. *Journal of Business Ethics*, *82*(2), 463–475.

Baden, D., & Harwood, I. (2013). Terminology matters: A critical exploration of corporate social responsibility terms. *Journal of Business Ethics*, *116*(3), 615–627.

Baden, D. A., Harwood, I. A., & Woodward, D. G. (2009). The effect of buyer pressure on suppliers in SMEs to demonstrate CSR practices: An added incentive or counter productive? *European Management Journal*, *27*(6), 429–441.

Battaglia, M., Bianchi, L., Frey, M., & Iraldo, F. (2010). An innovative model to promote CSR among SMEs operating in industrial clusters: evidence from an EU project. *Corporate Social Responsibility and Environmental Management*, *17*(3), 133–141.

Bebbington, J., Larrinaga, C., & Moneva, J. M. (2008). Corporate social reporting and reputation risk management. *Accounting, Auditing & Accountability Journal*, *21*(3), 337–361.

Botta, S., Comoglio, C., & Petrosillo, I. (2013). Implementing the environmental and social policies of a municipality through an integrated management system: theoretical framework and case study. *Journal of Environmental Planning and Management*, *56*(7), 1073–1095.

Bouma, J. J., & Kamp-Roelands, N. (2000). Stakeholders expectations of an environmental management system: Some exploratory research. *European Accounting Review*, *9*(1), 131–144.

Brammer, S., Hoejmose, S., & Marchant, K. (2012). Environmental management in SMEs in the UK: Practices, pressures and perceived benefits. *Business Strategy and the Environment*, *21*(7), 423–434.

Cambra-Fierro, J., Hart, S., & Polo-Redondo, Y. (2008). Environmental respect: Ethics or simply business? A study in the small and medium enterprise (SME) context. *Journal of Business Ethics*, *82*, 645–656.

Cassells, S., & Lewis, K. (2011). SMEs and environmental responsibility: Do actions reflect attitudes? *Corporate Social Responsibility and Environmental Management*, *18*(3), 186–199.

Castka, P., & Balzarova, M. A. (2008a). ISO 26000 and supply chains – On the diffusion of the social responsibility standard. *International Journal of Production Economics*, *111*(2), 274–286.

Castka, P., & Balzarova, M. A. (2008b). The impact of ISO 9000 and ISO 14000 on standardisation of social responsibility – An inside perspective. *International Journal of Production Economics*, *113*(1), 74–87.

Castka, P., Balzarova, M. A., Bomber, C. J., & Sharp, J. M. (2004). How can SMEs effectively implement the CSR agenda? A UK case study perspective. *Corporate Social Responsibility and Environmental Management*, *11*(3), 140–149.

Chiappetta Jabbour, C. J., & Puppim-de-Oliveira, J. A. (2012). Barriers to environmental management in clusters of small businesses in Brazil and Japan: From a lack of knowledge to a decline in traditional knowledge. *International Journal of Sustainable Development and World Ecology*, *19*(3), 247–257.

Choi, T. H., & Pae, J. (2011). Business ethics and financial reporting quality: Evidence from Korea. *Journal of Business Ethics*, *103*, 403–427.

Cisi, M., & Scagnelli, S. D. (2009). Behavioural models of Italian "ethical certified entities," a research study. *Economia Aziendale Online*, *1*(Special Issue), 43–60.

Cormier, D. J., & Gordon, I. (2001). An examination of social and environmental reporting strategies. *Accounting, Auditing & Accountability Journal*, *14*(5), 587–616.

Courrent, J. M., & Gundolf, K. (2009). Proximity and micro-enterprise manager's ethics: A French empirical study of responsible business attitudes. *Journal of Business Ethics*, *88*(4), 749–762.

Davies, I. A., & Crane, A. (2010). Corporate social responsibility in small-and medium-size enterprises: Investigating employee engagement in fair trade companies. *Business Ethics: A European Review*, *19*(2), 126–139.

Deegan, C. (2002). Introduction – The legitimising effect of social and environmental disclosures – a theoretical foundation. *Accounting, Auditing & Accountability Journal, 15*(3), 282–311.

Del Baldo, M. (2006). SMEs and corporate social responsibility. Some evidences from an empirical research. *Proceedings on Emerging Issues In International Accounting & Business Conference, 1*, 314–343.

Del Baldo, M. (2012). Corporate social responsibility and corporate governance in Italian SMEs: The experience of some "spirited businesses." *Journal of Management & Governance, 16*(1), 1–36.

Déniz, M. D. L. C. D., & Suárez, M. K. C. (2005). Corporate social responsibility and family business in Spain. *Journal of Business Ethics, 56*(1), 27–41.

DiMaggio, P. J., & Powell, W. W. (1983). The iron cage revisited: Institutional isomorphism and collective rationality in organisational fields. *American Sociological Review, 48*, 147–160.

Donaldson, T., & Preston, L. (1995). The stakeholder theory of the corporation – concepts, evidence, and implications. *Academy of Management Review, 20*(1), 65–92.

Dowling, J., & Pfeffer, J. (1975). Organisational legitimacy: Social values and organisational behaviour. *Pacific Sociological Review, January*, 122–136.

Enderle, G. (2004). Global competition and corporate responsibilities of small and medium-sized enterprises. *Business Ethics: A European Review, 14*(1), 51–63.

Epstein, E. M. (2007). The good company: Rhetoric or reality? Corporate social responsibility and business ethics redux. *American Business Law Journal, 44*(2), 207–222.

Eurobarometer survey. (2012, March 27). European Commission – MEMO/12/218. *SMEs are important for a smooth transition to a greener economy*. Brussels.

European Commission. (2011). *A renewed EU strategy 2011–14 for corporate social responsibility*. Brussels: European Commission.

European Union & CREM. (2011). *The state of play in sustainability reporting in the European Union. The publication is commissioned under the European Union's Programme for Employment and Social Solidarity – PROGRESS (2007–2013)*.

Evangelinos, K. I., & Skouloudis, A. (2012). European perspectives on corporate non-financial disclosure: Evidence from the Southeast. *International Journal of Disclosure and Governance*. Retrieved from http://dx.doi.org/10.1057/jdg.2012.13

Fassin, Y. (2008). SMEs and the fallacy of formalising CSR. *Business Ethics: A European Review, 17*(4), 364–378.

Fassin, Y., Rossem, A., & Buelens, M. (2011). Small-business owner-managers' perceptions of business ethics and CSR-related concepts. *Journal of Business Ethics, 98*(3), 425–453.

Fenwick, T. (2010). Learning to practice social responsibility in small business: Challenges and conflicts. *Journal of Global Responsibility, 1*(1), 149–169.

Fiedler, T., & Deegan, C. (2002). Environmental collaboration within the building and construction industry: A consideration of the motivations to collaborate. Paper presented at the critical perspective on accounting conference, New York, NY.

Fisher, K., Geenen, J., Jurcevic, M., McClintock, K., & Davis, G. (2009). Applying asset-based community development as a strategy for CSR: A Canadian perspective on a win-win for stakeholders and SMEs. *Business Ethics: A European Review, 18*(1), 66–82.

Fitjar, R. D. (2011). Little big firms? Corporate social responsibility in small businesses that do not compete against big ones. *Business Ethics: A European Review, 20*(1), 30–44.

Freeman, R. E. (1984). *Strategic management: A stakeholder approach.* Boston, MA: Pitman.

Freeman, R. E., & Reed, R. (1983). Stockholders and stakeholders: A new perspective on corporate governance. *Californian Management Review*, *25*(2), 88–106.

Friedman, M. (1962). *Capitalism and freedom.* Chicago, IL: University of Chicago.

Fuller, T., & Tian, Y. (2006). Social and symbolic capital and responsible entrepreneurship: An empirical investigation of SME narratives. *Journal of Business Ethics*, *67*, 287–304.

Gadenne, D., Kennedy, J., & McKeiver, C. (2009). An empirical study of environmental awareness and practices in SMEs. *Journal of Business Ethics*, *84*(1), 45–63.

Graafland, J., Van de Ven, B., & Stoffele, N. (2003). Strategies and instruments for organising CSR by small and large businesses in The Netherlands. *Journal of Business Ethics*, *47*(1), 45–60.

Gray, R., Collison, D., & Bebbington, J. (1998). Environmental and social accounting and reporting. *Financial Reporting Today*, 179–214.

Gray, R. H., Kouhy, R., & Lavers, S. (1995). Constructing a research database of social and environmental reporting by UK companies: A methodological note. *Accounting, Auditing and Accountability Journal*, *8*(2), 78–101.

Gray, R. H., Owen, D. L., & Adams, C. (1996). *Accounting and accountability: Changes and challenges in corporate social and environmental reporting.* London: Prentice Hall.

Grayson, D. (2004). *How CSR contribute to the competitiveness of Europe in a more sustainable world.* Netherlands: The World Bank Institute and the CSR Resource Centre, 1–15.

Guthrie, J., & Parker, L. (1989). Corporate social reporting: A rebuttal of legitimacy theory. *Accounting and Business research*, *9*, 76.

Hammann, E. M., Habisch, A., & Pechlaner, H. (2009). Values that create value: Socially responsible business practices in SMEs – Empirical evidence from German companies. *Business Ethics: A European Review*, *18*(1), 37–51.

Hasnas, J. (1998). The normative theories of business ethics: A guide for the perplexed. *Business Ethics Quarterly*, *8*(1), 19–42.

Hillary, R. (2000). Introduction. In R. Hillary (Ed.), *Small and medium-sized enterprises and the environment: Business imperatives.* Sheffield: Greenleaf Publishing.

Jamali, D., Safieddine, A. M., & Rabbath, M. (2008). Corporate governance and corporate social responsibility synergies and interrelationships. *Corporate Governance: An International Review*, *16*(5), 443–459.

Jämsä, P., Tähtinen, J., Ryan, A., & Pallari, M. (2011). Sustainable SMEs network utilization: The case of food enterprises. *Journal of Small Business and Enterprise Development*, *18*(1), 141–156.

Jenkins, H. (2004). A critique of conventional CSR theory: An SME perspective. *Journal of General Management*, *29*(4), 37–57.

Jenkins, H. (2006). Small business champions for corporate social responsibility. *Journal of Business Ethics*, *67*(3), 241–256.

Jenkins, H. (2009). A 'business opportunity' model of corporate social responsibility for small- and medium-sized enterprises. *Business Ethics: A European Review*, *18*(1), 21–36.

Jermier, J., & Forbes, L. (2003). Greening organisations: Critical issues. In M. Alvesson & H. Willmott (Eds.), *Studying management critically* (pp. 157–176). London: Sage.

Jirillo, R., Rocchi, A., & Martucci, O. (2003). EMAS and its local diffusion in Italy. *Corporate Social Responsibility and Environmental Management*, *10*(1), 40–49.

Jorgensen, A. L., & Knudsen, J. S. (2006). Sustainable competitiveness in global value chains: How do small Danish firms behave? *Corporate Governance*, *6*(4), 449–462.

Lange, E. A., & Fenwick, T. J. (2008). Moral commitments to community: Mapping social responsibility and its ambiguities among small business owners. *Social Responsibility Journal*, *4*(2), 41–55.

Lanis, R., & Richardson, G. (2012). Corporate social responsibility and tax aggressiveness: A test of legitimacy theory. *Accounting, Auditing and Accountability Journal*, *26*(1), 75–100.

Lawrence, S. R., Collins, E., Pavlovich, K., & Arunachalam, M. (2006). Sustainability practices of SMEs: the case of NZ. *Business Strategy and the Environment*, *15*(4), 242.

Lepoutre, J., & Heene, A. (2006). Investigating the impact of firm size on small business social responsibility: A critical review. *Journal of Business Ethics*, *67*(3), 257–273.

Lindblom, C. K. (1994). The implications of organisational legitimacy for corporate social performance and disclosure. Paper presented at the critical perspective on accounting conference, New York, NY.

Llach, J., Bagur-Femenías, L., Alonso-Almeida, M. D. M., & Perramon, J. (2013). Joint impact of quality and environmental practices on firm performance in small service businesses: An empirical study of restaurants. *Journal of Cleaner Production*, *44*, 96–104.

Longenecker, J., Moore, C., Petty, J., Palich, L., & McKinney, J. (2006). Ethical attitudes in small businesses and large corporations: Theory and empirical findings from a tracking study spanning three decades. *Journal of Small Business Management*, *44*(2), 167–183.

Longo, M., Mura, M., & Bonoli, A. (2005). Corporate social responsibility and corporate performance: The case of Italian SMEs. *Corporate Governance, The International Journal of Business in Society*, *5*(4), 28–42.

Lozano, R. (2012). Towards better embedding sustainability into companies' systems: An analysis of voluntary corporate initiatives. *Journal of Cleaner Production*, *25*, 14–26.

Lynch-Wood, G., Williamson, D., & Jenkins, W. (2009). The over-reliance on self-regulation in CSR policy. *Business Ethics: A European Review*, *18*(1), 52–65.

Matten, D., & Moon, J. (2008). "Implicit" and "explicit" CSR: A conceptual framework for a comparative understanding of corporate social responsibility. *Academy of Management*, *33*(2), 404–424.

McKeiver, C., & Gadenne, D. (2005). Environmental management systems in small and medium businesses. *International Small Business Journal*, *23*(5), 513–537.

Miles, M. P., & Munilla, L. S. (2004). The potential impact of social accountability certification on marketing: a short note. *Journal of Business Ethics*, *50*(1), 1–11.

Moore, G., Slack, R., & Gibbon, J. (2009). Criteria for responsible business practice in SMEs: An exploratory case of UK Fair Trade organizations. *Journal of Business Ethics*, *89*(2), 173–188.

Moore, S. B., & Manring, S. L. (2009). Strategy development in small and medium sized enterprises for sustainability and increased value creation. *Journal of Cleaner Production*, *17*(2), 276–282.

Morsing, M., & Perrini, F. (2009). CSR in SMEs: Do SMEs matter for the CSR agenda? *Business Ethics: A European Review*, *18*(1), 1–6.

Muller, A., & Kolk, A. (2009). CSR performance in emerging markets evidence from Mexico. *Journal of Business Ethics*, *85*(2), 325–337.

Murillo, D., & Lozano, J. M. (2006). SMEs and CSR: An approach to CSR in their own words. *Journal of Business Ethics*, *67*(3), 227–240.

Niehm, L. S., Swinney, J., & Miller, N. J. (2008). Community social responsibility and its consequences for family business performance. *Journal of Small Business Management*, *46*(3), 331–350.

Nielsen, A. E., & Thomsen, C. (2009). Investigating CSR communication in SMEs: A case study among Danish middle managers. *Business Ethics: A European Review*, *18*(1), 83–93.

Nooteboom, B. (2004). Governance and competence: How can they be combined? *Cambridge Journal of Economics*, *28*, 505–525.

O'Donovan, G. (1999). Managing legitimacy through increased corporate environmental reporting: An exploratory study. *Interdisciplinary Environmental Review*, *1*(1), 63–99.

O'Donovan, G. (2002). Environmental disclosures in the annual report: Extending the applicability and predictive power of legitimacy theory. *Accounting, Auditing & Accountability Journal*, *15*(3), 344–371.

O'Dwyer, B., Owen, D., & Unerman, J. (2011). Seeking legitimacy for new assurance forms: The case of assurance on sustainability reporting. *Accounting, Organizations and Society*, *36*(1), 31–52.

Parsa, S., & Kouhy, R. (2008). Social reporting by companies listed on the alternative investment market. *Journal of Business Ethics*, *79*(3), 345–360.

Perrini, F. (2006). SMEs and CSR theory: Evidence and implications from an Italian perspective. *Journal of Business Ethics*, *67*(3), 305–316.

Perrini, F., Russo, A., & Tencati, A. (2007). CSR strategies of SMEs and large firms. Evidence from Italy. *Journal of Business Ethics*, *74*(3), 285–300.

Petts, J., Herd, A., Gerrad, S., & Horne, C. (1999). The climate culture of environmental compliance within SMEs. *Business Strategy and the Environment*, *8*, 14–30.

Raar, J. (2007). Reported social and environmental taxonomies: A longer-term glimpse. *Managerial Auditing Journal*, *22*(8), 840–860.

Reddy, K., Locke, S., & Fauzi, F. (2013). Relevance of corporate governance practices in charitable organisations: A case study of registered charities in New Zealand. *International Journal of Managerial Finance*, *9*(2), 110–132.

Redmond, J., Walker, E., & Wang, C. (2008). Issues for small businesses with waste management. *Journal of Environmental Management*, *88*(2), 275–285.

Revell, A., & Rutherfoord, R. (2003). UK environmental policy and the small firm: Broadening the focus. *Business Strategy and the Environment*, *12*(1), 26–35.

Revell, A., Stokes, D., & Chen, H. (2010). Small businesses and the environment: Turning over a new leaf? *Business Strategy And The Environment*, *19*(5), 273–288.

Rivera-Lirio, J., & Muñoz-Torres, M. (2010). The effectiveness of the public support policies for the European industry financing as a contribution to sustainable development. *Journal of Business Ethics*, *94*(4), 489–515.

Roberts, S., Lawson, R., & Nicholls, J. (2006). Generating regional-scale improvements in SME corporate responsibility performance: Lessons from responsibility Northwest. *Journal of Business Ethics*, *67*(3), 275–286.

Russo, A., & Perrini, F. (2010). Investigating stakeholder theory and social capital: CSR in large firms and SMEs. *Journal of Business Ethics*, *91*(2), 207–221.

Russo, A., & Tencati, A. (2009). Formal vs. informal CSR Strategies. Evidence from Italian micro, small, medium-sized, and large firms. *Journal of Business Ethics*, *85*(Suppl. 2), 339–353.

Sabate, J. M. D. L. F., & Puente, E. D. Q. (2003). Empirical analysis of the relationship between corporate reputation and financial performance: A survey of the literature. *Corporate Reputation Review*, *6*(2), 161–177.

Sarbutts, N. (2003). Can SMEs "do" CSR? A practitioner's view of the ways small and medium-sized enterprises are able to manage reputation through corporate social responsibility. *Journal of Communication Management*, *7*(4), 340–347.

Schlierer, H. J., Werner, A., Signori, S., Garriga, E., von Weltzien Hoivik, H., Van Rossem, A., & Fassin, Y. (2012). How do European SME owner-managers make sense of "Stakeholder Management"? Insights from a cross-national study. *Journal of Business Ethics*, *109*(1), 39–51.

Shocker, A. D., & Sethi, S. P. (1973). An approach to developing societal preferences in developing corporate action strategies. *California Management Review*, *15*(4), 97–105.

Spence, L. J. (1999). Does size matter? The state of the art in small business ethics. *Business Ethics: A European Review*, *8*(3), 163–174.

Spence, L. J., & Rutherfoord, R. (2001). Social responsibility, profit maximisation and the small firm owner-manager. *Journal of Small Business and Enterprise Development*, *8*, 126–139.

Spence, L. J., & Rutherfoord, R. (2003). Small business and empirical perspectives in business ethics: Editorial. *Journal of Business Ethics*, *47*, 1–5.

Spence, L. J., Schmidpeter, R., & Habisch, A. (2003). Assessing social capital: Small and medium sized enterprises in Germany and the U.K. *Journal of Business Ethics*, *47*(1), 17–29.

Suchman, M. C. (1995). Managing legitimacy: Strategic and institutional approaches. *Academy of management review*, *20*(3), 571–610.

Tilley, F. (2000). Small firm environmental ethics: How deep do they go? *Business Ethics: A European Review*, *9*(1), 31–41.

Torugsa, N. A., O'Donohue, W., & Hecker, R. (2012). Proactive CSR: An empirical analysis of the role of its economic, social and environmental dimensions on the association between capabilities and performance. *Journal of Business Ethics*, *109*(4), 483–500.

Udayasankar, K. (2008). Corporate social responsibility and firm size. *Journal of Business Ethics*, *83*(2), 167–175.

Uhlaner, L. M., van Goor-Balk, H. A., & Masurel, E. (2004). Family business and corporate social responsibility in a sample of Dutch firms. *Journal of Small Business and Enterprise Development*, *11*(2), 186–194.

Ullmann, A. A. (1985). Data in search of a theory: A critical examination of the relationships among social performance, social disclosure, and economic performance of U.S. firms. *The Academy of Management Review*, *10*(3), 540–557.

Unioncamere. (2003). *Models of corporate social responsibility in Italy. Executive summary.* Rome: Italian Union of Chambers of Commerce, Industry, Craft and Agriculture.

van der Woerd, K. F. (1997). *Self-regulation in corporate environmental management: Changing interactions between companies and authorities.* Enschede/Utrecht: Febo.

Vives, A. (2006). Social and environmental responsibility in small and medium enterprises in Latin America. *Journal of Corporate Citizenship*, *21*, 39–50.

von Weltzien Høivik, H., & Shankar, D. (2011). How can SMEs in a cluster respond to global demands for corporate responsibility? *Journal of Business Ethics*, *101*(2), 175–195.

Vyakarnam, S., Bailey, A., Myers, A., & Burnett, D. (1997). Towards an understanding of ethical Behaviour in small firms. *Journal of Business Ethics*, *16*(15), 1625–1637.

Williamson, D., Lynch-Wood, G., & Ramsay, J. (2006). Drivers of environmental behaviour in manufacturing SMEs and the implications for CSR. *Journal of Business Ethics*, *67*, 317–330.

Woodward, D., Edwards, P., & Birkin, F. (2001). Some evidence on executives' views of corporate social responsibility. *British Accounting Review*, *33*(3), 357–397.

Worthington, I., Ram, M., & Jones, T. (2006). Exploring corporate social responsibility in the UK Asian small business community. *Journal of Business Ethics*, *67*(2), 201–217.

WATER MANAGEMENT AND ACCOUNTING: REMARKS AND NEW INSIGHTS FROM AN ACCOUNTABILITY PERSPECTIVE

Silvana Signori and Gerald Avondo Bodino

ABSTRACT

Purpose – *The aim of this chapter is to determine the need for water management and accounting.*

Design/methodology/approach – *This chapter first gives an overview of water-related business risks and exposes the need for sound corporate water management and accounting; it then critically examines water-related issues from an accountability perspective. Furthermore, it gives an overview of Australian Standardised Water Accounting (SWA) and General Purpose Water Accounting (GPWA) as possible practices to strengthen water disclosure.*

Findings – *The present study confirms the need for, and the importance of, transparent, high-quality, credible and comparable water disclosure. Water is considered a public good and involves a public interest and, consequently, public responsibility for its usage, management and protection.*

Accounting and Control for Sustainability
Studies in Managerial and Financial Accounting, Volume 26, 115–161

ISSN: 1479-3512/doi:10.1108/S1479-3512(2013)0000026004

Following this line of reasoning, the chapter draws attention to the need for accountability to be 'public' or at least shared between crucial stakeholders (government – at national and international levels, water industries, communities, environmentalists, NGOs, etc.).

Practical and social implications – *Company efforts are commonly focused on internal and self-referred operations. The different and conflicting uses that may be made of water, and the fact that water is geographically and temporally sensitive, necessitate a search for more flexible and more extended forms of accountability. An implication of these findings is the need and opportunity to switch focus from a single/private perspective to a more general/public one, with benefits for all the stakeholders.*

Originality/value – *This research enhances our understanding of water management and accounting and may serve as a sound base for future studies on this challenging topic.*

Keywords: Water management; water accounting; accountability; shared accountability; Australian Standardised Water Accounting (SWA); General Purpose Water Accounting (GPWA)

INTRODUCTION

In recent years, companies have received increasing pressure for greater transparency and clearer lines of responsibility and accountability on the use and management of natural resources (COAG, 2004; IIRC, 2010). The searches for 'systematic approaches to recording and reporting of that data in relevant, reliable, understandable and comparable ways have [therefore] gained prominence' (Chalmers, Godfrey, & Potter, 2012b, p. 275).

One of the most pressing global issues is without doubt water (WWAP, 2003, 2006, 2009, 2012). In fact, levels and variability of water quantity and quality are issues of major concern in many countries (Chalmers, Godfrey, & Lynch, 2012a).

Water is a basic human right (Human Rights Council of the United Nations, 2009; UN, 2010; UNCESCR, 2002): it is essential for survival ('water for life'), for 'public health' and 'the promotion of values of equity or social cohesion' ('water for citizens') and for economic activities ('water for development') (Dubreuil, 2006, p. 4). Water is, therefore, considered to be the 'foundation of a healthy economy' and its price reflects the 'problematic connection between communities, the economy and the environment' (Sofocleous, 2010, p. 294).

There is a need to take this issue seriously in the light of the fact that one fifth of the world's population lives in regions where water is in short supply; a quarter of the population is short of water because of inefficient infrastructures (Sofocleous, 2010, p. 294); about 92% of the total usage of water is for industrial and agricultural activities (Sofocleous, 2010, p. 295); current projections of water availability in the near future suggest a 40% supply deficit (Barton & Adrio, 2011); and recent studies have underlined that about 59% of companies feel exposed to water risks (Deloitte, 2011). High-quality and credible water-related information is of critical importance to address decision-making and to steer policy and management reforms (Chalmers et al., 2012b, p. 275). Thus, it is not surprising that, in the past decade, several water initiatives and guidelines have been developed internationally.

While Dubreuil (2006) advises that accountability and information are crucial for the realisation of all three types of water rights mentioned above (quoted in Hazelton, 2013, p. 281), Hazelton (2013) recently argues that not only is access to water a human right but also access to water-related information.

Recognising a right to water-related information calls for increased forms of accountability. Indeed, Williams (1987) refers to accountability as the requirement or duty to provide an account or justification for one's action to whoever has a right to ask for it.[1] Gray, Dey, Owen, Evans, and Zadek (1997), instead, describe accountability as the provision of information between two parties where the one who is accountable explains or justifies actions to the one to whom the account is owed.

The concept of accountability, even if a little 'murky' and difficult to define (Sinclair, 1995; Tello Melendez, Cummings, & Hazelton, 2012), has been widely used in management or business studies mainly as the basis for explaining and justifying the role and nature of the practices of social (and environmental) reporting (Gray, Owen, & Adams, 1996). More specifically, social accountability (henceforth accountability) is viewed as the assumption and the necessary condition to justify the existence and role of the practice of social accounting[2] (Contrafatto & Signori, 2012). In addition, social accounting and its techniques are the means by which it is possible to increase the democracy of society (Gray et al., 1996) and contribute to the idealisation, conceptualisation and implementation of economic and social systems based more on the principles of sustainable development

(Contrafatto, 2009; Contrafatto & Signori, 2012; Gray et al., 1996; Unerman, Bebbington, & O'Dwyer, 2007).

In particular Gray, Owen and Adams define accountability as

> The duty to provide an account (by no means necessarily a *financial* account) or reckoning of those actions for which one is held responsible.
>
> Thus, accountability involves two responsibilities or duties: the responsibility to undertake certain actions (or forbear from taking actions) and the responsibility to provide an account of those actions. (Gray et al., 1996, p. 38)

To understand the nature and conditions of accountability we should, therefore, refer to (1) the type and foundation of this responsibility; (2) the instruments of accountability; and (3) the role of accountability and its tools primarily for a company's sustainability. From this perspective, accountability requires a strong focus on responsibility: (1) the responsibility for the action (or non-action); (2) the responsibility to prepare a report; and (3) the responsibility to make these accounts and reports available, accessible, comparable and understandable to all parties involved (Contrafatto & Signori, 2012).

After a presentation of the risks and responsibilities connected with water issues (mainly from a business point of view), this chapter will focus on water management and accounting. Underlining the importance of the duty of accountability, a specific analysis will be dedicated to this aspect. In particular, the need for shared forms of water accountability will be highlighted and an analysis will be made of the potentials offered by the developments of the Australian General Purpose Water Accounting (GPWA) standard setting as a form of global and multi-stakeholder accountability.

WHY WORRY ABOUT WATER? A COMPANY'S PERSPECTIVE

Water is a peculiar good: its availability is sensitive to space (different countries or geographic areas have different water-related problems) and time (water availability is 'seasonal' and can fluctuate strongly and unpredictably at different times of the year); therefore, similar levels of water extraction may have different environmental and social impacts depending on their location.[3]

As outlined by a report written for the Carbon Disclosure Project by Irbaris, water provides a 'unique set of measurement and reporting challenges'. Water is a local as well as a global issue, there are 'different types of water' and different usages (Irbaris, 2009, p. 7).[4]

Although it is possible to adopt some forms of measurement and/or reporting for other environmental questions (as, e.g., CO_2 emissions), water measurement and disclosure is harder. The geographical dimension is critical. While the emission of a tonne of CO_2 has the same environmental impact in Sydney as in Stockholm, the usage of a litre of water does not. Furthermore, producing water-intensive foodstuffs in areas where there is a lot of blue water may be less of a problem than producing the same crops using scarce groundwater provisions (examples suggested by Irbaris, 2009).

Access to water is recognised as a precondition of universal human rights and indispensable for leading a life with dignity (Human Rights Council, 2009; UNCESCR, 2002, Art.1); however, freshwater resources are being degraded at an unprecedented rate (Barton & Adrio, 2011). Heavy pollution can render water sources, which in theory are renewable, as 'missing' until they return (either through a natural process or through expensive technological treatments) to an appropriate standard of quality. According to the *World Water Assessment Program* (2009), in developing countries 70% of industrial waste enters lakes and rivers untreated. The Chinese government's June 2011 announcement that one sixth of the country's major rivers were so polluted that the waters were regarded as no longer safe for agriculture, much less for human use (Blanchard, 2011) is emblematic. If we turn to the United States, an EPA (US Environmental Protection Agency) study identified agricultural activities as the main cause of water quality degradation in rivers and lakes and the second largest cause of impairment to wetlands, estuaries and groundwater (EPA, 2005, see also WWAP, 2012).

Even if agriculture accounts for 70% of the usage of freshwater (WWAP, 2012), water is a crucial resource for most industries around the world. Virtually every sector relies on it to develop and sustain its business. About 18% of water usage is destined for the industrial sector, which includes many forms of power plants requiring massive amounts of water for cooling, namely 41% of total water withdrawals in the United States and 44% in the European Union (2030 Water Resources Group, 2009; Barton & Adrio, 2011).

Business risks are closely linked to an increase in water demand and an insufficient water supply. As availability in water-stressed regions becomes scarcer, costs of water will be higher. Industries will have to face the uncertainty of regulatory caps on use, and safeguard probable conflicts with communities and other water users (WWAP, 2006). Consequently, due to a reduction or limit on water supply there will be a growing demand for water-efficient products and, according to Ceres (2010),[5] businesses will have to face operational disruptions and associated financial loss.

The deterioration in water quality may have, therefore, some serious impacts on business. According to a Ceres (2010) report, some of the implications may include increased costs for pre-treatment to achieve the desired water quality and for wastewater treatment to meet a more stringent regulation, which may also restrict water usage for specific industrial activities. All in all there will be greater uncertainty about the availability of water quality and supplies while, in the meantime, the demand for freshwater is growing at a rapid pace due to a variety of factors such as population growth, industrial activities and increasing standards of living, particularly in emerging economies (Morrison, Schulte, & Schenck, 2009b).

According to a recent study led by McKinsey (Boccaletti, Grobbel, & Stuchtey, 2010), even with accelerated investment in efficiency and improved water resource management, there will be major freshwater deficiencies in the next two decades. The authors estimate that by 2030 global water demand will exceed supply by 40%. This shortage will hit hard, especially in those countries that are already facing water scarcity scenarios, such as the southwest United States, Australia, Africa and East and Southeast Asia. With regard to Asia, water risks are even more troublesome as it is experiencing a vast population and economic growth (Barton & Adrio, 2011).

Moreover, besides this problem of water scarcity or quality, floods like those experienced in Australia, Brazil, Indonesia, Sri Lanka, and even in Italy, in 2011 and 2012, have demonstrated the need for information to respond effectively to water abundance as well.

BUSINESS RISKS RELATED TO WATER

Negative trends in water quantity and quality are directing companies' attention to the uncertainty that adverse water-scenarios may have on their business as well as increasing their awareness of the harmful impacts that their wastewater discharge and water use might have on communities and the ecosystem.

Companies are increasingly conscious of a strategic interest in proactively developing long-term water management plans in order to reduce these risks (Schulte, Morrison, & Gleick, 2012). A key finding from the CDP (Carbon Disclosure Project) *Water Disclosure Program 2011* is that the majority of companies have identified water as a substantial risk to their business. According to the report, 59% of respondents feel exposed to water-related risks and over one third has already incurred water-related business impacts, with financial costs amounting to US$200 million (Deloitte, 2011).

Furthermore, there is an increasing demand from investors for more robust corporate management and disclosure of the material risks and opportunities related to water. For example, in January 2010, after 6 years of lobbying by institutional investors, the US Securities and Exchange Commission (SEC) provided interpretative guidance on disclosures related to business or legal questions regarding climate change (SEC, 2010). The guidance clarifies what publicly listed companies need to disclose about material climate-related risks, including physical risks, such as water (ACCA, 2010).

Measuring and reporting corporate water-related risks and opportunities are complex. This complexity arises from issues such as 'the lack of a universally accepted methodology for calculating the risk impact of water, lack of mandate for corporate water reporting, the piecemeal ability to access reliable data from suppliers on water performance, as well as the dynamic variability of local and regional issues in water catchments' (ACCA, 2010, p. 5) but also on the very nature of water. While measuring the direct operations of an industrial user is straightforward, this becomes more complex when dealing with measuring non-meter use (e.g. from rainfall) or recycled water[6] (on this point see also Godfrey, 2007; Mudd, 2008; Sofocleous, 2010).

With these limits in mind, this paragraph discusses the main material business risks related to water issues, classifying them into four broad categories (Schulte et al., 2012): physical/operational, reputational/stakeholder, regulatory/political and litigation risk.

Physical/Operational Risk

Physical risks relate to the inability to manage a company's operations because of an inadequate water supply or service. This risk occurs when there is too little (scarcity), too much (flooding) or inadequate (quality) water. These are mostly problems for companies with water-intensive operations in water-scarce regions. Even where water is physically abundant, companies may have problems accessing it due to poor public water management or inconsistent water services. Reductions or disruptions in water supply can have serious effects on industrial operations where water is needed for production, irrigation, material processing, cooling, washing or cleaning (Barton, 2010). Clean water is critical to many industrial processes; contaminated water supply usually requires additional, and costly, investments and pre-treatments. Water quality is so critical in certain processes that in the absence of alternative water sources or treatment options, facility operations will be forced to relocate (Morrison, Morikawa, Murphy, & Schulte, 2009a).

Reputational/Stakeholder Risk

In water stressed regions, competition for clean water is high. The strife for water between businesses and local communities becomes more acute in developing countries, where local populations struggle to access safe and reliable drinking water. Stakeholders might oppose companies due to their perceived, or real, negative impacts on the quantity and quality of water resources, health and well-being of workers, aquatic ecosystems, communities and future business viability (Schulte et al., 2012). Tensions may arise suddenly and profoundly affect businesses (WWAP, 2006). Local conflicts can damage brand image or, in the worst cases, can cause the loss of license to operate. For example, in McCloud, California, Nestlé had to cancel plans to bottle water after years of opposition by local residents and advocacy groups concerned about the environmental impacts of the proposed bottling plan. The deal was supposed to create 240 jobs and bring US$350,000 annually to Small Town in northern California (Morrison et al., 2009a).

Following a greater acknowledgement of human rights to access water (Human Rights Council of the United Nations, 2009; UNCESCR, 2002), the last of which is the formal recognition of such rights by the United Nations in 2010 (UN, 2010), there is a growing awareness and concern over the impacts of water withdrawal and wastewater discharge on human life and the ecosystem. Consequently, companies' water practices are subjected to greater scrutiny from major media outlets. Furthermore, investors, in their decision-making, are taking increasing account of the extent to which companies are considering and planning for water-related risks. In 2008 Citi, JPMorgan, Merrill Lynch, and Morgan Stanley all issued water-focused research reports in which they highlighted the data gaps investors and analysts face when assessing corporate water risks (Schulte et al., 2012). Acknowledging this increased demand for disclosure on water practices and performance, shareholders' resolution on water issues has more than quadrupled over the last 10 years (Schulte et al., 2012

The authors refer to the activity of the Interfaith Center on Corporate Responsibility: on shareholder activism and resolutions interesting information are available at their website www.iccr.org and in the report ICCR, 2012. For investors studies on water issues, see also EIRIS, 2011).

Regulatory/Political Risk

There are growing concerns among local communities and stakeholders over the impacts on the ecosystem of water discharges and withdrawals. That, along with increasing water-scarcity scenarios, is putting pressure on local authorities and policymakers to consider a series of interventions to limit these growing issues. Governments and local authorities have at their disposal a number of tools to influence and manage business environment. For instance they might implement a stricter regulatory requirement as a result of water scarcity or conflicts among various needs (e.g. urban, agricultural, industrial, ecological). They may consider water reallocations or the development of water markets that cap usage, suspend permits to draw water and implement stricter water quality standards (Barton, 2010). All these measures can lead to a less stable or less inviting business environment and can affect a company's capacity to access water supplies and services, increase the cost of operations or make usage of water and its management more challenging.

According to Schulte et al. (2012), water scarcity is also driving pricing policies, which in turn aim at promoting greater efficiency in industrial operations. Moreover, a higher standard of water quality leads to new and more costly requirements for water plant treatments which, if not met, can lead to costly litigation, civil penalties or criminal fines. An example of regulation that governments may apply is given by Australia which, in 2005, decreed the Water Efficiency Labeling and Standards Act, which required certain products (e.g. taps and showers) to be registered and labelled according to their water-use efficiency (Commonwealth of Australia, 2010).[7]

As discussed in Schulte et al. (2012), a poor water management system in the public sector, due to a lack of will, experience or financial resources, might lead, in the long run, to the creation of an insufficient and inconsistent water service. In such a scenario, industries face a high risk due to uncertainty in water supplies and quality, exacerbating industrial water practices. These problems are most common in the global South, where governments typically have less money to manage water resources and where corruption is more widespread.[8]

Litigation Risk

Litigation risks refer to 'the consequences of lawsuit or other legal actions related to the company's impacts on water levels and water quality. As water challenges continue to gain more attention and water-related physical, reputational and regulatory risks increase, companies face increased litigation risks' (Adrio, 2012, p.10).

As discussed by Schulte et al. (2012), the above categories are the type of risks that companies may incur, but the extent to which a company is exposed to them depends on a multitude of other factors that may be more, or less, controllable. Companies, in fact, do not have direct control over each factor that creates risk. For example, a company cannot have

Table 1. Internal and External Factors of Water Risk.

Internal factors

- *Maturity of practice*: Industries that work in water-intensive sectors are those that more frequently face regulatory pressures or stakeholder discontent; therefore, because risk exposure is partly dependent on a facility's investment in technologies that improve the efficiency of water use and the treatment of wastewater effluent, companies with a long experience in the sector might have a competitive advantage or be less susceptible to new regulatory standards.
- *Nature of use and discharge*: Different sectors have different water needs. There are those, such as steelmaking or oil refining, that require large amounts of low-quality water for cooling purposes while others, particularly in high-tech industries, need smaller amounts of higher quality water. Furthermore one must take into consideration the quality of water after usage and before returning it to the watershed. Differences in the nature of water use determine the extent to which a company is more exposed to a certain risk over another.

External factors

- *Hydrological context*: Water quantity in a region has a great influence on the functioning of ecosystems and access to water. Therefore, less water means less availability for both the ecosystem and human needs. As the situation gets worse, negative feelings towards companies' use of water are going to exacerbate. The likelihood that water supplies for a company's operation are going to be capped is high. Moreover, reputational risks may lead to brand damage.
- *Social, political and institutional context*: Community plays a central role in water issues. A limited availability increases the likelihood that industrial presence in an area will contribute to this lack of access, in reality or as a perception. Although restrained access to water may be caused by a lack of political will or capacity related to water structure management, communities that have little water supply will hold a grudge against companies' availability, therefore, leading to reputational damage or opposition.

Source: Adapted from Schulte et al. (2012).

direct control over a supplier, even though there are ways to influence such practices. Table 1 shows internal and external factors that influence water risks.

CORPORATE WATER MANAGEMENT

For companies seeking to improve their sustainability efforts, effective use and management of water resources are becoming increasingly important. There is a growing awareness among companies that developing more coordinated and forward-looking water management strategies can enhance business value: 'Corporate water management is a complex, iterative process that requires companies to assess and reassess the water situation, evaluate and revaluate their impact, and determine the best course of action on a continual basis' (WBCSD, 2012, p.6).

Because water gives rise to a complex set of issues, and the responses by companies are necessarily just as complex, there is no one-size-fits-all approach. A widely accepted water management scheme must deal, in its iterative process, with four broad categories: measurement, management, engagement and disclosure.

Measurement

A common business saying is: 'you can't manage what you can't measure'. The application of measurement practices means adopting a particular lens for understanding policies, activities and outcomes (Chalmers et al., 2012b). Therefore, the first step in water management is measurement. Initially a company must measure the water performance of its various facilities and products. This process includes an assessment of water use, water reuse efficiency, volume and quality of wastewater discharge throughout the value chain, including suppliers and direct operations. Once a companies' water use and needs have been analysed, a company should assess how its water use affects the broader ecosystem. A successful impact assessment provides companies with the data and information to prioritise management practices and mitigate the impacts deemed most important. Data gathering should also be exercised on key suppliers for those companies that have water-intensive operations or that rely on water-intensive raw materials.

Management

Having a strong water management means having an all-round social responsibility awareness throughout the entire company. Robust governance begins in the boardroom with oversight and commitment and ends on the factory floor with consciousness and responsibility. For companies with significant water risk, water should be a priority issue; instead, according to the Ceres report (2010), executives underestimated this aspect. There should be a clear assessment of the goals and clear lines of responsibility between the committee and responsible site-level personnel. Moreover, different stakeholders, in particular investors, ask for remuneration systems linked to long-term targets and integrated social and environmental performances (EUROSIF, 2010; UNPRI, 2012).

Another aspect of management is ensuring that a company discloses its public policy agenda with respect to water. Setting performance standards and goals helps companies to raise awareness of water in addition to giving a better view of the performance trend over the years. Recognising the importance of water and stating publicly the company's policy on water usage, goals and performance are a first critical step towards more sound water management (Barton & Adrio, 2011).

Engagement

As water is a public good everyone shares its usage, risk, right and responsibility. There is a complex mix of political, social (also religious) and environmental values involved, and stakeholder management is vital to face these issues. Engaging with stakeholders can, in fact, be a powerful way of understanding key water-related issues from a different perspective, and therefore develop new strategies and solutions to water challenges. There must, however, be the will from the executive board not only to dialogue with stakeholders but to respond actively to their concerns and find, where possible, a common ground.

Operational and Employee Engagement

In order for a company to deal with long-term water-related business risks, it must develop a company-wide policy or strategy for water management. There is a series of tools that a company can implement to achieve corporate commitment: setting benchmarks for water management practices, wastewater discharge goals and facilitating specific water use are just some examples of such policies.

A successful example of employees' engagement to reduce water use and impacts is the programme promoted by Gerber Products Company, a producer of baby foods, a business unit of Novartis Consumer Health, Inc. (see Box 1).

Supply Chain Engagement

The impact of supply chains constitutes a large part of a company's water footprint. Water risks are often hidden in companies' raw materials inputs or intermediate suppliers. As reported by SABMiller, 98% of its water use for beer production in South Africa involves agricultural production, over which it does not have complete control (SABMiller et al., 2009).

In the CEO Water Mandate Survey (Morrison & Schulte, 2009) four criteria are listed that a company should meet to assess reporting on its supply chain: (1) assess prospective or current suppliers on environmental performance; (2) engage suppliers on matters of water impact and management; (3) follow specific policies for water-scarce regions; (4) measure supplier water performance. A key finding in the CEO Water Mandate Survey was that 80 companies (73% of the respondents) met at least one supply chain and watershed management criterion; however, only 2 companies (SABMiller and Unilever) met all four. The average aggregated company score was 0.96 (out of 4).

The assessment of water use from a large number of suppliers across different geographies is highly complex. Even just obtaining reliable information may be a challenge (Irbaris, 2009).

Community Engagement

To avoid reputational business risks and to obtain legitimacy to operate, companies have to engage with local communities. It is a difficult process because it largely depends on contextual factors. A company must describe local-, basin-, or national-level activities and advance goals based on one or more water challenges (CEO Water Mandate, 2012a). Furthermore, results and progress may be difficult to communicate given the 'broad concepts and intangible issues such as improving water governance capacity or alleviating water shortages' (CEO Water Mandate, 2012a, p.75). However, according to Schulte et al. (2012), facilitating access to water can often improve brand reputation and facilitate engagement with local communities, given the fact that, especially in the global South, local governments often have less capacity and funds to provide consistent access to water

Box 1. Engaging Employees to Reduce Water Use and Impacts: The Case of Gerber Products Company.

'Gerber Products Company, a producer of baby foods, discovered that employee education and involvement related to water management at its Fremont, Michigan plant can yield significant returns. Gerber is a business unit of Novartis Consumer Health, Inc. In January 2000, the plant's Water Team kicked off a year-long effort to cut water consumption. By year's end, they had saved 67.5 million gallons of water compared to 1999.

The Water Team worked with all areas of the plant to survey water use, collect water conservation suggestions from employees, and identify specific opportunities. Numerous projects emerged from the plant's water conservation initiatives, including:

- Installation of new equipment that uses 30% less water to cool jars of hot baby food;
- Recycling of wastewater to wash down the plant's floors, gutters, and drains;
- Recycling of wastewater to irrigate corn, oats, and alfalfa grown for animal feed on a 420-acre farm owned by Gerber four miles down the road.

Gerber health, safety and environment personnel found that employee education was key to the plant's success, making wise water use a habit. The Water Team produced a video to increase employees' awareness of water issues and plant water use. Among other topics, the video encourages employees to routinely check for leaks and drips to reduce wasted water. Employee involvement with Water Team activities, combined with the video and other awareness raising efforts, has helped to change employees' water management behaviors while enlisting them in company efforts to continually improve the plant's water-related performance'.

(Copyright GEMI's *Connecting the Drops Toward Creative Water Strategies: A Water Sustainability Tool.* Case study 'Novartis: Engaging Employees to Reduce Water Use and Impacts'. Global Environmental Management Initiative (GEMI). 2002. www.gemi.org/water/novartis.htm, accessed on 6 June 2013).

services. In the CEO Water Mandate Survey (Morrison & Schulte, 2009), when assessing the level of engagement of companies, two criteria were selected: (1) corporate action on water at the community level – that is, undertaking philanthropic projects that address community issues with regard to water, for example watershed restoration and (2) local water infrastructure development – report on any development project at community level regarding water infrastructure, such as water wells and water treatment plants.

Key findings in the report survey were that, 38 companies (35%) met at least one of the two Community Engagement criteria; only 6 companies conformed to both. The average aggregated score was 0.40 (out of a possible 2) and no companies were found to include local communities in decision-making relating to corporate-level water-related projects.

Public Policy Engagement

As stated in Schulte et al. (2012, p. 38), 'corporate engagement with public policy has often been understood as a direct policy advocacy and lobbying. However, engagement can be understood more broadly as initiatives that involve interaction with government entities, local communities, and/or civil society organisations with the goal of advancing two objectives: the responsible internal company management of water resources within direct operations and supply chains in line with policy imperatives, and the sustainable and equitable management of the catchment in which companies operate'.

In order to pull a company's action together under a common water strategy, there should be a unifying water policy. That is achieved by explaining how policies address the company's specific water-related risks and impacts, specifying in which regions water management activities are focused, supporting research, advocacy and monitoring, contributing to the development of effective and equitable policy and regulations – in short, working to align the company's objectives with the needs of local communities and stakeholders.

Participation in Global Initiatives and Partnerships

In order to have a better understanding of specific water challenges and find shared solutions, many companies decide to engage in water-related initiatives. Examples of water initiatives include UN CEO Water Mandate, the World Economic Forum's 2030 Water Resource Group, the World Business Council for Sustainable Development, the World Footprint Network and GEMI (see Appendix A). Adhering to one or more of these movements means explicating a commitment to that group's programme.

A company that participates demonstrates action and willingness in relation to water issues.

Another way to engage in water risks is through the creation of partnerships. Direct involvement with NGOs, intergovernmental agencies, universities and so on enhances a company's credibility, broadens its perspective on the matter and leads to shared solutions in addition to augmenting the pool of resources that are invested in water-related initiatives. Through a company's perspective partnerships can really build, or rebuild, credibility and change the stakeholders' perception of the company's commitment towards water issues. That said, Schulte et al. (2012) report that partnerships comprised solely of private-sector entities or that created to inhibit rather than boost transparency and sustainability are surely less credible than those with a variety of public entities and NGOs.

Most of the time, the final goal of a partnership is similar to that of engaging with stakeholders and local communities. It just works in another way. Instead of addressing direct issues, partnerships can be an indirect way for a company to work on a certain matter. Namely, funding an NGO programme or offering know-how, technologies and visibility to a small initiative can be a way for a company to reach on-the-ground results despite not engaging directly in the problem (Schulte et al., 2012).

A recent study of the World Business Council for Sustainable Development, Water for Business (WBCSD, 2012), lists as many as 18 water initiatives. As there is no such thing as the perfect tool, companies should evaluate what suits them best. The water initiatives are listed on the basis of the sponsoring organisation, the level of application (whether at site, corporate or product, process or organisation level), the activity they are focused on, that is, which of the stages of corporate water management the tools address, the geographic focus (global or regional), the primary corporate users (corporate communication, corporate finance, operations, sales and marketing, and so on), and lastly it discloses whether the tool is in use or under development.

In Appendix A, a brief description of widely used measurement and/or accounting water initiatives or tools is proposed (see also ACCA, 2010; CEO Water Mandate, 2012b; Chalmers et al., 2012b; ICCR, 2012; Morrison, Schulte, & Schenck, 2009b).

Disclosure

The final step of corporate water management consists of disclosing all the information in a concise and transparent way.

Corporate water disclosure is 'the act of collecting data on the current state of a company's water management, assessing the implications of this information for the business, developing a strategic response, and ultimately reporting this information to stakeholders (investors, NGOs, consumers, communities, suppliers, employees, and others)' (CEO Water Mandate, 2012a, p. 9).

As underlined above, disclosure improves the ability of stakeholders to evaluate a company's sustainability, and thus fosters greater corporate accountability and increases stakeholders' trust, confidence and goodwill. Water disclosure practice can also support business on the inside; for example, the CEO Water Mandate (2012a) states that companies that report their water uses and impacts improve their knowledge of water challenges and the effectiveness of their responses. In addition to that, it provides an opportunity to keep track of progress over the years, which can also be disclosed to improve the company's reputation and build investors' confidence. Furthermore, it establishes a dialogue with stakeholders, introducing the way towards shared water-related goals. However, reports need to answer the need for transparency. According to the transparency framework outlined in Morrison and Schulte (2009) there are three main transparency principles:

- *The Determination of Materiality*: that is the threshold that delimits the information considered to be relevant and that which is not. As it would be impossible to include all the information, companies need to determine which issues interest the public and to which extent. Assessing materiality proves to be useful also for determining the issues that pose the greatest business risks, as well as opportunities, and as such are valued by the investment community.
- *Stakeholder Inclusiveness*: determining which material water issues to include and deciding which information to report is a key decision in meeting different stakeholders' concerns. A first step is to assess who the company's stakeholders are and then decide which information to disclose in order to meet their needs. Therefore, it follows that the content of the report should be established according to stakeholder's needs (Morrison & Schulte, 2009).
- *Harmonisation and Convergence*: To ensure an increasing comparability among social reports, companies should use broadly accepted terminology and indicators/metrics. Unfortunately, at this time, according to the CEO report (Morrison & Schulte, 2009) there is no single standardised approach to corporate water accounting or reporting.

Although corporate reporting is, nowadays, becoming a baseline expectation of global companies and despite the urgency of good water management, according to recent studies (ACCA, 2010; Barton, 2010; CIMA, 2011; Egan & Frost, 2010; Irbaris, 2009; Morrison & Schulte, 2009), the majority of leading companies in water-intensive sectors still have weak management and disclosure of water-related risks and opportunities. The report issued by Ceres (2010), for example, evaluated the quality, depth and clarity of water risk disclosure of 100 companies over the fiscal year 2008 and ranked their water disclosure practice. The sectors classified as water intensive were beverages, chemicals, electricity, food, building, mining, oil and gas and semiconductors. Scores were given for five categories: water accounting, risk assessment, direct operations, supply chain and stakeholder engagement.

Results showed that corporate-wide data on direct water use was disclosed by 63% but only a few companies provided local-level data (14%). Because water risk is geographically dependent, this is a major shortfall in the reports, that does not allow a correct assessment of risk. Even though most companies have environmental policies on direct operations, only 15% disclosed goals to reduce wastewater discharge, and only 24% detailed having water-specific policies, standards or management systems. Regarding the supply chain no company provided comprehensive data on its suppliers' water performance. For sectors where a significant portion of the corporate water footprint is found in the supply chain, there was little information or discussion about relationships with suppliers to manage water risk.

As a whole, the Ceres report (2010) underlined the fact that even the disclosure and water management of companies working in water intensive sectors are still weak. Nonetheless, there are signs of increasing attention: the response to the Deloitte Water Disclosure's second annual questionnaire, for example, increased from 50% in 2010 to 60% in 2011 (Deloitte, 2012). That denotes increased awareness of water-related risks and the ability to provide water-related usage data.[9]

However, according to a recent Ceres study (2012) of corporate reporting on water risk, the majority of companies surveyed recognise some level of exposure to water risks. Disclosure of water-related risks and opportunities, since 2009, has increased, but much reporting still remains weak and inconsistent, especially with regard to data on overall water use, financial exposure and potential supply chain risk.

The greatest change over 3 years was the percentage of companies disclosing water-related physical risk. According to Ceres (2012), although there has been an improvement in the overall disclosure, data on company water use and the financial impacts of water-related risks remain infrequent in financial filings. This was also a key finding in the Ceres 2010 report: on a scale from 0 to 100 of the reliability of companies' water disclosure, no single company scored more than 43 points.

Similar results were found in a report of the Pacific Institute (Morrison & Schulte, 2009) which outlined that of the 110 companies studied (most of them signatories of the CEO Water Mandate) only 62% displayed conformity with one of three criteria: (1) describing a systemic materiality assessment process, (2) stakeholder engagement, and (3) using both GRI and AA1000 principles in their reports. Less than half (47%) utilised any form of stakeholder engagement, thereby effectively excluding local users of water resources (Sethi & Schepers, 2013). While companies were quite interested and able to measure their own water use, 'relatively few of them provided information on regional or local water use or any contextual information in which their water uses and/or impacts could be understood' (Morrison & Schulte, 2009, p. 7 quoted in Sethi & Schepers, 2013).

Similarly, the Association of Chartered Certified Accountants (ACCA, 2010) shows that, even with significant variation in performances, the overall scores of the 32 Australian companies included in their study on water reporting quality ranged from 56% to less than 10% with an average score of just 28%. While current disclosure practices continue to consist largely of qualitative and descriptive statements (ACCA, 2010; Egan & Frost, 2010), there is also responsiveness to calls for increased detail and for some indications of the ratios of water used per unit of production (Egan & Frost, 2010).

The results of this research demonstrate that there is significant progress still to be made on disclosing water-related data in a more uniform and comparable manner.

The Challenges in Water Disclosure

The main challenges in water disclosure, as identified also by CDP Water initiatives, are the following (quoted in ACCA, 2010, p. 9):

- *Ability to measure*: There is no universally accepted method for calculating the impact of water use by businesses.
- *Local/regional issues*: The impact of using one megalitre of water will vary for different geographical and climatic regions. Moreover, 'many factors need to be considered, including the water source; availability of water within the catchment; urban or rural infrastructure support and pricing; the volume and quality of water returned; and its impact on the surrounding environment, such as groundwater; and alternative beneficial uses'.

- *Water in the supply chain*: Companies need to consider the water use along their supply chain 'where there can be substantially larger, compounding impacts than from their own facilities. Supply chain considerations include both upstream issues with suppliers and downstream issues in terms of the water used when consumers use their products and services'.
- *Globally accepted standard*: At the moment, there is no universally accepted standard for measuring water use and its impact. This is due, in part, to complexities in 'collecting and disseminating meaningful water-related data and measuring the impact on surrounding environments'.

TOWARDS A SHARED WATER ACCOUNTABILITY

As emphasised in the introduction, the concept of accountability is strictly linked to a sense of responsibility: a subject will be held accountable for what he has (or has not) done to observe existing rules (legal, moral, quasi-legal, etc.) (the so-called 'responsibility for action' – see Gray et al., 1996). Furthermore, the nature and extension of accountability are strongly grounded on the 'vision' of corporate social responsibility (CSR) that is undertaken.

Following Garriga and Melè's classification of CSR theories, we have four main ways of interpreting the interaction between business and society: (1) *instrumental*, through which the corporation is seen as an instrument for the creation of wealth, and its social activities are only a means to achieve economic results; (2) *political*, focused on the power of corporations in society and the responsible use of this power in the political arena; (3) *integrative*, linked with the capability to satisfy social demands and to integrate them into the main company's purposes; and (4) *ethical*, based on values and ethical responsibilities of corporations to society (Garriga & Melé, 2004).

The authors outline how these four approaches have to be understood as four interconnected dimensions present in every social phenomenon. This is the case for water issues.

In the preceding paragraphs, we have highlighted the need for a water management and reporting system strongly focused on the recognition of water as a universal human right. Consequently, there is a strong *ethical*-based duty springing from the human rights and use of natural resources approaches that is strongly linked to the concept of sustainable development.

There could also be an 'instrumental' motivation for facing water issues: the previous discussion shows how a correct water management reduces the risks and, therefore, improves corporate economic, environmental and social performance. The importance given to stakeholders' engagement on the corporate water management model presented suggests the need to *integrate* different stakeholders' demands and expectations into the process of water management and reporting. Furthermore, all these considerations have also to be contextualised within the public nature of water and, as a consequence, on the public interests converging on it. A compelling accountability should contribute towards maintaining (or increasing) credibility and legitimacy and lead to a consequent stronger license to operate within a specific community (*political dimension*).

The duty of accountability is, as a result, grounded on different bases from which different instruments of accounting and reporting should arise. As underlined by Buhr (2007), reporting is driven by whoever the corporation thinks it is accountable to and what it is accountable for. Companies have to deal with and choose from a wide range of documents and tools that serve the needs of accountability, which comes as a response to the many pressures and expectations on companies from a wide array of stakeholders. Through reporting, corporations contribute towards shaping new public expectations and debate that, in turn, create a need for the disclosure of new information and, in the last instance, lead to the shaping of new laws (Buhr, 2007).

Even if the author believes that reporting alone is not the only way to 'save the planet', 'the very act of providing accounts has the potential to change behaviour. The process of reporting should serve to change management strategies and information systems and, in turn, lead to changes in management philosophies and practices' (Buhr, 2007, p. 67). Furthermore, Gray et al. (1996) suggest that accountability is a tool for a better informed and more just democracy. Accountability is an emancipatory and evolutionary process in which access to and control over information is an important way to build and rebalance power relationships (Gray et al., 1996). Bebbington (1997, p. 365) advocates environmental accounting as an 'enabling, empowering and emancipatory form of accounting in that it provides both a critique of existing practice and develops alternative accounting practices' (see also Bebbington & Gray, 2001).

Water use and water-related risks are shared among different parties: governments, businesses, communities, the environment, etc., all of which share a responsibility (the title of the second UN World Water Development Report is emblematic: *Water, a Shared Responsibility* WWAP, 2006). Although corporate (or organisational) reporting is essential to answer a duty of accountability, in the case of water it is insufficient: 'though information *about* corporate water use is critical, information *at the level of the corporation* is much less important' (Hazelton, 2013, p. 284).

Accountability should, therefore, be an ongoing process involving different parties. As emphasised by Hazelton (2013, p. 281), Dubreuil highlights that accountability and information are central to the realisation of the 'rights of users' and this includes 'access to information, consultation, participation' and the need to 'encourage information for and participation of users' (Dubreuil, 2006, p. 11).

These considerations also confirm the general statement of the Global Compact CEO Water Mandate, that is 'facilitating equitable processes through which all the affected parties can come together to mitigate these shared risks or pursue improvement opportunities is a powerful tool for combating this century's mounting water challenges' (CEO Water Mandate, 2012b, p. 1).

The recent initiatives labelled as 'Collective Action' and promoted by different bodies (CEO Water Mandate, 2012b; Deloitte, 2012) also move in this direction. Collective action leads to a strong sense of shared interests, shared responsibility and shared benefits. In particular, the Global Compact CEO Water Mandate promotes Integrated Water Resources Management (IWRM) as a 'widely accepted paradigm for balancing water demands with available supplies'. In this project, a considerable emphasis is placed on the 'equitable engagement' of all parties involved in water access, use and management (CEO Water Mandate, 2012b, p. 7). IWRM entails establishing a clear commitment to common purposes, to share interests and responsibilities, and to include an accountability structure to support implementation. This means identifying ways, rules and tools for making actual collective actions and building an effective shared accountability.

A promising experience in this sense is the development of the Australian GPWA to which the next section is dedicated.

GENERAL PURPOSE WATER ACCOUNTING (GPWA)

There is a general awareness that high-quality, credible and comparable information is of crucial importance to enable sound decision-making regarding water issues. This was also a key assumption in Australian water accounting developments (Chalmers et al., 2012a; Chalmers et al., 2012b).

In Australia, government commitment to water accounting (and later to the water accounting standard-setting process) has been considered necessary because of the awareness of the critical importance of the resource during a period of water scarcity. In particular, there has been a crisis over the public's and the government's confidence in the quality and consistency of information provided by different states and territories (Connell, Dovers, & Grafton, 2005; Fisher, 2007; Gardner & Bowmer, 2007, all quoted in Chalmers et al., 2012a) and public concern over the environment and the integrity of water management by various jurisdictions. The Council of Australian Governments (COAG) identified the need for consistent water resource accounting that could be standardised, compared, reconciled and aggregated. This has led to a series of reforms and developments, starting with an intergovernmental agreement on the National Water Initiative (NWI) signed at the COAG meeting in 2004 (Chalmers et al., 2012a). As supported by McKay and Marsden (2009, quoted in Chalmers et al., 2012a) it was the increasingly unsustainable exploitation of water in Australia that led to institutional and legal reforms.

With NWI 'the Parties' agreed that 'the outcome of water resource accounting is to ensure that adequate measurement, monitoring and reporting systems are in place in all jurisdictions, to support public and investor confidence in the amount of water being traded, extracted for consumptive use, and recovered and managed for environmental and other public benefit outcomes' (NWI, 2004, paragraph 80; NWC, 2010).

In 2007, the Commonwealth *Water Act* (2007) reaffirmed the national importance of water information and identified new functions for the Bureau of Meteorology in water accounting, including issuing national water information standards. In April 2009, the Water Accounting Standards Board (WASB) was established as an independent advisory board of the Bureau of Meteorology to oversee and coordinate water accounting standards development. In May 2009, the WASB issued the *Water Accounting Conceptual Framework for the Preparation and Presentation of General Purpose Water Accounting Reports* (WACF) and, in May 2012, the first *Australian Water Accounting Standard 1 – Preparation and Presentation of General Purpose Water Accounting Reports* (AWAS1).

The WACF requires that General Purpose Water Accounting Reports (GPWAR) must be audited or reviewed, but does not establish the framework for assurance commitments (Ernst & Young, 2012). Accordingly, the Auditing and Assurance Standards Board (AUASB) and the WASB agreed to work together to develop an assurance standard. In 2012, after receiving feedback from a range of stakeholders on the consultation paper, the AUASB and WASB released the *Proposed Standard on Assurance Engagements ASAE 3xxx Australian Water Accounting Standard 2: Assurance Engagements on General Purpose Water Accounting Reports* (AWAS2)[10] (http://www.bom.gov.au/water/standards/wasb/gpwareports.shtml, accessed 23 April 2013; for an overview of the chronology of Australia's water accounting developments, see Chalmers et al., 2012a; Tello Melendez & Hazelton, 2010; Tello Melendez et al., 2012; WASB & Bureau of Meteorology, 2012).

The way chosen by the Australian government was, therefore, a Standardised Water Accounting (SWA), i.e. a 'consistent and structured approach to identifying, measuring, recording and reporting information about water' (SKM, 2006, p. 2). SWA was developed to ensure comparability of water accounting reports over time and between different report entities to improve decision-making and stakeholder confidence.

A considerable aspect is that Australian SWA is a geographically focused set of reporting requirements as opposed to an organisationally focused one. Two key documents of SWA are the *Statement of Net Water Assets* and the *Statement of Changes in Net Water Assets*. The Australian government – Bureau of Meteorology's website (http://www.bom.gov.au/water/nwa/2011/) contains a set of water accounting reports for eight nationally significant water management regions; one of them is proposed also in Appendix B.

Prior to the release of AWAS1, it was important to evaluate the costs and benefits of adopting these standards to both preparers and users. A report, *Effects Analysis of AWAS Adoption*, was prepared by Deloitte Access Economics (2012) to estimate the costs of adopting AWAS1 and to identify benefits for users and preparers.

Understanding what types of benefits would be provided for each group was and is still important because of the voluntary nature of the standard. Report preparers are likely to choose to develop GPWAR for those water entities where the perceived benefits are at least equivalent to the costs. The real benefit generated by developing GPWAR, however, will, in part, be dependent on the popularity they achieve (Deloitte Access Economics, 2012; WASB & Bureau of Meteorology, 2012).

Costs and benefits – and the emphasis placed on them by report preparers – will vary depending on the type of organisation. The report identifies four main cost and three main benefit categories. The costs include education and training, purchasing of equipment, publication and documentation, and cost of assurance, while the benefit categories include reduced reporting, informed decision-making and stewardship of a publicly owned natural resource.[11] We would like to draw particular attention to this last point.

The report highlights how state and territory governments may place greater emphasis on demonstrating stewardship of a publicly owned natural resource. Transparency in reporting the management of a public resource is essential, and not only for governments.

As stated in the WASB and Bureau of Meteorology report (2012, p. 4), General Purpose Water Accounting Reports 'may improve public understanding of water resource planning and provide greater knowledge and confidence regarding water resource management, thus leading to improved community dialogue'. The availability of information prepared in a consistent and comparable way is likely to lead to greater public understanding of water resource planning and managing (WASB & Bureau of Meteorology, 2012).

Following the definition given by the WASB, a broad, public and ethical-based approach (based on rights and obligation) to water usage and accounting has been adopted. WASB, in fact, defines water accounting as 'a systematic process of identifying, recognising, quantifying, reporting, and assuring information about water, the rights and other claims to that water, and the obligations against that water' (WASB, 2009).

In developing GPWA, the Board has drawn from financial accounting concepts, principles and practices (see www.bom.gov.au/water/standards, accessed 24 April 2013) and has applied financial accounting methods of recording and reporting information to non-financial content (Chalmers et al., 2012a, p. 1002).[12]

Of considerable relevance, for the purpose of this chapter, is the 'general purpose' given to the water accounting reports. GPWA is 'designed to report information about water and rights to water to external parties who are otherwise unable to command that information from an entity, but who could be expected to need the information to make decisions about the allocation of resources' (WASB, 2010 quoted in Chalmers et al., 2012a, p. 1003).

The shift from a 'local' to a 'global and public' view of the problem was of fundamental importance:

> Public interest and public unrest gave rise to government intervention [...]. The first phase of the reform of water accounting institutional arrangements took responsibility for water accounting away from the individual vested State and Territory jurisdictional interests and gave it to a specially-established body that worked closely with staff

> responsible for Australia's largest river system and basin, the Murray-Darling Basin Authority. This was possibly the best initial publicly and politically acceptable way to facilitate a public interest approach to setting water accounting standards. The acceptability came from two sources. The first is removal of the responsibility from individual jurisdictions that previously had been unable to develop a national, systematic and consistent approach to reporting water information of interest to policy makers, federal government, interest groups and the public. This constituted the market failure crisis that gave rise to calls for regulation in the public interest. (Chalmers et al., 2012a, p. 1011).

Therefore, the lack of capability to be accountable to different stakeholders and the public nature of the water rights and obligations stimulate a general purpose approach. As underlined by Chalmers et al. (2012a, p. 1017), '[w]hile other systems labelled 'water accounting' exist, none matches the general purpose approach of the Australian system' (for a comparison of different types of water accounting see also Chalmers et al., 2012b and Hazelton, Cummings, Leung, & Wang, 2011).

GPWA seems, therefore, to have the potential to respond to the duty of accountability as stated in the previous paragraph. The general purpose approach should favour not only an inter-government but also a multi-stakeholder participation.

Although WAS in general, and GPWA in particular, were devised essentially for governments, their application should be extended to other water users. The focus, indeed, has been moved from a single legal entity to a geographical entity where different users are involved. Besides governments and policymakers, also water industry, water and more traditional financial accountants and advisors and other interest groups could enjoy the opportunity to have a high-quality, credible and comparable source of information. Furthermore, sharing the use also means sharing the responsibility and the relevant duty of accountability.[13]

It is important to note that this public approach does not conflict with the private one.[14] As Chalmers et al. (2012a, p. 1013) underline, for example, one benefit that has been prefigured is the 'rationalization of water reporting requirements in a similar fashion to a company producing one set of accounts using IFRS rather than multiple sets of accounts for listings in different countries that have different accounting standards and reporting requirements'. Moreover, '[h]aving to provide only one report each reporting period will provide relief to those report preparers who previously were required to produce multiple reports to satisfy an array of regulatory reporting responsibilities'.

In order to reduce the 'reporting burden', the various existing water reporting obligations and requirements must converge (Hazelton et al., 2011, p. 37).

Another criticism that could influence the adoption and diffusion of SWA is the different business structure of water organisations (companies, governments, NGOs, etc.). This diversity might determine different reactions under certain circumstances (Sofocleous, 2010). As this author suggests, water accounting standards should 'differentiate information requested from different business structure (government/non-government) users' (Sofocleous, 2010, p. 300). The idea proposed in this chapter is that this diversity should at the end converge on a shared process towards a common accountability. In this case, single organisational reports drawn up with a standardised language and approach would be a communal and useful basis for common and shared reporting.

The value of SWA will be determined by how useful this kind of report is to stakeholders (Hazelton et al., 2011). On this matter, Tello Melendez et al. (2012) conclude that even though there is a general agreement on the usefulness of SWA for potential users, there is also a need for more awareness of its benefits. At this stage of development their study suggests that accountability of water managers is unlikely to be fully realised by GPWAR.

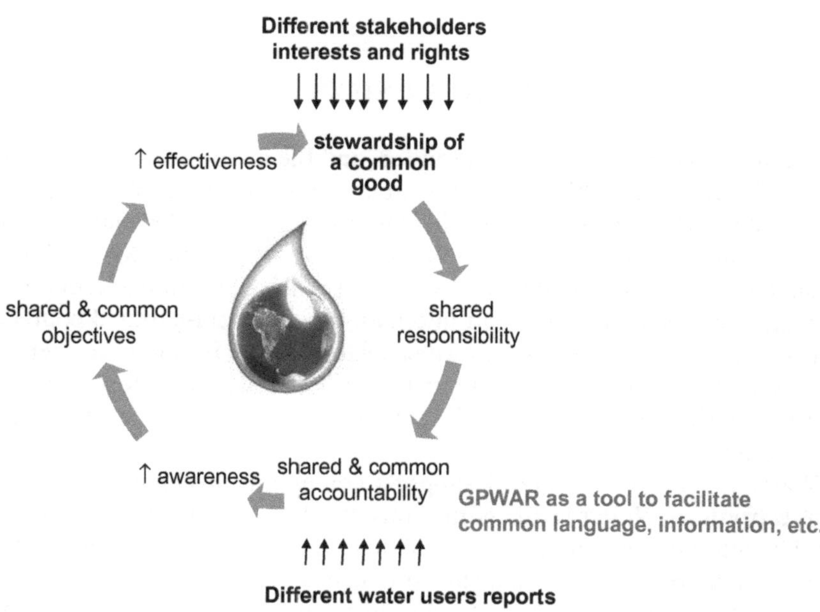

Fig. 1. Accountability Circle.

A shift from a single entity to a more collective (or public) point of view still has to be achieved. The awareness and active role of all the parties involved (governments, policymakers, water industries, water and financial accountants and other interest groups) in water usage and management will, therefore, be crucial.

Moreover, the participation of different stakeholders might also direct the predominantly historic information requirement towards 'more forward-looking, speculative disclosures' (Hazelton et al., 2011, p. 37) generating a virtuous circle illustrated in Fig. 1.

Notwithstanding the support for the development of a general purpose approach, much work has been and will have to be centred on implementation issues – including 'the development and a shared understanding of definitions and concepts to enable the asserted objectives of the framework to be achieved' (Chalmers et al., 2012b, p. 248). This is the main challenge also for an international and multi-stakeholder development (Chalmers et al., 2012a).

There is no experience in global water accounting standard setting or collaboration and this could be a limit but also an advantage. The absence of an extensive, deep-rooted culture might facilitate the adoption of a single, international approach to water accounting standard setting.

CONCLUSION

This chapter has pointed out the need for, and the importance of, transparent, high-quality, credible and comparable water disclosure. We have presented some considerations about the important role of water management and accounting mainly from a businesslike point of view. As Chalmers et al. (2012b, p. 282) highlight, 'water crises have generated economic, social and political hardship, and international and intra-national conflict. The world is seeking solutions to water-related issues. In doing so, there is increasing recognition of the potential for water accounting to contribute to the solution by providing relevant and faithfully represented water information'.

Water is required for life: it supports community livelihoods and sustains ecosystems. Water is, therefore, considered a public good and involves a public interest and, consequently, public responsibility for its usage, management and protection. Following this line of reasoning, we also draw attention to the need for accountability to be 'public' or at least shared by different stakeholders (government – at national and international levels, water industries, communities, environmentalists, NGOs, etc.).

Company efforts are commonly focused on internal and self-referred operations. The different and conflicting uses that may be made of water and the fact that water is geographically and temporally sensitive necessitate a search for more flexible and more extended forms of accountability. The reasons for this are *ethical*, *political* but also *instrumental*. In fact, even if a company optimises its own water use and minimises its impacts on others, the presence of challenges in the watersheds it uses can place conflicts or pressures on its own license to operate. This aspect opens the need and the opportunity to switch focus from a single/private perspective to a more general/public one.

In a recent study conducted by Deloitte for CDP (for the CDP Global Water Report 2012, see Deloitte, 2012) it is demonstrated that even if companies traditionally work independently to tackle water-related issues, 74% of respondents report taking some form of collective action.

Integrated Water Resources Management has emerged as a paradigm for balancing water demands and risks (CEO Water Mandate, 2012b). In this process, the definition and pursuit of common objectives, the alignment of interests and resources and the sharing of responsibilities are essential. To disclose and share information about water use and management is the first step. To be accountable also means being responsible and showing how this responsibility has been answered. An effective Integrated Water Management also implies shared accountability in the ways that better suit the specific contexts and situations.

A concrete way of seizing this opportunity is the development of the GPWA standard setting recently issued by accounting and water industry experts under the impulse of the Australian government. This is still an ongoing process but, for that very reason, it could lead to a promising improvement of a shared and public water accountability.

SWA is, in fact, a significant step forward for water accounting and reporting (in Australia but also all other the world) as it allows a standardisation of terminology, information content and presentation (on this point see also Hazelton et al., 2011). SWA could be considered a new form of *accounting* as referred to by Bebbington and Gray (2001), but to be a new form of *accountability* it also needs a shared sense of responsibility and the willingness to change behaviour in the search for better solutions to protect and preserve this common good. To seize this chance, the continual balancing of different interests (and power) is crucial; the commitment and active participation of all the different parties (governments, communities, companies, etc.) are essential.

NOTES

1. There are also more stringent definitions that conceive accountability as being pertinent to contractual arrangements only, asserting that if there is no legal bond, there can be no accountability (Tricker, 1983).

2. In this chapter, we refer to 'social accounting' or 'social reporting' including practices of environmental accounting or reporting.

3. We would like to thank one of the anonymous referees for this observation. On this point see also Hazelton (2013).

4. We can refer to 'green', 'blue' and 'grey' water use. Blue water is freshwater from surface or groundwater, green water is water from rainwater stored in the soil as soil moisture and grey water is polluted water associated with production. There are considerable differences on the impact of using water from different sources. For example, using water from recent rainfall is different from withdrawing water stored in an aquifer for millennia (Irbaris, 2009, pp. 2, 9).

5. CERES is a coalition of more than 130 member organisations with the purpose of mobilising investor and business leadership to build a thriving, sustainable global economy. These members include environmental and social nonprofit groups, institutional investors, public pension funds, socially responsible investors (SRIs), labour unions and other key stakeholders. Further information is available at www.ceres.org, accessed on April 7 2013.

6. We would like to thank the anonymous referee for this consideration.

7. An interesting essay on regulatory theories is Chalmers et al. (2012a).

8. Irbaris (2009, p. 5) suggests that 'regulation may relate to pricing, use or efficiency, pollution, withdrawal rights, reuse or recycling, process or product standards or licenses to operate'.

9. A sign of how awareness of water risks among companies is growing is the fact that 59% (113) of the respondents report that water-related risks have the potential to cause significant business impacts and 38% (73) have experienced water-related business impacts within the last 5 years (Deloitte, 2011).

10. The AUASB and WASB have invited comments on the Exposure Draft by 15 March 2013. It is intended that this proposed standard be operative for reporting periods commencing on or after 1 January 2014. (AWAS2).

11. Another important benefit mentioned in the report, in particular for companies, is the possibility to improve investor confidence and managing reputational risk leading, as a consequence, to a lower cost of capital, higher sales or reduced compliance expenditure.

12. The proposed SWA model includes, among other things, developing a conceptual framework to underpin the standard-setting process, preparing General Purpose Water Accounting Reports (GPWAR), the use of accrual basis of accounting, and the use of double-entry bookkeeping to ensure the reliability of reporting (Tello Melendez & Hazelton, 2010).

13. On the idea of a shared accountability for public services see Signori (2012).

14. The awareness and choice to follow a shared approach to water accountability could also help to overcome the risk of regulatory capture, that is the possibility for private interests to dominate public ones (a very interesting analysis of this point and of the regulatory theories on water accounting is presented in Chalmers et al., 2012a).

On public and private interests in relation to accounting see also Malsch (2013).

ACKNOWLEDGEMENTS

We are very grateful to the two anonymous referees for their very useful comments. Their suggestions have enabled us to improve the quality of the chapter.

NOMENCLATURE

AA1000	AccountAbility 1000
ACCA	Association of Chartered Certified Accountants
AUASB	Auditing and Assurance Standards Board
AWAS	Australian Water Accounting Standard
CDP	Carbon Disclosure Project
CIMA	Chartered Institute of Management Accountants
COAG	Council of Australian Governments
CSR	Corporate social responsibility
EIRIS	Ethical Investment Research Services
EPA	US Environmental Protection Agency
EUROSIF	European Social Investments Forum
GPWA	General Purpose Water Accounting
GPWAR	General Purpose Water Accounting Reports
GRI	Global Reporting Initiative
ICCR	Interfaith Center on Corporate Responsibility
IIRC	International Integrated Reporting Committee
IWRM	Integrated Water Resources Management
NGOs	Non-governmental organisations

NWC	Australian Government National Water Commission
NWI	National Water Initiative
SEC	US Securities and Exchange Commission
SWA	Standardised water accounting
UN	United Nations
UNCESCR	United Nations Committee on Economic Social and Cultural Rights
UNESCO	United Nations Educational, Scientific and Cultural Organization
UNPRI	United Nations Principles for Responsible Investments
WASB	Water Accounting Standards Board
WBCSD	World Business Council for Sustainable Development
WWAP	World Water Assessment Program
WWDR	Word Water Development Report
WWF	World Wildlife Fund

REFERENCES

2030 Water Resources Group. (2009). *Charting our water future. Economic frameworks to inform decision-making*. Retrieved from http://www.2030waterresourcesgroup.com/water_full/Charting_Our_Water_Future_Final.pdf. Accessed on 25 September 2012.

Adrio, B. (2012). *Clearing the water: A review of corporate water risk disclosure in SEC filings*. A Ceres Report. Retrieved from http://www.ceres.org/resources/reports/clearing-the-waters-a-review-of-corporate-water-risk-disclosure-in-sec-filings. Accessed on 20 September 2012.

Association of Chartered Certified Accountants (ACCA) & the Net Balance Foundation and the Sustainable Investment Research Institute (SIRIS) (2010). *Disclosures on water*. Retrieved from http://www.siris.com.au/newsfiles/WaterDisclosure SIRIS.pdf. Accessed on 2 April 2013.

Barton, B. (2010). *Murky waters? Corporate reporting on water risk. A benchmarking study of 100 companies*. A Ceres Report. Retrieved from http://www.ceres.org/resources/reports/corporate-reporting-on-water-risk-2010/view. Accessed on 15 September 2012.

Barton, B., & Adrio, B. (2011). *The Ceres Aqua Gauge: A framework for 21st century water risk management*. A Ceres Report. Retrieved from http://www.ceres.org/resources/reports/aqua-gauge. Accessed on 20 September 2012.

Bebbington, J. (1997). Engagement, education and sustainability: A review essay on environmental accounting. *Accounting, Auditing & Accountability Journal*, *10*(3), 365–381. doi:10.1108/09513579710178115

Bebbington, J., & Gray, R. (2001). An Account of sustainability: Failure, success and a reconceptualization. *Critical Perspectives on Accounting*, *12*(5), 557–587. doi:10.1006/cpac.2000.0450

Blanchard, B. (2011, June 3). *China gives bleak assessment of its battered environment*. Reuters. Retrieved from http://uk.reuters.com/article/2011/06/03/us-china-environmentidUKTRE7521FD20110603. Accessed 14 September 2012.

Boccaletti, G., Grobbel M., & Stuchtey, M. R. (2010). The business opportunity in water conservation. *McKinsey Quarterly*, 1. Retrieved from http://weef2010.files.wordpress.com/2010/01/mckinsey-the-business-of-water-dec-09.pdf. Accessed on 15 September 2012.

Buhr, N. (2007). Histories of and rationales for sustainability reporting. In J. Unerman, J. Bebbington, & B. O'Dwyer (Eds.), *Sustainability accounting and accountability* (pp. 57–69). Abingdon, Oxon: Routledge.

CEO Water Mandate. (2012a, August). *Corporate water disclosure guidelines. Toward a common approach to reporting water issues*. Report. Retrieved from http://ceowatermandate.org. Accessed on 15 September 2012.

CEO Water Mandate. (2012b, August). *Guide to water-related collective action. Beta 1.0*. Retrieved from http://pacinst.org/reports/water_related_collective_action/wrca_full_report.pdf. Accessed on 29 April 2013.

Chalmers, K., Godfrey, J. M., & Lynch, B. (2012a). Regulatory theory insights into the past, present and future of General Purpose Water Accounting Standard setting. *Accounting, Auditing & Accountability Journal*, *25*(6), 1001–1024. doi:10.1108/09513571211250224

Chalmers, K., Godfrey, J. M., & Potter, B. (2012b). Discipline-informed approaches to water accounting. *Australian Accounting Review*, *22*(3), 275–285. doi:10.1111/j.1835-2561.2012.00175.x

Chartered Institute of Management Accountants (CIMA). (2011). *Apocalypse H20:Case studies on Puma and Rio Tinto*. Retrieved from http://www.cimaglobal.com/Documents/Thought_leadership_docs/Sustainability and Climate Change/H20_case_studies_v7.pdf. Accessed on 15 April 2013.

Commonwealth of Australia. (2010). *About the Water Efficiency Labelling and Standards (WELS) scheme*. Retrieved from http://www.waterrating.gov.au/about/index.html. Accessed 14 February 2011.

Connell, D., Dovers, S., & Grafton, R. Q. (2005). A critical analysis of the National Water Initiative. *The Australasian Journal of Natural Resources Law and Policy*, *10*(1), 81–107.

Contrafatto, M. (2009). *Il social and environmental reporting e le sue motivazioni: teoria, analisi empirica e prospettive*. Milan: Giuffrè.

Contrafatto, M., & Signori, S. (2012). Responsabilità, accountability e sostenibilità aziendale: alcune riflessioni. In C. Rossi, G. Rusconi, & S. Servalli (Eds.), *Saggi di storia delle discipline aziendali e delle dottrine economiche. Scritti in onore di Antonio Amaduzzi Professore Emerito* (pp. 309–326). Rome: Rirea.

Council of Australian Governments (COAG). (2004). *Intergovernmental Agreement on a National Water Initiative*. Commonwealth of Australia, Canberra. pp. 1–39.

Deloitte. (2011). *CDP (Carbon Disclosure Project) Water Disclosure Global Report 2011: Raising corporate awareness of global water issues*. Retrieved from https://www.cdproject.net/CDPResults/CDP-Water-Disclosure-Global-Report-2011.pdf. Accessed on 15 September 2012.

Deloitte. (2012). *CDP (Carbon Disclosure Project) Global Water Report 2012: Collective responses to rising water challenges.* Retrieved from https://www.cdproject.net/CDPResults/CDP-Water-Disclosure-Global-Report-2012.pdf. Accessed on 25 April 2013.

Deloitte Access Economics. (2012). *Effects analysis of AWAS adoption.* Retrieved from http://www.bom.gov.au/water/standards/wasb/effects.shtml. Accessed on 2 April 2013.

Dubreuil, C. (2006). *The Right to Water: From concept to implementation.* World Water Council. Retrieved from www.worldwatercouncil.org/fileadmin/wwc/Programs/Right_to_Water/Pdf_doct/RightToWater_FinalText_Cover.pdf. Accessed on 2 April 2013.

Egan, M., & Frost, G. R. (2010). *Corporate water reporting: A study of the Australian food, beverage and tobacco sector.* Retrieved from http://www.cpaaustralia.com.au/cps/rde/xbcr/cpa-site/Corporate-water-reporting.pdf. Accessed on 15 April 2013.

EIRIS. (2011). *A drought in your portfolio: Are global companies responding to water scarcity?.* Retrieved from http://www.eiris.org/files/researchpublications/EIRISWaterRiskReport2011.pdf. Accessed on 15 April 2013.

Environmental Protection Agency (EPA). (2005, March). *Protecting water quality from agricultural runoff.* U.S. EPA Factsheet (841-F-05-001). Retrieved from www.epa.gov/owow/NPS/Ag_Runoff_Fact_Sheet.pdf. Accessed 14 September 2012.

Ernst & Young (2012). *General Purpose Water Accounting Report independent assurance cost estimate.* Retrieved from http://www.bom.gov.au/water/standards/wasb/effects.shtml. Accessed on 2 April 2013.

EUROSIF. (2010, January). *Remunerations.* Theme Report – 3rd in a Series. Retrieved from http://www.eiris.org/files/research%20publications/remunerationjan10.pdf. Accessed on 30 April 2013.

Fisher, D. (2007). Delivering the National Water Initiative: The emergence of innovative legal doctrine. In K. Hussey & S. Dovers (Eds.), *Managing water for Australia: The social and institutional challenges* (pp. 113–126). Collingwood: CSIRO.

Gardner, A., & Bowmer, K. H. (2007). Environmental water allocations and their governance. In K. Hussey & S. Dovers (Eds.), *Managing water for Australia: The social and institutional challenges* (pp. 42–58). Collingwood: CSIRO Publishing.

Garriga, E., & Melé, D. (2004). Corporate social responsibility theories: Mapping the territory. *Journal of Business Ethics, 53,* 51–71. doi:10.1023/B:BUSI.0000039399.90587.34

Global Environmental Management Initiative (GEMI). (2002). *Connecting the drops toward creative water strategies: A water sustainability tool.* Case study 'Novartis: Engaging Employees to Reduce Water Use and Impacts'. Retrieved from www.gemi.org/water/novartis.htm. Accessed on 6 June 2013.

Godfrey, J. M. (2007, November). *Drop by precious drop. In the black.* CPA Australia, pp. 59–61.

Gray, R., Dey, C., Owen, D., Evans, R., & Zadek, S. (1997). Struggling with the praxis of social accounting: Stakeholders, accountability, audits and procedures. *Accounting, Auditing and Accountability Journal, 10*(3), 25–364. doi:10.1108/09513579710178106

Gray, R., Owen, D., & Adams, C. (1996). *Accounting and accountability: Changes and challenge in corporate social and environmental reporting.* Hemel Hempstead, England: Prentice-Hall.

Hazelton, J. (2013). Accounting as a human right: The case of water information. *Accounting, Auditing & Accountability Journal, 26*(2), 267–311. doi:10.1108/09513571311303738

Hazelton, J., Cummings, L., Leung, P., & Wang, F. (2011). *Standardised water accounting: Effects analysis. Macquarie University.* Retrieved from http://www.bom.gov.au/water/standards/wasb/effects.shtml. Accessed on 2 April 2013.

Hoekstra, A. Y., & Chapagain, A. K. (2008). *Globalization of water. Sharing the planet's freshwater resources.* Malden: Blackwell.

Human Rights Council of the United Nations. (2009, July 1). *Promotion and protection of all human rights, civil, political, economic, social and cultural rights, including the right to development.* Report of the independent expert on the issue of human rights obligations related to access to safe drinking water and sanitation, Catarina de Albuquerque. Twelfth session, Agenda item 3. Retrieved from http://www2.ohchr.org/english/bodies/hrcouncil/docs/12session/A-HRC-12-24_E.pdf. Accessed on 14 September 2012.

Interfaith Center on Corporate Responsibility (ICCR). (2012). *Toward water disclosure: Recommended process tools.* Retrieved from http://www.iccr.org/issues/subpages/pdf/2012ICCRTowardWaterDisclosure.pdf. Accessed on 23 April 2013.

International Integrated Reporting Committee (IIRC). (2010). *What is integrated reporting?* Retrieved from http://integratedreporting.org/node/3. Accessed on 14 September 2012.

Irbaris. (2009). *CDP Water Disclosure – The case for water disclosure.* Retrieved from https://www.cdproject.net/CDPResults/CDP-Case-for-Water-Disclosure-2009.pdf. Accessed on 16 April 2013.

Lambooy, T. (2011). Corporate social responsibility: Sustainable water use. *Journal of Cleaner Production*, *19*(8), 852–866. doi:10.1016/j.jclepro.2010.09.009

Malsch, B. (2013). Politicizing the expertise of the accounting industry in the realm of corporate social responsibility. *Accounting, Organizations and Society*, *38*(2), 149–168. doi:10.1016/j.aos.2012.09.003

McKay, J., & Marsden, S. (2009). Australia: The problem of sustainability in water. In J. Dellapenna & J. Gupta (Eds.), *The evolution of the law and politics of water* (pp. 175–188). Dordrecht: Springer.

Molden, D. (1997). *Accounting for water use and productivity.* SWIM Paper 1. International Irrigation Management Institute, Colombo, Sri Lanka.

Molden, D., Sakthivadivel, R., & Habib, Z. (2001). *Basin use and productivity of water: Examples from South Asia.* Research Report 49. International Water Management Institute, Colombo, Sri Lanka.

Morrison, J., & Schulte, P. (2009). *Water disclosure 2.0. Assessment of current and emerging practice in corporate water reporting.* The CEO Water Mandate. Retrieved from http://www.pacinst.org/reports/water_disclosure/report.pdf. Accessed on 14 September 2012.

Morrison J., Schulte P., & Schenck R. (2009b). *Corporate water accounting. An analysis of methods and tools for measuring water use and its impacts.* The CEO Water Mandate. Retrieved from http://www.pacinst.org/topics/globalization_and_environment/ceo_water_mandate/UNEP_Corporate_Water_Accounting_Public_Draft.pdf. Accessed on 14 September 2012.

Morrison, J., Morikawa, M., Murphy, M., & Schulte P. (2009a). *Water scarcity & climate change: Growing risks for businesses & investors.* A Ceres Report. Ceres and Pacific Institute. Retrieved from http://www.ceres.org/resources/reports/water-scarcity-climate-change-risks-for-investors-2009/view. Accessed on 15 April 2013.

Mudd, G. M. (2008). Sustainability reporting and water resources: A preliminary assessment of embodied water and sustainable mining. *Mine Water and the Environment*, *27*(3), 136–144. doi:10.1007/s10230-008-0037-5

National Water Commission (NWC) (Australian government). (2010). *Australian environmental water management report 2010.* Retrieved from http://archive.nwc.gov.au/library/topic/environment/australian-environmental-water-management-report-2010. Accessed on 23 April 2013.

National Water Initiative (NWI). (2004). *Intergovernmental Agreement on National Water Initiative Between the Commonwealth of Australia and the Governments of New South Wales, Victoria, Queensland, South Australia, the Australian Capital Territory and the Northern Territory*. Retrieved from http://nwc.gov.au/__data/assets/pdf_file/0008/24749/Intergovernmental-Agreement-on-a-national-water-initiative.pdf. Accessed on 23 April 2013.

SABMiller plc, WWF-UK, & GTZ. (2009). *Water futures. Working together for a secure water future*. Report. Retrieved from http://www.wwf.org.uk/wwf_articles.cfm?unewsid = 4204. Accessed on 14 September 2012.

Schulte, P., Morrison, J., & Gleick, P. H. (2012). Corporate water management. In P. H. Gleick (Ed.), *The world's water* (Vol. 1, pp. 23–45). The Biennal Report on Freshwater Resources. Washington, DC: Island Press.

Securities and Exchange Commission (SEC) (United States). (2010, January 27). *Issues interpretive guidance on disclosure related to business or legal developments regarding climate change*. Online press release. Retrieved from http://www.sec.gov/news/press/2010/2010-15.htm. Accessed on 6 May 2013.

Sethi, S. P., & Schepers, D. H. (2013). United Nations Global Compact: The promise–performance gap. *Journal of Business Ethics*, published online 7 February 2013. doi:10.1007/s10551-013-1629-y

Signori, S. (2012). Sistemi di welfare e accountability delle aziende non profit: verso una rendicontazione condivisa e partecipata dei servizi alla persona. *Azienda Pubblica*, *4*, 423–442.

Sinclair Knight Merz (SKM). (2006). *Stocktake and analysis of Australia's water accounting practice*. Retrieved from http://www.bom.gov.au/water/about/consultation/document/SKM_Stocktake_Report_2006.pdf. Accessed on 3 April 2013.

Sinclair, A. (1995). The chameleon of accountability. *Organizations and Society*, *20*(2/3), 219–237. doi:10.1016/0361-3682(93)E0003-Y

Sofocleous, S. (2010). Will water accounting standards provide useful information to stakeholders?. *Interdisciplinary Environmental Review*, *11*(4), 293–302. doi:10.1504/IER.2010.038084

Tello Melendez, E., Cummings, L., & Hazelton, J. (2012). Stakeholders' perspectives on Standardised Water Accounting Reports: An accountability perspective. In *Proceedings of 11th Australasian Conference on Social and Environmental Accounting Research Wollongong*, Australia.

Tello Melendez, E., & Hazelton, J. (2010). Improving water information through standardised water accounting: Australian evidence. In *Proceedings of 9th Australasian Conference on Social and Environmental Accounting Research Albury Wodonga*, Australia.

Tricker, R. I. (1983). Corporate responsibility, institutional governance and the roles of accounting standards. In M. Bromwich & A. G. Hopwood (Eds.), *Accounting standards setting, an international perspective* (pp. 27–41). London: Pitman.

Unerman, J., Bebbington, J., & O'Dwyer, B. (2007). *Sustainability, accounting and accountability*. Abingdon, Oxon: Routledge.

United Nations (UN). (2007). *System of environmental economic accounting for water*. Final Draft. Retrieved from http://unstats.un.org/unsd/statcom/doc07/SEEAW_SC2007.pdf. Accessed on 14 September 2012.

United Nations (UN). (2009). *Global assessment of water statistics and water accounting*. Background Document to the 40th Session on the UN Statistical Commission. Retrieved from http://unstats.un.org/unsd/statcom/doc09/BG-WaterAccounts.pdf. Accessed on 14 September 2012.

United Nations (UN). (2010). *The human right to water and sanitation*. Sixty-fourth session, item 48, Resolution 64/292. Retrieved from http://www.un.org/ga/search/view_doc.asp?symbol=A/RES/64/292. Accessed on 16 September 2012.

United Nations Committee on Economic, Social and Cultural Rights (UNCESCR). (2002, January 20). *The Right to Water*. General Comment No. 15 – E/C.12/2002/11. Retrieved from http://www.unhchr.ch/tbs/doc.nsf/0/a5458d1d1bbd713fc1256cc400389e94. Accessed on 4 April 2013.

United Nations General Assembly (UN). (2010). *The human right to water and sanitation*. A/RES/64/292, Sixty-fourth session, Agenda item 48. Retrieved from http://www.un.org/ga/search/viewm_doc.asp?symbol=A/RES/64/292. Accessed on 4 April 2013.

United Nations Principles for Responsible Investments (UNPRI). (2012, June). *Integrating ESG issues into executive pay. Guidance for investors and companies*. Retrieved from http://www.unpri.org/viewer/?file=wp-content/uploads/IntegratingESGissues.pdf. Accessed on 30 April 2013.

Water Accounting Standards Board (WASB). (2009). *Water accounting conceptual framework for the preparation and presentation of General Purpose Water Accounting Reports*. Commonwealth of Australia, Canberra.

Water Accounting Standards Board (WASB). (2010). *Exposure draft of Australian Water Accounting Standard 1: Preparation and presentation of General Purpose Water Accounting Reports*. Commonwealth of Australia, Canberra.

Water Accounting Standards Board (WASB) and Bureau of Meteorology. (2012). *Analysis of effects of adopting Australian Water Accounting Standard 1*. Retrieved from http://www.bom.gov.au/water/standards/wasb/effects.shtml. Accessed on 2 April 2013.

Williams, P. F. (1987). The legitimate concern with fairness. *Accounting, Organizations and Society*, *12*(2), 169–189. doi:10.1016/0361-3682(91)90014-6

World Business Council for Sustainable Development (WBCSD). (2011). *The global water tool*. Retrieved from http://www.wbcsd.org/work-program/sector-projects/water/global-water-tool.aspx. Accessed on 3 October 2012.

World Business Council for Sustainable Development (WBCSD), Water Sustainability & IUCN. (2012, August). *Water for business. Initiatives guiding sustainable water management in the private sector*. Version 3. Retrieved from http://www.wbcsd.org/waterforbusiness3.aspx. Accessed 15 April 2013.

World Water Assessment Programme (WWAP). (2003). *Water for people, water for life*. The United Nations world water development report 1 (WWDR1). Retrieved from http://www.un.org/esa/sustdev/publications/WWDR_english_129556e.pdf. Accessed on 10 April 2013.

World Water Assessment Programme (WWAP). (2006). *Water, a Shared Responsibility*. The United Nations world water development report 2 (WWDR2). Retrieved from http://www.unesco.org/new/en/natural-sciences/environment/water/wwap/wwdr/wwdr2-2006/. Accessed on 10 April 2013.

World Water Assessment Programme (WWAP). (2009). *Water in a changing world*. The United Nations world water development report 3 (WWDR3). London: UNESCO & Earthsca. Retrieved from http://unesdoc.unesco.org/images/0018/001819/181993e.pdf. Accessed on 3 October 2012.

World Water Assessment Programme (WWAP). (2012). *Managing water under uncertainty and risk*. The United Nations world water development report 4 (WWDR4). Retrieved from http://www.unesco.org/new/en/natural-%20sciences/environment/water/wwap/wwdr/wwdr4-2012/. Accessed on 10 April 2013.

APPENDIX A: TOWARDS WATER DISCLOSURE: TOOLS AND GUIDELINES

(*Sources*: ACCA, 2010; CEO Water Mandate, 2012a, 2012b; Chalmers et al., 2012b; ICCR, 2012; Morrison et al., 2009b and specific tool and guideline websites).

Water Risk Mapping and Data Gathering

The System of Environmental-Economic Accounting for Water (SEEAW)
The United Nations (UN) Statistics Division, in collaboration with the London Group on Environmental Accounting, has developed a System of Environmental-Economic Accounting for Water (SEEAW). This system is described as 'a conceptual framework' for the organisation of physical and economic information related to water using concepts, definitions and classifications consistent with those of the System of National Accounts 1993 (UN, 2007). It is an extension of the UN's System of Environmental-Economic Accounting, recording information about environmental and related socioeconomic indicators in a manner similar to the way in which many countries' national accounts record information about economic transactions. SEEAW accounts are used to provide data for policymaking, water resource management, reporting to international agencies, and research and modelling (UN, 2009). They are used primarily at a macro-level (Chalmers et al., 2012b, pp. 278, 279).
http://unstats.un.org/unsd/envaccounting/seeaw/

Water Risk Filter
This tool developed by the World Wildlife Fund (WWF) and the German development bank DEG can be used to assess exposure to water-related risks globally and across industries. The tool contains country and basin level data that is used to identify and quantify physical, regulatory and reputational risks.
http://waterriskfilter.panda.org/

Aqueduct
Developed by the World Resources Institute (WRI), Aqueduct is a global database of water risk information that enables the creation of water risk

maps. Aqueduct's global water risk mapping tool helps companies, investors, governments, and other users to understand where and how water risks and opportunities are emerging worldwide.
http://insights.wri.org/aqueduct/atlas

The UN Global Compact CEO Water Mandate
Launched in July 2007 by the UN Secretary-General, the CEO Water Mandate is a unique public–private initiative designed to assist companies in the development, implementation and disclosure of water sustainability policies and practices. It offers a unique action platform to share best and emerging practices and to forge multi-stakeholder partnerships to address the problems of access to water and sanitation.

Its website, among other things, offers the business case for corporate water stewardship by describing global water challenges, water-related business risks, and corporate water stewardship; it identifies and explains the many potential uses of corporate water assessment and analyses the functionality, strengths and weaknesses of relevant assessment tools.
http://ceowatermandate.org

The Carbon Disclosure Project (CDP) Water Disclosure Initiative
CDP is an international, not-for-profit organisation providing the only global system for companies and cities to measure, disclose, manage and share vital environmental information.

They devise a questionnaire issued on behalf of 530 investors representing $57 trillion in assets. These signatories are requesting companies to disclose business critical water-related information to guide their decision-making processes and drive strategic investment.

By acting as a platform for information sharing they aim to:

- drive better measurement and transparency of water issues and make meaningful reporting on water standard corporate practice globally;
- work with other standard setting bodies to support and accelerate the development of standard metrics and performance benchmarks;
- provide data that informs decision-making by investors, companies and governments.

https://www.cdproject.net/en-US/Programmes/Pages/cdp-water-disclosure.aspx

Risk Self-Assessment and Management

The WBCSD Global Water Tool (GWT)

The Global Water Tool launched in 2007 by the World Business Council for Sustainable Development (WBCSD) is a free and easy-to-use tool for companies and organisations to map their water use and assess risks relative to their global operations and supply chains. It assesses the conditions of a watershed in which an industrial facility is located (WBCSD, 2011). According to WBCSD (2011) the tool provides GRI water indicators, inventories, risk and performance metrics and geographical mapping and enables effective communication with internal and external stakeholders on a company's water issue.

The GWT does not provide specific guidance on local situations. This requires more in-depth systematic analysis at plant level. That is why the WBCSD collaborated with GEMI to develop The Local Water Tool (LWT) – a free tool for companies and organisations to evaluate the external impacts, business risks, opportunities and management plans related to water use and discharge at a specific site or operation.
http://www.wbcsd.org/work-program/sector-projects/water/global-water-tool.aspx

GEMI Water Sustainability Tools

There are two of them which have been developed by the Global Environmental Management Initiative (GEMI). Released in 2002, GEMI water sustainability Tool is an online tool that helps organisations to create a water strategy. It evaluates the relationship between water and a company's business, identifies associated risk and sets forth a course of action to address specific needs and circumstances.

GEMI's Water Sustainability Tool contains five core analytical stages or modules. These include (1) Water Use, Impact, and Source Assessment; (2) Business Risk Assessment; (3) Business Opportunity Assessment; (4) Strategic Direction and Goal Setting; (5) Strategy Development and Implementation.

Collecting the Drops: A Water Sustainability Planner is a tool separated into three Modules that guides a facility user through: the process of assessing the facility's specific water uses/needs in comparison to the availability of water in the region, the impacts these operations pose on the available water resources and the identification of factors that may pose a risk on the operation's ability to produce. Case examples of how GEMI members

have identified opportunities to efficiently manage water resources are also provided.
http://www.gemi.org/water/overview.htm
http://www.gemi.org/waterplanner/

The International Water Management Institute Water Accounting (IWMI WA)
IWMI is one of 15 international research centres supported by the network of 60 governments, private foundations and international and regional organisations collectively known as CGIAR. It is a non-profit organisation with a staff of 350 and offices in over 10 countries across Asia and Africa and with its headquarters in Colombo, Sri Lanka.

Its mission is to improve the management of land and water for food, livelihoods and the environment, with a particular focus on developing countries. To assist with achieving this mission, a multidisciplinary and cross-cultural team led by hydrologists developed IWMI Water Accounting (IWMI WA) (Molden, 1997; Molden, Sakthivadivel & Habib, 2001). IWMI WA is a tool that helps identify effective strategies for water saving and enhancing the productivity of water, and also to ease the water-related dialogue between professionals and non-water professionals (Chalmers et al., 2012b, p. 280).
http://www.iwmi.cgiar.org/index.aspx

Aqua Gauge
Aqua Gauge was developed by Ceres to help companies to improve their qualitative disclosure to CDP Water Disclosure questions related to governance, management, policies and strategy.

This tool provides companies with an initial baseline self-assessment of core management practices and gaps with regards to water risk and opportunity.
http://www.ceres.org/issues/water/aqua-gauge/aqua-gauge

The Alliance for Water Stewardship (AWS)
The AWS is a collaboration between some of the world's leading players in sustainable water resource management who are committed to driving collective responses to shared water risk through a stakeholder-endorsed International Water Stewardship Standard.

On March 2013 they announced the release of the Beta AWS Standard, the world's first International Water Stewardship Standard.

The Standard is designed to give companies and utilities a roadmap to follow towards sustainable water use, including engagement with

stakeholders and others within their watershed. Building on other water-related tools, the Standard helps to reduce water risk and generate social, environmental and economic benefits across all sectors and regions.
http://www.allianceforwaterstewardship.org/

Measuring

The Global Water Footprint Standard
The Global Water Footprint Standard – developed by a joint effort of the Water Footprint Network, its partners, and scientists of the University of Twente in the Netherlands – has garnered international support from major companies, policymakers, NGOs and scientists. This is a methodology that measures the total annual volume of freshwater used to produce the goods and services consumed by any well-defined group of consumers (Hoekstra & Chapagain, 2008). A water footprint pinpoints the volume, location and timing of water uses and discharges. Water footprints are then divided into three components: blue, green and grey water. The first are waters taken from the surface and aquifers, the green measures water consumption taken from the soil or used directly as rainfall. The grey water footprint measures the volume of water needed to dilute pollutants discharged to water bodies to the extent that they do not exceed minimum regulatory standards. Water footprints can be calculated for individual processes and products, as well as for consumers, nations and businesses.
http://www.waterfootprint.org

Reporting guidelines

The Global Reporting Initiative (GRI)
The Global Reporting Initiative is among the pioneers in the development of a sustainability reporting framework. This framework sets out the principles and performance indicators that organisations can use to measure and report on their economic, environmental and social performance. The current generation guidelines (G4) provide an extensive chapter on environmental performance reporting. GRI advises companies to report on their direct water withdrawal from all available sources such as surface, ground and rainwater, waste water from other organisations and freshwater supplies from municipalities, which can all be measured from water bills and meters and calculations derived from other available water data (G4-EN8)

(Lambooy, 2011); furthermore, companies should report on water sources significantly affected by the withdrawal of water, and the percentage and total volume of water recycled and reused (G4-EN9 and G4-EN10). Total water discharge by quality and destination is captured by indicator G4-EN22, while G4-EN26 is a qualitative indicator on the impact of the water discharges on the ecosystem (identity, size, protected status, and biodiversity value of water bodies and related habitats significantly affected by the organisation's discharges of water and runoff).

https://www.globalreporting.org

Particular Sector's Initiatives

Minerals Council of Australia Water Accounting Framework for the Minerals Industry

In response to the business case for consistent water accounting for the minerals industry, the Minerals Council of Australia in conjunction with the Sustainable Minerals Institute of the University of Queensland has developed the Water Accounting Framework for the Minerals Industry. The member companies of the Minerals Council of Australia have endorsed an initial phase of framework adoption which includes (1) the alignment of company water metrics and definitions consistent with the Framework's Input Output Model and (2) using these metrics to meet an existing company water reporting requirement (e.g. Global Reporting Initiative Requirements).

To support the implementation of the Water Accounting Framework, a number of guidance tools have been developed to assist mineral industry users in applying the framework.

http://www.minerals.org.au/focus/sustainable_development/water_accounting

Oil, Gas and Electric Power Supplement Developed by International Petroleum Industry Environmental Conservation Association (IPIECA)

The IPIECA Global Water Tool for Oil and Gas is a customised version of the WBCSD Global Water Tool. The Tool will help oil and gas companies map their water use and assess risks for their overall global portfolio of sites considering each part of the oil and gas value chain.

http://www.ipieca.org/topic/water/global-water-tool

APPENDIX B: WATER ACCOUNTING STATEMENTS

We would like to acknowledge the Bureau of Meteorology of the Australian Government for the kind authorisation for the use and publication of these data.

Account Region of Adelaide

Water Assets and Water Liabilities

	2011 ML	2010 ML
Water assets		
Surface water	**120,57**	**93,753**
1.1 Storages	120,11	93,316
1.2 Unregulated river	460	437
1.4 Lakes and wetlands	–	–
Total Surface water	120,57	93,753
Groundwater	**88,252**	**87,833**
2.1 Water table aquifer	–	–
2.2 Underlying aquifers	–	–
2.5 Other groundwater assets	88,252	87,833
Total Groundwater	88,252	87,833
Urban water system	**18,323**	**18,31**
3.1 Urban water supply system	18,218	18,205
3.2 Wastewater collection system	95	95
3.3 Recycled water supply system	10	10
3.4 Urban inter-region claim on water	0	0
Total Urban water system	18,323	18,31
Irrigation scheme	**29**	**2,306**
4.1 Irrigation water supply system	29	29
4.2 Irrigation scheme inter-region claim on water	0	2,277
Total Irrigation scheme	29	2,306
Total water assets	227,174	202,202

(Continued)

	2011 ML	2010 ML
Water liabilities		
Surface water liability	**0**	**0**
5.1 Surface water allocation remaining	0	0
Total Surface water liability	0	0
Groundwater liability	**3,561**	**2,857**
6.1 Groundwater allocation remaining	3,561	2,857
Total Groundwater liability	3,561	2,857
Total water liabilities	3,561	2,857
Opening net water assets	199,345	196,209
Add/(Less): Change in net water assets	24,268	3,136
Closing net water assets	223,613	199,345

Changes in Water Assets and Water Liabilities

	2011 ML	2010 ML
Water asset increases		
Surface water increases	**609,014**	**492,061**
9.1 Precipitation on surface water	10,974	8,785
9.4 Runoff to surface water	598,04	483,276
9.6 Overbank flood return to river channel	–	–
Total Surface water increases	609,014	492,061
Groundwater increases	**693,76**	**382,352**
10.1 Groundwater inflow from outside region	22	13
10.2 Groundwater inflow from outside region at coast	2,051	1,651
10.3 Recharge from landscape	685,221	373,388
10.5 Leakage from off-channel water storage	1,011	–
10.8 Managed aquifer recharge – private user	5,455	7,3
Total Groundwater increases	693,76	382,352
Urban water system increases	**244,076**	**239,572**
11.1 Precipitation on urban water system	2,052	1,801
11.4 Wastewater collected	92,024	87,771
11.15 Increase of inter-region claim on water by urban water system	150	150
Total Urban water system increases	244,076	239,572

(Continued)

Irrigation scheme increases	**4,103**	**2,277**
12.1 Precipitation on irrigation scheme	–	–
12.12 Increase of irrigation scheme inter-region claim on water	3,85	2,277
12.18 Other irrigation water increases	253	–
Total Irrigation scheme increases	4,103	2,277
Total water asset increases	1,550,953	1,116,262
Water liability decreases		
Surface water liability decreases	**1,525**	**1,692**
13.1 Adjustment and forfeiture of surface water allocation	1,525	1,692
Total Surface water liability decreases	1,525	1,692
Groundwater liability decreases	**25,832**	**17,227**
14.1 Adjustment and forfeiture of groundwater allocation	25,832	17,227
Total Groundwater liability decreases	25,832	17,227
Total water liability decreases	27,357	18,919
Water asset decreases		
Surface water decreases	**323,864**	**146,349**
17.1 Evaporation from surface water	15,283	16,635
17.2 River outflow from the region	305,853	126,214
17.4 Leakage to landscape	–	–
17.5 Overbank flood spilling	–	–
17.6 Diversions – other statutory rights	2,728	3,5
Total Surface water decreases	323,864	146,349
Groundwater decreases	**131,019**	**87,217**
18.1 Groundwater outflow to outside region	390	408
18.2 Groundwater outflow to outside region at coast	1,363	1,243
18.3 Discharge to landscape	99,677	41,755
18.5 Discharge to off-channel water storage	–	–
18.7 Extraction – other statutory rights	29,589	43,811
Total Groundwater decreases	131,019	87,217
Urban water system decreases	**315,688**	**302,887**
19.1 Evaporation from urban water	3,289	3,826
19.4 Delivery to urban water system users	125,686	130,509
19.7 Wastewater discharge outside of region	70,836	60,139
19.11 Transfer of water outside of region	3,476	3,627
19.14 Decrease of urban inter-region claim on water	104,654	97,009
19.20 Other urban water decreases	7,747	7,777
Total Urban water system decreases	315,688	302,887

(*Continued*)

Irrigation scheme decreases	**18,615**	**4,89**
20.1 Evaporation from irrigation scheme	–	–
20.4 Delivery to irrigation scheme users	14,789	4,89
20.9 Decrease of irrigation scheme inter-region claim on water	3,826	–
Total Irrigation scheme decreases	18,615	4,89
Total water asset decreases	789,186	541,343
Water liability increases		
Surface water liability increases	**2,759**	**2,759**
21.1 Surface water allocation announcements	2,759	2,759
Total Surface water liability increases	2,759	2,759
Groundwater liability increases	**41,555**	**39,236**
22.1 Groundwater allocation announcements	41,555	39,236
Total Groundwater liability increases	41,555	39,236
Total water liability increases	44,314	41,995
Unaccounted-for difference	**720,542**	**548,707**
25.1 Unaccounted-for difference	720,542	548,707
Total unaccounted-for difference	720,542	548,707
Change in net water assets	24,268	3,136

PART II
INTEGRATING SUSTAINABILITY INTO BUSINESS PRACTICE: WHAT IS THE ROLE OF MANAGERIAL CONTROL SYSTEMS AND ACCOUNTANTS?

A REVIEW OF THE EMPIRICAL RESEARCH IN MANAGEMENT CONTROL, STRATEGY AND SUSTAINABILITY

Nathalie Crutzen and Christian Herzig

ABSTRACT

Purpose – *This chapter reviews empirical studies into the relationship between management control, strategy and sustainability.*

Approach – *The review explores the theoretical frameworks and models used in previous empirical research as well as the research questions and methods applied to empirically explore this emerging research area.*

Findings – *Even if a growing body of empirical research has emerged over the last decade, our knowledge of how companies design or use management control to support sustainability strategy appears to be limited, providing considerable scope for further research.*

Accounting and Control for Sustainability
Studies in Managerial and Financial Accounting, Volume 26, 165–195

ISSN: 1479-3512/doi:10.1108/S1479-3512(2013)0000026005

Originality of the chapter – *This review structures the state of our empirical knowledge in the area of management control, strategy and sustainability and makes suggestions for future research paths.*

Keywords: Management control; strategy; sustainability; literature review

INTRODUCTION

The role of management control for supporting strategies oriented towards sustainability has increasingly been discussed in the literature (e.g. Ballou, Casey, Grenier, & Heitger, 2012; Durden, 2008; Epstein & Roy, 2001; Galbreath, 2010; Gond, Grubnic, Herzig, & Moon, 2012; Maxwell, Rothenberg, Briscoe, & Marcus, 1997; Perego & Hartmann, 2009; Van der Woerd & Van den Brink, 2004). Considerable interest has revolved around the emergence of new forms of accounting and control for sustainability (such as eco-control, material flow cost accounting systems or stakeholder value concepts) and the way in which greater level of integration of environmental and social issues into management control systems can support strategic integration of sustainability into organisations. The latter has featured prominently for example in research on the balanced scorecard (e.g. Dias-Sardinha & Reijnders, 2005; Figge, Hahn, Schaltegger, & Wagner, 2002; Hubbard, 2009; Van der Woerd & Van den Brink, 2004). More broadly, evidence for an increased use and integration of sustainability indicators in the context of strategic planning and decision-making, performance measurement, monitoring and benchmarking is provided in Searcy's (2012) recent review of research on sustainability performance measurement systems. The roles and uses of control systems in the integration of sustainability within organisational strategy have also been accounted for in the framework developed by Gond et al. (2012). What this burgeoning body of literature management control has in common is that management control is expected to play a key role in shaping processes of sustainability strategy formulation and implementation, often attributed with a high capability to support decision-making.

This chapter reviews the empirical research that has focused on sustainability, strategy and management control. It uses the framework developed by Tucker, Thorne and Gurd (2009) to clarify how research questions developed in previous research can be positioned in relationship to each other. The framework suggests that the 'management control–strategy' association comprises four distinct 'relationships' which result from the juxtaposition of two central themes in management control (design and use) and two central themes in strategy (content and process). Our review shows that a disproportionate part of the empirical studies investigate how management control design supports (sustainability) strategy implementation and that other 'relationships' have been less frequently examined. Overall, we hope that our exploration of this emerging body of empirical literature is seen to be helpful in structuring the state of our knowledge in this area and in guiding future research efforts.

The remainder of this chapter is organised as follows. The section 'Management Control, Strategy and Sustainability' considers the terminology, frameworks and concepts used for this literature review. The section "Methodology" explains the research design which includes the analytical framework developed for organising and presenting the empirical literature. Then, in the section 'Findings' synthesise the findings in key issue areas. In the final section the insights provided by this review are discussed and future research paths are suggested.

MANAGEMENT CONTROL, STRATEGY AND SUSTAINABILITY

Management Control, Strategy and their Relationships

Controls have been defined in many ways. Traditionally, management control is most associated with formal, accounting-based controls (Anthony, 1965) which are easy to research (Langfield-Smith, 1997). While an extensive academic literature has explored formal controls such as planning, monitoring, and performance measurement and management, their relationship with and the role of more informal controls such as unwritten policies, values and beliefs of the organisational culture have also gained increased attention in management control research (Chenhall, 2003; Chenhall & Langfield-Smith, 2003; Ferreira & Otley, 2009; Kober, Ng, & Paul, 2007; Malmi & Brown, 2008). While in both of these areas the operation and performance of individual controls have been investigated by researchers, others have stressed the importance of broader conceptualisations of management control and the necessity to understand the integrative nature of these components (Berry, Coad, Harris, Otley, & Stringer, 2009; Malmi & Brown, 2008; Otley, Broadbent, & Berry, 1995). In their review of the recent literature on management control, Berry et al. (2009) describe an evolving and broadened agenda of management control which derives from developments in three areas, namely strategic performance measurement systems such as the balanced scorecard (Kaplan & Norton, 1992, 1996, 2001), Simons' (1987, 1990, 1991, 1995) levers of control framework and an integrative performance management and control framework (Ferreira & Otley, 2009; Otley, 1999).

Reflective of these developments, we use a broad and generic definition for our review and define management control as the 'evolving formal and informal mechanisms, processes, systems, and networks used by organisations for conveying the key objectives and goals elicited by management, for assisting the strategic process and on-going management through analysis, planning, measurement, control, rewarding, and broadly managing performance, and for supporting and facilitating organisational learning and change' (Ferreira & Otley, 2009, p. 264). In our review of literature, we also aim to follow Langfield-Smith (1997) and Tucker et al. (2009) in that we describe management accounting and control in terms of the design and the use of controls. According to this traditional distinction, studies that investigate the *design* of controls focus on their existence and potential configurations to support strategy-making while the *use* of controls refers to the adoption, utilisation and/or implementation of such control mechanisms. Both types of research questions appear to have relatively equally been addressed in empirical research on the relationship between management control systems and strategy since the end of the 1990s (Tucker et al., 2009).

Turning to the strategic management literature, it appears that much attention has been paid to the allocation of resources to convert competencies into competitive advantages (Porter, 1980). In alignment with this, Johnson, Scholes, and Whittington (2008) define strategy as 'the direction and scope of an organisation over the long-term, which achieves advantage for the organisation through its configuration of resources within a challenging environment, to meet the needs of markets and to fulfil stakeholders' expectations'. Based on the work of Mintzberg and Waters (1985), which distinguishes between 'intended' and 'emergent' strategies, researchers have also paid attention to the complexity and the variety in the form and nature of strategic processes within organisations (Dent, 1990). While deliberate and rational strategies are associated with precise intentions by the organisation and occur before action, 'emergent' strategies evolve rather incrementally and in the absence of intentions during action. Both types can ultimately lead to the notion of 'realised strategies' (Henri, 2006). With reference to the distinction between the deliberate and the emerging approaches of the strategic process (Mintzberg, 1979; Mintzberg & Waters, 1985), a growing number of researchers (e.g. Kober, Ng, & Paul, 2007; Langfield-Smith, 1997; Simons, 1987, 1990, 1991, 1994, 1995; Tucker et al., 2009) have conceptualised management controls not only as an outcome of strategy (to implement strategy) but also as relevant for strategy development and change. This broader and more dynamic view of strategic management recognises a complex two-way relationship between management control and strategy and stresses the importance of distribution of management attention to different controls (Simons, 1987, 1990, 1991, 1994, 1995).

Our aim is to synthesise findings from past research which has been receptive of the strategy themes addressed above and we seek clarification on the relationship between strategy and management control by, again, following Tucker et al.'s (2009) framework and distinguishing two central themes in strategy, namely content and process. Strategy content is regarded here as to be 'concerned with the product of the strategy process' (Chenhall, 2005, p. 11) and refers to different typologies of strategy. Strategy process is conceptualised as both strategy formulation and implementation. Studies into the process of strategy have featured less prominently in the past. One reason for this might be that process orientated research requires the immersion into the research context and analysis over time (Ryan, Scapens, & Theobald, 2002). The dominant view of management control being an outcome of strategy and the focus on survey-based research in this context represent other possible explanations (Tucker et al., 2009). We now turn to the emerging field of management control for *sustainability* strategy.

Management Control for Sustainability Strategy

Sustainability is concerned with the intra- and inter-generational justice (Brundtland, 1987) and the balance of multiple that means economic, social and environmental performance and impact criteria ('triple bottom line'; Elkington, 1997). In response to alternative paradigms to the financial profit maximisation and the attempt to blend the interests and needs of organisations with those of their stakeholders while protecting and enhancing the human and natural resources that will be needed in the future, we have experienced an emergence of new calculative practices. These can be viewed as either driving for example carbon trading markets (e.g. Bebbington & Larrinaga-González, 2008) and environmental/

sustainability accounting standardisation initiatives (e.g. Fries, McCulloch, & Webster, 2010; GRI, 2013; ISO, 2012) or being driven by (new forms of) assurance practices (Ballou et al., 2012; Owen & O'Dwyer, 2008; O'Dwyer, 2011; O'Dwyer, Owen, & Unerman, 2011) and enhanced accountability mechanisms (Gray, Owen, & Maunders, 1988; Gray, Owen, Adams, 1996).

The concept of sustainability is seen to have wide-ranging implications for management control and strategy. For example, previous research has elucidated its relationship with management control and the integration of multidisciplinary issues within decision-making (e.g. social cost–benefit analysis and non-market valuation techniques) and within education of accountants (Milne, 1996). Much attention has also been paid to the development of environmental/sustainability management accounting and control mechanisms including environmental budgeting, environmental/sustainability performance evaluation systems, eco-control or sustainability balanced scorecard (Burritt, Hahn, & Schaltegger, 2002; Gond et al., 2012; Herzig, Viere, Schaltegger, & Burritt, 2012). Overall, sustainability management control is viewed to provide support to organisations in considering the wider environmental and social impacts of their activities and in measuring and managing the interaction between business, society and environment (Bennett & James, 1998; Milne, 1996).

However, aligning with and responding to these demands for greater social responsibility and accountability represent a major challenge for organisations (Searcy, 2012) and involve organisational strategic renewal (Hart, 1995). As a consequence, there has been heightened interest in strategising sustainability through initiatives such as programs and policies to rethink and redesign business models, engaging with stakeholders, and measuring and communicating organisations' social and environmental performance and impact (e.g. Hart, 1997; Lovins et al., 2007; Porter & Van der Linde, 1995; Roome, 1998). The development and implementation of sustainability strategy have been viewed to include extensive organisational learning and change (Maon, Lindgreen, & Swaen, 2009), and to require the support of appropriate mechanisms such as management accounting and control (e.g. Milne, 1996). The extent of such change and the level of strategic renewal, however, depend on the level of an organisation's commitment to sustainability, its understanding of the responsibility for the impact of organisational activities, the power it allocates to stakeholders (Brown & Fraser, 2006) and the role ascribed to and actual use of management control systems (e.g. Gond et al., 2012). The focus of our literature review is on the latter. We are interested in how research has empirically investigated the relationship between management control, strategy and sustainability. Our review aims to describe the frameworks and models researchers have used to provide structure to this field of research, and to explore the research questions and methods applied to analyse this relationship. We explore the empirical literature which has responded to calls made by others for deeper investigations on the interrelation between control, strategy and sustainability (e.g. Chung & Parker, 2008; Parker, 2000) and we organise and present it according to the four dimensions of Tucker et al.'s (2009) framework, i.e. the design and use of management control, on the one hand, and the strategy content and process, on the other. The methodology is explained next.

METHODOLOGY

Selection of Studies

Our interest is in empirical studies conducted at the company (micro) level and published in academic journals (in English). Papers which focus on management control and strategy in the context of sustainability at the meso or macro level (e.g. city, county or country) are not included in the review. For our criteria-based search we relied on two databases, namely EBSCO and Pro Quest ABI/Inform Global. We defined three sets of keywords to identify relevant empirical studies dealing with the relationship between management control, strategy and sustainability. These are:

i. sustainab*, social* respons*, environment*, sustainable development;
ii. strateg*, planning, decision-making, decision support; and
iii. control*, performance, management system, measurement system, information management, accounting.

Keywords were used in different combinations. Our iterative search for relevant empirical studies included an initial review of abstracts and papers. The paper selection was then refined and completed through an analysis of the referencing section, revealing further publications. Even though some papers do refer to strategy in a less explicit way, we include them in our review. In these instances, the research provides useful insights into ways of designing and using management control for stakeholder oriented and socially responsive decision-making. As this literature is still in an emerging state, papers dealing with the environmental and/or social dimension(s) of the sustainable development only are also considered in this literature review.

Framework for Analysis

Criteria to analyse the papers are both derived from previous works such as other literature reviews or articles (Chenhall, 2003; Ferreira & Otley, 2009; Langfield-Smith, 1997; Thomson 2007; Tucker et al., 2009) and emerged from engaging with the selected articles. They can broadly be framed according to three dimensions: theoretical foundation, content and methodology. *Theoretical foundation* deals with the theories and frameworks used in the reviewed papers (Thomson, 2007). The *content* dimension focuses on the content of the papers in terms of research question(s) investigated (Langfield-Smith, 1997; Tucker et al., 2009), the control mechanisms studied as well as their operationalisation (Ferreira & Otley, 2009; Langfield-Smith, 1997) and the different dimensions of sustainability addressed by the research (Thomson, 2007). *Methodology* groups together all the criteria related to the methodological aspects of the research such as the type of research (conceptual paper or empirical paper), the research focus or the empirical methodology chosen (Langfield-Smith, 1997; Thomson, 2007; Tucker et al., 2009) (Table 1).

Table 1. Framework for Analysis.

Theoretical Foundation
Frameworks and understanding of strategy (e.g. emergent/deliberate strategy (Mintzberg & Waters, 1985); strategy-as-process, strategy-as-practice (Whittington, 1996))
Frameworks and understanding of management control (e.g. Kaplan & Norton, 1992, 1996, 2001)
Philosophical perspectives (Brown & Fraser, 2006; Gray, 2002; Burritt & Schaltegger, 2010)
Content
Themes and research questions
Parameters of management control (e.g. Abernethy & Chua, 1996; Ferreira & Otley, 2009; Otley, 1999)
Type of control mechanisms (e.g. formal – informal/accounting based – non-accounting based)
Dimensions (social, environmental and/or economic)
Methodology
Research method (case-based or survey-based studies) and number of cases
Research focus (country, type of organisation in terms of size and industry as well as respondents/interviewees (CSR managers, accountants or others))

FINDINGS

Our initial keyword search revealed a large proportion of conceptual papers, sometimes with empirical underpinnings such as case studies used for illustrative purposes (e.g. Epstein & Roy, 2001; Figge et al., 2002; Leon-Soriano et al., 2010; Schaltegger, 2011; Schaltegger & Wagner, 2006; Van der Woerd & Van den Brink, 2004). We identified 27 papers which empirically investigate the relationship between management control, strategy and sustainability. These papers build the basis for our review.

All papers, except one (Maxwell et al., 1997) were published over the last decade. Twelve papers were published in corporate social responsibility (CSR)/sustainability journals (*Journal of Business Ethics; Business Strategy and the Environment; Environmental Quality Management; Corporate Social Responsibility and Environmental Management; Journal of Cleaner Production* and *Sustainability Accounting, Management and Policy Journal*). Ten papers were published in accounting and management control journals (*Abacus; Accounting, Auditing and Accountability Journal; Accounting Forum; Accounting Horizons; Advances in Management Accounting; British Accounting Review; International Journal of Productivity and Performance Management; Management Accounting Quarterly* and *Qualitative Research in Accounting and Management*). Four papers come from management journals (*British Journal of Management*; *California Management Review* and *Corporate Governance*) and one paper comes from the information systems discipline (*Industrial Management and Data Systems*). To this extent, our analysis confirms Melville's (2010) observation, i.e. that few studies about sustainability incorporate the information systems perspective.

As far as authorship is concerned, researchers in accounting and management control author the majority of the papers. Researchers with a more 'technical' background (such as mechanical or chemical engineering) and researchers who are active in the field of sustainability/CSR studies (CSR, environmental studies or sustainability management) are less prominent in our sample (four studies each). Authors with other backgrounds constitute exceptions (two studies are authored by scholars from information systems and one study is authored by a practitioner/consultant).

These general observations show that most of the reviewed studies belong to the accounting/control and the sustainability/CSR literature and have been authored by scholars from these two fields, with a focus on the former. Interestingly, we could not identify any empirical study in the strategy literature and only one paper published in a journal from a different discipline (information systems; Leon-Soriano et al., 2010). However, the reviewed papers show that research on management control, strategy and sustainability is multidimensional in nature. Hence, these constructs could be studied through the lenses of various disciplines (Langfield-Smith, 1997; McWilliams, Siegel, & Wright, 2006; Milne, 1996).

Now we introduce our more specific findings following the three dimensions introduced earlier, namely theoretical foundation (section 'Theoretical Foundation'), content (section 'Content') and methodology (section 'Methodology').

Theoretical Foundation

As a general observation, it is interesting to mention that almost half of the studies do not refer explicitly to any prior theory or conceptual framework published in the literature. The other papers mobilise – to a varying extent – already existing theories or frameworks. However, as noted for example by Malmi and Granlund (2009), there is some debate about what might define theory (see also Llewelyn, 2003; Sutton & Staw, 1995). From the perspective of theories that have 'theory status' (Malmi & Granlund, 2009), most reviewed papers appear to lack substantial theoretical foundation. For example, traditional theories such as institutional theory, contingency theory or stakeholder theory are rarely used in our set of empirical papers. Explicit grounding of research in such theoretical frameworks is evident in Durden (2008), Lansiluoto and Jarvenpaa (2008) and Perego and Hartmann (2009). It is also a somewhat curious omission that the resource-based theory – given its influential role in the strategy literature over the past decades (e.g. Barney, 1991; Barney, Wright, & Ketchen, 2001) – has largely been ignored by our set of empirical studies.

In the main, and in conformance with Ferreira and Otley's (2009) observation on the traditional accounting and management control literature, we find a lacuna of strong and consistent theoretical foundations in most of the studies, which perhaps restrains the development of new knowledge in this emerging area of research (Chapman, 1997). When reference is made to a specific framework or theory, in most instances these appear to be practice-oriented 'theories' or frameworks (Malmi & Granlund, 2009), of which the balanced scorecard is most popular (e.g. Dias-Sardinha, Reijnders, & Antunes, 2002, 2007; Gates & Germain, 2010; Leon-Soriano et al., 2010; Van der Woerd & Van den Brink, 2004). Other practice-oriented frameworks include the Australian Business Excellence Framework or the Eco-Management and Audit Scheme (e.g. Khoo & Tan, 2002; Albelda, Correa, & Carrasco, 2007).

With regard to *frameworks and understanding of strategy*, most publications refer (explicitly or implicitly) to traditional strategy frameworks. This is most evident in the use of the deliberate view of strategy (Mintzberg & Waters, 1985) which dominates most of the reviewed articles. A large majority of the papers explore how management controls support strategy implementation in the context of sustainability (e.g. Albelda, 2011; Cramer, 2005; Epstein & Roy, 2007; Epstein & Wisner, 2005; Khoo & Tan, 2002). Similar to the observations made by Chenhall (2003) and Tucker et al. (2009), few studies have elaborated on the role of management control in formulating sustainability strategies. One exception can be observed in Dias-Sardinha et al. (2007). Our interest was also in reviewing whether the empirical studies were reflective of the importance of managers' perceptions in mediating the management control – strategy relationship (Langfield-Smith, 1997), which highlights the need for a strategy-as-practice view as a complement to the dominant process view (Whittington, 1996). However, none of the reviewed papers refers explicitly to the strategy as social practice or similar approaches. In the main, this suggests that Chenhall's (2003) argument, that strategy constructs used in accounting studies may be outdated, might hold also true for studies on management control, strategy and sustainability.

Turning to our interest in *frameworks and understanding of management control*, we found much evidence of the balanced scorecard concept of Kaplan and Norton (1992, 1996, 2001), mobilised in a large majority of the reviewed papers to explore the use of management control for sustainability strategy (e.g. Leon-Soriano et al., 2010; Van der Woerd & Van den Brink, 2004). It is seen to support a comprehensive approach to sustainability strategy implementation that links key success factors, key performance indicators and incentive systems to the improvement of performance. The levers of control framework developed by Simons (1987, 1990, 1991, 1994) have emerged as another influential framework in the management control and strategy literature, describing four 'levers' of control that help an organisation in deploying and developing strategy, namely belief systems, boundary systems, diagnostic control systems and interactive control systems. Although the levers of control framework is applied to the field of strategic control for sustainability in a few other papers (e.g. Bonacchi & Rinaldi, 2007; Gond et al., 2012; Perego & Hartmann, 2009), we did not identify any empirical study on management control, strategy and sustainability which has used Simons' work. A few papers such as the paper by Norris and O'Dwyer (2004) refer to traditional control theory (e.g. Falkenberg & Herremans, 1995; Merchant, 1985; Otley & Berry, 1980; Ouchi, 1977). Other more recent management control frameworks, such as those developed by Malmi and Brown (2008) or Ferreira and Otley (2009), have not been adopted yet in empirical studies on management control, strategy and sustainability – despite the widespread recognition that individual controls constitute only a part of an interacting package of controls, functioning as either complements or substitutes (Abernethy & Chua, 1996; Malmi & Brown, 2008; Otley, 1999).

Finally, in terms of *philosophical perspectives*, we observe that some empirical studies are anchored in a business-case perspective and are oriented towards the creation of value for shareholders (e.g. Epstein & Roy, 2007; Perego & Hartmann, 2009; Taplin, Bent, & Aeron-Thomas, 2006). However, there has been an increasing number of papers published in recent years which have adopted a broader stakeholder accountability perspective (e.g. Durden, 2008; Galbreath, 2010; Norris & O'Dwyer, 2004; Perrini & Tencati, 2006). Adopting a broader understanding of value creation and the relationship between business and society, these empirical papers investigate, for example, whether, how and to what extent companies design or use management control systems to control for stakeholder responsiveness and monitor whether the business is operating in accordance with broader social goals and expectations, and hence could be seen to apply a broader stakeholder accountability perspective (Brown & Fraser, 2006).

Content

Our review of *themes and research questions* is based on the four broad categories of Tucker et al.'s (2009) framework, namely strategy content and process as well as management control design and use. The results of our review are summarised in Table 2 while the appendix (columns 2 and 3) describes the research questions investigated in each publication and positions them in the framework. The first category (Case A) refers to empirical research that studies management control *design* in function of the *content* of specific sustainability strategies. The second type of research (Case B) investigates the *use* of management control in function of the *content* of particular sustainability strategies. The third category (Case C) brings together empirical studies which concentrate on the *design* of management control to support the sustainability strategy *process* (implementation and/or formulation). The fourth category (Case D) concerns studies into the *use* of management control to support the sustainability strategy *process* (implementation and/or formulation). Overall, there is diversity in elaborating to a different extent on strategy content and process, and management control design and use.

We note that Tucker et al. (2009) consider the four groups or cases of their framework to represent 'archetypes', i.e. four 'ideal' types of research questions. This means that some studies can belong to more than one archetype, as is the case for example for Epstein and Wisner (2005) or Perego and Hartmann (2009) (Table 2). In the main, the large majority of the papers of our literature review are located in Case C. The link between management control design and the sustainability strategy process (with a focus on strategy implementation rather than strategy formulation) has often been investigated. A large proportion of the papers examine how companies design management control to implement an environmental or sustainability strategy (e.g. Durden, 2008; Epstein & Wisner, 2005;

Table 2. Classification of the Research Questions (Based on Tucker et al., 2009).

MC Strategy	Design	Use
Content	*Case A* Dias-Sardinha et al. (2002); Van der Woerd and Van den Brink (2004)	*Case B* Dias-Sardinha and Reijnders (2005)
	Cases A and B Perego and Hartmann (2009)	
Process	*Case C* Ballou et al. (2012); Cramer (2005); Dias-Sardinha et al. (2005); Durden (2008); Epstein and Roy (2007); Gates and Germain (2010); Khoo and Tan (2002); Lansiluoto and Jarvenpaa (2008); Leon-Soriano et al. (2010); Maon et al. (2009); Masanet-Llodra (2006); Maxwell et al. (1997); Morsing and Oswald (2009); Panapanaan, Linnanen, Karvonen, and Phan (2003); Perego and Hartmann (2009); Riccaboni and Leone (2010); Taplin et al. (2006); White (2009)	*Case D* Adams and Frost (2008)
	Cases C and D Albelda (2011); Albelda et al. (2007); Epstein and Wisner (2005); Galbreath (2010); Norris and O'Dwyer (2004)	

Leon-Soriano et al., 2010; Riccaboni & Leone, 2010). In contrast, few research papers differentiate management control based on the content of environmental or sustainability strategy (e.g. Dias-Sardinha & Reijnders, 2005; Van der Woerd & Van den Brink, 2004) and a very limited number of studies address the use of management control in relationship with sustainability strategy (content and process) (e.g. Adams & Frost, 2008; Perego & Hartmann, 2009).

Our search for *parameters of management controls* shows that, first, there is no generally accepted definition of the parameters of management control and ways to operationalise them, rather many definitions of management control (from narrow to very broad) are used in the reviewed papers. As a consequence, research findings are difficult to compare. In addition, several papers are dedicated to one or more specific components of management control. For example, Bonacchi and Rinaldi (2007) and Perego and Hartmann (2009) concentrate on sustainability performance measurement systems while Epstein and Roy (2007) investigate the role of organisational structure in the implementation of an environmental corporate strategy. Galbreath (2010) examines the control mechanisms of planning and culture and Morsing and Oswald (2009) concentrate on culture and leadership. This selective analysis of particular aspects of management control (from a subjective and variable inventory of possible controls) complicates the comparison of the research findings. In contrast, very few papers (e.g. Durden, 2008; Norris & O'Dwyer, 2004) have adopted a broader approach of management control.

In terms of *types of control mechanisms*, as alluded to earlier, researchers in the traditional accounting and management control literature (Chenhall, 2003; Langfield-Smith, 1997; Otley, 1999; Tucker et al., 2009) argue that most research has adopted a formal and accounting-oriented view while calling for research on broader set of controls which include both formal and informal approaches. Our review of the 27 empirical studies shows that this does not hold true for empirical studies into sustainability strategy and control. While about half of the studies concentrate on formal and accounting-based control mechanisms, a large number of studies explore simultaneously, or solely, informal and non-accounting controls (e.g. Durden, 2008; Epstein & Wisner, 2005; Morsing & Oswald, 2009; Norris & O'Dwyer, 2004; Riccaboni & Leone, 2010). Researchers point towards the important role informal control plays in this context (e.g. Norris & O'Dwyer, 2004) and the interactions between formal and informal controls.

Finally, in conformance with other research published for example in the field of managing for sustainability (Schaltegger, Windolph, & Herzig,

2012), we observe a predominance of research dedicated to the environmental *dimension of sustainability*. More than one third of the studies concentrate on the environmental aspects of sustainability (e.g. Albelda et al., 2007; Ballou et al., 2012; Epstein & Wisner, 2005; Masanet-Llodra, 2006; Perego & Hartmann, 2009) and we cannot identify any research that is solely dedicated to social sustainability issues. Still, more than half of the research portrays itself as dealing with all three dimensions of sustainable development and applying a more integrated approach to sustainability (e.g. Leon-Soriano et al., 2010; Riccaboni & Leone, 2010; Taplin et al., 2006).

Methodology

Within the *research design* applied by the 27 empirical studies there is a strong orientation towards case-based research (see the appendix, column 4). The 19 case-based studies are roughly equally based on single, in-depth case study designs (10) and multiple case study designs (9). We identify only eight survey-based studies (Ballou et al., 2012; Dias-Sardinha et al., 2002; Epstein & Roy, 2007; Epstein & Wisner, 2005; Galbreath, 2010; Gates & Germain, 2010; Perego & Hartmann, 2009). While this observation is somewhat contrary to the observation made by Tucker et al. (2009) with regard to the traditional management control and strategy literature (they identified a higher proportion of survey-based studies (20 papers) than case-based studies (13 papers)), it is perhaps indicative of the early stage of development in this research area.

We analysed the research focus of the reviewed empirical studies according to the countries and the type of companies (size and industry) investigated by the authors of our set of papers as well as the departmental affiliations and functions of the respondents and interviewees, respectively. With respect to *countries*, 4 empirical studies take place in the Oceania region (Australia and New Zealand), 19 empirical studies concentrate on Europe (Denmark, Finland, France, Italy, Portugal, Spain, Sweden, the Netherlands and the United Kingdom), 3 studies focus on North America and 1 study focuses on Mexico. It is interesting to note that half of the empirical surveys were carried out in Australia and in America (Ballou et al., 2012; Epstein & Roy, 2007; Epstein & Wisner, 2005; Galbreath, 2010). Out of the 19 empirical studies exploring European companies, there are 4 surveys that were carried out among Dutch, French, Italian and Portuguese companies (Dias-Sardinha et al., 2002; Gates & Germain, 2010; Perego & Hartmann, 2009;

Van der Woerd & Van den Brink, 2004), of which only 1 study provides a multiple country analysis. However, although Van der Woerd and Van den Brink (2004) analyse the sustainability-related management control and strategy practices in the Dutch tourist and the Italian food industry, they do not elaborate on international differences in their work.

Turning to the *size and type of company*, the majority of the empirical papers focus on large private companies. Only three papers investigate smaller companies (Durden, 2008; Leon-Soriano et al., 2010; Perrini & Tencati, 2006) and no research has been carried out on public organisations in the area of management control, strategy and sustainability. Consistent with the observation made by Chung and Parker (2008), we observe a clear focus on manufacturing companies (such as the chemical, the food, the automotive or the ceramic-tile industry). As Chung and Parker (2008) argue, it seems that 'most research into corporate environmental strategy, control and reporting has focused on the mining, manufacturing and chemical industries, especially those heavy industries where the potential for direct pollution and degradation of the environment is most obvious and appears to be the most significant. Increasingly, however, community environmental concerns have begun to extend to businesses in the service industry'.

Clear conclusions also emerge concerning the *interview partners and respondents* in which the focus on perspectives of only one organisational member appears the most common approach. The research design of these studies considers organisational members such as the CSR or sustainability manager (e.g. Ballou et al., 2012; Dias-Sardinha & Reijnders, 2005; Epstein & Roy, 2007; Maon et al., 2009), the financial manager (Perego & Hartmann, 2009) or the CEO (Galbreath, 2010). However, there is also evidence of some broader conceptualisations in which a range of organisational members from different departments is being interviewed or surveyed (e.g. Albelda et al., 2007; Durden, 2008).

SYNTHESIS AND DIRECTIONS FOR FUTURE RESEARCH

Synthesis

Even if a growing body of empirical research has emerged over the last decade, our current knowledge about how companies design or use management control to support environmental or sustainability strategy appears to be limited in several ways, providing scope for further research. One observation is that most of the reviewed studies belong either to the accounting and control or to the sustainability and CSR literature. We could not identify any empirical study from the strategy literature and only one paper published in a journal from another discipline (Leon-Soriano et al., 2010). However, previous studies demonstrates that research on the relationship between management control, strategy and sustainability is multidimensional in nature and that these constructs could be studied through the lenses of various disciplines (Langfield-Smith, 1997; McWilliams et al., 2006; Milne, 1996). Relatedly, although it would probably bring original insights, we have not identified any real multidisciplinary research on the connection of these concepts. This observation underlines again the importance to develop research in other fields or, ideally, multidisciplinary research on this interrelationship in the future.

With regard to their theoretical foundations, almost half of the studies do not refer explicitly to prior theory or conceptual frameworks published in the literature. The other publications mobilise to a varying extent theories or frameworks presented or developed in previous research. The strategy and management control frameworks and models tend to be 'out-dated'. For example, we observe a huge predominance of the deliberate and process view of strategy and its relationship with management control. More recent strategy and management control frameworks and models – such as those developed by Whittington (1996) or Malmi and Brown (2008) – have not been used in any of the papers which we have reviewed.

We feel that our literature review reveals some useful findings with regard to the content of the empirical studies on management control, strategy and sustainability. First, a large proportion of the studies investigate how management control *design* supports environmental or sustainability strategy implementation in practice. However, only a few papers have examined empirically how management controls are *used* to support these strategies or how management control design or use *differs in function of the strategy content* (e.g. Dias-Sardinha & Reijnders, 2005; Van der Woerd & Van den Brink, 2004). We propose some research questions which could be investigated in future research in the next section. Second, several studies could be viewed as having adopted a 'shopping list' approach to management control. They investigate specific aspects of management control from a rather subjective and variable inventory of possible controls (Tucker et al., 2009) while very few papers have adopted a broader approach to management control which combine formal and informal controls and explore the interplay between these mechanisms (e.g. Durden, 2008; Norris & O'Dwyer, 2004). The disparate conceptualisation and operationalisation of management control hamper the integration of research findings and we see a need to develop consistent classifications for controls and other contingent variables and to use established classifications and parameters in future research (Tucker et al., 2009). Third, there is a high proportion of papers which investigate simultaneously, or solely, informal and non-accounting controls (Durden, 2008; Epstein & Wisner, 2005; Morsing & Oswald, 2009; Norris & O'Dwyer, 2004; Riccaboni & Leone, 2010). The importance of informal control (e.g. Norris & O'Dwyer, 2004) and the interactions between formal and informal controls appear to be well recognised appear to be well recognised in this field of study. Finally, consistent with other research on sustainability, we observe a predominance of research dedicated to the environmental dimension of sustainability. Still, more than half of the research portrays itself as dealing with all three dimensions and applying a more integrated approach to researching sustainability (e.g. Perego & Hartmann, 2009; Riccaboni & Leone, 2010; Taplin et al., 2006).

In terms of methodology, there is a strong bias towards case-based research designs. Similarly, there is also a strong focus (more than two third of the studies) on Europe (Denmark, Finland, France, Italy, Portugal, Spain, Sweden, the Netherland, and the United Kingdom). Comparative studies into management control, strategy and sustainability are non-existent. The majority of the studies focus on large private manufacturing companies and often consider only one group of organisational members when collecting data through interviews or surveys. However, we also observe a broader range of interviewees and respondents (i.e. a set of representatives from different departments) in some studies (e.g. Albelda et al., 2007; Durden, 2008).

Overall, our literature review shows that our (empirical) knowledge on the relationship between management control, strategy and sustainability is still at a developmental stage. Especially, a limited number of conceptual models and theories have been utilised, the majority of the studies have researched the same category of research questions, and the use of diverse concepts and operationalisation of management control has restricted comparison of empirical findings on how companies control for sustainability strategy in practice. We expect that further studies addressing these gaps could create a stronger body of knowledge on the relationship between management control, strategy and sustainability. Some potential directions for future research are outlined in the next section.

Directions for Future Research

With regard to the theorisation of our knowledge on management control, strategy and sustainability, it could be useful to clarify the conceptual foundations of future empirical studies and to mobilise new approaches to strategy (such as the emerging strategy approach, (Mintzberg & Waters, 1985) or the strategy-as-practice approach (Whittington, 1996)) and to management control (e.g. Malmi & Brown, 2008, Simons, 1990, 1994). Research anchored in a more critical perspective could also extend our knowledge.

In terms of research content and questions, it could be interesting to further investigate research questions derived from the model by Tucker et al. (2009) which have been neglected in previous studies so far (in particular use and content). A non-exhaustive list of research questions that could be examined by future research might include questions such as the following:

- How does management control design vary according to the sustainability strategy pursued?
- What kind of design is the more adequate in function of the strategy pursued?
- How is the sustainability strategy pursued influenced by management control design?
- What are the main implications of changes in sustainability strategy for management control design?
- How are informal controls combined with formal controls to support particular sustainability strategies?
- Are some informal/formal controls adapted more than others to support specific sustainability strategies?
- How does management control use vary in function of the sustainability strategy?
- How is the sustainability strategy pursued and/or the sustainability strategy process influenced by the use of management control systems (diagnostic vs. interactive use – Simons, 1987, 1990, 1994)?
- How are management controls used in the process of formulating and implementing sustainability strategy?
- How do perceptions of actors involved in strategising sustainability through management control vary according to management level (Tessier & Otley, 2012) and/or departmental unit?

Due to the disparate conceptualisation and operationalisation of management control, we think it is essential to develop consistent classifications for controls and other contingent variables and to use established classifications and parameters in future research. Broader approaches to management control including both formal and informal controls and the interplay between these mechanisms (Durden, 2008; Norris & O'Dwyer, 2004) provide further scope for future research, using models such as those developed by Malmi and Brown (2008) or Ferreira and Otley (2009).

A stronger focus on surveys might also help in producing more generalisable findings (Ryan et al., 2002). As far as continents and countries are concerned, it would be interesting to examine other continents like Asia or Middle East or to focus on important American or European countries which have not been, or only to a minor extent, investigated by previous studies (e.g. France, Germany, the United Kingdom or the United States). Studies providing comparative perspectives would also be of interest. Furthermore, research dedicated to other types of companies such as small and medium sized companies, public organisations or companies operating in other industries like the service or commerce industries would add new empirical knowledge to this body of literature.

Finally, we see it as essential to continue engaging with different and a broader range of organisational members in empirical studies on management control, strategy and sustainability (especially with controllers). Indeed, as management control, strategy and sustainability are multidisciplinary notions, understanding the role of management control for sustainability strategy could benefit from engaging with and understanding the perspectives of different organisational members.

REFERENCES

Abernethy, M. A., & Chua, W. F. (1996). A field study of control system 'redesign': The impact of institutional processes on strategic choice. *Contemporary Accounting Research, 13* (2), 569–606.

Adams, C. A., & Frost, G. R. (2008). Integrating sustainability reporting into management practices. *Accounting Forum, 32*, 288–302.

Albelda, E. (2011). The role of management accounting practices as facilitators of the environmental management: Evidence from EMAS organisations. *Sustainability Accounting, Management and Policy Journal, 2*(1), 76–100.

Albelda, E., Correa, C., & Carrasco, F. (2007). Environmental management systems as an embedding mechanism: A research note. *Accounting, Auditing and Accountability Journal, 20*(3), 403–422.

Anthony, R. (1965). *Planning and control systems: A framework for analysis.* Cambridge, MA: Harvard University Press.

Ballou, B., Casey, R., Grenier, J., & Heitger, D. (2012). Exploring the strategic integration of sustainability initiatives: Opportunities for accounting research. *Accounting Horizons, 26*(2), 265–288.

Barney, J. B. (1991). Firms resources and sustained competitive advantage. *Journal of Management*, *17*, 99–120.

Barney, J., Wright, M., & Ketchen, D. J. (2001). The resource-based view of firm: Ten years after 1991, *Journal of Management* (*27*, 625–641).

Bennett, M., & James, P. (1998). *The green bottom line: Environmental accounting for management: Current practice and future trends*. Sheffield, UK: Greenleaf Publishing.

Berry, A., Coad, A., Harris, E., Otley, D., & Stringer, C. (2009). Emerging themes in management control: A review of recent literature. *The British Accounting Review*, *41*, 2–20.

Bonacchi, M., & Rinaldi, L. (2007). DartBoards and clovers as new tools in sustainability planning and control. *Business Strategy and the Environment*, *16*, 461–473.

Brown, J., & Fraser, M. (2006). Approaches and perspectives in social and environmental accounting: An overview of the conceptual landscape. *Business, Strategy and the Environment*, *15*, 103–117.

Brundtland, G. (1987). *Our common future: The world commission on environment and development*. Oxford: Oxford University Press.

Burritt, R. L., Hahn, T., & Schaltegger, S. (2002). Towards a comprehensive framework for environmental management accounting: Links between business actors and environmental management accounting tools. *Australian Accounting Review*, *12*(2), 39–50.

Burritt, R., & Schaltegger, S. (2010). Sustainability accounting and reporting: Fad or trend? *Accounting, Auditing and Accountability Journal*, *23*(7), 829–846.

Castro, N., & Chousa, J. (2006). An integrated framework for the financial analysis of sustainability. *Business Strategy and the Environment*, *15*, 322–333.

Chapman, C. (1997). Reflections on a contingent view of accounting. *Accounting, Organizations and Society*, *22*, 189–205.

Chartered Institute of Management Accountants (CIMA) and Accenture. (2011). Sustainability performance management: How CFOs can unlock value. Retrieved from http://www.accenture.com/us-en/Pages/insight-sustainability-performance-management.aspx

Chenhall, R. (2003). Management control systems design within its organizational context: Findings from contingency-based research and directions for the future. *Accounting, Organizations and Society*, *28*(2–3), 127–168.

Chenhall, R. H. (2005). Integrative strategic performance measurement systems, strategic alignment of manufacturing, learning and strategic outcomes: An exploratory study. *Accounting, Organizations and Society*, *30*, 395–422.

Chenhall, R. H., & Langfield-Smith, K. (2003). Performance measurement and reward systems, trust, and strategic change. *Journal of Management Accounting Research*, *15*, 117–144.

Chung, L., & Parker, L. (2008). Integrating hotel environmental strategies with management control: A structuration approach. *Business Strategy and the Environment*, *17*, 272–286.

Cramer, J. (2005). Experiences with structuring corporate social responsibility in Dutch industry. *Journal of Cleaner Production*, *13*, 583–592.

Dent, J. F. (1990). Strategy, organization and control: Some possibilities for accounting research. *Accounting, Organizations and Society*, *15*(1–2), 3–25.

Dias-Sardinha, I., & Reijnders, L. (2005). Evaluating environmental and social performance of large portuguese companies: A balanced scorecard approach. *Business Strategy and the Environment*, *14*, 73–91.

Dias-Sardinha, I., Reijnders, L., & Antunes, P. (2002). From environmental performance evaluation to eco-efficiency and sustainability balanced scorecards. *Environmental Quality Management*, *Winter*, 51–64.

Dias-Sardinha, I., Reijnders, L., & Antunes, P. (2007). Developing sustainability balanced scorecards for environemntal services: A study of three large portuguese companies. *Environmental Quality Management, Summer*, 13–34.

Durden, C. (2008). Towards a socially responsible management control system. *Accounting, Auditing & Accountability Journal, 21*(5), 671–694.

Elkington, J. (1997). *Cannibals with forks: The triple bottom line of 21st century business.* Oxford: Capstone.

Epstein, M., & Roy, M. (2001). Sustainability in action: Identifying and measuring the key performance drivers. *Long Range Planning, 34*, 585–604.

Epstein, M., & Roy, M. (2007). Implementing a corporate environmental strategy: Establishing coordination and control within multinational companies. *Business Strategy and the Environment, 16*, 389–403.

Epstein, M., & Wisner, P. (2005). Managing and controlling for environmental performance: Evidence from Mexico. *Advances in Accounting, 14*, 115–136.

Falkenberg, L., & Herremans, I. (1995). Ethical behaviours in organizations: Directed by the formal or informal systems?. *Journal of Business Ethics, 14*(2), 133–145.

Ferreira, A., & Otley, D. (2009). The design and use of performance management systems: An extended framework for analysis. *Management Accounting Research, 20*, 263–282.

Figge, F., Hahn, T., Schaltegger, S., & Wagner, M. (2002). The sustainability balanced scorecard – linking sustainability management to business strategy. *Business Strategy and the Environment, 11*, 269–284.

Fries, J., McCulloch, K., & Webster, W. (2010). The Prince's accounting for sustainability project: Creating 21st-century decision-making and reporting systems to respond to 21st-century challenges and opportunities. In A. Hopwood, J. Unerman & J. Fries (Eds.), *Accounting for sustainability: Practical insights*. Earthscan.

Galbreath, J. (2010). Drivers of corporate social responsibility: The role of formal strategic planning and firm culture. *British Journal of Management, 21*, 511–525.

Gates, S., & Germain, C. (2010). Integrating sustainability measures into strategic performance measurement systems: An empirical study. *Management Accounting Quarterly, 11*(3), 1–7.

Global Reporting Initiative (GRI). (2013). *G4 Sustainability reporting guidelines*. Amsterdam: GRI.

Gond, J. P., Grubnic, S., Herzig, C., & Moon, J. (2012). Configuring management control system: Theorizing the integration of strategy and sustainability. *Management Accounting Research, 23*, 205–223.

Gray, R. (2002). The social accounting project and accounting, organizations and society: Privileging engagement, imaginings, new accountings and pragmatism over critique?. *Accounting, Organizations and Society, 27*, 687–708.

Gray, R., Owen, D., & Maunders, K. (1988). Corporate social reporting: Emerging trends in accountability and the social contract. *Accounting, Auditing & Accountability Journal, 1*(1), 6–20.

Gray, R. H., Owen, D. L., & Adams, C. (1996). *Accounting and accountability*. Harlow: Prentice Hall Europe.

Hart, S. (1995). A natural resource-based view of the firm. *Academy of Management Review, 20*(4), 986–1014.

Henri, J.-F. (2006). Management control systems and strategy: A resourcebased view. *Accounting, Organizations and Society, 31*, 529–558.

Herzig, C., Viere, T., Schaltegger, S., & Burritt, R. L. (2012). *Environmental management accounting: Case studies of South East-Asian companies*. London: Routledge.

Hubbard, G. (2009). Measuring organizational performance: Beyond the triple bottom line. *Business Strategy and the Environment*, *18*(3), 177–191.

International Organization for Standardization (ISO). (2012). *ISO 14051 environmental management – Material flow cost accounting – General framework*. ISO.

Johnson, G., Scholes, K., & Whittington, R. (2008). *Exploring corporate strategy*. London, UK: Pearson.

Kaplan, R. S., & Norton, D. P. (1992). *The balanced score card – measures that drive performance*. Boston, MA: Harvard Business School Press.

Kaplan, R. S., & Norton, D. P. (1996). *The balanced scorecard: Translating strategy into action*. Boston, MA: Harvard Business Review Press.

Kaplan, R. S., & Norton, D. P. (2001). *The strategy-focused organisation: How balanced scorecard companies thrive in the new business environment*. Boston, MA: Harvard Business Review Press.

Khoo, H., & Tan, K. (2002). Using the Australian business excellence framework to achieve sustainable business excellence. *Corporate Social Responsibility and Environmental Management*, *9*, 196–205.

Kober, R., Ng, J., & Paul, B. J. (2007). The interrelationship between management control mechanisms and strategy. *Management Accounting Research*, *18*(4), 425–452.

Langfield-Smith, K. (1997). Management control systems and strategy: A critical review. *Accounting, Organizations and Society*, *22*(2), 207–232.

Lansiluoto, A., & Jarvenpaa, M. (2008). Environmental and performance management forces: Integrating "greenness" into balanced scorecard. *Qualitative Research in Accounting and Management*, *5*(3), 184–206.

Leon-Soriano, R., Muñoz-Torres, M., & Chalmeta-Rosaleñ, R. (2010). Methodology for sustainability strategic planning and management. *Industrial Management & Data Systems*, *110*(2), 249–268.

Llewelyn, S. (2003). What counts as "theory" in qualitative management and accounting research? Introducing five levels of theorizing. *Accounting, Auditing & Accountability Journal*, *16*(4), 662–708.

Malmi, T., & Brown, D. A. (2008). Management control systems as a package – opportunities, challenges and research directions. *Management Accounting Research*, *19*(4), 287–300.

Malmi, T., & Granlund, M. (2009). In search of management accounting theory. *European Accounting Review*, *18*(3), 597–620.

Maon, F., Lindgreen, A., & Swaen, V. (2009). Designing and implementing corporate social responsibility: An integrative framework grounded in theory. *Journal of Business Ethics, and Practice*, *87*, 71–89.

Masanet-Llodra, M. (2006). Environmental management accounting: A case study research on innovative strategy. *Journal of Business Ethics*, *68*(4), 393–408.

Maxwell, J., Rothenberg, S., Briscoe, F., & Marcus, A. (1997). Green schemes: Corporate environmental strategies and their implementation. *California Management Review*, *39*(3), 118–134.

McWilliams, A., Siegel, D., & Wright, P. (2006). Corporate social responsibility: Strategic implications. *Journal of Management Studies*, *43*(1), 1–18.

Melville, N. (2010). Information systems innovation for environmental sustainability. *MIS Quarterly*, *34*(1), 1–21.

Merchant, K. (1985). *Control in business organizations*. Boston, MA: Pitman Press.

Milne, M. (1996). On sustainability: The environment and management accounting. *Management Accounting Research*, *7*, 135–161.

Mintzberg, H. T. (1979). *The structuring of organizations*. Englewood Cliffs, NJ: Prentice Hall.

Mintzberg, H. T., & Waters, J. A. (1985). Of strategies, deliberate and emergent. *Strategic Management Journal*, *6*, 257–272.

Morsing, M., & Oswald, D. (2009). Sustainable leadership: Management control systems and organizational culture in Novo Nordisk A/S. *Corporate Governance*, *9*(1), 83–99.

Norris, G., & O'Dwyer, B. (2004). Motivating socially responsive decision making: The operation of management controls in a socially responsive organisation. *The British Accounting Review*, *36*, 173–196.

O'Dwyer, B. (2011). The case of sustainability assurance: Constructing a new assurance service. *Contemporary Accounting Research*, *28*(4), 1230–1266.

O'Dwyer, B., Owen, D., & Unerman, J. (2011). Seeking legitimacy for new assurance forms: The case of assurance on sustainability reporting. *Accounting, Organizations and Society*, *36*(1), 31–52.

Otley, D. T. (1999). Performance management: A framework for management control system research. *Management Accounting Research*, *10*, 363–382.

Otley, D. T., & Berry, A. J. (1980). Control, organisation and accounting. *Accounting, Organizations and Society*, *5*(2), 231–246.

Otley, D. T., Broadbent, J., & Berry, A. J. (1995). Research in management control: An overview of its development. *British Journal of Management*, *6*, 31–44.

Ouchi, W. G. (1977). The relationship between organizational structure and organizational control. *Administrative Science Quarterly*, *22*, 95–113.

Owen, D., & O'Dwyer, B. (2008). Corporate social responsibility: The reporting and assurance dimension. In A. Crane, A. McWilliams, J. Moon & D. S. Siegel (Eds.), *The Oxford handbook of corporate social responsibility* (pp. 384–409). New York, NY: Oxford University Press.

Panapanaan, V., Linnanen, L., Karvonen, M., & Phan, V. (2003). Roadmapping corporate social responsibility in finnish companies. *Journal of Business Ethics*, *44*(2/3), 133–148.

Parker, L. (2000). Environmental costing: A path to implementation. *Australian Accounting Review*, *10*(3), 43–52.

Perego, P., & Hartmann, S. (2009). Aligning performance measurement systems with strategy: The case of environmental strategy. *Abacus*, *45*(4), 397–428.

Perrini, F., & Tencati, A. (2006). Sustainability and stakeholder management: The need for new corporate performance evaluation and reporting systems. *Business Strategy and the Environment*, *15*, 296–308.

Porter, M. (1980). *Competitive strategy*. New York, NY: Free Press.

Porter, M., & van der Linde, C. (1995). Green and competitive. *Harvard Business Review*, (September/October), 121–134.

Riccaboni, A., & Leone, E. (2010). Implementing strategies through management control systems: The case of sustainability. *International Journal of Productivity and Performance Management*, *59*(2), 130–144.

Roome, N. J. (1998). Sustainability strategies for industry. *The future of corporate practice*. Washington, DC: Island.

Ryan, R., Scapens, R., & Theobald, M. (2002). *Research methods and methodology in finance and accounting* (2nd ed.). London, UK: Thomson.

Schaltegger, S. (2011). Sustainability as a driver for corporate economic success – consequences for the development of sustainability management control. *Society and Economy*, *33*(1), 15–28.

Schaltegger, S., Bennett, M., & Burritt, R. (2006). Sustainability accounting and reporting: Development, linkages and reflection: An introduction. In S. Schaltegger, M. Bennett, & R. Burritt (Eds.) *Sustainability accounting and reporting* (pp. 1–33). Dordrecht: Springer.

Schaltegger, S., & Wagner, M. (2006). Integrative management of sustainability performance, measurement and reporting. *International Journal of Accounting, Auditing and Performance Evaluation*, *3*(1), 1–19.

Schaltegger, S., Windolph, S., & Herzig, C. (2012). A longitudinal analysis of the knowledge and application of sustainability management tools in large German companies. *Society and Economy*, *34*(4), 549–579.

Searcey, C. (2012). Corporate sustainability performance measurement systems: A review and research agenda. *Journal of Business Ethics*, *107*, 239–253.

Simons, R. (1987). Accounting control systems and business strategy: An empirical analysis. *Accounting, Organizations and Society*, *24*, 107–125.

Simons, R. (1990). The role of management control systems in creating competitive advantage: New perspectives. *Accounting, Organizations and Society*, *15*(1/2), 127–143.

Simons, R. (1991). Strategic orientation and top management attention to control systems. *Strategic Management Journal*, *12*, 49–62.

Simons, R. (1994). How new top managers use control systems as levers of strategic renewal. *Strategic Management Journal*, *15*, 169–189.

Simons, R. (1995). *Levers of control, how managers use innovative control systems to drive strategic renewal.* Boston, MA: Harvard Business School Press.

Sutton, R. I., & Staw, B. M. (1995). What theory is not. *Administrative Science Quarterly*, *40*(3), 371–384.

Taplin, J., Bent, D., & Aeron-Thomas, D. (2006). Developing a sustainability accounting framework to inform strategic business decisions: A case study from the chemicals industry. *Business Strategy and the Environment*, *15*, 347–360.

Tessier, S., & Otley, D. (2012). A conceptual development of Simons' Levers of Control framework. *Management Accounting Research*, *23*, 171–185.

Thomson, I. (2007). Mapping the terrain of sustainability accounting. In J. Unerman, J. Bebbington, & B. O'Dwyer (Eds.), *Sustainability accounting and accountability*. London, UK: Routledge.

Tucker, B., Thorne, H., & Gurd, B. (2009). Management control systems and strategy: What's been happening? *Journal of Accounting Literature*, *28*, 123–133.

Van der Woerd, F., & Van den Brink, T. (2004). Feasibility of a responsive business scorecard – a pilot study. *Journal of Business Ethics*, *55*, 173–186.

White, P. (2009). Building a sustainability strategy into the business. *Corporate Governance*, *9*(4), 386–394.

Whittington, R. (1996). Strategy as practice. *Long Range Planning*, *29*(5), 731–735.

APPENDIX 1: SUMMARY OF THE 27 EMPIRICAL STUDIES ON MANAGEMENT CONTROL, STRATEGY AND SUSTAINABILITY

Name of the Author(s) (Publication Date)	Research Theme(s) and Research Objective(s)	Operationalisation of Management Control (Design/Use) and Strategy (Content/Process) (Tucker et al., 2009)	Empirical Research and Methodology
Maxwell et al. (1997)	This article examines the environmental strategies and implementation schemes of three companies in different industries (Volvo, Polaroid, and Procter & Gamble)	*Design* of controls as an important part of environmental strategies implementation (*process*) – Case C	Case-based research (three cases – large multinational corporations)
Dias-Sardinha et al. (2002)	This paper analyses different types of environmental strategic objectives and related management control (MC) design	*Design* of MC in function of the environmental strategy *content* (environmental strategic objectives) – Case A	Survey-based research (35 cases – industrial and service SMEs – Portugal)
Khoo and Tan (2002)	This paper presents different stages to transform a company towards sustainability	*Design* of controls as an important part of environmental strategies implementation (*process*) – Case C	Case-based research (one case – one manufacturing plant – Australia)
Panapanaan et al. (2003)	This paper presents a roadmap of Finnish companies adopting and managing corporate social responsibility (CSR). It discusses the companies' views on CSR and highlights the practices that Finnish companies have adopted or are currently adopting. It also presents a	*Design* of controls (structure, planning, monitoring and evaluation) as an important part of environmental strategies implementation (*process*) – Case C	Case-based research (12 cases – large companies – Finland)

	framework that outlines the CSR processes and management prospects		
Norris and O'Dwyer (2004)	The authors examine the perceived influence of control systems on socially responsive managerial decision-making	*Design and use* of MC to support decision-making *process* – Case B	Case-based research (one single case study – one large retail company – the United Kingdom
Van der Woerd and Van den Brink (2004)	The authors assess the practical feasibility of a responsive scorecard in food and tourist industries	*Design* of a Balanced Score Card to integrate sustainability into strategy in function of the sustainability strategy *content* – Case A	Survey-based research (small and large companies operating in the Dutch tourist and Italian food industry)
Cramer (2005)	The author investigates how to implement CSR into an organisation	*Design* of controls as an important part of environmental strategies implementation (*process*) – Case C	Case-based research (19 cases – diverse companies in the Netherlands)
Dias-Sardinha and Reijnders (2005)	A thematic balanced scorecard format was used to address environmental and social performance evaluation of 13 large companies operating in Portugal.	*Use* of management control (performance evaluation) in function of the environmental strategy (content) – Case B	Case-based research (13 cases – large companies in Portugal)
Epstein and Wisner (2005)	The authors test the relationship between management control systems and structures and environmental compliance	*Design and use* of management control to support (environmental) strategy implementation (*process*) – Cases C and D	Survey-based research (236 manufacturing companies – Mexico)
Masanet-Llodra (2006)	The main objectives of the research are two. The first one consists in determining the relationship between companies and environment, analysing environmental positions in companies assumed in their environmental strategy and their environmental behaviour reflected in facts, while the second one attempts	*Design* of control to support strategy *process* – Case C	Case-based research (1 case – ceramic-tiles industry – Spain)

Appendix (*Continued*)

Name of the Author(s) (Publication Date)	Research Theme(s) and Research Objective(s)	Operationalisation of Management Control (Design/Use) and Strategy (Content/Process) (Tucker et al., 2009)	Empirical Research and Methodology
	to establish the role played by the accounting information system in the environmental management systems of the companies in the sector		
Taplin et al. (2006)	This paper proposes to help ChemCo develop a framework for business decision-making	*Design* of MC to support the strategy *process* – Case C	Case-based research (1 case – large company operating in Chemical industry – the United Kingdom)
Albelda et al. (2007)	The purpose of this paper is to explore the interplay between strategy, environmental management systems and environmental accounting, and their role in improving environmental performance	*Design and use* ('presence and usage') of MC (strategic planning, environmental accounting) to support strategy *process* – Cases C and D	Case-based research (10 cases – Spanish EMAS registered sites)
Dias-Sardinha et al. (2007)	The papers aim at designing a sustainability BSC in three large Portuguese companies	*Design* of management control to support the strategy *process* (implementation + formulation) – Case C	Case-based research (three cases – large companies – Portugal)
Epstein and Roy (2007)	This article presents the results of an empirical study that investigated coordination and control within multinational companies over six key aspects of their environmental strategy	*Design* of management control (organisational structure – centralisation) to implement an environmental strategy (*process*) – Case C	Survey-based research (98 cases – multinational corporations – North America)
Adams and Frost (2008)	The paper studies the process of developing key performance	*Use* of MC to support decision-making *process* (// strategy) – Case D	

	indicators for measuring sustainability performance and the way in which sustainability KPIs are used in decision-making, planning and performance management		Case-based research (seven cases – Australia/the United Kingdom)
Durden (2008)	The purpose of this paper is to investigate the measurement and monitoring of social responsibility within the management control system (MCS) of an organisation that subscribes to a stakeholder and social responsibility approach and to propose a framework that provides for the integration of the MCS with social accounting and social responsibility aspects	*Design* of management controls to support decision-making (strategy implementation – *process*) – Case C	Case-based research (one case – small manufacturing company in New Zealand)
Lansiluoto and Jarvenpaa (2008)	The authors analyse the forces that prompted a Finnish food manufacturing company to implement an EMS and PMS. Furthermore, they describe how and why environmental issues were integrated into a BSC	*Design* of MC to support strategy implementation (*process*) – Case C	Case-based research (one case – Food manufacturing company – Finland)
Moan et al. (2008)	This article introduces an integrative framework of CSR design and implementation	*Design* of controls as an important part of environmental strategies implementation (*process*) – Case C	Case-based research (three cases – large multinational)
Perego and Hartmann (2009)	This paper addresses the following research question: How environmental strategy affects the design and use of performance measurements systems?	*Design and use* of management control (performance measurement) in function of environmental strategy *content* (proactive/reactive) – Cases A and B	Survey-based research (81 cases – small and large manufacturing companies – the Netherlands)
Morsing and Oswald (2009)	This paper explores to what extent it is possible to influence sustainability at the operational level by contemporary management control systems as it	*Design* of management control to support sustainability (strategy) *process* – Case C	Case-based research (one case – large pharmaceutical company – Denmark)

Appendix *(Continued)*

Name of the Author(s) (Publication Date)	Research Theme(s) and Research Objective(s)	Operationalisation of Management Control (Design/Use) and Strategy (Content/Process) (Tucker et al., 2009)	Empirical Research and Methodology
	proposes to integrate the perspective of organisational culture		
White (2009)	This paper provides a new and broad overview of how sustainability has been implemented in a global consumer goods company	*Design* of controls as an important part of environmental strategies implementation (*process*) – Case C	Case-based research (one case – one large global consumer company)
Galbreath (2010)	This paper addresses the role of formal planning and company culture as drivers of corporate social responsibility	*Design and use* of management control (strategic planning and culture) to support strategy implementation (*process*) – Cases C and D	Survey-based research (280 cases – manufacturing and services companies in Australia)
Gates and Germain (2010)	The authors study to which extent sustainability measures are integrated into SPMS and align with strategy as well as which factors (strategy, industry, stock market listing, nationality) explain this	*Design* of management control to support strategy implementation (*process*) – Case C	Survey-based research (79 companies – France)
Leon-Soriano et al. (2010)	The paper describes the process of designing and implementing a sustainability BSC for sustainability strategic planning and management	*Design* of management control to support strategy implementation (*process*) – Case C	Case-based research (one case – manufacturing SME – Spain)
Riccaboni and Leone (2010)	The paper aims at exploring two categories of research questions RQ1. How MCS supports the implementation of sustainability focused strategies? How formal and informal controls work together in order to allow the	*Design* of management control to support strategy implementation (*process*) – Case C	Case-based research (one case – large consumer good producer – the United States)

	achievement of sustainable goals as well as the integration of sustainable principle with organisation culture? RQ2. What pattern of change is followed by MCS when a strategic change in a 'sustainable' direction occurs?		
Albelda (2011)	This paper addresses the link between social/environmental strategies and management control systems	*Design and use* of management control to support strategy *process* – Cases C and D	Case-based research (six sites – Spain)
Ballou et al. (2012)	This paper examines how three areas of accounting expertise (risk identification and measurement, financial reporting, and independent review/assurance) contribute to the strategic integration of sustainability initiatives	*Design* of (accounting) controls to support the strategic integration of sustainability initiatives (*process*) – Case C	Survey-based research (178 cases – the United States)

ENVIRONMENTAL MANAGEMENT ACCOUNTING SYSTEMS: A REVIEW OF THE EVIDENCE AND PROPOSITIONS FOR FUTURE RESEARCH

Giovanni Battista Derchi, Michael Burkert and Daniel Oyon

ABSTRACT

Purpose – *Organizations' increasing concern for environment shows the interest in appropriate mechanisms that account for relevant flows of environment-related information. Today managers and researchers are promoting environmental management accounting (EMA) systems mechanisms as a means to incorporate the full spectrum of ecological data into day-to-day business decisions and foster green management execution. However implementation remains a challenge and many of the difficulties are associated with conceptual and practical problems in integrating 'green' information and providing guidance on effective implementation. In this context academics might investigate on further explanations on how to achieve excellence in both environmental and*

Accounting and Control for Sustainability
Studies in Managerial and Financial Accounting, Volume 26, 197–229

ISSN: 1479-3512/doi:10.1108/S1479-3512(2013)0000026006

financial performance. Hence this chapter substantiates the need for more theoretical and empirical studies on EMA practices and proposes avenues for future research.

Approach – *We review the growing body of EMA research to inform the reader of what has been studied to date and indicate the necessity for further investigation. In addition, we suggest areas for future research.*

Findings – *Our synthesis highlights the relevant aspects of EMA examined in prior studies. The review reveals unexplored facets that need to be investigated to complement existing knowledge. In particular researchers might explore the concept of environmental performance and the application of different forms of EMA within organizations. Moreover academics have the opportunity to further examine the role of EMA mechanisms in companies that do not pursue environmental results for economic benefits.*

Value – *The chapter sheds some light on EMA literature and emphasizes the opportunities that new theoretical developments and appropriate research designs offer in the investigation of the remaining gaps in the literature.*

Keywords: Environmental management accounting; environmental and economic performance; environmental costing; eco-practices

INTRODUCTION

The organizational focus on environmental sustainability has changed considerably in the past 30 years – from a side topic in the early 1980s to a dominant theme today. Beyond the moral reasons for 'green' development (Marcus & Fremeth, 2009), demands for environmental management also originate from a variety of sources. From a managerial perspective, we can identify a combination of external social and internal business-related factors (Burritt & Schaltegger, 2010).

On the one hand calls for green management arise from social forces outside the organization. Corporations must show material commitment to environmental sustainability in order to comply with 'green' regulations and avoid the deterioration of their reputation, which could potentially result in loss of sales (Marcus & Fremeth, 2009). On the other hand managers are committed to environmental sustainability on the basis of an internally developed business strategy. Decisions aimed at solving environmental problems are business-related in nature because they are made to strengthen the competitive position of the company in the marketplace (Burritt & Schaltegger, 2010; Carroll & Shabana, 2010).

As a result management leaders and academic researchers alike have generally accepted that corporate environmental aspects must be integrated into business strategy and thus into operational and capital-investment decisions in order to more effectively manage leading corporations (Berns et al., 2009; CIMA, 2011; Epstein, 2008). So 'it is no longer a discussion of why, what or whether to focus on sustainability, but how' (Epstein, 2010, p. 4). Nevertheless effective execution remains volatile (Epstein, 2010), creating challenges for both managers and academics. Several studies indicate that organizations have difficulty integrating green management into day-to-day decision-making and ascribe this implementation gap to defects and breakdowns in planning and execution (Berns et al., 2009; CIMA 2011; Epstein, 2010; Mankins & Steele, 2005). Some authors suggest that many of these difficulties are associated with conceptual and practical problems of management control and performance measurement systems which seem to be unable to incorporate environment-related information and provide guidance on how to succeed in environmental sustainability (Burritt, 2004; Epstein, 2010). So far major barriers to effective corporate action have been attributed to conventional management accounting (Berns et al., 2009; Burritt, 2004; Epstein, 2010). First, environmental costs are generally lumped in with business overheads and 'green' externalities are not accounted for. As a result companies fail to understand what green management means, largely because of a lack of information for decision-making. Second, 'performance appraisal techniques are too narrow and short term in their focus' (Burritt, 2004, p. 18), whereas environmental performance is multidimensional and long term in nature. As such companies find it difficult to model the business case for environmental sustainability because of difficulties in identifying, measuring and controlling 'green' impacts. Third, rewarding systems do not include the environmental impacts of individuals and organizational units. Poorly motivated organizations are unlikely to deliver targeted outcome. Finally firms encounter many organizational obstacles in adapting existing control systems to environmental concerns. When companies act, the implementation of sustainable practices is constrained or even blocked by scepticism originating from managerial inertia, lack of requisite skills, organizational and cultural factors, and the reluctance to change.

It is in this context that academics have room to contribute to management accounting research and provide further explanations on how to successfully implement environmental sustainability (Burritt, 2004; Epstein, 2010; Henri & Journeault, 2010).

This work focuses on environmental management accounting (EMA), which refers to the development and implementation of appropriate accounting practices that identify and measure the full spectrum of relevant environment-related information to support business decisions (IFAC, 2005; UNDSD, 2001). EMA is concerned with the entire set of formal and informal control systems that use financial and ecological information to establish patterns in corporate environmental activity (Burritt, 2004; Henri & Journeault, 2010). Several recent studies have shed light on the importance of these systems, arguing that EMA represents one of the tools adopted by firms to profit from the potential benefits of environmental performance (Schaltegger & Burritt, 2000).

Our central aim is to substantiate the claim for more theoretical and empirical work in the field of EMA and to propose directions for future research.

As such we review existing literature on EMA and identify avenues for further investigation. Our analysis indicates that extant research has provided many relevant insights into the various aspects of 'green' management control practices adopted by organizations. We also reveal interesting, unexplored facets of EMA that need to be investigated. We additionally elaborate on the increasing enthusiasm and consensus on green management (Marcus & Fremeth, 2009), providing researchers with the opportunity to explore innovative theories and models to better explain the concept of EMA and its applications.

The remainder of this chapter is organized as follows. The following section introduces the background of the study. The next section reviews literature on EMA substantiating the need for additional research. We then propose new theoretical developments and research designs that accounting scholars might consider when setting up and structuring future work concerning innovative aspects of 'green' management control. Finally we summarize the results of our investigation and conclude the study.

BACKGROUND

The managerial view of environmental sustainability provides various explanations about corporate needs for green management. We can distinguish two main theories in the related academic research.

Some authors adopt a sociopolitical approach to justify why managers are called for contributing to environmental development. As such corporations engage with external green-oriented stakeholders to demonstrate that they operate within the bounds of society and behave with 'legitimacy' to the extent that their activities are transparent and congruent with societal expectations and managers are fully accountable for their decisions (Mathews, 1993; Parsons, 1960). In this context several empirical studies provide evidence of green management tools used by companies to address their exposure to social, legal and political pressures (Cho & Patten, 2007; Cho, Freedman, & Patten, 2012a; Cho, Guidry, Hageman, & Patten, 2012b; Marquis & Toffel, 2012; O'Sullivan & O'Dwyer, 2009).

In parallel other academics agree on an economics-based paradigm to explain what drives corporate environmental behaviour. According to this line of thought, companies incorporate 'green' aspects into their internal business strategies because of the potential financial benefits related to environmental performance. These business-case arguments contend that firms engaging in environmental activities are rewarded by the market in monetary terms (Carroll & Shabana, 2010; Schaltegger, Ludeke-Freund, & Hansen, 2012). More specifically, organizations allocate resources to responsible eco-efficient activities as they realize that it is possible to increase economic performance while simultaneously strengthening environmental performance. Ecological improvements such as waste reduction, energy conservation, material reutilization and a life-cycle perspective increase productive efficiency, thereby reducing costs (Porter & Van der Linde, 1995). Also, superior 'green' performance provides a basis for enhancing corporate reputation and for increasing revenues by satisfying the needs of 'green' consumers (Hart, 1995). Finally the positive association between environmental and economic performance can also be explained by the potential to reduce compliance and liability costs (i.e. by reducing emissions below the required level) as well as to diminish long-term risks associated with resource depletion, pollution, waste management and fluctuations in energy costs and product liabilities (Shrivastava, 1995). Thus far, much of the literature has empirically shown that the more enlightened corporations recognize environmentally responsible activities as value-relevant. Firms engage with green-oriented stakeholders to help improve corporate economic performance through cost reductions and ecological efficiencies, as well as new-market development, first-move advantage, better community relations and an improved image (Berns et al., 2009; Burnett & Hansen, 2008; CIMA, 2011, 2010; Clarkson, Li, & Richardson, 2004; Clarkson, Li, Richardson, & Vasvari; 2008; Dhaliwal, Radhakrishnan,

Tsang & Yang, 2012; Ditz, Ranganathan, & Banks, 1995; Epstein, 2008; Henri & Journeault, 2010; Hughes, 2000; Schaltegger & Burritt, 2000).

'As changes occur in corporate concepts and accountability for the environment, the demands for different flows of information – accounting and otherwise – are also growing' (Hopwood, 2009a, p. 433). While organizational concern about caring for the environment is increasing, so is interest in accounting for the environment (Burnett & Hansen, 2008; Gray, 2010). In this context managerial professionals have widely requested management control and performance measurement systems that support organizations in managing environment-related information and allow firms to foster green management execution. At an institutional level, for example, the United Nations Division of Sustainable Development has promoted EMA systems by providing government agencies, industry management, accounting professionals and all others with detailed guidelines and frameworks for effective application (UNDSD, 2001). Additionally, from a corporate perspective, practitioner studies have identified firms that are investing resources to develop new organizational capabilities, including a culture that stimulates and rewards long-term vision and managerial tools to support performance measurement, business modeling and reporting (Berns et al., 2009; CIMA, 2011). Similarly one line of academic research has focused on defining the concept of EMA and has reported current issues related to ecologically oriented control systems (Burritt, 2004; Epstein, 2008; IFAC, 2005; Schaltegger & Burritt, 2000).

According to this research EMA refers to the design and implementation of appropriate accounting techniques that identify and measure the full spectrum of physical and monetary, environment-related information to support day-to-day business decisions (IFAC, 2005; UNDSD, 2001). In particular, 'as a specific application of management control systems, EMA has attracted growing attention in recent years as a means of driving firm-wide environmental strategy' (Henri & Journeault, 2010, p. 63). EMA is concerned with the entire set of formal and informal control systems that use financial and ecological information to model environmental decisions (Burritt, 2004; Henri & Journeault, 2010). As pointed out by Henri and Journeault (2010, p. 64), ecological management accounting tools are 'used to supply information for decision-making to ensure the attainment of environmental objectives and to provide persuasive evidence supporting the benefits of such actions'.

'If the business case for environmental sustainability is valid, then companies are more likely to establish EMA systems aimed at quantifying costs and benefits of proactive green management' to support day-to-day business decisions (Burnett & Hansen, 2008, p. 552). This often includes redesigning cost estimation systems with an ecological focus, integrating environment-related information into both capital and operating budgeting, adopting a balanced scorecard approach to manage and report green sustainability information, developing a variety of green metrics related to ecologically oriented internal and external value drivers for managerial use and linking managers' performance incentives to environmental objectives. However both researchers and professionals have recently highlighted the difficulty that corporations face when incorporating 'green' aspects into business processes and have particularly indicated the existence of a divide between good intentions and execution (Berns et al., 2009; Epstein, 2010). Some authors suggest that many of these challenges are associated with conceptual and practical problems with management control and performance measurement systems integrating environment-related information and providing guidance on how to succeed in environmental sustainability (Burritt, 2004; Epstein, 2010). So far major barriers to effective corporate action have been attributed to traditional management control tools. Burritt (2004) outlines several 'environmental' criticisms to conventional management accounting. Environmental costs are assumed to be unimportant, and indirect expenses are usually aggregated with general business overheads. Performance evaluation techniques are dominated by short-term financial accounting rules, which contrast with the multidimensional and long-term nature of environmental performance. Performance measurement and rewarding mechanisms often do not include measures and weights that congruently assess environmental impacts of individuals and organizational units (profit centres and cost objects), thereby resulting in poor motivation during planning, implementation and control. Finally there is an absence of accounting for externalities and social cost issues. On this matter, Berns et al. (2009) illustrate three main roadblocks to successfully implement environmental management. First, companies often do not understand what green management is and what it means concretely, largely because of a lack of information for decision-making. Second, companies struggle to model the business case for environmental sustainability because of difficulties identifying, measuring and controlling the tangible and intangible 'green' aspects of their business. Third, when companies do act, the execution of sustainable policies is often hampered by scepticism of how to institutionalize the eco-agenda throughout the company. Finally, Epstein (2010) highlights the significant role of organizational culture, leadership and people as informal controls to drive green management execution. Managerial inertia, costs, lack of requisite skills, organizational and cultural factors, and the reluctance to change may significantly influence the decision to adopt any application of formal eco-control tools.

As a result academics have the opportunity to invest more in EMA research to complement existing knowledge and provide further explanations on how to successfully implement green management (Burritt, 2004; Epstein, 2010; Henri & Journeault, 2010).

LITERATURE REVIEW

As demands for green management have prompted businesses to adopt EMA systems that facilitate environmental decision-making, academics and managerial professionals have focused their attention on the design of tools and their application. In this review article we analyse the literature with the aim to summarize the key contributions and highlight interesting areas that need to be further explored in order to complement existing knowledge. For this we assess both extant theoretical research and empirical work on EMA practices published between 1992 and 2013 in leading accounting journals and academic book series including: *The Accounting Review*; *Journal of Management Accounting Research*; *Accounting, Organizations and Society*; *Journal of Accounting and Public Policy*; the *European Accounting Review*; *The British Accounting Review*; *Management Accounting Research*; *Accounting Forum*; *Accounting, Auditing and Accountability Journal*; *Abacus*; *Australian Accounting Review*; *Advances in Management Accounting*; and *Advances in Environmental Accounting and Management*. In addition, given the continuous publication of new research, we extend our investigation to related scientific manuscripts and professional reports and articles published in the main practitioner journals in order to capture a more comprehensive picture of this novel domain. Despite practical limits on the number of studies included, we believe that the selected sample contains a broad diversity of EMA research published in English and properly covers the relevant literature. Indeed we structure our analysis around the following three main issues:

i. studies analysing the design of EMA practices and the level of diffusion of these tools across firms;
ii. studies analysing the antecedents influencing the decision to adopt effective EMA mechanisms; and
iii. studies examining the effects of EMA systems on organizational performance.

Overview of the Literature

Studies analysing the design of EMA practices and the level of diffusion of these tools across firms

Main Contributions. As outlined in the introduction, in the last 20 years research linking accounting to the concept of environmental sustainability has received growing attention in both academic and professional accounting literature. Table 1 reports a series of articles analysing the design of EMA practices and the level of diffusion of these tools across firms. The majority of these works were published after 2000, indicating the newness of the field. In particular more than 50% of these publications were published post-2005, indicating the even stronger attention given to ecologically oriented control in the last 5 years. Empirical and normative papers have been equally distributed throughout the period, while conceptual studies have been less diffused and mostly concentrated before 2000, when environmental managerial control was still at an embryonic stage. Prescriptive commentaries and (multiple) case studies have been the most used methodologies equally adopted throughout the time span analysed.

One sustained group of studies adopts a broader approach examining the diffusion of the concept of EMA across firms and addressing some of the main conceptual and practical problems encountered while designing and implementing green management-control systems. More specifically, the first publications linking accounting with sustainability focus on the deficiencies of conventional accounting in measuring and managing sustainability-related information (Gray, 1992; Mathews, 1997; Milne, 1996; Schaltegger & Burritt, 2000). The studies also highlight the limits of the underlying philosophy of accounting, which conventionally focuses on financial measures of corporate economic activities (Gray, 1992; Mathews, 1997; Milne, 1996). Some authors report current practices and provide guidance on how to model effective EMA tools. For instance, Bartolomeo et al. (2000) report and analyse the results of a trans-European project to investigate actual and future links between environmental management and management accounting functions of a company. Later Burritt, Hahn, and Schaltegger (2002) propose a comprehensive framework providing a structure for managers to understand and assess the variety of EMA tools that have been developed, with the intention of encouraging their adoption. Epstein (2004) provides a review of the progress made in both academic literature and corporate practice starting from 1970, finding little evidence of advances in the integration of social and environmental impacts into management decisions. More generally Lamberton (2005) consolidates

Table 1. Articles Published from 1992 to 2012 on the Design and Level of Diffusion of EMA Systems.

Author(s)	Year	Type of Study	Methodology	Main Analysed Issues
Gray	1992	Conceptual	Commentary	Environmental accounting
Milne	1996	Conceptual	Literature review	EMA systems
Mathews	1997	Conceptual	Literature review	EMA
Parker	2000a	Empirical	Multiple case study	Environmental costing
Parker	2000b	Normative	Multiple case study	Environmental costing
Bartolomeo et al.	2000	Empirical	Survey	EMA systems
Burritt et al.	2002	Normative	Commentary	EMA framework
Epstein	2004	Conceptual	Literature review	EMA systems
Antheaume	2004	Empirical	Case study	Full-cost environmental accounting
Lamberton	2005	Normative	Commentary	Sustainability accounting
Lockhart and Taylor	2007	Normative	Case study	Environmental activity-based costing
Beiman	2008	Normative	Commentary	Environmental balanced scorecard
Adams and Frost	2008	Empirical	Multiple case study	Sustainability management control systems
Durden	2008	Empirical	Case study	Sustainability management control systems
Deegan	2008	Empirical	Case study	Environmental capital budgeting
Dutta and Lawson	2009	Normative	Commentary	Environmental managerial rewarding
Joshi and Krishnan	2010	Normative	Commentary	Sustainability management control systems
Schaltegger	2011	Normative	Commentary	Sustainability balanced scorecard
O'Rourke	2011	Normative	Commentary	Sustainability balanced scorecard
Butler et al.	2011	Normative	Commentary	Sustainability balanced scorecard
Cooper and Pearce	2011	Empirical	Multiple case study	Environmental performance measurement systems
Bowen and Wittneben	2011	Empirical	Review + Opinion workshop	Carbon accounting
Burritt et al.	2011	Empirical	Multiple case study	Carbon management control systems
Horváth and Berlin	2012	Normative	Case study	Environmental target costing
Gond et al.	2012	Conceptual	Commentary	Sustainability management control systems
Deegan and Islam	2012	Empirical	Content analysis	Environmental managerial rewarding

the various approaches taken by researchers to link accounting to sustainability, proposing a broad sustainability accounting framework aimed at measuring performance and producing consistent information for potential internal and external users. Adams and Frost (2008) interview managers from four British and three Australian companies in different industries and describe high variation in how firms develop and use key performance indicators for decision-making, planning and performance management. Durden (2008) analyses the case of a small, privately owned New Zealand manufacturing business that explicitly subscribes to social responsibility and stakeholder principles, and finds that formal management control systems of the observed organization do not measure or monitor social responsibility. By elaborating on the case evidence, he proposes a framework aimed at integrating both formal and informal control mechanisms with social responsibility. Recently Gond, Grubnic, Herzig, and Moon (2012) have adopted a configuration approach to develop different organizational patterns that reflect the various roles and uses of management control tools for the integration of sustainability within organizational strategy. The integration encompasses three specific dimensions: technical, organizational and cognitive. The authors elaborate on eight configurations to show how management accounting systems and sustainability control mechanisms can be linked, and how these tools can prevent or facilitate the emergence of sustainability at a strategic level.

Another stream of research investigates issues related to EMA by focusing on the current diffusion and appropriate design of specific eco-practices such as cost accounting (Antheaume, 2004; Bebbington, Gray, Hibbitt, & Kirk, 2001; Deegan, 2008; Ditz et al., 1995; Horváth & Berlin, 2012; Joshi, Krishnan, & Lave, 2001; Lockhart & Taylor, 2007; Parker, 2000a, 2000b), performance measurement (Cooper & Pearce, 2011) and management incentives (Deegan & Islam, 2012; Dutta & Lawson, 2009). By taking a broader view, some studies call for an expanded role of management control and speculate on a more structured concept of sustainability management control on the basis of the balanced scorecard approach that accounts for business-relevant market and non-market factors (Joshi & Krishnan, 2010; O'Rourke, 2011; Schaltegger, 2011). This leads in particular to the use of balanced scorecard and strategy mapping practices to address 'green' challenges (Beiman, 2008; Butler, Henderson, & Raiborn, 2011).

Other contributions focus on management control approaches dealing with specific environmental concerns. As such, carbon management control is maybe the most prominent theme. Burritt, Schaltegger, and Zvezdov

(2011), through field work, elaborate on the practices of 10 leading German companies to create a dedicated framework, while Bowen and Wittneben (2011) highlight the tensions between accuracy, consistency and certainty in carbon emission computation both within and across distinct organizational fields.

Open Issues. Four relevant areas for research can be identified with this literature review. First, while contributing to the development of tools, this literature is mostly prescriptive or based on case studies. Hence there is room to complement existing knowledge by examining large-scale empirical evidence. Recent studies have addressed this gap by exploring the empirical aspects of EMA practices in extensive cross-sectional settings. Some initial surveys have examined the characteristics and level of diffusion of EMA systems in a number of countries and cultures (Berns et al., 2009; CIMA, 2011; Gates & Germain, 2010). Nevertheless accounting scholars have recently reported that there is still not a great deal of extensive and longitudinal empirical evidence published in scientific journals examining the applicability of these ecological practices recommended by professionals and researchers (Henri & Journeault, 2010). Additionally most studies have focused their investigations primarily on materially sensitive environmental industries, while the demand for green management originates from all organization types (Berns et al., 2009; Sinkin, Wright, & Burnett, 2008). Thus there is a need for large-scale studies to test whether and to what extent green control patterns and propositions developed for single-organizational or industrial case studies could be generalized and applied to different samples.

Second, much of the work on management control and performance measurement in the field of environmental sustainability has focused on the role and design of formal systems rather than informal ones, despite the widely recognized reliance on soft or informal mechanisms such as organizational culture, leadership, learning and people (Berns et al., 2009; CIMA, 2011; Durden, 2008; Epstein, 2010; Hart, 1995). Empirical evidence from leading corporations suggests that informal controls may be more important than formal systems and processes in driving sustainability implementation. Additionally results demonstrate that soft controls are probably more important than previously thought (Epstein, 2010; Norris & O'Dwyer, 2004).

Third, recent surveys have indicated that environmental accounting is now practiced by more than just accountants (Berns et al., 2009; CIMA, 2011). Some authors have suggested that, as environmental decisions are distributed throughout organizations, managers at all levels are being asked to simultaneously manage environmental and financial performance (Burritt et al., 2002; Epstein, 2010). Indeed the forms of economic calculation that 'green' accounting creates are now a part of most managerial functions. However as mentioned by Hopwood (2007, p. 1370), 'we still lack understanding of the processes and pressures underlying the shifting locations of economic calculation and control in the wider management accounting area'. Also, both theoretical contributions and empirical evidence indicate that accountants are 'equipped with tools and techniques that ensure businesses understand the scale of environment-related problems, create viable solutions and implement these solutions properly' (CIMA, 2011, p. 2; Hopwood, 2009a). Some studies have suggested that management accountants have a 'pivotal role in providing business intelligence to support strategic decision-making' (CIMA, 2011, p. 2; Henri & Journeault, 2010; IFAC, 2005; UNDSD, 2001). Indeed 'without the rigor and business acumen of the accounting and control function, it may result impossible to embed environmental sustainability into day-by-day business life' (CIMA, 2011, p. 2). Burritt and Schaltegger (2010) in particular have indicated that the failure of management accountants to provide necessary guidance to other departments or to get involved in key decisions on ecological initiatives and climate-change compliance could result in higher costs, lost opportunities and, thereby, poor execution.

Finally while environmental sustainability is viewed as a growing priority for businesses of all sizes at a global level, only a few empirical studies have focused on how small and medium-sized enterprises (SMEs) can implement sustainable business practices to benefit the environment, their communities, their customers and their bottom lines (Burritt, 2004; CIMA, 2011; Durden, 2008). Moreover relevant topics such as the design and level of diffusion of EMA practices within organizations operating in developing countries remain largely unexplored. As such there is an opportunity to complement the existing EMA knowledge by investigating the role and different applications of eco-control tools used by SMEs and firms in developing countries.

Studies Analysing the Antecedents Influencing the Decision to Adopt Effective EMA Mechanisms

Main Contributions. Another group of studies focuses on the antecedents that explain the decision to adopt EMA tools for managing environment-related information appropriately. As can be seen in Table 2, all studies are

Table 2. Articles Published from 1992 to 2012 on Antecedents of EMA Systems.

Author(s)	Year	Methodology	Main Analysed Issues
Frost and Wilmhurst	2000	Survey	EMA systems
Bouma and Kamp-Roelands	2000	Case study	Environmental management information systems
Gago	2002	Multiple case study	Environment-related make or buy decision
Ball	2005	Case study	Environmental accounting
Perego and Hartmann	2009	Survey	Environmental performance measurement systems
Gates and Germain	2010	Survey	Sustainability performance measurement systems

conducted post-2000, with the majority post-2005. Overall they are approximately equally distributed between case study and survey methodologies.

More specifically some studies adopt a contingency approach to identifying and testing significant factors that fit corporate uses of different EMA systems in a variety of contexts. For instance, Frost and Wilmhurst (2000) report and analyse survey data from CFOs of Australian companies to examine the environmental sensibility of the industry as a factor associated with the adoption of environmental cost accounting and management control practices. Their findings indicate that although environmental practices are more likely to occur in environmentally sensitive firms, the adoption of EMA procedures does not appear to be driven solely by the environmental sensitivity of the industry. Hence both the authors conclude that further research is needed to identify what other determinants cause organizations to adopt eco-control practices. In the context of a single production site of a Dutch multinational chemical company, Bouma and Kamp-Roelands (2000) report that expectations of different stakeholders influence the content of the set of green information that managers choose to collect and measure while designing and implementing a structured environmental management system. Gago Rodriguez (2002) examines an ecologically oriented 'make-or-buy' decision taken in 11 Spanish environment-sensitive companies and finds financial considerations are the main determinants of structured use of cost and benefit analysis. Similarly Gates and Germain (2010) use survey data from financial controllers of 79 big firms operating in France and find that industry type and stock-market listings influence the choice of integrating sustainability metrics into strategic performance measurement systems. However the authors do not find any association between the presence of sustainability measures and organizational strategy or nationality of the company. Pistoni and Songini (2009) adopt a case-study approach focusing on one of the largest Italian enterprises in the energy sector to analyse why and how the firm decides to align its performance measurement and evaluation systems to its formulated environmental strategy within a broader corporate social responsibility approach. Finally Perego and Hartmann (2009) combine contingency theory with an agency perspective and examine a sample of manufacturing firms in the Netherlands. In particular they observe that the relationship between environmental strategy and the use of performance measurement systems is mediated by some attributes of EMA tools and specific properties of the measures adopted.

Other contributions focus on the public sector and adopt an institutional perspective to shed some light on company motivations that drive the decision to introduce EMA tolls for green management execution. For instance, Ball (2005) finds that environmental accounting is used by UK local officers to measure relevant eco-aspects of their activities and externally report on the basis of gradual political, functional and social pressures. More recently Qian, Burritt, and Monroe (2011) have conducted a field analysis over 12 local councils in New South Wales (Australia) investigating the main motivations that drive the use of EMA information for waste management in local government. The authors combine an institutional and contingency-based approach and find that social structural pressures (regulatory pressures from different environmental regulatory bodies, 'green' expectations from local communities and influences from peer councils) and organizational contextual factors (uncertainty in waste and recycling management facing the council, and the council's strategic position for waste management) contribute to explain the development of EMA practices in a complementary manner.

Open Issues. Much of this literature has adopted an economic perspective and identified relevant drivers that influence the decisions to implement and design EMA tools that facilitate and maximize economic value creation. However previous management accounting research has indicated that economic models do not themselves constitute a valuable assessment instrument to explain phenomena in case of departures from their implied assumptions (Ball & Brown, 1968; Hopwood, 2007). For instance, 'some capital budgeting literature has suggested that accounting information may be used more to justify decisions that have already been taken rather than being an aid to decision-making' (Drury & Tayles, 1995, p. 272). If environmental cost information is used mainly for legitimizing/rationalizing purposes, then organizational participants should perceive it as accurate or reliable rather than simply meeting the accuracy requirements specified by rational economic theory (Drury & Tayles, 1995). Furthermore some companies may have chosen not to make fundamental changes in their control processes by means of integrating environmental data into their managerial control practices, even when facing substantial changes in their competitive environment. Notably academics have suggested that 'there are many barriers to adopting or changing accounting systems, including management inertia, high costs, lack of requisite skills, organizational and cultural factors, and reluctance to abandon existing systems' (Drury & Tayles, 1995, p. 278). 'Hence it is dangerous to conclude, in the absence of further empirical testing, that a lack of substantive meaning implies a lack of utility' (Ball & Brown, 1968, p. 160). Therefore explanations for variations in the role and different applications of the observed eco-control practices must be explored also by using other theories that are beyond the win-win perspective. Indeed as we argue about these remaining gaps in the literature, we can also appreciate the importance of having in managerial accounting a tradition of research that focuses on the organizational, social and political facets of the subject (Hopwood, 2007). In fact previous research in the area of management control has illustrated 'the need for an understanding of how the wider political context, organizational structure and culture, and individual psychological factors mediate the use of accounting data and thereby its consequences' (Hopwood, 2007, p. 1368). Indeed as mentioned by Hopwood (2009b, p. 890), 'a diversity of understanding is fundamental in a complex and changing world where knowledge is an emergent process rather than a more static straightforward endeavour'.

Studies Examining the Effects of EMA Systems on Organizational Performance

Main Contributions. The last group of studies (Table 3) examines the role of EMA tools by focusing on the most relevant implications related to the design and adoption of the observed green control practices. More specifically this part of the literature has examined the relevance of EMA practices to helping organizations achieve excellence in terms of both environmental and financial performance. Except for Lanen (1999), all articles were written post-2000 and are highly concentrated post-2005. The majority adopted a survey-based methodology.

Table 3. Articles Published from 1992 to 2012 on Consequences of EMA Systems.

Author(s)	Year	Type of Study	Methodology	Main Analysed Issues
Lanen	1999	Empirical	Archival research	Environmental performance measurement systems
Norris and O'Dwyer	2004	Empirical	Case study	Formal and informal environmental controls
Epstein and Wisner	2005	Empirical	Survey + Interviews	EMA systems
Dunk	2005	Empirical	Survey	EMA systems
Wisner et al.	2006	Empirical	Survey	Environmental planning
Campbell et al.	2007	Empirical	Survey + Archival research	Environmental managerial rewarding
Perez et al.	2007	Empirical	Multiple case study	EMA systems
Henri and Journeault	2010	Empirical	Survey	EMA systems
Wisner et al.	2010	Empirical	Survey	EMA systems
Ferreira et al.	2010	Empirical	Survey	Environmental costing
Neumann et al.	2012	Conceptual	Commentary	Sustainability performance measurement systems
Eccles et al.	2012	Empirical	Archival research	Environmental managerial rewarding

Consistent with the rationale behind the managerial case for 'green' sustainability, several normative statements and professional studies provide prescriptive indications of the three central functions performed by ecologically oriented control tools when embedded in an organization, its strategy and operations (CIMA, 2011; German Federal Ministry, 2003; IFAC, 2005; UNDSD, 2001). First, EMA mechanisms safeguard and stimulate corporate strategy by taking into account capital environmental expenses and by supporting the marketing of 'green' products, services and reputation-reinforcing initiatives. Second, they promote eco-efficiency by controlling operating practices for material and energy flows. Finally they support environmental protection by helping to ensure the cost-effective implementation of ecological initiatives and monitoring to avoid safety and environmental incidents. Other lines of research empirically test the effectiveness of EMA mechanisms and their impact on environmental and economic performance.

Some authors focus on specific EMA mechanisms. For instance, Lanen (1999) finds that the adoption of non-financial, environment-related performance metrics at 3M Corporation is positively linked to the successful results of a 5 year project on waste minimization in 55 plants. However

Lanen does not detect any association between the incentives to monitor plant performance and waste ratio. Similarly other scholars examine the role of environment-related information on top management compensation. Campbell, Selfik, and Soderstrom (2007) find a positive relationship between environmental performance and the 'green' components of CEOs' compensation plans implemented across a sample of US-based corporations. More specifically the authors note the existence of a risk premium in compensating CEOs for incremental personal, environmental and economic risks in more environmentally sensitive industries. Also, using archival data from a sample of 207 S&P 500 firms in the United States, Cordeiro and Sarkis (2009) find a significant impact of firm-level environmental performance on CEO remuneration levels in firms that explicitly report the presence of a contractual link between 'green' performance metrics and executive compensation. Alternatively Wisner, Epstein, and Bagozzi (2006) examine the role of environmental planning using survey data from a sample of 215 large-base firms. The authors find a positive relationship between environmental strategic planning and 'green' economic performance. Moreover they identify a number of techniques, systems and managerial attitudes that form a package of formal and informal EMA mechanisms. Ferreira, Moulang, and Hendro (2010) examine a sample of large Australian businesses in various industries and report a positive association between the extent of use of environmental cost accounting systems and process innovation level. However they do not find any link with product innovation intensity. Additionally strategy does not seem to affect green costing use and innovation.

In contrast other academics adopt a broader approach to investigate the concept of eco-control. Norris and O'Dwyer (2004) examine a case study in a UK retail company and indicate the dominant influence of informal controls such as organizational culture and personal values in driving socially responsive decision-making in managers. Epstein and Wisner (2005) study a random sample of 236 Mexican manufacturing plants and find that environmental compliance is positively influenced by various eco-controls, such as plans and procedures, belief systems, measurement systems and reward systems. In addition, using a sample of 119 area managers from manufacturing companies across Australia, Dunk (2005) indicates that, at organizational level, the integration of environmental information into management control mechanisms is positively linked to non-financial performance. Perez, Ruiz, and Fenech (2007) elaborate on evidence from managers of 10 Spanish EcoManagement and Audit Scheme (EMAS) registered production sites and illustrate how the use of 'green' data in strategic planning and other management accounting practices drives environmental performance improvement. Henri and Journeault (2010) investigate a large sample of Canadian manufacturing firms and observe the manner in which formal eco-control tools contribute to organizational performance. Their results indicate that, in a context of high environmental exposure, high public visibility, high environmental concern, and larger size, eco-control practices have no direct impact on financial outcomes but there appears to be a mediating effect of environmental performance on the link between eco-control and economic performance. Wisner, Epstein, and Bagozzi (2010) examine data from a cross-section of US-based industrial firms and demonstrate a positive indirect relation between the use of green information in capital equipment decision-making and firms' environmental performance, mediated by the level of corporate environmental proactivity. Neumann, Cauvin, and Roberts, (2012) speculate on prior experimental literature and argue that adding environmental and societal information into managerial reports contributes to managers' information overload and bias the interpretation and the use of performance measures. Finally, Eccles, Ioannou, Xin Li, & Serafeim (2012) examine a large cross-industry sample of multinational organizations between 2007 and 2010, analysing the effectiveness of monetary and non-monetary incentives provided by companies to their managers and employees to reduce carbon emissions. Specifically, consistent with monetary crowding-out motivation theory, their findings report that the use of financial incentives is associated with higher carbon emissions, while the provision of non-monetary rewards is related to lower carbon emissions.

Open Issues. We distinguish two sets of interesting open areas when examining this body of research. First, much of the work examining EMA as the causal factor associated with organizational characteristics has analysed EMA practices primarily at a corporate level. Additionally the studies have focused on testing exclusively for the presence of linear, explanatory relations between the design and adoption of these tools and companies' performances. On the one hand few empirical studies have investigated the role of individuals' attitudes and organizational culture in the link between green management control and organizational performance, or analysed the conditions under which EMA practices drive managers' behaviour within firms (Campbell et al., 2007; Norris & O'Dwyer, 2004; Wisner et al., 2006). As a result we still only have partial understanding of how managers' personal characteristics influence how firms use EMA systems and moderate the extent to which these mechanisms contribute to organizational performance. On the other hand the existing empirical literature provides little information on how ecologically oriented control tools create value. Few empirical studies have examined how EMA simultaneously contributes to environmental and economic performance (Henri & Journeault, 2010). Moreover, other than causal linear form, explanatory links between green control practices and organizational performance remain unexplored. As such we still do not know whether particular EMA tools improve performance only up to a certain point and then make it worse, conditional on certain contextual factors and specific individual characteristics of the managers using them. As stated in prior research, businesses do not merely want to know that more or less EMA is better, but how much EMA is optimal (Luft & Shields, 2003). Therefore there seems to be opportunity to further investigate these questions.

Second, prior research has emphasized the lack of consensus on the definition and operationalization of environmental performance (Henri & Journeault, 2010; Ilinitch, Soderstrom, & Thomas, 1998; Xie & Hayase, 2007). More specifically academic researchers have recognized the complexity and multidimensional nature of the concept. In particular Ilinitch et al. (1998) have mentioned that 'green' performance appraisal requires measurement of non-financial performance, evaluation under significant levels of uncertainty, assessment over a long-term time frame and aggregation of multiple types of metrics. Burritt (2001, 2004) has accordingly highlighted the long-term time dimensions of environmental performance. Burritt and Schaltegger (2010) have mentioned the corporate need for identifying and measuring environmental externalities that may influence organizational behaviour. Other authors have suggested that 'the notion of "green" performance covers various dimensions, analogous to the broad concept of performance that is not limited only to financial aspects but also integrates other aspects such as customer satisfaction, productivity, quality and innovation' (Henri & Journeault, 2010, p. 65). Moreover the accounting profession appears to be a natural candidate to establish such metrics because its domain typically includes measuring, communicating and regulating information about company performance. However few studies in the EMA literature have developed comprehensive 'green' performance measurement models (Epstein, 1996; Henri & Journeault, 2010; Ilinitch et al., 1998; Xie & Hayase, 2007). Specifically much of the empirical work on EMA has continued to examine 'green' performance mainly in terms of the environmental impact of business or environmental compliance (Burnett & Hansen, 2008; Campbell et al., 2007; Cordeiro & Sarkis, 2009; Joshi et al., 2001; Wisner et al., 2006). A notable exception is the work of Epstein (2008), who has conducted a field project to explore four successful companies operating in different industries and developed a broader model that provides details on the various drivers and the multiple measures used to successfully manage corporate sustainability. Another exception is the work of Henri and Journeault (2010), who has examined a sample of Canadian manufacturing firms and adopted different effectiveness models to define environmental performance. For this purpose they have identified four key dimensions that collectively constitute the concept of 'green' performance: (i) environmental impact and corporate image, (ii) stakeholder relations, (iii) financial impact and (iv) process and product improvements. Both theoretical and empirical studies have collectively indicated that 'green' sustainability is still subject to a general lack of understanding and thereby inaccurate measurability (Berns et al., 2009; Burritt & Schaltegger, 2010; CIMA, 2011). Hence accounting scholars have the opportunity to develop more congruent and inclusive environmental performance metrics aimed at defining, measuring and controlling this broad corporate domain.

Summary of the Findings

All told, this emerging stream of literature has provided many relevant insights into the various aspects of EMA practices implemented within firms. This literature review reveals interesting unexplored facets of environment-related control systems that need to be further investigated. In particular we have built on the increasing managerial enthusiasm and consensus on green management (Marcus & Fremeth, 2009) to provide researchers with the opportunity to complement existing EMA knowledge. Similarly researchers have the opportunity to explore innovative theories and models that further explain the concept of ecological control, its role and applications. Academics could cumulate knowledge by improving and testing new frameworks, examining novel aspects of the tools, and investigating different applications of these practices. This phase of knowledge development shares some characteristics with the concept of 'normal science' as mentioned by Sims (1996, p. 112): 'textbooks are written and frameworks developed; researchers pose and solve puzzles; and there is a general sense of powerful theories and methods being extended to cover unexplored areas of application'. Hence more research is needed in order to accumulate a stock of solutions for green management implementation and to contribute to management accounting and EMA literature.

RECOMMENDATIONS FOR FUTURE RESEARCH

As discussed in the preceding section, the extant research on EMA has produced partial explanations about the role and design of ecologically oriented control systems adopted by firms for green management implementation. As such, further research is needed to accumulate the stock of solutions necessary to provide the right guidance and clarification on how to successfully execute green management.

In this section we derive propositions for future explanatory studies and address some recommendations about research design.

Theoretical Developments

Exploring Alternative Theoretical Propositions

Causal-model forms, used to predict and test organizational causes and effects of EMA tools within firms, are mainly based on economic theories and are linear in nature. As such a multiplicity of approaches, rather than pure, neoclassical economics, would be required to complement existing knowledge.

On the one hand researchers could adopt alternative perspectives or combine different approaches to increase theories' explanatory and predictive ability as to how the broader political context, organizational cultural, and managers' psychological characteristics mediate the use made of environmental and accounting data and thereby its consequences.

From an organizational point of view, two relevant questions arise: (1) whether EMA is a voluntary management tool designed to help managers, or a tool of social policy by which governments impose their will and (2) under which conditions it can perform both functions simultaneously. Several studies on the corporate role of environmental disclosure have adopted legitimacy considerations to explain companies' use of external reporting as a tool to reduce exposure to the social and political environment as opposed to a means for signalling an unobservable proactive strategy towards 'green' objectives (Cho & Patten, 2007; Cho et al., 2012a, 2012b). Sociopolitical arguments might similarly shed some light on why some firms do not introduce fundamental changes in their control processes by integrating environmental data into their accounting practices, even amid significant change in their competitive environment. Additionally a mix of economic and societal interpretations could contribute to explaining green control implementation as a means of obtaining environmental and economic gains simultaneously.

From an individual perspective, EMA is considered to have at its disposal 'the right tools to motivate managers' commitment to implement and stimulate positive attitudes towards 'green' initiatives, but it might not produce the expected results due to behavioral problems' (Burritt, 2004, p. 13). People today 'expect managers to use resources wisely and responsibly, protect the environment, eliminate harmful toxins in the workplace and communities, and reduce greenhouse gas emissions' (Marcus & Fremeth, 2009, p. 17). Accordingly the moral obligations for green management and environmental social incentives might influence the manner in which managers make effort-level and effort-allocation choices (Norris & O'Dwyer, 2004). Moreover, as pointed out by Perego and Hartmann (2009, p. 406), 'managerial effort towards environmental sustainability can only be inferred indirectly and imperfectly through some measures of "green" performance'. The high uncertainty in measuring pollution or any harmful ecological effect as well as stochastic 'green' events risk placing environmental performance outside of the direct control of management (Perego & Hartmann, 2009). In this context environmental psychology could provide innovative insights explaining the interrelationships between the environment and human behaviour. In particular individual ecological knowledge and 'green' conservation attitudes might shed some light on how managers subjectively use environmental information to make judgements and decisions.

On the other hand, accounting scholars could investigate explanatory links other than linear relations in order to explore how ecologically oriented control creates value and to what extent EMA is required for green management execution. Additional theories must to be considered to predict and test non-linear relations. Indeed much of the theory underlying empirical management accounting research assumes curvilinear relations. With this regard, Luft and Shields (2003) mentioned that economic perspectives predict curvilinear functions for individual utility and for organizational costs and profits, while cognitive psychology assumptions predict U-shaped or inverted-U response curves. Accordingly reward designers would be practically interested in the shape of the curve and try to identify the point at which the expected costs of further environmental incentives outweigh the diminishing expected benefits. Moreover individual attitudes and values towards 'green' sustainability might affect how corporate use of specific environmental performance measures influences managers' learning curves and, in turn, the effectiveness of 'green' business decisions.

Looking at Different Levels of Analysis

So far most explanatory links examined in scientific journals have analysed antecedents and effects of EMA practices across companies, firms' subunits and other organization entities. As a result accounting scholars could complement existing EMA knowledge by investigating how managers individually use environmental and accounting information to make 'green' decisions (Norris & O'Dwyer, 2004). Researchers might also analyse how the design and use of different green management control practices could be associated with different characteristics of the managers who use them (i.e. values, skills, knowledge and abilities). Hence researchers could focus on examining EMA systems at the individual level of analysis to further understand how to design and use control tools that shape managers' decisions for green management execution. According to extant research in managerial accounting (Luft & Shields, 2003), theories from social psychology of organizations and predictions based on information economics and cognitive psychology would be appropriate to examine various aspects of EMA practices at the managerial level. Moreover these perspectives could help academics further explore the debate about individual rationality for environmental management implementation.

Research Designs

Potential of Case-Based and Field Study Design

Researchers have the opportunity to focus on innovative aspects of the role and design of green management control tools within organizations. They would ideally opt for qualitative case or field study designs to allow for the investigation of relevant unexplored facets of EMA. Indeed managerial scholars need to define new constructs and operationalize new variables in order to draw a more complete picture of the concept of ecologically oriented control. For this purpose, academics could start spending time 'performing systematic observation, description and classification, which lie at the foundation of knowledge creation' (Kaplan, 2011, p. 371). A more informed basis for these aspects would lead to stronger modelling, theory-building and hypothesis-testing activities (Kaplan, 2011).

We identify three specific new areas for investigation. First, accounting researchers should further examine the role of informal control systems, such as organizational culture, leadership, learning and people, to drive green management execution. For instance, as suggested in the literature (Epstein, 2010), soft factors such as managerial inertia, lack of requisite skills, corporate culture and the reluctance to change might be associated with different applications of eco-control tools and success in performing 'green' initiatives. As such field-based explorations would be conducted with the purpose of understanding environmental management implementation approaches beyond formal incentives.

Second, research scholars need to know more about the practical aspects of EMA when green management control is practiced by business professionals other than accountants. Indeed non-accountants could be equipped with different knowledge, skills and abilities that could influence how EMA mechanisms are used and thereby the effects related to their application. Additionally prior studies have indicated that management accountants are shifting towards the top of the organization as business partners in top level decision-making (Sorensen, 2008). Therefore researchers are required to examine whether the changing role of management accountants fits with the pivotal function they are required to perform for green management (Henri & Journeault, 2010).

Finally accounting researchers could develop metrics to accurately measure 'green' costs and benefits in line with the holistic concept of environmental performance. To do so they need to overcome the several limitations potentially hindering the informativeness and contractibility associated with the measures, and the goal congruence between the environmental and organizational objectives (Burritt, 2004; Burritt & Schaltegger, 2010; Henri & Journeault, 2010; Ilinitch et al., 1998). Keeping this in mind, as suggested by Kaplan (1986, 2011) managerial scholars could start by observing, documenting and describing leading practices and innovations. They could next identify where a specific set of 'green' performance metrics seems to be effective and where the measures fail in execution. They would finally be able to formulate general principles that drive the choice for the 'right' environment-related performance measures. As a result new convincing variables reflecting the multiple dimensions of corporate environmental performance (financial/non-financial, internal/external, direct/indirect, tangible/intangible, process/results) could be operationalized, tested and proposed.

Relevance of Large-Scale Empirical Evidence

Conclusive empirical evidence on the design and level of diffusion of EMA mechanisms should be large scale in nature and consider businesses of all sizes in all industries. Consequently extensive survey designs represent an appropriate method to investigate EMA systems in broader settings. In particular more cross-country and cross-industry studies would validate the correlation paths and causal associations examined to date in single organizational or industrial case analyses, allowing for better generalization of the findings (Henri & Journeault, 2010). Moreover a more complete understanding of the diffusion level of 'green' control mechanisms within firms requires both academic researchers and managerial professionals to consider implementation characteristics across SMEs and within organizations operating in developing countries (Burritt, 2004).

Additionally a longitudinal research design should be selected to allow for investigating changes in EMA practices over time. However, given the high costs and difficulties associated with longitudinal studies, cross-sectional surveys also constitute an appropriate method (Burkert, Davila, & Oyon, 2010).

CONCLUSIONS

The aim of this study was to substantiate the need for more theoretical and empirical research on innovative aspects of EMA practices adopted by firms to foster green management execution. The point of departure for our reasoning in the second section was that today both corporate leaders and academic researchers agree upon the relevance of green management in leading organizations. Indeed managerial scholars and professionals call for the integration of corporate environmental considerations into business strategy, thus into operational and capital investment decisions. Accordingly EMA represents one of the mechanisms used by firms to incorporate environment-related information into day-to-day decision-making and take advantage of the potential benefits of environmental performance. Hence, as stated by Schaltegger & Burritt (2000) ecologically oriented management control tools serve as a means of executing environmental strategy throughout the organization. However successful implementation remains challenging and defined targets are hardly fully reached (CIMA, 2011; Epstein, 2008). Several lines of evidence have indicated that many of these difficulties are associated with conceptual and practical problems with management control systems in integrating environmental information into decision-making and providing guidance on how to effectively implement green management (Berns et al., 2009; Burritt, 2004; Epstein, 2010).

In the third section we therefore reviewed extant literature on EMA practices published in both scientific and practitioner journals, exposing the important findings and shedding some light on interesting, unexplored issues that need to be further investigated in order to complement existing knowledge. First, in relation to the diffusion of the concept of EMA, academics have the opportunity to examine whether and to what extent green control mechanisms can be generalized to all types of businesses in cross-cultural settings. Additionally researchers might invest more in analysing the role of informal control systems to drive green management implementation, as well as cases where environmental accounting is practiced by various business professionals other than management accountants. Second, while investigating significant antecedents influencing the decision to adopt and how to design effective EMA mechanisms, accounting scholars should attempt to further explain variations in the role and different applications of the observed green control practices in cases of departure from the win-win economic prediction. Finally when examining the potential effects produced by the use of ecologically oriented control tools, researchers have the opportunity to investigate more how EMA systems contribute to organizational performance. Moreover academics have the opportunity to further explore the concept of environmental performance and develop more inclusive metrics to define, measure and control this broad corporate domain.

In the fourth section we identified avenues for future explanatory studies and addressed recommendations for research design. On the one hand we suggested innovative theoretical developments to establish and investigate new causal links. Researchers could accordingly use sociopolitical argumentation and psychological considerations to explain applications of corporate EMA practices either only partially or entirely not justified by profit-maximization theories. Similarly a multiple theoretical approach might serve to investigate the extent to which EMA is required for effective green management. We also proposed the adoption of theories from organizational social psychology, information economics and cognitive psychology to investigate the various aspects of EMA at an individual level and examine the debate about managers' individual rationality in green management implementation. On the other hand we derived recommendations for appropriate research designs to address specific open issues outlined in the review. In particular we proposed the qualitative case/field study approach as appropriate for the further examination of those relevant facets of EMA practices that today remain partly unexplored. For this purpose researchers could start with the systematic observation, description and classification of practical aspects of EMA, possibly defining appropriate constructs and new convincing variables to further explore the role of informal green control mechanisms, the case of environment-related control systems practiced by non-accountants and the multiple dimensions of corporate environmental performance. We finally indicated large-scale, cross-sectional surveys and longitudinal studies for the empirical investigation of the design of EMA mechanisms and the level of diffusion of these tools across SMEs, non-manufacturing organizations and firms operating in developing countries.

In conclusion we think that academics should play an important role in investigating challenging aspects of EMA practices that today remain partly unexplored. More research is therefore required in order to accumulate a stock of solutions to better explain the design and role of effective green control tools adopted by organizations for green management execution. There is a need for new theoretical developments as well as empirical evidence with regard to eco-control and we hope that this chapter stimulates the debate on innovative approaches to the appropriate design of such research.

REFERENCES

Adams, C. A., & Frost, G. R. (2008). Integrating sustainability reporting into management practices. *Accounting Forum*, *32*, 288–302.

Antheaume, N. (2004). Valuing external costs – From theory to practice: Implications from full cost environmental accounting. *The European Accounting Review*, *13*(3), 443–464.

Ball, A. (2005). Environmental accounting and change in UK local government. *Accounting, Auditing & Accountability Journal*, *18*(3), 346–373.

Ball, R., & Brown, P. (1968). An empirical evaluation of accounting income numbers. *Journal of Accounting Research*, *6*, 159–178.

Bartolomeo, M., Bennett, M., Buoma, J. J., Heydkamp, P., James, P., & Wolters, T. (2000). Environmental management accounting in Europe: Current practice and future potential. *The European Accounting Review*, *9*(1), 31–52.

Bebbington, K. J., Gray, R. H., Hibbitt, C., & Kirk, E. (2001). *Full cost accounting: An agenda for action*. London: ACCA.

Beiman, I. (2008). Economic and environmental sustainability: A modest proposal – Part II. *Cost Management*, *22*(5), 18–28.

Berns, M., Townend, A., Khayat, Z., Balagopal, B., Reeves, M., Hopkins, M., & Krushwitz, N. (2009, September). The business of sustainability. Findings and insights from the first annual business of sustainability survey and the global thought leaders' research project. *MIT Sloan Management Review*. Special report.

Bouma, J. J., & Kamp-Roelands, N. (2000). Stakeholders' expectations of an environmental management systems: Some exploratory research. *The European Accounting Review*, *9*(1), 131–144.

Bowen, F., & Wittneben, B. (2011). Carbon accounting. Negotiating accuracy, consistency and certainty across organizational fields. *Accounting, Auditing & Accountability Journal*, *24*(8), 1022–1036.

Burkert, M., Davila., A., & Oyon, D. (2010). Performance consequences of balanced scorecard adoptions: Claim for large-scale evidence and propositions for future research. In M. J. Epstein, J.-F. Manzoni, & A. Davila (Eds.), *Performance measurement and management control: Innovative concepts and practices*. Bingley, UK: Emerald.

Burnett, R. D., & Hansen, D. R. (2008). Ecoefficiency: Defining a role for environmental cost management. *Accounting, Organizations and Society*, *33*(6), 582–602.

Burritt, R. L. (2004). Environmental management accounting: Roadblocks in the way to green and pleasant land. *Business Strategy and the Environment*, *13*(1), 13–32.

Burritt, R. L., Hahn, T., & Schaltegger, S. (2002). Towards a comprehensive framework for environmental management accounting – links between business actors and environmental management accounting tools. *Australian Accounting Review*, *12*(2), 39–50.

Burritt, R. L., & Schaltegger, S. (2010). Sustainability accounting and reporting: Fad or trend? *Accounting, Auditing, & Accountability Journal*, *23*(7), 829–846.

Burritt, R. L., Schaltegger, S., & Zvezdov, D. (2011). Carbon management accounting: Explaining practice in leading German companies. *Australian Accounting Review*, *21*(1), 80–98.

Butler, J. B., Henderson, S. C., & Raiborn, C. (2011). Sustainability and the balanced scorecard: Integrating green measures into business reporting. *Management Accounting Quarterly*, *12*(2), 1–10.

Campbell, K., Selfik, S. E., & Soderstrom, N. S. (2007). Executive compensation and non-financial risk: An empirical examination. *Journal of Accounting and Public Policy*, *26*(4), 436–462.

Carroll, A. B., & Shabana, K. M. (2010). The business case for corporate social responsibility: A review of concepts, research and practice. *International Journal of Management Reviews*, *12*(1), 85–105.

Cho, H. C., Freedman, M., & Patten, D. M. (2012a). Corporate disclosure of environmental capital expenditures: A test of alternative theories. *Accounting, Auditing, & Accountability Journal*, *25*(3), 486–507.

Cho, H. C., Guidry, R., Hageman, A., & Patten, D. M. (2012b). Do actions speak louder than words? An empirical investigation of corporate environmental reputation. *Accounting, Organizations and Society*, *37*(1), 14–25.

Cho, H. C., & Patten, D. M. (2007). The role of environmental performance as tools of legitimacy: A research note. *Accounting, Organizations and Society*, *32*(7/8), 639–647.

CIMA (2010). *Accounting for climate change. How management accountants can help organizations mitigate and adapt to climate change.* London: Chartered Institute for Management Accountants (CIMA).

CIMA (2011). *Sustainability performance management: How CFOs can unlock the value.* London: Chartered Institute for Management Accountants (CIMA).

Clarkson, P. M., Li, Y., & Richardson, G. D. (2004). The market valuation of environmental capital expenditures by pulp and paper companies. *The Accounting Review*, *79*(2), 329–353.

Clarkson, P. M., Li, Y., Richardson, G. D., & Vasvari, F. P. (2008). Revisiting the relation between environmental performance and environmental disclosure: An empirical analysis. *Accounting, Organizations and Society*, *33*(3–5), 303–328.

Cooper, S., & Pearce, G. (2011). Climate change performance measurement, control and accountability in English local authority areas. *Accounting, Auditing & Accountability Journal*, *24*(8), 1097–1118.

Deegan, C. (2008). Environmental costing in capital investment decisions: Electricity distributors and the choice of power poles. *Australian Accounting Review*, *18*(44), 2–15.

Deegan, C., & Islam, M. A. (2012). Corporate commitment to sustainability – Is it all hot air? An Australian review of the linkage between executive pay and sustainable performance. *Australian Accounting Review*, *22*(4), 384–397.

Dhaliwal, D. S., Radhakrishnan, S., Tsang, A., & Yang, Y. G. (2012). Nonfinancial disclosure and analyst forecast accuracy: International evidence on corporate social responsibility disclosure. *The Accounting Review*, *87*(3), 723–759.

Ditz, D. J., Ranganathan, J., & Banks, R. D. (1995). *Green ledgers: Case studies in corporate environmental accounting*. Washington, DC: World Resources Institute.

Drury, C., & Tayles, M. (1995). Issues arising from surveys of management accounting practice. *Management Accounting Research*, *6*(3), 267–280.

Dunk, A. S. (2005). Financial and non-financial performance: The influence of quality of information system information, corporate environmental integration, product innovation, and product quality. *Advances in Management Accounting*, *14*, 91–114.

Durden, C. (2008). Towards a socially responsible management control system. *Accounting, Auditing & Accountability Journal*, *21*(5), 671–694.

Dutta, S. K., & Lawson, R. A. (2009). Aligning performance evaluation and reward systems with corporate sustainability goals. *Cost Management*, *23*(6), 15–23.

Eccles, R. G., Ioannou, I., Xin Li, S., & Serafeim, G. (2012). *Pay for environmental performance: The effect of incentive provision on carbon emissions*. Harvard Business School Working Paper No. 13-043. Harvard Business School, Harvard.

Epstein, M. J. (1996). *Measuring corporate environmental performance*. New York, NY: McGraw-Hill.

Epstein, M. J. (2004). The identification, measurement, and reporting of corporate social impacts: Past, present, and future. *Advances in Environmental Accounting and Management*, *2*, 1–29.

Epstein, M. J. (2008). *Making sustainability work: Best practices in managing and measuring corporate social, environmental and economic impacts*. Sheffield, UK: Greenleaf.

Epstein, M. J. (2010). The challenge of simultaneously improving social and financial performance: New research results. In M. J. Epstein, J.-F. Manzoni, & A. Davila (Eds.), *Performance measurement and management control: Innovative concepts and practices*. Bingley, UK: Emerald.

Epstein, M. J., & Wisner, P. S. (2005). Managing and controlling environmental performance: Evidence from Mexico. *Advances in Management Accounting*, *14*, 115–137.

Ferreira, A., Moulang, C., & Hendro, B. (2010). Environmental management accounting and innovation: An exploratory analysis. *Accounting, Auditing & Accountability Journal*, *23*(7), 920–948.

Frost, G. R., & Wilmhurst, T. D. (2000). The adoption of environment-related management accounting: An Analysis of corporate environmental sensitivity. *Accounting Forum*, *24*(4), 344–365.

Gago Rodriguez, S. (2002). Management information for ecologically-oriented decision-making. A case study of the introduction of co-generation in eleven Spanish companies. *Accounting Forum*, *26*, 191–218.

Gates, S., & Germain, C. (2010). Integrating sustainability measures into strategic performance measurement systems: An empirical study. *Management Accounting Quarterly*, *11*(3), 1–7.

German Federal Ministry (2003). *Guide to corporate environmental cost management*. Berlin: German Federal Ministry for Environment/Federal Environmental Agency.

Gond, J.-P., Grubnic, S., Herzig, C., & Moon, J. (2012). Configuring management control systems: Theorizing the integration of strategy and sustainability. *Management Accounting Research*, *23*, 205–223.

Gray, R. H. (1992). Accounting and environmentalism: An exploration of the challenge of gently accounting for accountability, transparency and sustainability. *Accounting, Organizations and Society*, *17*(5), 399–425.

Gray, R. H. (2010). Is accounting for sustainability actually accounting for sustainability … and how would we know? An exploration of narratives of organizations and planet. *Accounting, Organizations and Society*, *35*(1), 47–62.

Hart, S. L. (1995). A natural-resource-based view of the firm. *Academy of Management Review*, *20*(4), 986–1014.

Henri, J.-F., & Journeault, M. (2010). Eco-control: The influence of management control systems on environmental and economic performance. *Accounting, Organizations and Society*, *35*(1), 63–80.

Hopwood, A. G. (2007). Whither accounting research? *The Accounting Review*, *82*(5), 1365–1374.

Hopwood, A. G. (2009a). Accounting and the environment. *Accounting, Organizations and Society*, *34*(3/4), 433–439.

Hopwood, A. G. (2009b). Reflections and projections – and many, many thanks. *Accounting, Organizations and Society*, *34*(8), 887–894.

Horváth, P., & Berlin, S. (2012). Green target costing: Getting ready for green challenge!. *Cost Management*, *26*(3), 25–36.

Hughes II, K. E. (2000). The value relevance of nonfinancial measures of air pollution in the electric utility industry. *The Accounting Review*, *75*(2), 209–228.

IFAC (2005). *Environmental management accounting*. New York, NY: International Guidance Document.

Ilinitch, A. Y., Soderstrom, N. S., & Thomas, T. E. (1998). Measuring corporate environmental performance. *Journal of Accounting and Public Policy*, *17*(4/5), 383–409.

Joshi, S., & Krishnan, R. (2010). Sustainability accounting systems with a managerial decision focus. *Cost Management*, *24*(6), 20–30.

Joshi, S., Krishnan, R., & Lave, L. (2001). Estimating the hidden costs of environmental regulation. *The Accounting Review*, *26*(2), 171–198.

Kaplan, R. S. (1986). The role for empirical research in management accounting. *Accounting, Organizations and Society*, *11*, 4–5.

Kaplan, R. S. (2011). Accounting scholarship that advances professional knowledge and practice. *The Accounting Review*, *86*(2), 367–383.

Lamberton, G. (2005). Sustainability accounting: A brief history and conceptual framework. *Accounting Forum*, *29*(1), 7–26.

Lanen, W. (1999). Waste minimization at 3M company: A field study of nonfinancial performance measurement. *Journal of Management Accounting Research*, *11*, 29–43.

Lockhart, J., & Taylor, A. (2007). Environmental considerations in product mix decisions using ABC and TOC. *Management Accounting Quarterly*, *9*(1), 13–21.

Luft, J., & Shields, M. D. (2003). Mapping management accounting: Graphics and guidelines for theory-consistent empirical research. *Accounting, Organizations and Society*, *28*, 169–249.

Mankins, M. C., & Steele, R. (2005). Turning great strategy into great performance. *Harvard Business Review*, *83*(7/8), 64–71.

Marcus, A., & Fremeth, A. (2009). Green management matters regardless. *Academy of Management Perspectives*, *23*(3), 17–26.

Marquis, C., & Toffel, M. W. (2012). *When do firms greenwash? Corporate visibility, civil society scrutiny, and environmental disclosure*. Harvard Business School Working Paper, No. 11–115.

Mathews, M. R. (1993). *Socially responsible accounting*. London: Chapman & Hall.

Mathews, M. R. (1997). Twenty-five years of social and environmental accounting research: Is there a silver jubilee to celebrate. *Accounting, Auditing and Accountability Journal*, *10*(4), 481–531.

Milne, M. J. (1996). On sustainability: The environment and management accounting. *Management Accounting Research*, *7*, 135–161.

Neumann, B. R., Cauvin, E., & Roberts, M. L. (2012). Management control systems dilemma: Reconciling sustainability with information overload. *Advances in Management Accounting*, *20*, 1–28.

Norris, G., & O'Dwyer, B. (2004). Motivating socially responsive decision making: The operation of management controls in a socially responsive organization. *The British Accounting Review*, *36*, 173–196.

O'Rourke, J. (2011). Sustainability matters. *Cost Management*, *25*(5), 6–15.

O'Sullivan, N., & O'Dwyer, B. (2009). Stakeholder perspectives on financial sector legitimation process: The case of NGOs and the equator principles. *Accounting, Auditing & Accountability Journal*, *22*(4), 553–587.

Parker, L. D. (2000a). Green strategy costing. *Australian Accounting Review*, *10*(1), 46–55.

Parker, L. D. (2000b). Environmental costing: A path to implementation. *Australian Accounting Review*, *10*(3), 43–51.

Perego, P., & Hartmann, F. (2009). Aligning performance measurement systems with strategy: The case of environmental strategy. *Abacus*, *45*(4), 397–426.

Perez, E. A., Ruiz, C. C., & Fenech, F. C. (2007). Environmental management systems as an embedding mechanism: A research note. *Accounting, Auditing & Accountability Journal*, *20*(3), 403–422.

Pistoni, A., & Songini, L. (2009). ENEL: CSR and performance measurement. In N. C. Smith & G. Lenssen (Eds.), *Mainstreaming corporate responsibility: Cases and texts for integrating corporate responsibility across the business school curriculum*. Hoboken: Wiley.

Porter, M. E., & Van der Linde, C. (1995). Toward a new conception of the environment-competitiveness relationship. *Journal of Economic Perspectives*, *9*(4), 97–118.

Qian, W., Burritt, R., & Monroe, G. (2011). Environmental management accounting in local government. A case of waste management. *Accounting, Auditing & Accountability Journal*, *24*(1), 93–218.

Schaltegger, S. (2011). *Sustainability as a driver for corporate economic success. Consequences for the development of sustainability management control*. Centre for Sustainability Management, Leuphana University of Lueneburg.

Schaltegger, S., & Burritt, R. (2000). *Contemporary environmental accounting*. Sheffield, UK: Greenleaf.

Shrivastava, P. (1995). The role of corporations in achieving ecological sustainability. *Academy of Management Review*, *20*(4), 936–960.

Sims, C. A. (1996). Macroeconomics and methodology. *Journal of Economic Perspectives*, *10*(1), 105–120.

Sinkin, C., Wright, C. J., & Burnett, R. D. (2008). Layoff announcements and stockholder wealth. *Journal of Accounting and Public Policy*, *27*(2), 167–176.

Sorensen, J. E. (2008). Management accountants in the United States: Practitioner and academic views of recent developments. In C. S. Chapman, A. G. Hopwood, & M. D. Shields (Eds.), *Handbook of management accounting research*. Oxford, UK: Elsevier.

United Nations Division for Sustainable Development (UNDSD). (2001). *Environmental management accounting, procedures and principles*. Retrieved from http://www.un.org/esa/sustdev/publications/proceduresandprinciples.pdf

Wisner, P. S., Epstein, M. J., & Bagozzi, R. P. (2006). Organizational antecedents and consequences of environmental performance. *Advances in Environmental Accounting and Management*, *3*, 143–167.

Wisner, P. S., Epstein, M. J., & Bagozzi, R. P. (2010). Environmental proactivity and performance. *Advances in Environmental Accounting and Management*, *4*, 105–127.

Xie, S., & Hayase, K. (2007). Corporate environmental performance evaluation: A measurement model and a new concept. *Business Strategy and the Environment*, *16*(2), 148–168.

THE USE OF CAUSAL MAPPING IN THE DESIGN OF SUSTAINABILITY PERFORMANCE MEASUREMENT SYSTEMS: EVIDENCE FROM NOVO NORDISK

Cristiana Parisi

ABSTRACT

Purpose – *The purpose of this study is to illustrate the use of the ad hoc methodology of causal mapping to support the process of quantifying the financial returns related to sustainability investments. The present study uses two methods to build causal maps, that is aggregate and congregate mapping, in order to capture managerial cognition and derive a model that reflects companies' competitive advantages. The resulting causal map is a prerequisite and serves as a building block for the design of the organisation's performance management systems for sustainability.*

Design/methodology/approach – *This study relies on qualitative, deductive research undertaken at the leading international pharmaceutical company Novo Nordisk. This chapter presents the results of a*

Accounting and Control for Sustainability
Studies in Managerial and Financial Accounting, Volume 26, 231–264

ISSN: 1479-3512/doi:10.1108/S1479-3512(2013)0000026007

longitudinal study developed through an action research approach conducted at the Company over a four-year period.

Findings – *This study illustrates how the described approach for developing causal maps can facilitate the elicitation of managerial tacit knowledge and the consequent identification of indicators to quantify the investments in sustainability.*

Practical implications – *This chapter proves the relevance of causal mapping as a comprehensive, articulated basis for developing and improving organisations' strategic performance measurement systems (SPMSs).*

Originality/value – *This study's main contribution is the triangulation of multiple qualitative methods to enhance the reliability of causal maps. This innovative approach supports the use of causal mapping to extract managerial tacit knowledge in order to identify indicators for the evaluation of investments in sustainability.*

Keywords: Sustainability; social and environmental performance; strategic performance measurement systems; performance management; causal maps; managerial cognition

INTRODUCTION

The concept of 'sustainability' rose to prominence due to the Brundtland report in 1987 in which it was defined as 'the development that meets the needs of the present without compromising the ability of the future generations to meet their own needs' (WCED, 1987, p. 8). While there is extensive agreement about the basic idea of sustainability, the identification of the exact meaning of the concept and the assessment of its impact are points of contention in the literature (Gadenne, Lokman, Sands, Winata, & Hooi, 2012). In this chapter, in concurrence with Laszlo and Zhexembayeva (2011), sustainability is defined from a value creation perspective as 'a dynamic state that occurs when a company creates ongoing value for its shareholders and stakeholders' (2011, p. 42; see also Porter & Kramer, 2011). This definition, which is in line with the triple bottom line (TBL) approach, encompasses social welfare, protection of the environment, efficient use of resources and economic well-being (Elkington, 1997).

While some of the literature maintains that sustainability can be considered a mere drain on an organisation's profit (Kim & Statman, 2012; Reich, 2007), most authors support the hypothesis that there might be a 'business case' for it based on the results of qualitative and quantitative analyses (Hahn & Figge, 2011; Salzmann, Ionescu-Somers, & Steger, 2005). As some influential meta-analyses suggest, to date, existing empirical evidence does not support any conclusion on the association between sustainability and financial results, even though a number of exemplary cases of a positive relationship can be found in the literature (Margolis & Walsh, 2003; Orlitzky, Schmidt, & Rynes, 2003; Orlitzky, 2011). For this reason, several researchers have called for contributions aiming at shedding a light on the dynamics of the sustainability–financial returns relationship (Griffin & Mahon, 1997; Lungu, Caraiani, & Dascalu, 2012; Margolis & Walsh, 2003; Porter & Kramer, 2011; Rowley & Berman, 2000; Surroca, Tribó & Waddock, 2010; Wagner, Schaltegger, & Wehrmeyer, 2002; Wood & Jones, 1995). More specifically, Margolis and Walsh (2003) emphasised the relevance of creating models that incorporate variables that have been omitted in the past and test mediating mechanisms and contextual conditions to clarify the relationship between the described forms of performance.

The debate over the expected returns on investments in sustainability, defined as 'investments driven by the long-term economic, environmental, and social risks and opportunities facing the global economy' (Krosinsky & Robins, 2008, p. xxiii), has led to the creation of strategic performance measurement systems (SPMSs) for sustainability aimed at identifying the mediating elements of the relationship between sustainability and financial performance in order to quantify and manage these investments. SPMSs for sustainability are part of the broader category of comprehensive SPMSs, examples of which are Otley's (1999) Performance Management model, Kaplan and Norton's (1996) Balanced Scorecard (BSC), and Epstein, Kumar, and Westbrook's (2000) APL model. These models include financial and non-financial performance measures and also emphasize the importance of the relationship among diverse performance measures in a SPMS (Hansen, 2010; Vaivio, 2005). Perhaps the most well-known sustainability SPMS is the 'Sustainability Balanced Scorecard': an adaptation of Kaplan and Norton's (1996) framework, in which an additional 'non-market perspective' was added to the traditional BSC to capture the value of social and environmental sustainability (Figge, Hahn, Schaltegger, & Wagner, 2002).

Apart from reports concerning the use of the above-mentioned models, little empirical evidence exists to evaluate their impact (Searcy, 2012). For this reason, the practical effectiveness of SPMSs for sustainability is questionable due to, among other reasons, the intangible nature of sustainability activities and the long-term returns generally associated with these investments (Andriessen, 2004).

While the management accounting literature is beginning to improve our understanding of the functions of SPMSs for sustainability, the same cannot be said concerning how their components, that is their metrics and interrelationships, are identified effectively and how their linkage to organisational outcomes can be measured. The existing literature suggests the need for an effective SPMS for sustainability that is linked to a company's strategy (Hansen, 2010; Kaplan & Norton, 2003; Vaivio, 2005), but empirical research has shown that the main source for the identification of indicators for the SPMS is data mining of existing archival sources (Porac, Mishina, & Pollock, 2002; Rucci, Kirn, & Quinn, 1998). Even though this method is feasible for gathering data that are relevant to performance and for performing longitudinal analyses of the company's performance, it can also be considered somewhat unsound. Building a performance measurement model based solely on indicators that show the evolution of currently available data might create gaps in the definition of companies' competitive advantages. This could result in the gathering of data that are unrelated to the actual drivers of the organisation's performance.

Even though top management might understand the organisation's intended strategy and policies, it might be unable to formally represent and diffuse its perception of the company's competitive advantages, which can be considered as the mediators between organisations' investments and the desired financial outcomes (Waddock, Bodwell, & Graves, 2002). This is critical for investments in sustainability, the outcomes of which are particularly difficult to estimate.

A possible solution could be to build a specific model that is independent of current practice for the measurement of performance and is aimed only at capturing companies' competitive advantages and their relationships with valued organisational outcomes. This method can provide a more complete foundation for the design and development of performance measurement systems by identifying all performance drivers, some of which currently may not be included in existing SPMSs. Once the performance drivers, or mediators, which can be defined as competitive advantages, are determined, the performance measures that are currently used can be compared with those derived directly from the new model.

However, in the management accounting literature, the question of the elicitation of competitive advantages and their relationships from top managers' perceptions and beliefs still remains unclear (Gonzáles, Calderón, & Gonzáles, 2012).

This study advances the understanding of the relationship between sustainability and financial results in three ways, that is theoretically, empirically and methodologically. On the theoretical side, this study aims at opening the black box of the resource-based view (RBV) to extend the literature on the operationalisation of sustainability. More specifically, a model is presented in which ethical and sustainable practices are analysed as mediating factors in the relationship between sustainability and financial returns. To support the definition of the empirical model, the study drew upon the recent formulation of the RBV framework linking social and environmental challenges to organisational resources, that is the so-called 'natural RBV' (Aragon-Correa & Sharma, 2003; Hart, 1995; Russo & Fouts, 1997; Sharma & Vredenburg, 1998). Even though the mainstream RBV focuses only on intangible assets as a source of competitive advantage, studies that use the natural view have supported the concept that ethical and sustainable practices can also be a source of competitive advantage (Hart, 1995). According to the mentioned literature stream, investments in sustainability might lead to competitive advantage through various mediating factors, for example sustainable organisations might have more opportunities to innovate (Helfat, 1997) and to make investments for generating human capital (Wright, Gardner, Moynihan, & Allen, 2005), reputation (Roberts & Dowling, 2002) and culture (Denison & Mishra, 1995).

Methodologically, the study aimed at overcoming the lack of consensus on the relationship between sustainability and financial results, which also relates to measurement issues (Griffin & Mahon, 1997), the omission of variables (McWilliams & Siegel, 2000), and a lack of clear direction of causality between social and financial performance (Brammer & Millington, 2008; Orlitzky et al., 2003; Simpson & Kohers, 2002; Surroca et al., 2010) by using a multi-method approach: causal mapping.

Attempts to derive models that reflect companies' competitive advantages are problematic due to the difficulty of capturing tacit managerial knowledge (Abernethy, Horne, Lillis, Malina, & Selto, 2005). The present study uses two methods to build causal maps, that is aggregate and congregate mapping, in order to capture managerial cognition. The resulting causal map is a prerequisite and serves as a building block for the design of the organisation's SPMS for sustainability. Finally, this study showed that the use of the ad hoc methodology of causal mapping can support the process of quantifying the financial returns related to sustainability.

Empirically, this study relied on qualitative, deductive research that was undertaken at a leading international pharmaceutical company, Novo Nordisk. This setting is particularly relevant for the risk associated to the management of sustainability in the pharmaceutical industry and the related problems of designing an effective SPMS. In addition, as will be discussed in the case analysis, Novo Nordisk's unique ownership structure, which is controlled by the Novo Nordisk Foundation that has a purely humanitarian mission, allows the company to focus on sustainability beyond the boundaries of a traditional normative approach (Searcy, 2012), making it a relevant case for the present research.

To investigate the matter at hand, this chapter is structured into four sections. The second section consists of a literature review of the two main areas of focus of this chapter. The first area is the literature on the business case for sustainability and related performance measurement systems. The focus is on the influence of top management's decision-making processes on the effective design of SPMSs for sustainability. The second area is the literature on causal mapping models and the process of deriving social and environmental indicators from these models.

The third section describes the methodology used in the case study to illustrate how the use of causal maps can improve companies' SPMSs for sustainability. The fourth section contains the analysis and discussion of the case study of Novo Nordisk, while the final section summarises the findings of the developed analysis, presents the implications that were derived and suggests extensions for future research.

LITERATURE REVIEW

The management accounting literature has a long tradition of advocating performance-based management control systems (Kaplan & Norton, 1996; Merchant, 1998; Simons, 2000). In recent years, there has been increased discussion of the particular problems associated with using such systems for the measurement of sustainability and intellectual capital (IC) (Hahn & Figge, 2011; Hansen, 2010; López-Gamero, Zaragoza-Sáez, Claver-Cortés, & Molina-Azorín, 2011; Surroca et al., 2010).

IC, which traditionally has been described as the basis of an organisation's competitive advantage (Barney, 1991; Dierickx & Cool, 1989;

Wernerfelt, 1984), may have a vital role in determining the organisation's competitive advantage and its financial performance. The introduction of IC reflects the idea that corporate responsibilities are integral to corporate resolutions, actions and impacts. Therefore, the United Nations' (UN's) definition of sustainable development (WCED, 1987) has been translated into an actionable model in which the future generations' needs are considered alongside those of today's societies.

The literature analyses the possibility of investments in sustainability to produce a positive financial return and, in that case, whether IC can be considered as a mediating factor in the relationship and how effective metrics can be developed to capture the said value (Epstein, 1996; Kaplan & Norton, 2003).

In order to analyse the above-mentioned literature, this section is divided into two sub-sections that examine the contributions of SPMSs for sustainability and the alternative use of the causal mapping technique.

Environmental and Social Performance Measurement Systems

Since the literature on the relationship between sustainability and financial returns presents contradictory results (McWilliams & Siegel, 2000), academics and practitioners have developed models that encompass diverse mediating elements in order to clarify this relationship. Exemplary results were presented in the study by McWilliams and Siegel (2000), which included the variable 'research and development' (R&D) as the key mediating factor that explains the contradictory results of the extant literature. Other scholars have suggested misspecification is due to exogenous factors, such as the growth rate of the specific industry that is being analysed (Russo & Fouts, 1997). In fact, according to the authors, the said factor has a direct, positive effect on the relationship between sustainability and financial results (Russo & Fouts, 1997).

The literature focused on environmental accounting suggests the need for development of comprehensive systems divided into: environmental management accounting (EMA), external environmental accounting (EEA), both monetary and physical, and other environmental accounting systems (Schaltegger, Burritt, & Petersen, 2003). EMA can be defined as a generic term that included both monetary and physical EMA (Bennett & James, 1998; Burritt, Hahn, & Schaltegger, 2002; IFAC, 1998). Environmentally related impacts are reflected through monetary information and address all organisational-related effects on the past, present and future financial stocks and flows of a corporation and are expressed in monetary terms. The impacts of corporate activities on environmental systems are reflected in physical environmental information. Thus, at organisational level, physical environmental information includes all the past, present and future material and energy amounts that have an impact on ecological systems. (Bartolomeo et al., 2000).

Other authors have taken a broader approach on the relationship between sustainability and financial returns by focusing on the three aspects of sustainability: environmental, social and economic in line with the TBL perspective (Elkington, 1997) and by selecting a number of intangible resources, such as innovation resources, human resources, reputation and culture to complement them (Surroca et al., 2010). Part of the literature has tried to integrate the three dimensions of IC and sustainability to theorise the existence of a 'sustainable intellectual capital' at a conceptual level (Lungu et al., 2012). The latter view suggests that organisations can be described as dynamic systems of financial, tangible and intangible resources, including sustainability investments, which, among other resources, are a source of the long-term creation of value (Hansen, 2010; Vaivio, 2005). As a result, only the combination of all company resources can create wealth, even though, contrary to financial capital, the unit of measurement of intangible resources is not uniform and often difficult to define (Epstein et al., 2000). In most cases, targets for the performance of sustainability are included in economic decisions in the form of restrictions. Hence, the objective of the companies' SPMSs is to obtain maximum economic return, given a list of environmental and social requirements that are perceived as burdens. The managers of most companies believe that many of their sustainability investments have long-term, positive financial returns in spite of the negative short-term effects. That is why attempts have been made to evaluate these effects in a more systematic way and to include them in the SPMSs of companies.

Academics and practitioners have developed theoretical frameworks in order to integrate the determinants of the long-term process for creating value within traditional managerial models, with one such determinant being investments in sustainability. This multi-dimensional perspective has resulted in the proliferation of performance measurement systems the aim of which is to provide more holistic strategic thinking (Crawford & Scaletta, 2005; Korhonen, 2003). Some examples are Otley's (1999) Performance Management model, Kaplan and Norton's (1996) BSC, Epstein et al.'s (2000) APL, the Scandia Navigator (Edvinsson & Malone,

1997), the frameworks created by the Danish Agency for Trade and Industry (DATI, 2000) and the Danish Ministry of Science, Technology and Innovation (DMSTI, 2002), and the Performance Prism (Neely, Adams, & Kennerley, 2002). Other scholars also have described similar models in the management accounting literature (Ittner & Larcker, 2001). With regard to the measurement of sustainability based on a multi-dimensional approach, relevant examples are the BSC (Epstein & Wisner, 2001; Kaplan & Norton, 1996), the Sustainability Balanced Scorecard (Figge et al., 2002), and the Performance Prism (Neely et al., 2002).

It has been argued that a framework for the assessment of value created by sustainability investments should describe how financial and non-financial resources jointly support corporate strategy (Hansen, 2010; Kaplan & Norton, 2003, 2006). Even though the expected returns on sustainability investments are not likely in the near future and even though they are of an intangible nature, they should be integrated in the SPMS of an organisation. Aligning sustainability resources is expected to improve process performance, which, in turn, should create value for the company (Kaplan & Norton, 2003).

Although several indicators often are collected to give a better and more useful insight into critical value drivers of social and environmental performance, results are usually poor. These studies fail to support organisations in the definition of performance measurement systems that take into consideration the dynamic interdependencies and trade-offs between performance measures and, ultimately, the process that underlies performance (Rusjan, 2005) externally as well as internally to the organisation (Brunklaus, Malmqvist, & Baumann, 2009). In addition, the intangible nature of sustainability investments and the long-term returns that generally are associated with those investments can be considered to be important causes for the limited impact of scorecard models in integrating sustainability activities into the organisation's overall strategy (Hahn & Figge, 2011).

More specifically, the scorecard models have received some criticism related to the interrelationships between measures (Marr, 2006; Nørreklit, 2000). Recently, scholars in the performance management field recommended that establishing great clarity concerning the linkages between the different dimensions of organisational performance should receive significant emphasis during the process of designing performance measurement systems (Banker, Chang, & Pizzini, 2011; Malina & Selto, 2004; Malina, Norreklit, & Selto, 2007). For example, Ittner and Larcker (2003) suggested that the lack of explicit causal relationships between measures creates difficulties in evaluating the relative importance of performance measures, and it hinders the development of a viable definition of the extent and timing of the associations among the said measures. Therefore, causal models are critically important for reducing the ambiguity in the relationships between actions and results (Kunc, 2008; Marr, 2006). By reducing this ambiguity, causal models support the effective implementation of scorecard models (Kaplan & Norton, 2003). However, traditional causal models, such as the strategy map of the BSC (Kaplan & Norton, 2000), fail to support the implementation of scorecard models due to the rigidity of their structure, which assumes linear, reinforcing, and predefined causal linkages (Brunklaus et al., 2009; Nørreklit, 2000; Rusjan, 2005).

It also has been argued that managers are critical agents in promoting responsible business practices within companies. For instance, Weaver, Treviño, and Cochran (1999) found that the moral stance of top management is likely to affect the content and structure of companies' ethics programmes. Moreover, Kaplan and Norton (2003) saw the commitment of management as a precondition for the successful development and use of sustainability initiatives and the implementation of environmental management systems. In addition, Waddock et al. (2002) supported top management's critical role in enforcing responsibility initiatives and attributed the failure to integrate responsibility issues within the organisation's management systems to management's lack of support.

As a consequence, the analysis of top management perceptions towards social and environmental issues appears to be critical in the analysis of the business case for sustainability. However, existing SPMSs do not allow for effective elicitation of top management's perceptions of sustainability-related, competitive advantages. If managers do not give sustainability a priority status and, consequently, are unwilling to allocate the necessary resources for its implementation, sustainability will almost certainly continue to remain in its present, rhetorical context. In this chapter, based on the analysis of the extant literature concerning sustainability management, accounting, and control, the point is made that the current SPMSs for sustainability fail to support management's ability to perceive the relevance of sustainability, which is essential if its social and environmental aspects are to be integrated within the organisation's strategy. Further, this failure results in a lack of the resources and commitment required to support the identification of the mediating factors and the relative indicators that must be accomplished to fully capture the outcomes of investments in sustainability.

Using Causal Mapping to Improve the Measurement of the Performance of Sustainability

The extant literature in the fields of psychology and strategic management elicits mental models from individuals to build formal cognitive maps. A cognitive map is a representation of an individual's personal knowledge, experience and beliefs (Bougon, 1992). During the mapping process, individuals are asked to reveal their opinions and knowledge, disclosing facets of their beliefs that were previously tacit and possibly not fully understood. The in-depth probing allows tacit knowledge, that is the knowledge that goes unspoken in the organisation to be 'mapped'. Cognitive maps visualise knowledge and communicate it as an image to different people within organisations (Axelrod, 1976; Eden, 1988).

A specific category of cognitive map, which captures judgments about the link between actions and outcomes, is referred to as a causal map. Creating a causal map allows for the conversion of individuals' tacit knowledge to a model of explicit constructs and their interrelationships. In causal maps, the nodes are the constructs that the individual perceives as being important, and the arrows illustrate the believed relationships among the nodes (Abernethy et al., 2005).

Constructs and arrows represent the links among inputs, processes, and value outcomes. In this manner, cognitive mapping provides data to support the development of a performance measurement system by analysing competitive advantages or mediators between investments in sustainability and companies' outcomes (Gonzáles et al., 2012). By eliciting the knowledge of individuals within an organisation, a causal map describes the constructs and relationships among them. Then, from this map, it is possible to define measures that are potential candidates for inclusion in a performance measurement system. In fact, the importance of causal maps in supporting the formulation of strategy and strategic control has been supported consistently by a vast range of literature (Eden & Ackerman, 1998; Narayanan & Armstrong, 2005). Numerous methodologies have been proposed for constructing causal maps, but only a few attempts to use the causal mapping technique for identifying performance indicators have been reported in the literature (Gonzáles et al., 2012).

Numerous researchers have proposed possible ways of developing causal maps, but no single method is dominant in the literature (Bougon, 1992; Langfield-Smith, 1992; Lant & Shapira, 2001; Laukkanen, 1994; Nicolini, 1999; Schneider & Anglemar, 1993; Weick & Bougon, 1986). The literature presents three common mapping methods for constructing collective mental models, that is aggregate, congregate, and workshop mapping methods (Vo, Poole, & Courtney, 2005). Given the relative strengths and weaknesses of the above methodologies to derive causal maps, in the present study, aggregate and congregate mapping techniques were combined in an attempt to overcome the respective limitations.

The first method, 'aggregate mapping', aims to represent individual maps of a group of interviewees as completely as possible in the collective map. This can result in a complex, aggregate causal map, but, at the same time, it provides the most complete representation of a social system, allowing all views to be represented. The 'congregate mapping' approach is focused on the identification of key causal loops that drive system dynamics (Bougon, 1992). This methodology stresses the cause-and-effect relationships among metrics. Congregate maps are simpler than the sum of individual maps, but they do not fully represent all of the possible conflicting views of the social system. Last, the 'workshop mapping' approach focuses on a consensual model built at the group level. Workshops, or group meetings, aggregate all participants with the aim of creating a collective map with the facilitation of the researcher, whose role is central for the success of the session. The last methodology is difficult for large groups or organisations to use, and it presents the limit of subjectivity in the elicitation of the model (Eden & Ackerman, 1998).

The present study was focused on the first two methodologies, that is aggregate and congregate mapping. Aggregate mapping starts from an ethnographic study, in which a traditional coding technique of interviews is used to derive constructs and to create the causal maps. Ethnographic interpretation allows the researcher to elicit single causal maps from interviews conducted with top managers. Then, single causal maps are discussed with each individual and aggregated by the researcher. The final aggregated map reflects the nodes captured by the researcher and the relative importance of the causal linkages. It has to be approved by all of the interviewees to ensure that the researcher's interpretations are correct.

A disadvantage of this ethnographic interpretation is the tendency to focus on confirming evidence. Psychology studies have actually found that people place more weight on confirming evidence than on refuting evidence and that they tend to ignore or forget information that does not follow their line of reasoning (Nisbett & Ross, 1980). This is one of the main reasons that traditional strategy maps of the BSC (Kaplan & Norton, 2003) were not considered in the present study. In fact, the literature mentions the rigidity of the described narrative of value creation presented by those tools, which suggest that the process of creating value can be described by aggregating the indicators of the four perspectives of the BSC in a specific order (Banker et al., 2011). Strategy maps can lead to the creation of inaccurate narratives of organisations' value creation due to the confirming evidence problem that may suggest that top managers not alter the tools' predetermined causal linkages in the narrative of the organisation's strategy.

The cognitive complexity related to the creation of an aggregated causal map also can lead to the creation of incomplete and inaccurate portrayals of organisations' strategic causal linkages. Moreover, scholars question the reliability of scorecard models due to the lack of an explicit time dimension, which is needed to help top management understand the effects of time intervals in the implementation of the organisations' strategy (Nørreklit, 2000).

In order to overcome the limitations of the aggregate mapping technique, in the present study, it is suggested that congregate maps, derived from a qualitative system dynamic approach, should be used. This approach consists of the use of a conceptual framework to make the full patterns of the system's behaviour clearer by showing the structures that underlie complex situations (Eden & Ackerman, 1998; Parisi, 2010). In their first book, Kaplan and Norton (1996) recommended a 'systems thinking' approach, but, according to the literature related to the measurement of performance, no attempts have been made to implement their recommendation.

The use of congregate maps to implement strategies has been proposed by a number of authors (Franco-Santos & Bourne, 2005; Tapinos & Dyson, 2007). The specific benefit related to the use of this technique is to avoid the linear logic that is typical of traditional strategy maps and aggregate maps (Kunc, 2008). In fact, those models tend not to consider the information feedback processes in which outcome performance measures (effects) are used to change processes identified in the leading performance indicators (causes). Thus, the information in the strategy and aggregate maps is not neutral to the process of decision making and can affect the future value of the performance indicators leading to a circular process, that is causes – effects – causes. The design of the causal relationships should consider the feedback processes that exist between the information given by the performance indicators and the likely intervention in the organisation to correct deviations. Causal loop diagrams can illustrate the feedback processes that exist between performance indicators and related organisational processes and evaluate the time intervals.

However, the complex nature of organisations makes the design of an effective set of performance measures highly dependent upon the ability to effectively unveil the most relevant determinants of organisations' competitive advantage. The literature suggests that congregate mapping is limited for this task and indicates the superiority of aggregated maps and their brainstorming technique (Vo et al., 2005).

While the literature on system dynamics describes the role of congregate causal maps in supporting the scorecard models, improving the causal relationships of the model, and selecting better indicators following a positivistic approach (Othman, 2006; Schoeneborn, 2003), the effective definition of the nodes in the congregate mapping still is not considered adequately in the literature. For this reason, in this chapter, it is suggested that aggregate and congregate mapping techniques be integrated in order to overcome the limitations of both approaches and provide an effective tool to support the selection of indicators for systems that are intended to measure social and environmental performance.

Causal mapping can improve the SPMS for sustainability of the organisation overall, and it also can be used to derive performance indicators in order to measure the long-term financial impact of investments in sustainability. The application of these maps is expected to improve the selection of indicators used in SPMSs for sustainability. Actions aimed at increasing the value of investments in sustainability can be evaluated financially even if short-term calculations do not demonstrate the profitability of those actions.

Through the implementation of causal maps, the strategic hypotheses that form the basis for the implementation of sustainability investments can be identified, prioritised, and analysed. Furthermore, indicators can be derived and included in the existing internal reporting system in order to obtain quantification of the expected financial costs and benefits.

The elicitation of indicators from aggregated causal maps has been suggested by a few authors (Eden & Ackerman, 1998; Suwignjo, Bititci, & Carrie, 2000), who emphasised the capacity of causal maps to communicate the definition of performance measures in a tailored manner.

METHODOLOGY

The above literature review supported the definition of the research question that was tested using a single, explorative, in-depth, case study (Yin, 2003). The case study was developed through an action research approach (McKernan, 1991), conducted at a leading pharmaceutical company over a number of years beginning in 2008 with follow-up in 2011. Therefore, this contribution is the result of the work conducted by the author of this chapter at Novo Nordisk A/S, based in Copenhagen, DK.

The setting was selected for several reasons. Firstly, pharmaceutical companies represent archetypical, knowledge-based organisations, since the medicine production process is well understood. Thus, organisational outcomes are easily quantifiable if the development of new drugs is taken into account, but this is not the case when the effects on stakeholders are considered. These conditions create a management control environment in which it is particularly problematic to monitor and measure the performance of sustainability and its impact on the company's stakeholders. It is also a setting in which the upper echelon's knowledge of the company's strategy and competitive advantage related to sustainability is at risk. The elicitation of managerial aggregate and congregate maps can lead to the creation of a more effective system for measuring sustainability performance, and it can foster the diffusion of strategic knowledge throughout the entire organisation. Secondly, Novo Nordisk is characterised by a distinctive ownership structure in the industry, as described in the following section. This allows the organisation to have a unique focus on its social and environmental performance.

Both the aggregate and the congregate causal mapping approaches were selected for the Novo Nordisk case since strategic hypotheses are more likely to emerge from a full representation of diverse viewpoints. The contribution of investments into sustainability to the overall process of value creation can be identified more easily when the causal linkages that describe Novo Nordisk's strategy are clearly represented.

The use of causal maps at Novo Nordisk linked environmental and social performance with a set of competitive advantages or mediators. Novo Nordisk's strategic programmes and actions were mapped by the researcher during semi-structured interviews. Following Yin (2003), the researcher used an interview protocol that was based on a generic performance model in which inputs are converted into outputs through a transformation process. This model served as a preliminary explanation to facilitate the participants' understanding of the causal mapping technique and to motivate the selection of the questions in the interview protocol. However, questions did not constrain the respondents to fit the exemplary model. Conversely, they were designed to elicit successful stories of sustainability performance. By telling stories of how the organisation functioned and the factors that led to success, the participants explicated and clarified goals, processes, performance, and outcomes (Abernethy et al., 2005).

More specifically, participants were asked to identify certain relevant positive and negative attributes of environmental and social performance. Then, they were prompted to state the reasons the company had chosen to engage in such practices and whether they felt that such activities created a competitive advantage. Through this process, the first collection of sustainability activities with corporate strategy was achieved, and, in the second phase of the analysis, congregated causal maps were created based on the initials results that were obtained. Data from the interviews also were triangulated with archival data provided by the Company. The Company's internal management control documents were consulted in order to improve the reliability of the analysis (Tegarden, Tegarden, & Sheetz, 2005). More specifically, the researcher had access to the Company's annual report, including sustainability reporting; to the TBL BSC of Novo Nordisk in Copenhagen; to documents that described the 'Novo Nordisk Way of Management', and to internal presentations on sustainability created by the Company for internal purposes.

The merging operation was an iterative process. Single causal maps were constructed during the interviews with individual managers using Decision Explorer® software, while aggregation was conducted by the researcher. The interviews involved managers responsible for corporate social responsibility (CSR), BSC and financial management, and external communication. Each interview lasted an hour and a half to two hours. The interviews were recorded, and, subsequently, they were transcribed and coded. During successive interview sessions, the aggregate map was presented to each interviewee and eventually changed to fit the manager's beliefs. The workshop mapping approach was not used due to the numerous possible shortcomings and the difficulty of aggregating all the interviewees at the same time. In the second phase of the research, the congregate map was created, and indicators were derived when the definitive causal map was approved by the participants. The first phase of the study was conducted by the researcher, who was supported by an expert in the use of Decision Explorer® software. The researcher followed up on the study with the participants to further test the model and to improve the congregate mapping, which was developed further at this stage. The results presented in this work were produced in the second phase of the research.

CASE STUDY AND DATA ANALYSIS

Novo Nordisk

Novo Nordisk is active in 179 countries, with production facilities in six countries and affiliates in 178 countries. Novo Nordisk has over 91,000 employees and a sales turnover of over €3,900 million (Novo Nordisk, 2011).

Since its foundation in 1923, Novo Nordisk has specialised in biotechnology. The company operates in two fields. The first field, biopharmaceuticals, provides around 30% of the Company's income. In this field, the Company occupies a leading position in the market in the areas of homeostasis management, growth disorders, and hormone replacement therapy. The second field, diabetes care, constitutes 70% of the Company's income, and Novo Nordisk also occupies a leading position in this area, with a current market share of 51%.

Novo Nordisk is globally renowned for its sustainability investments and performance. On more than 50 occasions, the Company has won prizes and awards for its sustainability activities and social and environmental reporting. Novo Nordisk is listed on both the Ethibel Sustainability Index (ESI) and the Dow Jones Sustainability Index (DJSI), on which, in 2008, it was ranked as best-in-class in healthcare – one of 18 global DJSI super sectors (Novo Nordisk, 2011).

Novo Nordisk is characterised by a value-based, holistic approach to business. There are two main reasons that it has taken this value-based approach and focused on sustainability. Firstly, it was a specific, strategic decision that related to the cost and duration of developing new drugs. It should be noted that, today, the average cost of developing a new drug is estimated to be around €3,900 million, and the average time it takes to develop and market a new drug is in the range of 10–12 years.

The second reason for Novo Nordisk's business approach is its unique ownership structure. The Company is controlled financially by the Novo Nordisk Foundation, which holds a large majority of voting rights through its holding Company, Novo A/S (Morsing & Oswald, 2006; Novo Nordisk, 2011). The Novo Nordisk Foundation is a private, self-governing institution that secures long-term financial independence and guarantees its value-based approach to business (Novo Nordisk, 1997).

Novo Nordisk and Sustainability

The analysis that was undertaken at Novo Nordisk indicated that, like many other organisations in the same field, it had gradually attributed value to sustainability investments through a learning process (Morsing & Oswald, 2006). Sustainability and the management of stakeholder relationships evolved from being, in the beginning, a mere response to specific business crises (Novo Nordisk, 1997, 2011) to forming part of the Company's management system (Novo Nordisk, 1997, 2011) and finally to being a main objective of corporate strategy (Novo Nordisk, 1997, 2011).

In 1997, new guidelines, called 'Novo Nordisk Way of Management' (Novo Nordisk, 1997) were introduced in order to balance the conflicting interests between corporate control and decentralised decision making. The guidelines are an important instrument for putting management's commitment towards responsible business practices into operation.

Following its 'Way of Management', and in order to implement its corporate values throughout the organisation, Novo Nordisk proposed a methodology that originated from the Company's vision, values, commitments, and fundamentals. This methodology consists of a combination of three managerial tools, that is *Sustainability Reporting, the Balanced Scorecard*, and *Facilitators*. The vision and values of Novo Nordisk reflect the Company's engagement towards sustainable development. Novo Nordisk adopts the term 'sustainable development', which, although conceptually different, includes the same elements as sustainability at the current time. Sustainable development, operationalised through Novo Nordisk's TBL approach, clearly states Novo Nordisk's commitment towards financial, environmental and social responsibility.

Novo Nordisk's 'Way of Management' also includes the use of 'Facilitators', a group of about 15 high-profile, corporate-level professionals whose task it is to evaluate, assist, and help business units in implementing corporate strategy and in improving their general performance through on-site auditing activities. Since 2004, sustainability reporting has been integrated into the annual report, and it delivers a comprehensive documentation of the Company's aspirations, objectives, and actions aimed at improving its environmental and social performance. It also accounts for costs and targets related to the implementation of sustainability actions.

Financial, environmental and social performance is implemented through the BSC model (Kaplan & Norton, 1996), and it was first used by the Company in 1996. This serves as a means for cascading corporate objectives throughout the different organisational levels and to each of the sub-units that compose each business unit. The BSC at Novo Nordisk is currently composed of 24 objectives, divided into four dimensions, that is 'Customers and Society', 'Finance', 'Business Processes' and 'People and Organisations'.

Problems with Novo Nordisk's 'Way of Management'

Through facilitation, sustainability reporting, and the BSC, the Novo Nordisk 'Way of Management' guidelines guarantee the implementation of sustainability policies and actions. However, the decentralised approach might cause misalignment in the management of sustainability initiatives across the Company, since management at the local unit level primarily are responsible for prioritising the different sustainability actions. The situation is managed by imposing different sustainability targets on the business units at the corporate level. However, the selection of different sustainability policies and the adoption of the related actions imply a weighting system that assesses different, and often contrasting, costs and benefits and the effects on different stakeholders and shareholders. Clearly prioritising the selected actions would imply an in-depth analysis of those trade-offs through a quantification of the expected returns on the Company's investment in sustainability actions.

Due to the difficulties in quantifying the external objectives of different stakeholders and the lack of a management instrument to effectively internalise environmental and social costs and benefits, attempts are only made in specific areas. The resulting normative attitude prevents the Company from an in-depth evaluation of the expected long-term effects of sustainability on its financial performance. It is recognised that sustainability-driven investments have a positive financial impact on performance (Novo Nordisk, 2003), but the difficulty of measuring these activities in financial terms is also acknowledged. In 2003, attempts were made to recognise the potential financial impacts of sustainability-driven activities (Novo Nordisk, 2003). Mediators that have been identified in the increment of shareholders' value include cost efficiency, lower costs for employee retention, productivity benefits, lower insurance costs and higher market values to name but a few.

No systematic attempts were made to arrange these actions and competitive advantages hierarchically in relation to the Company's strategic priorities or to identify indicators to be included in the BSC. The relevance of deriving indicators from the Company's strategic hypothesis and for the internal reporting system somewhat collides with the normative attitude adopted by the Company towards sustainability. This chapter demonstrates that, through the implementation of causal maps, the strategic hypotheses that form the basis for investments in sustainability can be identified, prioritised and analysed. Furthermore, indicators can be derived and included in the existing reporting system in order to reach a financial quantification of the expected costs and benefits. In fact, the indicators in the BSC's four perspectives are related in such a way as to quantify the organisation's performance in different areas of interest and to synthesize the overall result in a single, aggregated, financial indicator (Kaplan & Norton, 1996).

The Construction of Novo Nordisk's Causal Maps

The creation of causal maps at Novo Nordisk followed the procedure described in the methodology section. Firstly, an aggregated causal map was elicited, which captured managers' tacit knowledge and beliefs with regard to the Company's competitive advantages related to sustainability, their importance and how they were to be achieved. The resulting map expresses the assumptions about interrelationships between elements and the coherence of the strategy, providing, in turn, a coherent rationality. It should be noted here that the results of this case study are consistent with the four critical success factors defined by existing literature (Parisi & Hockerts, 2008). All activities related to sustainability were aimed at reducing business risk, increasing operational efficiency, pursuing product differentiation and creating a new market space. The resulting map illustrates the strategic actions identified by the managerial team in the sustainability area. Examples are the focus on reducing pollution, which is translated in the project of building windmills in developing countries in order to become clean energy producers and, in so doing, creating new markets for the company. Another critical area of interest is the 'Healthy Novo' programme, which aims at improving the lives and working conditions for employees in order to increase their motivation and internal operational efficiency, as well as the Company's image. The aggregated causal map portrays the causal relationships perceived by the interviewees. At this stage, the aim was to capture the tacit knowledge and beliefs of the managers (Fig. 1).

When the first description of the competitive advantages related to investments in sustainability was completed, the qualitative system dynamic approach was chosen in order to improve the managers' perceptions of which sustainability investments effectively contribute to the organisation's overall process of creating value (Parisi, 2010).

In order to build a congregate causal map, two steps were needed. Firstly, causal loops had to be identified, which, according to the System

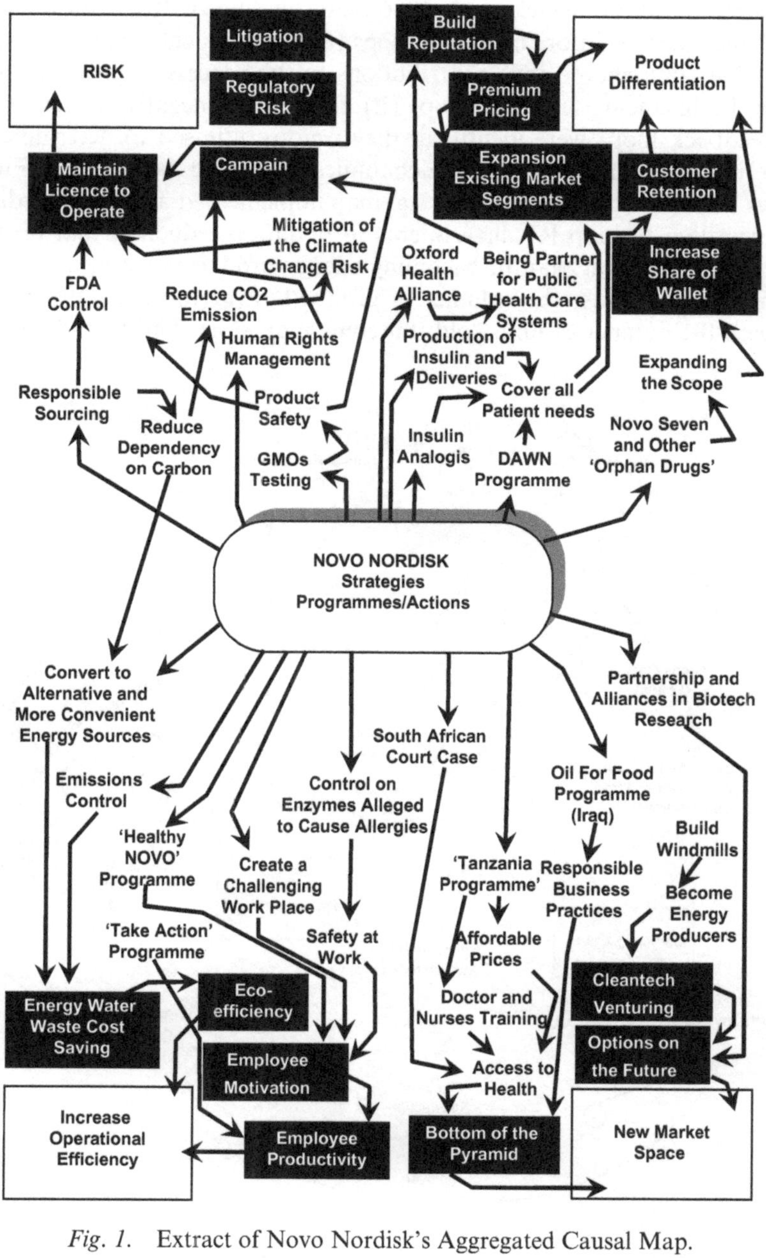

Fig. 1. Extract of Novo Nordisk's Aggregated Causal Map.

Dynamic tradition (Weick et al. 1986), can be named 'R' (reinforcing) or 'B' (balancing). Reinforcing causal loops (R) are characterised by a positive sign. They describe positive contributions to the process of creating value, while the balancing feedback loops (B) describe the negative effects. Once the feedback loops were identified, they were scrutinised to determine the most important nodes, after which indicators could be derived. Fig. 2 shows a simplified version of a causal map implemented at Novo Nordisk.

According to loop R1, investments in pollution reduction that resulted from the investment plan of becoming energy producers would enable the Company to increase the volumes of production (performance driver) and increase the number of units sold (outcome indicator). This would result in

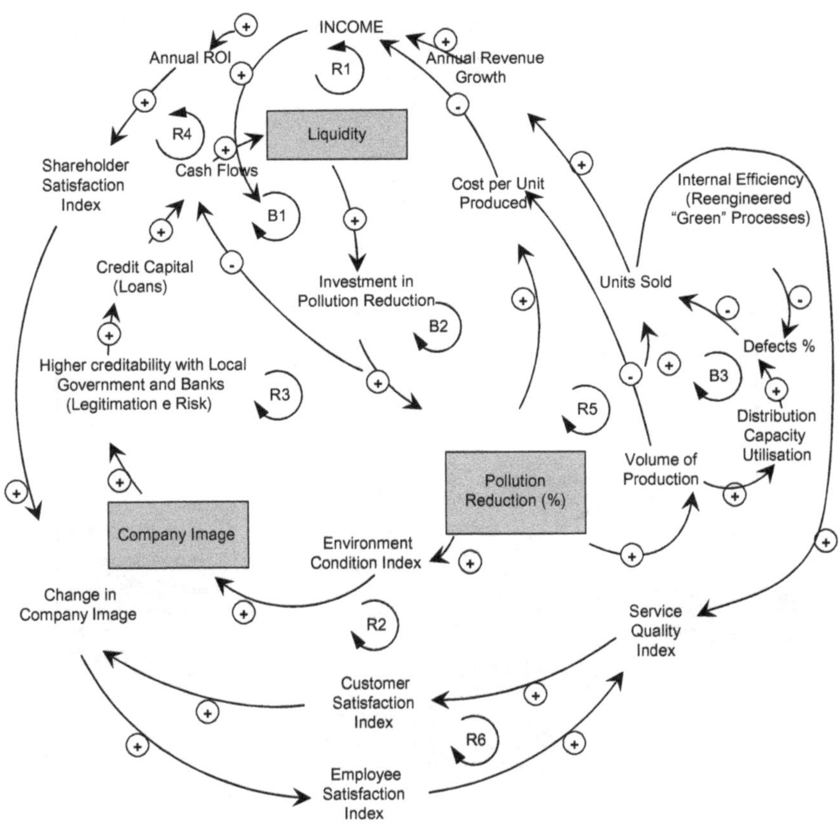

Fig. 2. Extract from Novo Nordisk's Congregate Map.

higher revenues (outcome indicator). An increase in the percentage of revenue growth would lead to a higher income and, other conditions being equal, cash flows (outcome indicator). A higher cash flow leads to an increase in available financial resources to reinvest in the acquisition of more pollution reduction capacity.

Furthermore, the higher the volume of production becomes the higher the experience and the better the quality of service and customer satisfaction (outcome indicators) will be. This will improve the Company's image, which, in turn, will increase the perceived credibility of Novo Nordisk in the financial markets and among local governments (performance driver). The Company's higher credibility will allow business decision makers to better negotiate funds to borrow from different stakeholders, thereby increasing cash flows to reinvest in pollution reduction capacity (loop R2).

Another effect of a higher pollution reduction capacity (performance driver) associated to a pollution reduction investment policy is an improvement in the environment condition index, leading to a higher Company image, better credibility among investors, and higher cash flows available for more investments in pollution reduction capacity, implying a further increase in the percentage of pollution reduction (loop R3).

A higher volume of units sold also implies, other conditions being equal, an increase in income and in the annual return on investment (ROI), resulting in an improvement in shareholders' satisfaction. Higher shareholders' satisfaction would increase the Company's image and, again, increase the funds the organisation can attain to finance its environmental policy (loop R4).

According to loop R5, the larger the production volume is, the larger the basis will be for spreading overhead costs and, all other conditions being equal, the lower the production unit cost will be. This should increase the Company's income and liquidity to reinvest in environmental protection, which, in turn, is likely to increase employees' satisfaction (loop R6).

Fig. 2 also shows a number of balancing loops (B), the dominance of which could undermine business growth. These balancing loops must be detected promptly and counteracted properly so they will not evolve into crises. Loop B1 shows how higher investments in pollution reduction result in reductions in the Company's total cash flow. This provides a possible limit to growth in investment policy, if the Company's returns from higher income and borrowed funds are not able to provide higher cash flows.

Loop B2 describes how the increase in the percentage of pollution reduction would result in an increase in the cost per unit produced because of the additional variable costs. An increment in cost per unit produced would have a negative effect on income. This could cause a reduction in financial resources and, hence, could prevent the Company from acquiring additional pollution reduction capacity.

Finally, as shown in loop B3, if the volume of production increases faster than the distribution capacity, an increase in the utilisation of distribution capacity could occur. This can lead to higher defect rates, negatively impacting the numbers of units sold to customers. In fact, the cost per unit sold would be higher, reducing the amount of financial resources that could be invested in pollution reduction.

The congregate map represents both positive and negative causal linkages and aims at simplifying and rationalising the results obtained by the congregate map. The causal linkages, as opposed to other methodologies, for example strategy maps (Kaplan & Norton, 2000), do not assume linear and predefined causal linkages. This overcomes the limitations of scorecard models identified in the literature (Nørreklit, 2000). Moreover, it identifies possible negative effects of balancing loops, which are not considered by traditional systems. It can be argued that different interpretations of the causal linkages could be suggested, for example that the causal relationship between pollution reduction and the cost per unit produced in loop B2 could be negative and not positive, that is that pollution reduction performed through an innovative sustainable technology could reduce costs per unit and not vice versa. The model must be tested and adjusted through a regular, double-feedback-loop process (Kaplan & Norton, 2006), which analyses the differences between what was foreseen and the actual results and accordingly changes the model and the strategic assumptions at the basis of its construction. The strength of the model lies in the fact that it is more reliable and comprehensive than traditional models.

Deriving Indicators from Novo Nordisk's Causal Map

This chapter presents a generalizable, qualitative approach to identifying a conceivable and articulate causal map in a pharmaceutical company. Creating causal maps is the first step of designing effective SPMSs, especially aimed at measuring the returns on investments in sustainability due to the intrinsic difficulty of quantifying their outcomes. Developing the company's causal map enables management to disclose and gather further knowledge about the competitive advantages, the activities, and the processes necessary to increase the returns of investments in sustainability. Causal maps also support organisations with dispersed knowledge such as pharmaceutical companies (Porter, 2004).

However, the maps shown in Fig. 1 and 2 provide a highly complex representation of competitive advantages. The desirability of implementing an SPMS that includes indicators for all the competitive advantages identified is questionable. The use of an excessive number of performance metrics can lead to information overload or selective focus on the most easily achievable measures (Feltham & Xie, 1994). For this reason, the selection of the most relevant competitive advantages must be performed with considerable care, also taking the patterns and feedback loops of the congregate maps into consideration, that is the impacts on the whole system of using or not using a specific indicator.

In Novo Nordisk's case, the use of causal maps paved the way for managerial teams to develop effective indicators that focused on the Company's value drivers to support the existing Balance Scorecard. This result was obtained as the competitive advantages were clearly identified by the causal map. This allowed the testing of the existing indicators in the Company's SPMS based on the analysis of the competitive advantages that they measure. Moreover, it allowed for the identification of indicators that were potentially measurable. These indicators were related to relevant competitive advantages, which were not yet measured by the Company.

The above-mentioned indicators had to be evaluated by Novo Nordisk's top management for inclusion in the Company's SPMS, depending on cost/benefit and a feasibility assessment. For example, in the case of the strategic objective 'increase employee motivation', the action chosen by the Company was to implement training programmes and increase the percentage of staff involved. Through the combined use of the causal and congregate mapping techniques, this strategic objective was combined to its positive and negative effects within the reinforcing and balancing loops. This circumstance allowed the managerial team to decide whether or not to include the relative indicator in the BSC of the Company.

On a more general level, the indicators drawn from causal maps constitute one step in the building of an SPMS (e.g. the BSC) based on performance measures. Over the years, these socio-economic models have been developed in order to evaluate the impact of sustainability investments on different stakeholders, grouped in economic terms. Still, they emphasise that, in most cases, it is not possible to internalise these effects in financial calculations and that such economic measures are not used for balancing dilemmas between stakeholders. However, causal maps also can incorporate preference information on acceptable trade-offs between performance in different dimensions. This preference information attempts to solve the problems related to discrepancies between different stakeholders' evaluations of the costs and benefits to be derived from the Company's actions. The continuous process of revising the strategy and the indicators based on the feedback of corporate management (Gonzáles et al., 2012; Kaplan & Norton, 2006) is expected to improve the precision of the model.

CONCLUSIONS

In this chapter, the aim was to illustrate the use of causal mapping for improving environmental and social performance measurement systems. To that end, first, the extant literature on performance measurement and sustainability was reviewed. The results showed that, even though there have been previous attempts to study and evaluate the link between environmental social performance and financial performance, the current literature is not capable of establishing this link with enough validity due to the lack of a sound methodology that can identify the mediating factors or the competitive advantages related to the adoption of sustainability actions. Consequently, the use of SPMSs for sustainability was suggested, but previous research has highlighted several limitations concerning this approach, including the lack of instruments that can represent managerial perceptions of the competitive advantages related to the implementation of sustainability strategies. Moreover, the traditional performance management tools, such as the strategy maps of the BSC (Kaplan & Norton, 2000), were unable to represent the complexity of causal linkages, because they cannot be adequately portrayed by a rigid and linear causal logic that does not take into account reinforcing and balancing loops (Brunklaus et al., 2009; Nørreklit, 2000; Rusjan, 2005).

To overcome these limitations, the use of the causal mapping technique was evaluated and tested. Causal maps, when combined with the existing SPMSs of companies, allow for an evaluation of the indicators that are used and can constitute a solid base for the design of new SPMSs for sustainability. In order to illustrate the use and validity of the causal mapping technique, an exemplary case study was analysed, in which the elicitation of causal maps from managerial tacit knowledge allowed the identification of the Company's competitive advantages linked to sustainability. Finally, it allowed for the definition of indicators for the quantification of the outcomes of the Company's investments in sustainability through the subsequent elicitation of a congregate mapping.

When constructing causal maps or, more generally, cognitive maps, most qualitative studies rely on one of the several available methods, but a single qualitative method might not identify all of the organisation's important performance factors and causal relationships. In this study, the results of aggregate and congregate mapping techniques were integrated, and merging these two methodologies resulted in a unique causal map that overcame the limitations of the different methodologies considered.

To create a consistent final map in this study, the data gathered in an aggregate map were organised by the subsequent use of a congregate map. Congregate maps are derived from qualitative system dynamics and allow for a structured, complete representation of all of the patterns that underlie complex processes. However, the accuracy and completeness of the patterns described by congregate maps are highly dependent upon the reliability of the respondents' perceptions. An inaccurate or limited conceptualisation of a phenomenon will result in an inexact map. The literature suggests the superiority of aggregate mapping over congregate mapping in creating a comprehensive portrayal of the participants' perceptions and to elicit their tacit knowledge. For this reason, in the present study, the integration of the two methodologies was tested. To the researcher's knowledge, no previous study has integrated and triangulated these methods as a means of validating the causal modelling of qualitative data.

The study's primary contribution is the development and illustration of an approach for developing performance models by using causal maps in which the elicitation of managerial tacit knowledge allows for the identification of indicators for investments in sustainability, the outcomes of which are difficult to quantify. The study's secondary contribution is the triangulation of multiple qualitative methods to enhance the reliability of causal maps. This approach supports the use of causal mapping to extract managerial and stakeholders' tacit knowledge. Moreover, it illustrates the extensive array of possible competitive advantages and related performance-relevant variables that arise from the causal mapping technique. Finally, it proves the potential for using causal mapping as a comprehensive, articulated basis for developing and improving existing SPMSs.

Empirically, this study relied on a qualitative analysis of a case study tested over a four-year time period in order to provide more robust findings than previous studies. In so doing, the present research contributes to the literature in the areas of sustainability management accounting and control in which the returns on investments in sustainability are evaluated.

Finally, the present work provides a theoretical contribution for the sustainability and IC literature by suggesting a possible theoretical framework that combines the two concepts. In fact, in this study, this was done by expanding the traditional, RBV and the stakeholder theory. More specifically, traditional RBV logic assumes that IC and intangible assets, in general, lead to the more effective use of resources (Orlitzky et al., 2003). This, in turn, has a positive impact on financial results (Hillman & Keim, 2001). Sustainable practices usually are not considered to be mediators in the relationship. The main argument of traditional stakeholder theory is that good management implies positive relationships with key stakeholders, which, in turn, improves financial results (Freeman, 1984; Waddock & Graves, 1997). Organisation-based IC, as well as sustainable practices, traditionally have not been not analysed as mediator factors between sustainability and financial results, but they can be combined through the methodology used in this chapter.

Given this project's focus on a single company in a specific critical industry from a sustainability perspective, there might be limitations in generalising or interpreting the findings. The chapter, however, was aimed at developing analytical, not statistical, generalisations. In fact, the objective of the present research was to develop an effective methodology to derive indicators for the evaluation the financial returns of investments in sustainability rather than to develop a generalizable causal map. However, the method used to generate the causal performance map is generalizable.

The study is based on the assumption that causal maps are distinctive to specific settings. It is possible, however, that the basic elements of causal maps are generalizable across peer organisations or even industries. Future research can be directed towards the verification of this assumption. The outcome of such research has the potential to make a significant contribution to the literature related to the management of sustainability performance.

The study involved a limited number of managers to develop the causal map. Thus, it is possible that the map is not truly representative of the entire company and reflects only the views of the respondents. The model also was developed using qualitative data, so it may be subject to both the interviewees' and the interviewer's biases. The researcher attempted to address these data limitations by integrating two different methodologies to extract the causal model. The findings also were triangulated using archival data from the Company in order to limit inaccuracies in the participants' maps. Future research should be aimed at overcoming these limitations by extending the research to other organisations and by mapping stakeholders' perceptions of sustainability in addition to managers' perceptions. This will improve the quality of the map and its ability to predict future financial performance of the Company.

Finally, future research should focus on proving additional evidence of the effectiveness of causal mapping in the design of SPMSs for sustainability. A longitudinal analysis in different industry settings should be performed, which would require the cyclical creation of causal maps in order to improve the SPMSs of specific organisations operating in different environments and would require top management to assess the financial burdens and potential accuracy of ongoing measurement of the organisations' sustainability competitive advantages. While there are costs associated with the design and implementation of a sustainability performance measurement system based on causal performance mapping, the process, in itself, ensures that the tacit knowledge in managers' and key stakeholders' cognition is converted to explicit organisational knowledge. This process allows for the continuous improvement of organisations' strategies through the identification of specific performance drivers, and it is an important approach that organisations can use to build their internal capabilities.

REFERENCES

Abernethy, M., Horne, M., Lillis, A., Malina, M. A., & Selto, F. H. (2005). A multi-method approach to building causal performance maps from expert knowledge. *Management Accounting Research*, *16*, 135–155.

Andriessen, D. (2004). *Making sense of intellectual capital: Designing a method for the valuation of intangibles*. Boston, MA: Butterworth-Heinemann.

Aragon-Correa, J. A., & Sharma, S. (2003). A contingent resource-based view of proactive corporate environmental strategy. *Academy of Management Review*, *28*(1), 71–88.

Axelrod, R. (1976). *Structure of decision*. Princeton, NJ: University of Princeton Press.

Banker, R. D., Chang, H., & Pizzini, M. (2011). The judgmental effects of strategy maps in balanced scorecards performance evaluations. *International Journal of Accounting Information Systems*, *12*, 259–279.

Barney, J. (1991). Firm resources and sustained competitive advantage. *Journal of Management*, *17*(1), 771–792.

Bartolomeo, M., Bennett, M., Bouma, J., Heydkamp, P., James, P., & Wouters, T. (2000). Environmental management accounting in Europe: Current practice and future potential. *European Accounting*, *1*, 31–52.

Bennett, M., & James, P. (Eds.). (1998). *The green bottom line. environmental accounting for management: Current practice and future trends*. Sheffield: Greenleaf Publishing.

Bougon, M. G. (1992). Congregate cognitive maps: A unified dynamic theory of organization and strategy. *Journal of Management Studies*, *29*(3), 369–389.

Brammer, S., & Millington, A. (2008). Does it pay to be different? An analysis of the relationship between corporate social and financial performance. *Strategic Management Journal, 29*(12), 1325–1343.

Brunklaus, B., Malmqvist, T., & Baumann, H. (2009). Managing stakeholders or the environment? The challenge of relating indicators in practice. *Corporate social responsibility and environmental management, 16*(1), 27–37.

Burritt, R. L., Hahn, T., & Schaltegger, S. (2002). Towards a comprehensive framework for environmental management accounting: Links between business actors and EMA tools. *Australian Accounting Review, 12*(2), 39–50.

Crawford, D., & Scaletta, T. (2005, October). The balanced scorecard and corporate social: Aligning values. *CMA Management, 17*(3), 20–27.

Danish Agency for Trade and Industry (DATI). (2000). *A guideline for intellectual capital statements: A key to knowledge management.* Copenhagen, Danish Agency for trade and Industry.

Danish Ministry of Science, Technology and Innovation (DMSTI). (2002). *Intellectual capital statements – The new guideline.* Copenhagen, Danish Ministry of Science, Technology and Innovation.

Denison, D. R., & Mishra, A. K. (1995). Toward a theory of organizational culture and effectiveness. *Organization Science, 6*(2), 204–223.

Dierickx, I., & Cool, K. (1989). Asset stock accumulation and sustainability of competitive advantage. *Management Science, 35*, 1504–1511.

Eden, C. F. (1988). Cognitive mapping: A review. *European Journal of Operational Research, 36*, 1–13.

Eden, C. F., & Ackerman, F. (1998). *Making strategy: The journey of strategic management.* London: Sage.

Edvinsson, L., & Malone, M. S. (1997). *Intellectual capital: The proven way to establish your company's real value by measuring its hidden brainpower.* London: Judy Piatkus Publishers.

Elkington, J. (1997). *Cannibals with forks.* Oxford: Capstone.

Epstein, M., Kumar, P., & Westbrook, R. (2000). The drivers of customer and corporate profitability: Modeling, measuring, and managing the causal relationships. *Advances in Management Accounting, 9*, 43–72.

Epstein, M. J. (1996). *Measuring corporate environmental performance: best practices for costing and managing an effective environmental strategy.* Chicago, IL: Irwin.

Epstein, M. J., & Wisner, P. S. (2001, Winter). Using a balanced scorecard to implement sustainability. *Environmental Quality Management, 11*(2), 1–10.

Feltham, G. A., & Xie, J. (1994). Performance measure congruity and diversity in multi-task principal-agent relations. *The Accounting Review, 69*, 429–453.

Figge, F., Hahn, T., Schaltegger, S., & Wagner, M. (2002). The sustainability balanced scorecard: Linking sustainability management to business strategy. *Business Strategy and the Environment, 11*(5), 269–284.

Franco-Santos, M., & Bourne, M. (2005). An examination of the literature relating to issues affecting how companies manage through measures. *Production Planning & Control, 16*(2), 114–124.

Freeman, R. E. (1984). *Strategic management: A stakeholder approach.* Boston, MA: Pitman.

Gadenne, D., Lokman, M., Sands, J., Winata, L., & Hooi, G. (2012). The influence of sustainability performance management practices on organisational sustainability performance. *Journal of Accounting & Organizational Change, 8*(2), 210–235.

Gonzáles, J. M. H., Calderón, M. A., & Gonzáles, L. G. (2012). The alignment of managers' mental models with the balanced scorecard strategy map. *Total Quality Management and Business Excellence*, *23*(5/6), 613–628.

Griffin, J. J., & Mahon, J. F. (1997). The corporate social performance and corporate financial performance debate. Twenty-five years of incomparable research. *Business and Society*, *36*(1), 5–31.

Hahn, T., & Figge, F. (2011). Beyond the bounded instrumentality in current corporate sustainability research: Toward an inclusive notion of profitability. *Journal of Business Ethics*, *104*, 325–345.

Hansen, A. (2010). Nonfinancial performance measures, externalities and target setting – A comparative case study of resolutions through planning. *Management Accounting Research*, *21*(1), 17–39.

Hart, S. L. (1995). A natural-resource-based view of the firm. *Academy of Management Review*, *20*(4), 986–1014.

Helfat, C. (1997). Know-how and asset complementarity and dynamic capability accumulation: The case of R&D. *Strategic Management Journal*, *18*(5), 339–360.

Hillman, A. J., & Keim, G. D. (2001). Shareholder value, stakeholder management, and social issues: what's the bottom line? *Strategic Management Journal*, *22*(2), 125–139.

International Federation of Accountants (IFAC). (1998). *The consideration of environmental matters in the audit of financial statements*. International Auditing Practices Committee, IFAC, New York, NY.

Ittner, C., & Larcker, D. (2001). Assessing empirical research in management accounting: A value-based management approach. *Journal of Accounting and Economics*, *32*, 349–410.

Ittner, C., & Larcker, D. (2003). Coming up short on nonfinancial performance measurement. *Harvard Business Review*, *18*(November), 88–95.

Kaplan, R. S., & Norton, D. P. (1996). *The balanced scorecard: Translating strategy into action*. Boston, MA: Harvard Business School Press.

Kaplan, R. S., & Norton, D. P. (2000, September/October). *Having trouble with your strategy? Then map it. Harvard Business Review*, *78*(5), 167–176.

Kaplan, R. S., & Norton, D. P. (2003). *Strategy maps: Converting intangible assets into tangible outcomes*. Boston, MA: Harvard Business School Press.

Kaplan, R. S., & Norton, D. P. (2006). *Alignment: Using the balanced scorecard to create corporate synergies*. Boston, MA: Harvard Business School Press.

Kim, Y., & Statman, M. (2012). Do corporations invest enough in environmental responsibility? *Journal of Business Ethics*, *105*, 115–129.

Korhonen, J. (2003). Should we measure corporate social responsibility. *Corporate Social Responsibility and Environmental Management*, *10*(1), 25–39.

Krosinsky, C., & Robins, N. (2008). *Sustainable investing: The art of long term performance*. London: Earthscan.

Kunc, M. (2008). Using system thinking to enhance strategy maps. *Management Decision*, *46* (5), 761–778.

Langfield-Smith, K. (1992). Exploring the need for a shared cognitive map. *Journal of Management Studies*, *29*(3), 349–368.

Lant, T. K., & Shapira, Z. (2001). *Organization cognition: Computation and interpretation*. Mahwah, NJ: Lawrence Erlbaum Associates.

Laszlo, C., & Zhexembayeva, N. (2011). To the desert and back: A brief history of value. In C. Laszlo & N. Zhexembayeva (Eds.), *Embedded sustainability: The next big competitive advantage* (pp. 30–51). Sheffield UK: Greenleaf Publishing Ltd.

Laukkanen, M. (1994). Comparative cause mapping of organizational cognitions. *Organization Science*, *5*(3), 322–343.

López-Gamero, M. D., Zaragoza-Sáez, P., Claver-Cortés, E., & Molina-Azorín, J. F. (2011). Sustainable development and intangibles: Building sustainable intellectual capital. *Business Strategy and the Environment*, *20*, 18–37.

Lungu, C. I., Caraiani, C., & Dascalu, C. (2012). Intellectual capital research through corporate social responsibility: (Re)Constructing the agenda. *International Journal of Economics and Management Sciences*, *6*, 139–146.

Malina, M. A., & Selto, F. A. (2004). Choice and change of measures in performance measurement models'. *Management Accounting Research*, *15*, 441–60.

Malina, M. A., Norreklit, H., & Selto, F. H. (2007). Relations among measures, result control and performance measurement models. *Contemporary Accounting Research*, *24*, 935–982.

Margolis, J. D., & Walsh, J. P. (2003). Misery loves companies: Rethinking social initiatives by business. *Administrative Science Quarterly*, *48*(2), 268–305.

Marr, B. (2006). *Strategic performance management: Leveraging and measuring your intangible value drivers*. London: Butterworth-Heinemann.

McKernan, J. (1991). *Curriculum action research: A handbook of methods and resources for the reflective practitioner*. London: Kogan Page.

McWilliams, A., & Siegel, D. (2000). Corporate social responsibility and financial performance: Correlation or misspecification? *Strategic Management Journal*, *21*(5), 603–609.

Merchant, K. (1998). *Modern management control systems: Text and cases*. Upper Saddle River, NJ: Prentice Hall.

Morsing, M., & Oswald, D. (2006). Novo Nordisk A/S: Integrating sustainability into business practice. In A. Kakabadse & M. Morsing (Eds.), *Corporate social responsibility: Reconciling aspiration*. New York, NY: Palgrave Macmillan.

Narayanan, V. K., & Armstrong, D. J. (2005). *Causal mapping for research in information technology*. London: Idea Group Publishing.

Neely, A., Adams, C., & Kennerley, M. (2002). *The performance prism: The scorecard for measuring and managing business success*. Upper Saddle River, NJ: Pearson Education.

Nicolini, D. (1999). Comparing methods for mapping organizational cognition. *Organization Studies*, *20*(5), 833–860.

Nisbett, R., & Ross, L. (1980). *Human inference: Strategies and shortcomings of social judgment*. Englewood Cliffs, NJ: Prentice Hall.

Nørreklit, H. (2000). The balance on the balanced scorecard a critical analysis of some of its assumptions. *Management Accounting Research*, *11*, 65–88.

Novo Nordisk. (1997). *Way of management*. Internal documents (Novo Nordisk).

Novo Nordisk. (2003). *Progress and change: Two diabetes scenarios towards 2020*. Internal documents (Novo Nordisk).

Novo Nordisk. (2011). *Annual report 2011*. Retrieved from http://www.novonordisk.com/. Accessed on December 2012.

Orlitzky, M. (2011). Institutional logics in the study of organizations: The social construction of the relationship between corporate social and financial performance. *Business Ethics Quarterly*, *21*(3), 409–444.

Orlitzky, M., Schmidt, F. L., & Rynes, S. L. (2003). 'Corporate social and financial performance': A meta-analisis. *Organisation Studies*, *24*(3), 403–441.

Othman, R. (2006). Balanced scorecard and causal model development: Preliminary findings. *Management Decision*, *44*(5), 690–702.

Otley, D. (1999). Performance management: A framework for management controls systems research. *Management Accounting Research, 10*, 363–382.

Parisi, C. (2010). Using qualitative system dynamics to enhance the performance measurement of sustainability. In P. Taticchi (Ed.), *Business performance measurement and management* (Chapter 8, pp. 115–130). Berlin: Springer.

Parisi, C., & Hockerts, K. N. (2008). Managerial mindsets and performance measurement systems of sustainability related intangibles. *Measuring Business Excellence, 12*(2), 51–67.

Porac, J., Mishina, Y., & Pollock, T. (2002). Entrepreneurial narratives and the dominant logics of high-growth firms. In A. Huff & M. Jenkins (Eds.), *Mapping strategic knowledge* (pp. 112–136). Thousand Oaks, CA: Sage.

Porter, M. E. (2004). Redefining competition in health care. *Harvard Business Review, 82*(6), 5–16.

Porter, M. E., & Kramer, M. R. (2011). 'Creating shared value: Redefining capitalism and the role of the corporation in society'. *Harvard Business Review, 89*(1/2), 62–77.

Reich, R. (2007). *Supercapitalism: The transformation of business, democracy, and everyday life.* New York, NY: Alfred A. Knopf.

Roberts, P. W., & Dowling, G. R. (2002). Corporate reputation and sustained superior financial performance. *Strategic Management Journal, 23*(12), 1077–1093.

Rowley, T., & Berman, S. (2000). A brand new brand of corporate social performance. *Business and Society, 39*(4), 397–418.

Rucci, A., Kirn, S., & Quinn, R. (1998). The employee-customer-profit chain at Sears. *Harvard Buiness Review, 76*, 82–97.

Rusjan, B. (2005). Usefulness of the EFQM excellence model: Theoretical explanation of some conceptual and methodological issues. *Total Quality Management, 16*(3), 363–379.

Russo, M. V., & Fouts, P. A. (1997). A resource-based perspective on corporate environmental performance and profitability. *Academy of Management Journal, 40*(3), 534–559.

Salzmann, O., Ionescu-Somers, A., & Steger, U. (2005). The business case for corporate sustainability: Literature review and research options. *European Management Journal, 23*(1), 27–36.

Schaltegger, S., Burritt, R., & Petersen, H. (2003). *An introduction to corporate environmental management*. Sheffield: Greenleaf Publishing.

Schneider, S., & Anglemar, R. (1993). Cognition in organizational analysis: Who's minding the store? *Organization Studies, 14*, 347–374.

Schoeneborn, F. (2003). Linking balanced scorecard to system dynamics. *Proceedings of 2003 International System Dynamics Conference*, New York, NY.

Searcy, C. (2012). Corporate sustainability performance measurement systems: A review and research agenda. *Journal of Business Ethics, 107*, 239–253.

Sharma, S., & Vredenburg, H. (1998). Proactive corporate environmental strategy and the development of competitively valuable organizational capabilities. *Strategic Management Journal, 19*(8), 729–753.

Simons, R. (2000). *Performance measurement and control systems for implementing strategy*. Upper Saddle River, NJ: Prentice Hall.

Simpson, W. G., & Kohers, T. (2002). The link between corporate social and financial performance: evidence from the banking industry. *Journal of Business Ethics, 35*(2), 97–109.

Surroca, J., Tribó, J. A., & Waddock, S. (2010). Corporate responsibility and financial performance: the role of intangible resources. *Strategic Management Journal, 31*, 463–490.

Suwignjo, P., Bititci, U. S., & Carrie, A. S. (2000). Quantitative models for performance measurement system. *International Journal of Production Economics*, *64*, 231–241.

Tapinos, E., & Dyson, R. (2007). Performance measurement. In F. O'Brien & R. Dyson (Eds.), *Supporting strategy: Frameworks, methods and models*. Chichester, UK: Wiley.

Tegarden, D. P., Tegarden, L. F., & Sheetz, S. D. (2005). Using causal mapping to uncover cognitive diversity within a top management team. In V. K. Narayanan & D. J. Armstrong (Eds.), *Causal mapping for research in information technology*. London: Idea Group Publishing.

Vaivio, J. (2005). Mobilizing knowledge with 'provocative' non-financial measures of performance. *European Accounting Review*, *13*(1), 39–71.

Vo, H. V., Poole, M. S., & Courtney, J. F. (2005). An empirical comparison of collective causal mapping approaches. In V. K. Narayanan & D. J. Armstrong (Eds.), *Causal mapping for research in information technology*. London: Idea Group Publishing.

Waddock, S. A., & Graves, S. B. (1997). The corporate social performance-financial performance link. *Strategic Management Journal*, *18*(4), 303–319.

Waddock, S. A., Bodwell, C., & Graves, S. B. (2002). Responsibility: The new business imperative. *Academy of Management Executive*, *16*, 132–147.

Wagner, M., Schaltegger, S., & Wehrmeyer, W. (2002). The relation between the environmental and economic performance of firms: What does theory propose and what does empirical evidence tell us? *Greener Management Internaltional*, *34*(Summer), 95–108.

Weaver, G. R., Treviño, L. K., & Cochran, P. L. (1999). Integrated and decupled corporate social performance: Management commitments, external pressures, and corporate ethics practices. *Academy of Management Journal*, *42*, 539–552.

Weick, K. E., & Bougon, M. G. (1986). Organizations as cognitive maps: Charting ways to success and failure. In H. Sims Jr., & D. Gioia (Eds.), *The thinking organization*. San Francisco, CA: Jossey-Bass.

Wernerfelt, B. (1984). A resource-based view of the firm. *Strategic Management Journal*, *5*(2), 171–180.

Wood, D. J., & Jones, R. E. (1995). Stakeholder mismatching: a theoretical problem in empirical research on corporate social performance. *International Journal of Organizational Analysis*, *3*(3), 229–267.

World Commission on Economic Development (WCED). (1987). *Our common future*. Oxford: Oxford University Press.

Wright, P. M., Gardner, T. M., Moynihan, L. M., & Allen, M. R. (2005). The relationship between HR practices and firm performance: examining the causal order. *Personnel Psychology*, *58*(2), 409–446.

Yin, R. K. (2003). *Case study research* (3rd ed.). Thousand Oaks, CA: Sage.

IN CONTROL OF SUSTAINABILITY INFORMATION: UNTANGLING THE ROLE OF ACCOUNTANTS

Stefan Schaltegger and Dimitar Zvezdov

ABSTRACT

Purpose – *Accountants' involvement in environmental and sustainability management has merely been investigated to date. With the continuous take-up of sustainability issues by companies and with the growing experience companies gain in dealing with this topic, this chapter raises the question whether accountants are involved in a way different than previously reported and if yes, what their role is in social accounting practice.*

Methodology – *Based on 58 interviews with corporate practitioners, this chapter firstly explores the roles involved in the social accounting practice in companies which are considered to be leading in sustainability reporting in the United Kingdom and Germany. Secondly, the role of professional accountants is analysed from a power theory perspective.*

Findings – *The main findings suggest that professional accountants are partially involved in social accounting practice but mainly exert a gate-keeping role between sustainability managers and higher management.*

Accounting and Control for Sustainability
Studies in Managerial and Financial Accounting, Volume 26, 265–296

ISSN: 1479-3512/doi:10.1108/S1479-3512(2013)0000026008

Practical implications – *Investigating the observed behaviour empirically can help improve social accounting. Should it turn out that the accountants have no other option but to act like gatekeepers, accounting education will play a major role in overcoming this deficiency in the pursuit of improved sustainability knowledge and performance. If, on the other hand, it is the defensive stance of accounting professionals and the fear of losing power in corporate structures which motivates them to act as gatekeepers, mechanisms to motivate them to cooperate should be researched.*

Value of chapter – *The chapter empirically investigates and discusses the accountant's contribution to sustainability information management. This can help overcome organisational challenges impeding companies to successfully implement sustainability measures.*

Keywords: Social accounting; role of accountants; environmental accounting; sustainability reporting

INTRODUCTION

For the last two decades social accounting and reporting and related management accounting and control approaches have been developed to create transparency in the unsustainability of corporate impacts (e.g. Ball, Owen, & Gray, 2000; Gray, Owen, & Adams, 1996) and to provide decision support for managing sustainability challenges (e.g. Henry & Journeault, 2010). Whereas the understanding of what social accounting encompasses differs (e.g. Parker, 2011) and its contribution in practice of tackling sustainability challenges is disputed (e.g. Medley, 1997; Bebbington & Gray, 2001), most of the extant literature agrees that accountants need to be involved in environmental and sustainability management (e.g. Carter, Burritt, & Pisaniello, 2011; Davey & Coombes, 1996; Evans, Burritt, & Guthrie, 2011; Gray, Bebbington, & Walters, 1993; Mathews, 1997).

From a practical viewpoint, the involvement of the accountant cannot be neglected. Managers are increasingly challenged to make decisions that are influenced by social and environmental aspects of business. Informed decisions depend on the timely preparation and interpretation of information – expertise that belongs to the domain of the accounting profession (CIMA, 1981). Hence, accountants' role in sustainability accounting may be a significant one.

The role and involvement of accountants in conventional accounting have been well researched for several decades (e.g. Byrne & Pierce, 2007).

Much less research examines the role of accountants in social accounting and reporting. The few publications in the area reveal that accountants are not sufficiently, if at all, involved in managing environmental and sustainability information (e.g. Benston, 1982; Carter et al., 2011; Davey & Coombes, 1996; Gray, Bebbington, & Walters, 1993; Mathews, 1997; Schreuder & Ramanathan, 1984; Wilmshurst & Frost, 2001).

However, similarly to the changing role of accounting professionals in general (Burns & Baldvinsdottir, 2007; Caglio, 2003) a change in the role of management accountants in sustainability information management can be anticipated. On the one hand, the growing importance of sustainability aspects of business (Salzmann, Ionescu-Somers, & Steger, 2005) requires collecting managing and reporting sustainability-related information. Reasons for producing such information include regulation compliance, market demand and media attention. On the other hand, new accounting tools and approaches have recently emerged (e.g. Weygandt, Kimmel, & Kieso, 2009). The combination of the former and the latter suggests that the accountant's role in social and environmental accounting needs to be explored.

By highlighting the capabilities of accountants and the potential benefits of their involvement as well as the drawbacks and problems associated with the identified ignorance, extant literature has called for more involvement of accountants in social accounting (e.g. Evans et al., 2011). Although interest in the topic has been regained (e.g. Evans et al., 2011) empirical research on what role accountants actually play in corporate social accounting practice is missing.

For the last decades social accounting research has dealt with a broad range of issues such as transparency (e.g. Ball et al., 2000; Gray et al., 1996), accountability (e.g. Burritt, 2012; Gray et al., 1996), stakeholder engagement (e.g. Bebbington, Brown, Frame, & Thomson, 2007; Gray, Bebbington, & Collison, 2006), the role of accounting for organisational change (e.g. Burritt, 2004; Larrinaga-González, Carrasco-Fenech, Caro-González, Correa-Ruíz, & Páez-Sandubete, 2001), the development of accounting and management control methods (e.g. Henry & Journeault, 2010) and the increasing number of companies dealing with sustainability reporting (e.g. Bebbington, Larrinaga, & Moneva, 2008; Milne, Tregidga, & Walton, 2009).

With the increasing number of academic, professional and practitioner-oriented literature on social accounting and reporting (e.g. Owen, 2008; Parker, 2005; Schaltegger, Gibassier, & Zvezdov, 2013) and the continuous take-up of sustainability issues by companies, it can be expected that many organisations have gained more experience in dealing with sustainability accounting (e.g. Bennett, Schaltegger, & Zvezdov, 2013). Given these developments since the early empirical publications on the role of accountants in social accounting, this chapter raises the question whether accountants have now (finally) started to get more involved than previously reported and if yes, what their role is in social accounting.

This chapter explores the involvement of accounting professionals in corporate social accounting practice and distinguishes three kinds of engagement – adaptive, constructive and defensive involvement – depending on the observed pattern of activities and the potential rationale behind these observations. The analysis is based on 58 interviews with employees who are specifically managing social and environmental information in companies with good sustainability reputation in the United Kingdom and Germany. The analysis draws on the literature of power in organisations (e.g. Mintzberg, 1983; Pfeffer, 1993, 2010) and the classification of promoter roles for innovations in organisations (e.g. Chakrabarti, 1974; Hauschildt & Schewe, 2000; Hauschildt & Kirchmann, 2001; Hauschildt, 2003; Fichter, 2009; Witte, 1977) and is used to develop an analytical framework for exploring the roles of accountants in social accounting practice.

Researching the accountants' involvement may help to understand drivers and barriers of engagement and contribute to improving social accounting and its application in corporate practice. Depending on the kind of current involvement of accountants and the reasons that lead to it, conclusions may be drawn for accounting education or the communication to motivate accountants to get more involved.

The chapter is structured as follows: The second section draws on the extant literature and highlights the demand for investigating the role of accountants in environmental and sustainability management. The third section gives an overview of the empirical research approach. The results are presented and discussed in the fourth section. The concluding section outlines the importance of the findings and delivers recommendations for practice and further research.

HOW THE ACCOUNTANT CAN CONTRIBUTE TO SUSTAINABILITY MANAGEMENT

Social and Environmental Accounting Literature

An ignorant approach to sustainability has inflicted serious financial damage upon numerous companies globally, including large ones. Sustainability issues have sometimes even threatened the existence of companies as, for example, illustrated for in the well-documented case of BP and its oil platform accident in the Gulf of Mexico (e.g. Hoffman & Jennings, 2011; Hopkins, 2011; Lustgarten, 2012; Lee & Garza-Gomez, 2012; Lüdeke-Freund & Zvezdov, 2013; Moerschbaecher & Day, 2011). The relevance of social and environmental performance for business cannot be denied any longer. Whilst managers are aware of the importance of informed decision making, accounting as a central information system of the company is recognised as an approach for tackling sustainability challenges (e.g. Burritt & Schaltegger, 2010; Bebbington & Gray, 2001). The generation of information provides a means by which organisations try to reduce uncertainty about their environment (e.g. Daft & Lengel, 1986). The accountants, being the professionals dealing with corporate accounting, are thus expected to potentially play an important role, firstly, in improving the information stakeholders receive about the social and environmental impacts of a company and, secondly, in improving how well managers are informed about sustainability issues (Schaltegger & Burritt, 2000; Zvezdov, Schaltegger, & Bennett, 2010).

Social and environmental accounting has enjoyed a growing popularity since the beginning of the 1990s (e.g. Parker, 2011) and the potential contribution of accountants in improving information management practices for sustainability management has been a research subject for well over a decade. The contributions range from what needs to be and what can be measured (Gray et al., 1996), to identifying what areas of business need to be revised (Burritt, 2004; Scavone, 2006) and to establishing corporate-wide social accounting systems. The case for engaging accounting professionals in environmental and sustainability management has been made by a number of authors (e.g. Benston, 1982; Carter et al., 2011; Davey & Coombes, 1996; Gray et al., 1993; Mathews, 1997; Medley, 1997; Schreuder & Ramanathan, 1984; Zvezdov et al., 2010) There are also a few exceptions of authors expressing a less enthusiastic view about accountants' involvement in social accounting practice (O'Dwyer, 2001; O'Dwyer & Owen, 2007). The understanding of what comprises social accounting and what the role of accountant could or should be, has however varied, as have the interpretations of potential benefits to organisations and society (Burritt & Schaltegger, 2010; Gray et al., 1996).

Also the relevance of social and environmental accounting for company's internal decision making has been addressed in literature. An improved information basis to make more sustainable decisions, the recognition of important business aspects, higher efficiency and lower costs of production and a potential legitimacy gain are some of the most commonly cited benefits (e.g. Bennett & James, 2000; Burritt, Hahn, & Schaltegger, 2002; Bennett, Schaltegger, & Zvezdov, 2011; Milne, 1996; Schaltegger & Burritt, 2010). Consequently, various social accounting tools and methods have been developed and adaptations of conventional accounting tools to fit the needs of sustainability managers have been made (e.g. Burritt et al., 2002; Finnveden & Moberg, 2005). From such a decision-oriented perspective, the role of accountants is to design social management accounting systems, collect sustainability information and inform management to make more sustainable decisions.

In summary, prior social accounting research provides societal as well as business reasons to involve accountants in social accounting. Whether for external (accountability and transparency) reasons or for internal (decision making and performance management) reasons, accountants are called for involvement in collecting social and environmental information.

Earlier empirical research observed a discrepancy between the professionals engaged in environmental and sustainability management and those dealing with accounting; and it concluded that accountants are not or merely involved in dealing with sustainability (e.g. Bebbington, Gray, Thomson, & Walters, 1994; Gray et al., 1993; Mathews, 1997). Newer empirical research on the involvement and role(s) of accountants in social accounting is however missing. In spite of recognising the potential benefits of adopting and applying social accounting, the role of accountants in today's corporate practice remains empirically under-researched.

To create a better understanding of potential roles of accounts in social accounting, the conventional accounting literature on the accountants' roles is reviewed.

The 'Conventional' Accounting Literature

For conventional accounting, Byrne and Pierce (2007, p. 471) identify that research on the 'roles of accountants and management accounting is fragmented in nature.' In spite of this fragmentation, quite a substantive number of publications can be found on the role of accountants in conventional accounting. The reasons developed in the literature for the engagement of accountants in a company are manifold and can be summarised in three major streams of research: accountants as knowledge experts, as methodological experts and as authorities.

Numerous authors found evidence that accountants have *knowledge on what kind of information is relevant* for managing a company successfully

(Davey & Coombes, 1996; Scapens, Jazayeri, & Scapens, 1998; Jack & Kholeif, 2008; Granlund & Malmi, 2002; Scapens and Jazayeri, 2003). Accountants can provide essential support on what information should be created to support management in decision making. They play an important role in deciding what kind of key performance indicators are helpful (e.g. Nanni, Dixon, & Vollman, 1992), thus giving guidance on achieving the goals of the company. Management accounts can help to develop performance measures and to create the needed information (Back-Hock, 1992; Nanni et al., 1992; Shank, 1989; Shields & Young, 1992). Accounting professionals also possess knowledge of which information can be handled by managers and is useful for their decision making and performance management control. Particularly their function as providers of cost information and scorekeepers has been acknowledged (Burns & Vaivio, 2001). Accountants provide future- and profit-orientated information to managers (Markus, 1983).

Accounting as a function is, however, not restricted to professional accountants. The decentralisation of accounting knowledge has resulted in a decreasing relevance of reports with 'historical information' provided by accountants (Scapens & Jazayeri, 2003). With non-accountants knowing their own spend, knowing their own budgets, controlling their own budgets far more than they ever did in the past, several jobs which were traditionally been assigned to professional accountants have become redundant. Related to the observed decrease of the information and knowledge creating role of accountants, Scapens and Jazayeri (2003) identify a need for more forward-looking information provided by accountants.

A second stream of research has looked into the accountants' *organisational and methodological expertise* (e.g. Byrne & Pierce, 2007, p. 492f.). Designing information management, organising data and information flows, processing large information quantities, reducing large data quantities to a reasonable set of indicators, securing good data quality, knowing about adequate methods of collection, etc. have been acknowledged as a particularly valuable expertise of accountants (e.g. Pierce & O'Dea, 2003; Yazdifar & Tsamenyi, 2005).

The third field of research has addressed the accountants' *authority within the organisation* (Markus & Pfeffer, 1983; Mintzberg, 1983). The established formal access to decision makers has enabled accountants to act as information providers for decision makers, including top management (Dezaley & Sugarman, 1995; Markus, 1983). Particularly the power of information has been a recognised topic in earlier (Bariff & Galbraith, 1978; Introna, 1997; Galbraith, 1974; Zand, 1981) as well as in more recent publications (e.g. Abernethy & Vagnoni, 2004; Braman, 2006). The power of the accountant's role has also led to the observation that accountants are increasingly becoming internal business consultants (Burns & Vaivio, 2001) and business advisors (Francis & Minchington, 1999). Collier (1984, p. 9) argues already in 1984 that 'the classical functions of accumulation, analysis and interpretation are shifting towards interpretation, evaluation, control and involvement in decision making.' Accountants have motivated employees to work for the goals of the firm (Benston, 1963) and to maintain 'a coexistence between the ideology of public service and the logic of profit' (Dezaley, 1995, p. 341). These capabilities partly arise from the fact that management accountants add a different viewpoint to other management or staff functions. Being often seen as external to daily business processes, accountants have been considered unaware of the details in operational processes (e.g. Byrne & Pierce, 2007; Johnson, 2002). Whereas this can be seen as a conflict, it also provides accountants with a fresh viewpoint and can be advantageous, for example, in identifying weakness and improvement potentials of projects, etc. Having various departments involved in a project may result in behaviour that seeks to maximise the available resources to the department while minimising the expected time and effort that need to be invested (Porter, 1985; Tjosvold, 1988). Accountants as actors who are not a party in the project or process are likely to support the adherence to a formally defined organisational rationality. Having an actor without specific interests other than those of the company itself can serve to maximise the rationality of operational business activities (Montagna, 1986).

The above streams of research are summarised in Table 1 which distinguishes three roles of accountants, that is, knowledge and information management expert, expert of organisation and methods and power promoter.

Further documented abilities of accountants include the development of new areas of advice and mediation from a traditional base in auditing, tax and insolvency (Power, 1997) and the support of managing 'shifting processes of commercialisation' (Radcliffe et al., 1994, p. 602). Accountants have thus become powerful social actors who, far from performing merely calculative and verificatory services, increasingly shape 'the whole apparatus of intervention' (Dezaley, 1995, p. 338) across a wide range of activities and organisations.

Table 1. Overview of the Literature on the Three Roles of Accountants.

Role	Stream of Research	Related Publications
Knowledge and information expert	Knowledge about what information matters; expertise in information properties	Back-Hock, 1992; Davey & Coombes, 1996; Jack & Kholeif, 2008; Granlund & Malmi, 2002; Nanni et al., 1992; Scapens & Jazayeri, 2003; Scapens et al., 1998; Shank, 1989; Shields & Young, 1992
Methodological expert	Organisational and methodological expertise and capabilities	Bennett et al., 2013; Burritt et al., 2002; Burritt, Schaltegger, Kokubu & Wagner, 2003; Byrne & Pierce, 2007; Caglio, 2003; Drury, 1985; Finnveden & Moberg, 2005; Francis & Minchington, 1999; Gray et al., 1996; Pierce & O'Dea, 2003; Scavone, 2006; Williams, Wilmshurst & Clift, 2010; Yazdifar & Tsamenyi, 2005
Authority and gatekeeper	Authority and power of linking information providers with decision makers	Benston, 1963; Braman, 2006; Byrne & Pierce, 2007; Collier, 1984; Dezaley, 1995; Dezaley & Sugarman, 1995; Francis & Minchington, 1999; Galbraith, 1974; Introna 1997; Johnson, 2002; Markus, 1983; Markus & Pfeffer, 1983; Mintzberg, 1983; Power, 1997; Radcliffe, Cooper, & Robson, 1994; Zand, 1981

Innovation Literature

Innovation literature has a long tradition of explaining organisational behaviour (e.g. Burns & Stalker, 1961) and has long recognised the role (as opposed to a formal responsibility) of individuals in the success or failure of corporate activities (e.g. Lindsay, Chadee, Mattsson, Johnston, & Millett, 2003; Tushman & Scanlan, 1981). The importance of the involvement of certain roles can be exemplified by top management, whose main role is often signalling commitment (Rodgers, Hunter, & Rogers, 1993).

Given the novel nature of social and environmental accounting (Schaltegger & Burritt, 2010) and its relative recent emergence in practice (Bennett et al., 2013), researching the role of the individuals involved in it may reveal important information about design and implementation issues of sustainability accounting.

The three different types of roles of accountants distinguished above resonate with the innovation management literature which addresses actors as innovation 'champions' or 'promotors' (the original Greek notion 'promotor' is used in this literature instead of 'promoter' to emphasise the supporting aspect of these actors rather than an advertising activity; see e.g. Allen, 1970; Coffee, 2006; Cox, 2006; Hauschildt & Schewe, 2000; Hauschildt & Kirchmann, 2001; Tushman & Katz, 1980; for strategic management see also Kraakman, 1986).

The promotor perspective distinguishes technological, process and power promotors or gatekeepers. The first group, the technological promotors, are actors serving the company as knowledge experts and inventors introducing new aspects into the organisation whereas the process promotors are project champions who apply organisational knowhow using existing procedures or introducing new methods to establish an innovation (Hauschildt & Schewe, 2000). Power promotors or gatekeepers, in turn, are 'sponsors' supporting or preventing an organisational innovation through hierarchical and network relationship power (Coffee, 2006). The power of a gatekeeper is largely based on selecting what information is used by decision makers on higher hierarchy levels of the organisation (Tushman & Scanlan, 1981).

In this chapter the introduction and implementation of sustainability accounting processes and methods is treated as an innovation. Whereas the promotor theory is concerned with various actors promoting or impeding innovations, this chapter focuses on the roles of accountants in corporate sustainability accounting practice as a sustainability management innovation.

DEVELOPING AN EXPLORATORY RESEARCH FRAMEWORK

By combining a technical view (Section 'Steps of the Management Accounting Process') with a power theory informed perspective of information management (Section 'Accounting Roles from a Promoter Perspective') this section develops a framework (Section 'Research Framework') to structure the following empirical analysis of the role of accountants in the management and the use of sustainability information in corporate practice.

Steps of the Management Accounting Process

No matter whether social accounting is applied for transparency and accountability purposes relating to the reporting and communication to external stakeholders or whether it is adopted for purposes of internal management decision support, some basic technical steps of information management are needed. In terms of the information management process, CIMA (1981) defines management accounting as the identification, measurement, accumulation, analysis, preparation, interpretation and communication of (financial) information used by management for planning, evaluation and control within an organisation. As some of these steps may be conducted almost inseparably in corporate practice, they can be merged into four categories of deciding what information should be collected, defining the information properties, collecting the data and providing the information to decision makers (Table 2).

The conventional information management view of accounting thus highlights the role of accountants in supporting these information management steps.

Different from the technical view of creating sustainability information, the involvement of accountants and their role can also be analysed from a power perspective.

Accounting Roles from a Promoter Perspective

The power and expertise functions identified with regard to the adoption and implementation of sustainability accounting as shown in Table 1 have not been subject to an extensive discussion so far. Jones (1992) observed that practitioners do not see accounting as a purely technical activity which is objective, factual and neutral. Instead, they see it as a social activity and draw on the differentiation of objective, subjective, inter-subjective and positional meanings in explaining how accountants construct practice within specific social contexts. 'It is this which constitutes management accounting rationality in practice,' claims Jones (1992, p. 225). By interpreting sustainability information into a language understood by senior management (e.g. Dierkes & Preston, 1977), the uptake of sustainability issues and the importance of sustainability performance are brought to the immediate attention of senior management, whose commitment is essential for the success of activities.

The following analysis of the accountants' roles in social accounting is informed by the literature on power in management (e.g. Mintzberg, 1983;

Table 2. Four Groups of Information Management Steps (Adapted from Bhimani et al., 2011; CIMA, 1981).

Step	Description
Deciding what information is collected	In this role accountants decide what sustainability aspects (e.g. carbon dioxide emissions and carbon performance of products) are considered and measured.
Defining the information properties	After the decision has been made about what aspects are to be considered, this role is about deciding what measures and metrics are used to tangibly depict that aspect. For example, carbon impacts and performance can be measured based on per employee emissions, per employee reductions, operation or cost centre emissions/reductions, etc. Also the method of data collection needs to be defined: is information collected regularly in a system or upon request, what is the basis for the calculations, etc.
Collecting the data	This role focuses on the actual collection of the data (e.g. CO_2 emissions). It may include the use of measurement techniques and the frequency, time and place of measurement as well as managing data quality, for example, by cross-checking plausibility, etc.
Providing the information (information selection)	Once the data has been collected the key performance figures are calculated and the information is prepared for presentation and reporting to decision makers. This role includes setting priorities of what is presented and what is omitted, the choice of format (e.g. time frame, denominator, absolute or relative figures) in which the information is shown and the interpretation (e.g. the qualitative comments accompanying the information).

Pfeffer, 1993, 2010) and research on the role of champions (e.g. Jervis, 1975; Howell & Higgins, 1990; Markham, Green, & Basu, 1991; Kimberly & Evanisko, 1981; Taylor, 1975) and promotors (e.g. Fichter, 2009; Hauschildt & Kirchmann, 2001; Witte, 1977) for organisational and innovation development in organisations.

As discussed above, in their supportive function, accountants can be seen as experts and methodological promoters who create awareness in an organisation that sustainability information should and can be collected. Champions of organisational innovations unveil problems in the organisation. An example of such organisational problems in the case of social accounting is the lack of sustainability information. Champions also support the introduction of innovations (e.g. Fichter, 2009; Hauschildt & Kirchmann, 2001), such as social accounting processes and methods. As juxtaposition to these promotion roles, accountants can also act as gatekeepers.

> It is my thesis that problems of implementation are, in many instances, problems in developing political will and expertise – the desire to accomplish something, even against opposition, and the knowledge and skills that make it possible to do so. (Pfeffer, 1992, pp. 7–8)

Particularly Jeffrey Pfeffer's notable research on power in organisations has been a source of motivation for extended research in the field. His work summarises various organisational phenomena related to power. Against this background, accounting departments have been identified as loci of enhanced control and power because of the potential 'uncertainty-reducing' information which they are able to define, possess, or generate (Bloomfield & Coombs, 1992). The establishment of information management systems in other departments such as marketing or production could therefore be read as an instance of decentralisation and a shift in relative power away from accounting as a centre of organisational power. Accountants, being a part of what Abbott (1988) describes as 'the system of professions', have strived to defend and expand their area of jurisdiction and power in competition with rival professions.

Challenges to the accountancy profession do not, however, come only from those who seek to occupy its territory. Challenges also come from journalists, academics, politicians and others who have no desire to occupy the territory of accountants but can nevertheless advance some competing discourses that may disrupt and weaken the profession's capacity to secure and expand its domain (Sikka & Willmott, 1995). In the process of defining, defending and extending its jurisdiction, the accountancy profession attaches considerable importance to its image of 'independence'. Thus accountants need to develop mechanisms to retain their power in organisations. One such possibility is by acting as gatekeepers.

Perceived as a small group of organisational actors whose structural position suggests that they share an interest in coordination and community organisation (Galaskiewicz & Krohn, 1984), gatekeepers and the phenomenon of *gatekeeping* have been subject to extensive research in both managerial and social science (e.g. Cranefield & Yoong, 2007; Klobas & McGill, 1995; Tushman & Katz, 1980). In both cases, gatekeeping is considered a form of brokerage, that is, a process 'by which intermediary actors facilitate transactions between other actors lacking access to or trust in one another' (Marsden, 1982, p. 202).

Any brokered exchange can thereby be thought of as a relation involving three actors, two who are the actual parties of the transaction and one who is the intermediary or broker. Brokerage as the act of facilitating exchange is usually rewarded with a 'commission' but can also be used to obtain or exert power. There are numerous examples of intermediaries whose reward for brokerage services is diffuse or even non-existent (see e.g. Blok, 1974; Boissevain, 1974). Since accountants clearly facilitate transactions or information and resource flows, they can be viewed as brokers regardless of whether or not they attempt to extract a commission as direct reward. Furthermore, the existence of empirical evidence that brokerage potential is actually an accurate predictor of influence, and thus power (Gould, 1989), makes the investigation of the accountant's role in the context of sustainability accounting even more relevant.

With very few exceptions (e.g. Coffee, 2006) the gatekeeping function of the accountant has hardly been subject to research. On the contrary, a few studies implicitly identify the necessity to involve management accountants in various emerging areas (such as sustainability management and accounting) precisely for their potential as gatekeepers (Davey & Coombes, 1996; Flesher & Zanzig, 2000; Wilmshurst & Frost, 2001). Thus, in analysing the accountants' roles in social accounting, it seems necessary to also consider the role of being a gatekeeper of sustainability information in the organisation.

This raises the essential question whether the accountants' involvement in sustainability accounting may constitute more of a gatekeeping power role than a promotion role as often emphasised with regard to their technical abilities, acquired during studies, training, etc.

Research Framework

The steps of information management as defined by CIMA (1981; see also Bhimani, Horngren, & Datar, 2011) can be related to the three main conventional roles of accountants as described as discussed in Section 'Steps of the Management Accounting Process', including the promoter and gatekeeping roles. The rows in Table 3 represent the information management steps and the columns the three roles of accountants as identified in the second section. As the activities of accountants can be explored through interviews and observations with regard to their involvement in the steps in the accounting process, Table 3 provides an analytical framework for the empirical identification of the actual roles of accountants in corporate social accounting practice.

Table 3. Expertise in and Power Through Managing Sustainability Information.

Steps of the Accounting Process	Accounting Roles		
	Knowledge and information expert	Expert of organisation and methods	Authoritative power promoter/gatekeeper
Deciding what information is to be collected	✓		
Defining information properties, KPIs and methods applied		✓	
Collecting data		✓	
Providing information to others			✓

The *decision of what information* should be created to capture the relevant sustainability issues mostly relates to the accountant's role as a *knowledge and information management expert.* Apart from sustainability expertise, knowledge is required regarding what data and information reflect this knowledge and may be of management relevance (Pierce & O'Dea, 2003). In the next step decisions are needed to define the *kind of (key performance) indicators* which may be useful for managers to support their decision making processes and to choose the accounting methods to collect the needed data (Davey & Coombes, 1996). In their role as *organisational and methodological experts*, professional accountants define key performance and other indicators, how the information shall be measured and its format, and they handle the collection of data and its transformation to management relevant information. This role is concerned with the *creation of information* which is of particular importance in areas such as sustainability where little practice, standardisation and experience may exist (e.g. Rao & Perry, 2003). People exercising this role will typically need expertise about sustainability topics as well as data availability and management relevance.

The *information provision to decision makers,* however, serving as a link between information creators and information seekers, is characterised by *information selection* (Collier, 1984). In this role as information providers accountants serve to link information creators with information users. Once the data has been collected for the chosen topics, the key performance figures are calculated and the information is prepared for presentation and reporting to decision makers. Information selection includes setting priorities of what is presented and what is omitted (Bhimani et al., 2011; Collier, 1984), the choice of format (e.g. time frame, denominator, absolute or relative figures) in which the information is shown and the interpretation of quantitative figures (e.g. the qualitative comments accompanying the information). Selecting and providing information to decision makers can be characterised as a *gatekeeping role*, thus exercising power in information management (Coffee, 2006).

Using this framework we identify the roles of accountants in a company's social accounting practice on the basis of their actual sustainability information management activities (Table 3):

- *Accountants using their technical expertise of defining what information* shall be collected and in producing information in accordance with established accounting principles can be considered to practice the *role of knowledge and information experts*. The knowledge and information expert role is based on the application of technical expertise. Such an involvement of accountants serves to improve data and information quality and decision usefulness.
- Accountants who *engage in defining indicators, designing methods, and collecting* sustainability information are seen to take a *methodological expert role* of promoting and supporting social accounting in the organisation. The knowledge of accounting methods and techniques in collecting, preparing, analysing and interpreting information is seen as a technical expertise, since it is largely subject to formal accounting training and education.
- *Providing information to decision makers,* particularly top management, and thus linking information creation with information use can be seen as a *power role of gatekeeping*. This role includes the choice of key and accompanying information properties such as what information is communicated with what indicators and how it is presented. The presentation includes choices like time period, denominators, graphical presentation, qualitative interpretation, etc.

All roles, as all human activities, can of course be interpreted from a power perspective. For example, the knowledge and information expert role can be seen as a combination of applying technical expertise and exerting power, since accountants exert power through their choice of what information shall be collected, provided or retained; thus enabling or preventing decision makers from using it. A similar argumentation is also possible for the definition of indicators, the design of methods and the collection of data. Acknowledging that different shades of intentions and perspectives are possible, it nevertheless seems appropriate to assume that providing information to decision makers has a much stronger power aspect involved whereas developing expertise on sustainability information, indicators and social accounting methods are less attractive and directly useful for gatekeeping purposes but more strongly related to knowledge and methodological expertise.

RESEARCH APPROACH AND DATA

Data Collection and Analysis

To explore the corporate practice of social accounting, a research project was set up and conducted between 2009 and 2010, whereby 58 respondents in 16 British and German-based companies were interviewed in person. The interviews had an average duration of 90 minutes and were guided by a structured interview agenda. Two researchers were present during each interview. Some of the interviewees had more than one role. In several companies, some roles were occupied by more than one person. Overall 103 management roles in 16 companies were observed. Data on the roles and the related activities of each interviewee were collected by asking the interviewees what their role was. To achieve data triangulation, the other interviewees were asked to describe the role of their colleagues. Last but not least, internal as well as publicly available information was considered.

One of the objectives of the research was to explore the role of accountants in corporate social accounting in companies leading in the area of sustainability reporting. Hence, an accounting professional was interviewed in each company. The focus is on companies with acknowledged sustainability reports which received awards, were ranked well in sustainability rankings, as this is where such involvement in social accounting could be expected.

Motivated by the sporadic research in the field, we opted for an exploratory research design (Stebbins, 2001), looking at social accounting practice without former development of hypotheses. Thus, the focus was on identifying aspects that had been neglected to this moment. For example, the type of information, the methods of data collection and preparation and the involved actors were the topics that were raised during the interviews. The analysis of the roles of the accountants in social accounting was deducted from the type of activities and the function which the accountants described in the interviews.

The data was collected in semi-structured interviews. Initial interviews were held in each company with the sustainability manager, whereby subsequent interviewees were identified. These were providers or users of sustainability information. By following the flow of sustainability information from users to providers, key actors in the social accounting practice were identified and interviewed. For the purpose of data triangulation, corporate data (where available) and publicly available information such as reports were used. Furthermore data was triangulated by using the interviewee's own perception of their role, the other interviewee's perception of this person's role, and factual information such as internal documents showing responsibility and external reports.

To identify the roles of the accountants in social accounting practice we applied the framework shown in Table 3 and analysed the interview data with regard to the activities which the corporate practitioners reported and the steps of social accounting.

The Role of the Accountant in Sustainability Information Management and Use

To be able to identify the involvement of accountants, we first looked at what people and professions are involved in social accounting practice. This included a large number of employees, who were subsequently grouped into four categories: accountants, people with accounting function, sustainability managers, and general managers (Table 4).

Involvement of accountants has been defined and measured based on tangible proxies such as the number of accountants involved in environmental projects (Davey & Coombes, 1996), or the number of information management activities supported by accountants. Previous literature (e.g. Bebbington et al., 1994; Burritt & Schaltegger, 2010; Davey & Coombes, 1996; Schaltegger & Burritt, 2000; Schaltegger & Burritt, 2010; Zvezdov et al., 2010) observed that professional accountants appear to be underrepresented in corporate social accounting. Applying the narrower definition of an accountant as shown in Table 4, this observation is supported by the data collected during the interviews as only 14 of the total of 58 interviewed corporate practitioners were accountants dealing with social accounting. As shown in Table 4 the definition of an accountant, however, can be more narrow or broader and thus the level and kind of involvement in social

Table 4. Information on the Sampled Companies. The Legal form of Some of the Researched Companies does not Require that They Disclose the Above Information.

Company	Industry	Turnover (2010)	Employees (2010)
1	Publishing	€ 2.8 billion	11.000
2	Insurance	€ 106.45 billion	151.000
3	Finance	€ 170.0 billion	4.200
4	Manufacturing	€ 14.88 billion	47.000
5	Utilities	€ 53.2 billion	74.000
6	Logistics	€ 51.5 billion	275.000
7	Services	NA	2.500
8	Mining	€ 14.0 billion	52.000
9	Utilities	€ 72.7 billion	155.000
10	Services	NA	NA
11	Services	NA	5.000
12	Sports	NA	NA
13	Telecommunications	€ 18.9 billion	107.000
14	Telecommunications	€ 46.9 billion	83.900
15	Retail	€ 12.9 billion	82.100
16	Oil and gas	€ 388.0 billion	87.000

accounting can vary depending on the applied definition. People with accounting function, not being accountants though, are mostly in subordinate positions, sometimes are trainees or in student jobs, and serve in various departments of the organisation.

Apart from the absolute numbers, particularly the relative involvement of different types of actors is revealing. Table 5 provides a summary of the actual sustainability information management activities each of the four types of actors explained in the interviews as being part of their social accounting activities. The table shows *for each group of actors* the percentages of activities (figure on the upper left in each cell). When reading the table in lines from left to right the underlying question is what is the main focus of all activities of the accountants, people with accounting function, sustainability, and general managers?

Table 5 in addition shows *for each social accounting activity* the percentages of actors involved in a certain activity (lower right percentage figure in each cell). Reading the table in columns top down the question is who, which group of actors, deals mainly with a certain social accounting activity?

To investigate in which activities accountants are mainly involved in social accounting, we examined their relative involvement, that is, how

Table 5. Types of Actors Involved in Corporate Sustainability Accounting.

Type of Actors	Definition of Function
Accountants	Accountants have an accounting background through extensive training, an education degree or a professional focus, or an explicit accounting title. It has become difficult to define precisely what an accountant is other than trivially in terms of membership of a professional body, which is in any case fragmented (Willmott, 1986; Sikka & Willmott, 1995, p. 550) and ill-defined (Kirkham & Loft, 1993, p. 508).
People with accounting function	People with an accounting function are those professionals who do not fall in either of the above category but fulfil accounting functions, that is, information management beyond the collection of information in their own field. This is often the case with sustainability managers who are in charge of analyzing sustainability performance based on numbers. These people are thus often in charge of establishing information flows, ensuring information quality, extracting conclusions based on the information, or presenting this information to decision makers (typically senior management).
Sustainability managers	Sustainability managers are people who are in charge of social or environmental performance, or financial performance that is managed by means of social and environmental measures.
General managers	In this study the category of general managers refers to all other roles that do not fall in one of the above three categories (e.g. communications, HR, ideas management, etc.).

many of the involved accountants identify, collect, and provide information? The first line in Table 5 depicts the percentage of accountants focussing on a specific information management activity. These figures express the main interest and focus of accounting professionals in social accounting. The results reveal an interesting observation. Whereas, for example, the activities of sustainability managers are distributed evenly across the process of sustainability information identification, generation and provision, the accountants concentrate on the identification of information that is generated and on the provision the final output of the information to higher hierarchy decision makers (Table 6).

Depending on the proxies applied to measure the involvement, accountants appear to be more or less actively involved in social accounting. Compared to other professionals such as sustainability managers, clearly fewer (in numbers) accountants are involved. However, investigating the

Table 6. Table Based on 103 Roles of 58 Interviewees. The Figures are Expressed as a *Percentage* of the Total Involvement of Each Role: for example, 7% of the Involved Accountants are in Charge of Deciding what Aspects are Covered.

Activity in Social Accounting Practice	Who Decides What Aspects are Covered?	Who Defines the Indicators?	Who Collects the Data?	Who Provides the Final Information to Others?	Total
Role	Knowledge expert	Expert of organisation and methods		Gatekeeper	
Accountants	7%	47%	3%	43%	100%
	11%	33%	6%	30%	
Sustainability managers	27%	28%	14%	31%	100%
	40%	20%	28%	22%	
General managers	16%	33%	18%	33%	100%
	24%	23%	38%	23%	
People with accounting functions	17%	34%	14%	35%	100%
	25%	24%	28%	25%	
Total	100%	100%	100%	100%	

type of involvement of the various professionals reveals a specific inclination of the accountant – towards information provision – who thus exposes the role of an information gatekeeper together with defining indicators as one aspect of a methods expert or process promotor.

Reading Table 5 from activity perspective top down reveals that the knowledge expert activity of deciding what sustainability issues should be captured is dominated by sustainability managers whereas general managers are the main organisation and methods expert activity through collecting the required data. The methods expert and gatekeeper activities are in turn dominated by accountants. Further employees conducting accounting functions seem to not play a dominant role in either of the activities, thus reflecting a serving function to the other types of actors. This is in line with the observation that these actors are spread over different departments in most organisations and mostly in subordinate positions.

In summary and as previous research implicitly indicates, accountants seem to be less involved in terms of technical contribution than other positions such as sustainability or general managers. In our sample, the methods applied and the organisation of workflows are more often than not shaped by sustainability managers. Experts in environmental and sustainability affairs are thus perceived as the main actors in charge of sustainability accounting activities. Accountants, on the other hand, focus their efforts on information communication, which is a gatekeeping role. This gatekeeping role has been described only sparsely in existing literature and needs to be further researched.

DISCUSSION

The empirically observed activities of accountants in social accounting practice reveal an interesting trait. The accountant's involvement in directing data generation and communicating information to higher management shows that accountants are in fact involved in sustainability accounting, although less compared to other professionals such as sustainability or general managers. The results suggest that accountants are involved in social accounting in a way that has not been investigated in literature to date: accountants act as gatekeepers and as methods and organisational experts.

From a gatekeeper viewpoint, the definition of indicators and the provision of this information to decision makers on higher hierarchy levels can be seen as exercising power. Applying technical capabilities in the process of information management, on the other hand, can be mainly attributed to general and sustainability managers. Whereas various studies (e.g. Bennett et al., 2013; Burritt, Schaltegger, & Zvezdov, 2011) reveal that other functions such as sustainability or middle managers are largely in charge of social accounting, these studies do not analyse the gatekeeping function of accounting professionals.

Based on the empirical findings we propose three possible *complementary* explanations for the observed behaviour of accountants. The interpretation of the results is based on Wilson and distinguishes between three types of involvement is presented in Table 7.

The first possible reaction pattern of accounts is *defensive involvement*. This interpretation relates to a strict gatekeeping role of accountants which could be observed in some companies where professional accountants focused on providing sustainability information to decision makers in higher hierarchy positions. Due to the increasing legal and economic relevance of social and environmental issues in many countries and markets sustainability information has a large and often growing influence on many companies. Assuming accountants fear losing power in organisational structures, they may tend to occupy and use an essential position in the information flows. This allows accountants to retain or tweak (in the

Table 7. Main Traits of Adaptive, Constructive and Defensive Involvement of Accountants in Managing and Using Sustainability Information.

Type of Involvement	Main Contribution	Need to Exercise Power
Defensive	Retain or tweak information	High
Adaptive	Interpretation into 'management terms'	Low
Constructive	Act as mediators	Average

extreme even beyond legal boundaries) information to avoid changes in power structures. Indication of such behaviour is found in existing literature that deals with the accountants' attempt to strengthen their positions. Power (1997) describes this and other 'strategies by which they [accountants] have attempted to represent themselves as relevant experts [in environmental audit].' Such behaviour is clearly reactive, as it is likely to occur only when the power structures in the organisation are on the verge of being reshaped. Defensive strategies often tend to only work for a limited time until the legal, economic, or social pressure are too high or new employees with different values and education may want to act differently.

The second interpretation of the observed role of the accountants is that gatekeeping combined with the application of some methodological expertise is the result of the appended nature (e.g. Epstein, 2008; Quinn & Dalton, 2009) of the sustainability department and the subsequent need of translating the results into 'management language'. We refer to this observation as *adaptive involvement* to reflect the situation that accountants communicate the information they are fed in. This behaviour can be explained with the accountants' willingness to contribute towards improving the overall performance of the company and achieving strategic and operational objectives. The need to exercise power is low as in this case accountants make use of their formal authority without pursuing objectives beyond that authority. Although expertise to define indicators and introduce methods is fed into the social accounting process, this activity is given lower priority than the role of providing information to decision makers.

The third interpretation of our empirical observations is that accountants are willing and interested to support the social accounting process, but the lack of sustainability expertise of accounting professionals may leave them no other option but to act as mediators in sustainability information management with their authoritative and methods expertise. We call this *constructive involvement while recognising the own limitations in sustainability knowledge* when accountants acknowledge the importance of sustainability and major deficiencies in the communication of sustainability information thus trying to support overcoming these information deficiencies in their own limited scope of expertise. The recognition of improvement potentials requires *pro-active behaviour* as opposed to a decision to not actively engage in social accounting which characterises adaptive or defensive involvement. The need to exercise formal and informal power exists since improvement attempts may face resistance and involve changes of existing management systems, the introduction of new measures and methods, or even affect the remuneration of senior management (Bennett et al., 2013). Although the same general activity pattern involving methodological and organisational expertise and providing sustainability information to decision makers can be observed as with a defensive and particularly adaptive behaviour, the accountants contribute substantially to the introduction and establishment of social accounting by actively developing and engaging with other professionals in institutionalizing social accounting procedures in the organisation.

CONCLUSIONS

With the sustainability discussion gaining relevance for corporate activities, a change in accounting is observed to be taking place. A change in accounting systems and methods, however, results in a shift in power (e.g. Bariff & Galbraith, 1978; Markus & Pfeffer, 1983). Thus, sustainability information and information handled by social accounting not only has the potential to affect the performance of a company but also to change its power order. Although sustainability management is designed and should be carried out in the best interest of the company – that is, to improve its overall performance – separate individuals or groups of individuals may not perceive the involved necessary changes as desirable. Hence, certain actors, such as accountants, may focus on gatekeeping (Bloomfield & Coombs, 1992; Pettigrew, 1972; Mechanic, 1982) of sustainability information in an attempt to influence the practice and relevance of social accounting – for example, the information collected, the type of information certain recipients get, the ways in which the information is generated, etc.

The research findings face some limitations. On the provision of information it needs to be discerned between information provision to higher management or to general management. Whereas the provision of information to higher management can be linked well to the power promotor role and gatekeeping, the information provision to general management is likely to have more pragmatic reasons such as whether the sustainability information relates well to the functional area of the manager.

Another research limitation may be the differentiation between roles. Since one person may assume several roles it is difficult to precisely separate the attributes of the different roles; for example, is information provided due to a person's engagement as quality manager or as their engagement as procurement manager? Whereas this limitation is not likely to result in major data misinterpretation, obtaining additional data resolution might provide a more persuasive explanation for the observed phenomena.

Last but not least our findings are limited to information gained from interviews with corporate sustainability accounting practitioners in companies with good sustainability reputation. The results may thus differ for companies who have started more recently and are less publically exposed to sustainability expectations.

Investigating the observed behaviour empirically can help improve social accounting. Should it turn out that the accountants have no other option but to act like gatekeepers, accounting education will play a major role in overcoming this deficiency in the pursuit of improved sustainability knowledge and performance. If, on the other hand, it is the defensive stance of accounting professionals and the fear of losing power in corporate structures which motivates them to act as gatekeepers, mechanisms to motivate them to cooperate should be researched. An example of the latter could be the motivation to improve overall sustainability performance rather than focusing on purely financial measures.

A hesitant involvement of accountants in social accounting may not be seen as problem. If accounting is a set of skills taught in accounting education, the social accounting skills can also be learnt and applied by other functions with sufficient interest in sustainability issues. This view, however, neglects both the role and the power of accountants in the organisational networks, information management and management decision making. It is not necessarily accountants who develop the sustainability equivalent to the complex return on investment (ROI) model, as accountants lack expertise in what constitutes good sustainability performance (Schaltegger & Burritt, 2000). Mathews (1997, p. 504) goes as far as to criticise management for authorising 'the accounting function to produce social and environmental information, even when the accounting profession does not show any interest' – and we might add, the accountants may neither be willing nor sufficiently trained to understand sustainability issues.

An important consideration may thus be the large (or excessive) power of accountants who play a major role in providing sustainability information to decision makers on higher hierarchy levels. Although this has not been considered problematical (Hopper, 1980), our empirical findings suggest that this statement might need rethinking.

REFERENCES

Abbott, A. (1988). *The system of the professions*. London: University of Chicago Press.

Abernethy, M. A., & Vagnoni, E. (2004). Power, organization design and managerial behaviour. *Accounting, Organization and Society*, *29*, 207–25.

Allen, T. (1970). Communication networks in R&D laboratories. *R&D Management*, *1*, 14–21.

Back-Hock, A. (1992). Towards strategic accounting in product management: Implementing a holistic approach to a date and methods base for managerial accounting. *European Journal of Operations Research*, *61*, 98–105.

Ball, A., Owen, D., & Gray, R. (2000). External transparency or internal capture? The role of third-party statements in adding value to corporate environmental reports. *Business Strategy and the Environment*, *9*(1), 1–23.

Bebbington, J., Brown, J., Frame, B., & Thomson, I. (2007). Theorizing engagement: The potential of a critical dialogic approach. *Accounting, Auditing & Accountability Journal*, *20*(3), 356–381.

Bariff, M. L., & Galbraith, J. R. (1978). Intraorganizational power considerations for designing information systems. *Accounting, Organizations and Society*, *3*, 15–27.

Bebbington, J., & Gray, R. (2001). An account of sustainability: Failure, success and a reconceptualization. *Critical Perspectives on Accounting*, *12*(5), 557–588.

Bebbington, J., Gray, R., Thomson, I., & Walters, D. (1994). Accountants' attitudes and environmentally-sensitive accounting. *Accounting and Business Research*, *24*, 109–120.

Bebbington, J., Larrinaga, C., & Moneva, J. (2008). Corporate social reporting and reputation risk management. *Accounting, Auditing & Accountability Journal*, *21*(3), 337–361.

Bennett, M., & James, P. (2000). *The green bottom line: Environmental accounting for management: Current practice and future trends*. Sheffield, UK: Greenleaf Publishing.

Bennett, M., Schaltegger, S., & Zvezdov, D. (2011). Environmental management accounting. In M. Abdel-Kader (Ed.), *Review of Management Accounting Research* (pp. 53–84). Hampshire, London: Palgrave Macmillan.

Bennett, M., Schaltegger, S., & Zvezdov, D. (2013). *Exploring corporate practices in management accounting for sustainability*. Institute for Chartered Accountants of England and Wales (ICAEW).

Benston, G. J. (1963). The role of the firm's accounting system for motivation. *The Accounting Review*, *38*(2), 347–354.

Benston, G. J. (1982). Accounting and corporate accountability. *Accounting, Organizations and Society*, *7*(2), 87–105.

Bhimani, A., Horngren, C. T., & Datar, S. M. (2011). *Management and cost accounting* (5th Revised ed.). Harlow et al.: Prentice Hall International.

Blok, A. (1974). *The mafia of a sicilian village, 1860–1960*. New York, NY: Harper and Row.

Bloomfield, B. P., & Coombs, R. (1992). Information technology, control and power: The centralization and decentralization debate revisited. *Journal of Management Studies, 29*, 459–484.

Boissevain, J. (1974). *Friends of friends. Networks, manipulators and coalitions.* Oxford: Basil Blackwell.

Braman, S. (2006). *Change of state: Information, policy, and power.* Cambridge: The MIT Press.

Burns, J., & Baldvinsdottir, G. (2007). The changing role of management accountants. *Issues in Management Accounting, 3*, 117–132.

Burns, J., & Vaivio, J. (2001). Management accounting change. *Management Accounting Research, 12*(4), 389–402.

Burns, T., & Stalker, G. M. (1961). *The management of innovation.* Il, USA: University of Illinois.

Burritt, R. (2004). Environmental management accounting: Roadblocks on the way to the green and pleasant land. *Business Strategy and the Environment, 13*, 13–32.

Burritt, R. (2012). Environmental performance accountability: Planet, people, profits. *Accounting, Auditing, and Accountability Journal, 25*(2), 370–405.

Burritt, R., Hahn, T., & Schaltegger, S. (2002). Towards a comprehensive framework for environmental management accounting. Links between business actors and environmental management accounting tools. *Australian Accounting Review, 12*(2), 39–50.

Burritt, R. L., & Schaltegger, S. (2010). Sustainability accounting and reporting: Fad or trend? *Accounting, Auditing & Accountability Journal, 23*(7), 829–46.

Burritt, R., Schaltegger, S., Kokubu, K., & Wagner, M. (2003). Environmental management accounting for staff appraisal. Evidence from Australia, Germany and Japan. In M. Bennett, P. Rikhardsson, & S. Schaltegger (Eds.), *Environmental management accounting. Purpose and progress* (pp. 151–188). Dordrecht: Kluwer Academic Publishers.

Burritt, R., Schaltegger, S., & Zvezdov, D. (2011). Carbon management accounting. *Australian Accounting Review, 21*(1), 80–98.

Byrne, S., & Pierce, B. (2007). Towards a more comprehensive understanding of the roles of management accountants. *European Accounting Review, 16*(3), 469–498.

Caglio, A. (2003). Enterprise resource planning systems and accountants: Towards hybridization? *European Accounting Review, 12*(1), 123–153.

Carter, A. J., Burritt, R. L., & Pisaniello, J. D. (2011). *Accountants as mental health workers: The public interest in regional and remote areas.* Adelaide: CAGS.

Chakrabarti, A. K. (1974). The role of champions in product innovation. *California Management Review, 17*, 58–62.

CIMA (Chartered Institute of Management Accountants). (1981). *CIMA official terminology.* London: CIMA.

Coffee, J. C. (2006). *Gatekeepers: The role of the professions in corporate governance: The Professions and corporate governance.* New York, USA: Oxford University Press.

Collier, P. A. (1984). *The impact of information technology on the management accountant.* London: Institute of cost and management accountants.

Cox, J. D. (2006). *The Oligopolistic Gatekeeper: The U.S. Accounting Profession. After Enron: improving corporate law and modernizing securities regulation in Europe and the U.S.* Legal Studies Paper No. 117. Duke Law School, Oxford. (Chapter 9).

Cranefield, J. & Yoong, P. (2007). The role of the translator/interpreter in knowledge transfer environments. *Knowledge and Process Management, 14*(2), 95–103.

Daft, R. L., & Lengel, R. H. (1986). Organizational information requirements, media richness and structural design. *Management Science*, *32*(5), 554–571.

Davey, H., & Coombes, R. (1996). A review of accountant and corporate involvement in environmental accounting in New Zealand. *Asian Review of Accounting*, *4*(2), 100–124.

Dezaley, Y. (1995). 'Turf battles' or 'class struggles': The internationalization of the market for expertise in the 'professional society'. *Accounting, Organizations and Society*, *20*, 331–344.

Dezaley, Y., & Sugarman, D. (1995). *Professional competition and professional power: Lawyers, accountants and the social construction of markets*. London: Routledge.

Dierkes, M., & Preston, L. E. (1977). Corporate social accounting reporting for the physical environment: A critical review and implementation proposal. *Accounting, Organizations and Society*, *2*(1), 3–22.

Drury, C. (1985). *Management and cost accounting*. London: Thomson Learning.

Epstein, M. J. (2008). Implementing corporate sustainability: Measuring and managing social and environmental impacts. *Strategic Finance*, *89*(7), 25–31.

Evans, E., Burritt, R., & Guthrie, J. (2011). *Bridging the gap between academic accounting research and professional practice*. Sydney: University of South Australia.

Fichter, K. (2009). Innovation communities. The role of networks of promotors in open innovation. *R&D Management*, *39*(4), 357–371.

Finnveden, G., & Moberg, A. (2005). Environmental systems analysis tools – An overview. *Journal of Cleaner Production*, *13*(12), 1165–1173.

Flesher, D. L., & Zanzig, J. S. (2000). Management accountants express a desire for change in the functioning of internal auditing. *Managerial Auditing Journal*, *15*(7), 331–337.

Francis, G., & Minchington, C. (1999). Quantitative skills: Is there an expectation gap between the education and practice of management accountants? *Accounting Education*, *8*(4), 301–319.

Galaskiewicz, J., & Krohn, K. R. (1984). Positions, roles, and dependencies in a community interorganization system. *The Sociological Quarterly*, *25*, 527–550.

Galbraith, J. R. (1974). Organization design: An information processing view. *Interfaces*, *4*(3), 28–36.

Gould, R. V. (1989). Power and social structure in community elites. *Social Forces*, *68*, 531–52.

Granlund, M., & Malmi, T. (2002). Moderate impact of ERPS on management accounting: A lag or permanent outcome? *Management Accounting Research*, *13*(3), 299–321.

Gray, R. H., Bebbington, K. J., & Walters, D. (1993). *Accounting for the environment: The greening of accountancy. Part II*. London: Paul Chapman.

Gray, R. H., Owen, D., & Adams, C. (1996). *Accounting & accountability*. Harlow et al.: Prentice Hall.

Gray, R., Bebbington, J., & Collison, D. (2006). NGOs, civil society and accountability: Making the people accountable to capital. *Accounting, Auditing & Accountability Journal*, *19*(3), 319–348.

Hauschildt, J. (2003). Promotors and champions in innovation. Development of a research paradigm. In L. Shavinina (Ed.), *The international handbook on innovation* (pp. 804–814). Oxford: Elsevier.

Hauschildt, J., & Kirchmann, E. (2001). Teamwork for innovation. The "troika" of promotors. *R&D Management*, *31*(1), 41–49.

Hauschildt, J., & Schewe, G. (2000). Gatekeeper and process promotor: Key persons in agile and innovative organizations. *International Journal of Agile Management Systems*, *2*(2), 96–103.

Henry, J., & Journeault, M. (2010). Eco-control. The influence of management control systems on environmental and economic performance. *Accounting, Organizations and Society*, *35*, 63–80.

Hoffman, A., & Jennings, D. (2011). The BP oil spill as a cultural anomaly? Institutional context, conflict, and change. *Journal of Management Inquiry*, *20*(2), 100–112.

Hopkins, A. (2011). Management walk-arounds. Lessons from the Gulf of Mexico oil well blowout. *Safety Science*, *49*, 1421–1425.

Hopper, T. M. (1980). Role conflicts of management accountants and their position within organisation structures. *Accounting, Organizations and Society*, *5*(4), 401–411.

Howell, J., & Higgins, C. (1990). Champions of technological innovation. *Administrative Science Quarterly*, *35*, 317–341.

Introna, L. D. (1997). *Management, information and power: A narrative of the involved manager*. Basingstoke: Macmillan.

Jack, L., & Kholeif, A. (2008). Enterprise resource planning and a contest to limit the role of management accountants: A strong structuration perspective. *Accounting Forum*, *32*(1), 30–45.

Jervis, P. (1975). Innovation and technology transfer. The roles and characteristics of individuals, IEEE Transactions on Engineering Management. *EM*, *22*, 19–27.

Johnson, H. T. (2002). A former management accountant reflects on his journey through the world of cost management. *Accounting History*, *7*(9), 9–21.

Jones, T. C. (1992). Understanding management accountants: The rationality of social action. *Critical Perspectives on Accounting*, *3*(3), 225–257.

Kimberly, J., & Evanisko, M. (1981). Organisation innovation. The influence of individual, organisational and contextual factors of hospital adoption of technological and administrative innovations. *Academy of Management Journal*, *24*, 689–713.

Kirkham, L., & Loft, A. (1993). Gender and the construction of the professional accountant. *Accounting, Organizations and Society*, *18*(6), 507–558.

Klobas, J. E., & McGill, T. (1995). Identification of technological gatekeepers in the information technology profession. *Journal of the American Society for Information Science*, *46*(8), 581–589.

Kraakman, R. (1986). Gatekeepers: The anatomy of a third-party enforcement strategy. *Journal of Law, Economics & Organization*, *2*, 53–104.

Larrinaga-González, C., Carrasco-Fenech, F., Caro-González, F., Correa-Ruíz, C., & Páez-Sandubete, J. (2001). The role of environmental accounting in organizational change. An exploration of Spanish companies. *Accounting, Auditing & Accountability Journal*, *14*(2), 213–239.

Lee, Y., & Garza-Gomez, X. (2012). Market-based approximation of the cost of non-conformance associated with the 2010 Gulf of Mexico oil spill. *Total Quality Management and Business Excellence*, *23*(2), 221–236.

Lindsay, V., Chadee, D., Mattsson, J., Johnston, R., & Millett, B. (2003). Relationships, the role of individuals and knowledge flows in the internationalisation of service firms. *International Journal of Service Industry Management*, *14*(1), 7–35.

Lüdeke-Freund, F. & Zvezdov, D. (2013). The Manager's job at BP: Decision making and responsibilities on the high seas. *International Journal of Case Studies in Management*, *11*(2), 1–32.

Markham, S., Green, S., & Basu, R. (1991). Champions and antagonists. Relationships with R&D project characteristics and management. *Journal of Engineering and Technology Management*, *8*, 217–242.

Markus, M. L. (1983). Power, politics, and MIS implementation. *Communications of the ACM*, *26*, 430–444.

Markus, M. L., & Pfeffer, J. (1983). Power and the design and implementation of accounting and control systems. *Accounting, Organizations and Society*, *8*(2–3), 205–218.

Marsden, P. (1982). Brokerage behavior in restricted exchange networks. In P. Marsden & N. Lin (Eds.), *Social structure and network analysis*. Beverly Hills Calif, CA: Sage.

Mathews, M. R. (1997). Twenty-five years of social and environmental accounting research: Is there a silver jubilee to celebrate? *Accounting, Auditing & Accountability Journal*, *10*(4), 481–531.

Mechanic, D. (1982). Sources of power of lower participants in complex organization. *Administrative Science Quarterly*, *7*, 349–364.

Medley, P. (1997). Environmental accounting. What does it mean to professional accountants? *Accounting, Auditing and Accountability Journal*, *10*(4), 594–600.

Milne, M. J. (1996). On sustainability, the environment and management accounting. *Management Accounting Research*, *7*, 135–161.

Milne, M., Tregidga, H., & Walton, S. (2009). Words not actions! The ideological role of sustainable development reporting. *Accounting, Auditing & Accountability Journal*, *22*(8), 1211–1257.

Mintzberg, H. (1983). *Power in and around organizations*. Englewood Cliffs, NJ: Prentice-Hall.

Moerschbaecher, M., & Day, J. (2011). Ultra-deepwater Gulf of Mexico oil and gas: Energy return on financial investment and a preliminary assessment of energy return on energy investment. *Sustainability*, *3*, 2009–2026.

Montagna, P. (1986). Accounting rationality and financial legitimation. *Theory and Society*, *15* (1–2), 103–138.

Nanni Jr., A. J., Dixon, J. R., & Vollman, T. E. (1992). Integrated performance measurement: management accounting to support the new manufacturing realities. *Journal of Management Accounting Research*, *4*, 1–19.

O'Dwyer, B. (2001). The legitimacy of accountants' participation in social and ethical accounting, auditing and reporting. *Business Ethics: A European Review*, *10*(1), 27–39.

O'Dwyer, B., & Owen, D. (2007). Assurance statement practice in environmental, social and sustainability reporting: a critical evaluation. *The British Accounting Review*, *37*, 205–229.

Owen, D. (2008). Chronicles of wasted time? A personal reflection on the current state of, and future prospects for, social and environmental accounting research. *Accounting, Auditing & Accountability Journal*, *21*(2), 240–267.

Parker, L. D. (2005). Social and environmental accountability research: A view from the commentary box. *Accounting, Auditing & Accountability Journal*, *18*(6), 842–860.

Parker, L. D. (2011). Twenty-one years of social and environmental accountability research: A coming of age. *Accounting Forum*, *35*, 1–10.

Pettigrew, A. M. (1972). Information control as a power resource. *Sociology*, *6*, 187–204.

Pfeffer, J. (1992). *Managing with power: Politics and influence in organizations*. Boston, MA: Harvard Business School Press.

Pfeffer, J. (2010). *Power: Why some people have it – And others don't*. New York, USA: HarperBusiness.

Pierce, B., & O'Dea, T. (2003). Management accounting information and the needs of managers: Perceptions of accountants and managers compared. *The British Accounting Review*, *35*(3), 257–290.

Porter, M. (1985). *Competitive advantage*. New York, NY: Free Press.

Power, M. (1997). Expertise and the construction of relevance: Accountants and environmental audit. *Accounting, Organizations and Society*, *22*(2), 123–146.

Quinn, L., & Dalton, M. (2009). Leading for sustainability: Implementing the tasks of leadership. *Corporate Governance*, *9*(1), 21–38.

Radcliffe, V. S., Cooper, D., & Robson, K. (1994). The management of professional enterprises and regulatory change: British accountancy and the financial services act, 1986. *Accounting, Organizations and Society*, *19*(7), 601–628.

Rao, S., & Perry, C. (2003). Convergent interviewing to build a theory in under-researched areas: principles and an example investigation of internet usage in inter-firm relationships. *Qualitative Market Research: An International Journal*, *6*(4), 236–247.

Rodgers, R., Hunter, J. E., & Rogers, D. L. (1993). Influence of top management commitment on management program success. *Journal of Applied Psychology*, *78*(1), 151–171.

Salzmann, O., Ionescu-Somers, A., & Steger, U. (2005). The business case for corporate sustainability: Literature review and research options. *European Management Journal*, *23*(1), 27–36.

Scapens, R., & Jazayeri, M. (2003). ERP systems and management accounting change: Opportunities or impacts? A research note. *European Accounting Review*, *12*(1), 201–233.

Scapens, R. W., Jazayeri, M., & Scapens, J. (1998). SAP: Integrated information systems and the implications for management accountants. *Management Accounting*, *76*(September), 46–48.

Scavone, G. M. (2006). Challenges in internal environmental management reporting in Argentina. *Journal of Cleaner Production*, *14*(14), 1276–1285.

Schaltegger, S., & Burritt, R. L. (2000). *Contemporary environmental accounting: Issues, concept and practice*. Sheffield: Greenleaf.

Schaltegger, S., & Burritt, R. (2010). Sustainability accounting for companies. Catchphrase or decision support for business leaders? *Journal of World Business*, *45*(4), 375–384.

Schaltegger, S., Gibassier, D., & Zvezdov, D. (2013). Is environmental management accounting a discipline? A bibliometric literature review. *Meditari Accountancy Research*, *21*(1), 4–31.

Schreuder, H., & Ramanathan, K. (1984). Accounting and corporate accountability: A postscript. *Accounting, Organizations and Society*, *9*(3–4), 421–423.

Shank, J. (1989). Strategic management accounting: New wine, or just new bottles. *Journal of Management Accounting Research*, *1*, 47–65.

Shields, M. D., & Young, S. M. (1992). Effective long-term reduction: A strategic perspective. *Journal of Cost Management*, *6*(1), 16–30.

Sikka, P., & Willmott, H. (1995). The power of "independence": Defending and extending the jurisdiction of accounting in the United Kingdom. *Accounting, Organizations and Society*, *20*(6), 547–581.

Stebbins, R. A. (2001). *Exploratory research in the social sciences*. London: Sage Publications.

Taylor, R. (1975). The technological gatekeeper. *R&D Management*, *5*, 239–143.

Tjosvold, D. (1988). Cooperative and competitive interdependence: Collaboration between departments to serve customers. *Group & Organization Management*, *13*, 274–289.

Tushman, M. L., & Katz, R. (1980). External communication and project performance: An investigation into the role of Gatekeepers. *Management Science*, *26*(11), 1071–1085.

Tushman, M. L., & Scanlan, T. J. (1981). Boundary spanning individuals: Their role in information transfer and their antecedents. *Academy of Management Journal*, *24*(2), 289–305.

Weygandt, J. J., Kimmel, P. D., & Kieso, D. E. (2009). *Managerial accounting: Tools for business decision making*. Oxford: Wiley.

Williams, B., Wilmshurst, T., & Clift, R. (2010). The role of accountants in sustainability reporting – A local government study. Paper presented at the 6th Asia-Pacific Interdisciplinary Research in Accounting Conference, July 11–13, University of Sydney, Australia.

Willmott, H. (1986). Organising the profession: A theoretical and historical examination of the development of major accountancy bodies in the UK. *Accounting, Organizations and Society*, *11*(6), 555–580.

Wilmshurst, T. D., & Frost, G. R. (2001). The role of accounting and the accountant in the environmental management system. *Business Strategy and the Environment*, *10*(3), 135–147.

Witte, E. (1977). Power and innovation: A two center theory. *International Studies of Management and Organization*, *7*, 47–70.

Yazdifar, H., & Tsamenyi, M. (2005). Management accounting change and the changing roles of management accountants: A comparative analysis between dependent and independent organizations. *Journal of Accounting and Organizational Change*, *1*(2), 180–198.

Zand, D. (1981). *Information, organization, and power: Effective management in the knowledge society*. New York: McGraw.

Zvezdov, D., Schaltegger, S., & Bennett, M. (2010). The Increasing Involvement of Accountants in Corporate Sustainability Management. *Journal of the Asia-Pacific Centre for Environmental Accountability*, *16*(4), 20–31.